CONSTITUTIONAL LABOUR RIGHTS IN CANADA

Farm Workers and the *Fraser* Case

CONSTITUTIONAL LABOUR RIGHTS IN CANADA

Farm Workers and the *Fraser* Case

edited by

Fay Faraday, Judy Fudge, & Eric Tucker

IRWIN LAW

Published in 2012 by

Irwin Law Inc.
14 Duncan Street
Suite 206
Toronto, ON
M5H 3G8

www.irwinlaw.com

ISBN: 978-1-55221-291-2

Library and Archives Canada Cataloguing in Publication

Constitutional labour rights in Canada : farm workers and the Fraser case / edited by Fay Faraday, Judy Fudge & Eric Tucker.

Includes bibliographical references.

Issued also in electronic format.

ISBN 978-1-55221-291-2

1. United Food and Commercial Workers Canada—Trials, litigation, etc. 2. Ontario—Trials, litigation, etc. 3. Agricultural laborers—Legal status, laws, etc.—Canada. 4. Migrant agricultural laborers—Legal status, laws, etc.—Canada. 5. Employee rights—Canada. 6. Collective bargaining—Law and legislation—Canada. 7. Freedom of association--Canada. I. Faraday, Fay, 1966- II. Fudge, Judy III. Tucker, Eric

KE3196.A37C65 2012 344.71'01890463 C2012-901168-1
KF3409.A42C65 2012

The publisher acknowledges the financial support of the Government of Canada through the Canada Book Fund for its publishing activities.

We acknowledge the assistance of the OMDC Book Fund, an initiative of Ontario Media Development Corporation.

Printed and bound by CPI Group (UK) Ltd, Croydon, CR0 4YY

1 2 3 4 5 16 15 14 13 12

TABLE OF CONTENTS

DEDICATION *vii*

PREFACE *ix*

CHAPTER ONE
Introduction: Farm Workers, Collective Bargaining Rights, and the Meaning of Constitutional Protection *1*
Judy Fudge

CHAPTER TWO
Farm Worker Exceptionalism: Past, Present, and the post-*Fraser* Future *30*
Eric Tucker

CHAPTER THREE
The Roots of Organizing Agriculture Workers in Canada *57*
Wayne Hanley

CHAPTER FOUR
Development as Remittances or Development as Freedom? Exploring Canada's Temporary Migration Programs from a Rights-based Approach *81*
Kerry Preibisch

CHAPTER FIVE
Envisioning Equality: Analogous Grounds and Farm Workers' Experience of Discrimination *109*
Fay Faraday

CHAPTER SIX
Harvest Pilgrims: Migrant Farm Workers in Ontario *139*
Vincenzo Pietropaolo

CHAPTER SEVEN
The *Fraser* Case: A Wrong Turn in a Fog of Judicial Deference *155*
Paul JJ Cavalluzzo

CHAPTER EIGHT
What *Fraser* Means For Labour Rights in Canada *190*
Steven Barrett and Ethan Poskanzer

CHAPTER NINE
Labour Rights: A Democratic Counterweight to Growing Income Inequality in Canada *234*
Derek Fudge

CHAPTER TEN
The International Constitution *261*
Patrick Macklem

CHAPTER ELEVEN
Giving Life to the ILO—Two Cheers for the SCC
KD Ewing and John Hendy, QC *286*

CONTRIBUTORS *319*

DEDICATION

On the afternoon of 6 February 2012, a van carrying thirteen migrant farm workers collided with another vehicle on Perth County Road No 107 near Hampstead, Ontario. Ten of the workers and the driver of the other vehicle were killed. This book is dedicated to all those who died or were injured in this tragic accident:

Christopher Fulton
David Armando Blancas-Hernandez
Jose Mercedes Valdiviezo-Taboa
Cesar Augusto Sanchez-Palacios
Enrique Arturo Leon
Corsino Jaramillo
Mario Abril
Oscar Compomanes-Corzo
Juan Castillo
Elvio Bravo-Suncion
Fernando Correa
Edgar Sulla-Puma
Juan Ariza
Abelardo Alba-Medina

PREFACE

Like all books, this one is simultaneously a collective endeavour and a deeply personal undertaking. Without our contributors, who put aside other projects and personal obligations to meet tight deadlines, this book would not exist. Our dedicated publisher, Jeffrey Miller, and superb editor, Lesley Steeve, ensured that this is a timely book, and one that we are confident will stand the test of time. Vincenzo Pietropaolo's wonderful photographs provide a special tribute to the thousands of migrant workers who produce the food we eat and sell in Ontario. Our diligent research assistants, Natalie Smith and Mike Bilski, gave the book the rigorous attention to detail that every good book requires. We are deeply indebted to all of these people for helping us with this book, and we would like to thank them for their work in making this a book of which we are very proud. It was a pleasure to work with them.

As editors, we were all involved in the *Fraser* case in various capacities, and we are all committed to ensuring that agricultural workers in Ontario, regardless of their migration status, enjoy the same suite of labour rights and standards that are available to the vast majority of other workers in the province. For all of us, the hard work and perseverance of agricultural workers was an inspiration. But, for each of us, our commitment to social justice for agricultural workers has different sources and sustenance. Fay Faraday offers love and gratitude to Jim, Robbie, and Alex for their support and inspiration. Judy Fudge would like to thank her family for their example that decency is an essential part of the fabric of life, and her students and teachers for always reminding her that social justice is not simply an academic matter. Her most heartfelt thanks go to Ken Massicotte, for providing her with love and support so that she can spend her time as she pleases, which is (mostly) reading, teaching, and writing about workers, their struggles, and labour rights. Eric Tucker would like to dedicate this book to his father, William Tucker, who passed away suddenly on 12 November 2011 at the age of 92. His commitment to the pursuit of world peace and social justice was and remains an inspiration for his family. He is missed.

CHAPTER ONE
Introduction: Farm Workers, Collective Bargaining Rights, and the Meaning of Constitutional Protection

Judy Fudge

A. Farm Workers, Freedom of Association, and the Supreme Court of Canada

On 29 April 2011, the Supreme Court of Canada released its much-anticipated decision in *Attorney General of Ontario v Fraser*.[1] It was the first case after *Health Services and Support—Facilities Subsector Bargaining Association v British Columbia*[2] in which the Supreme Court addressed the scope of constitutionally protected collective bargaining rights. It was also the third decision in twenty years that the United Food and Commercial Workers Union Canada (UFCW) had obtained from the Supreme Court of Canada as part of the campaign it began in the late 1970s to secure collective bargaining rights for agricultural workers, workers who historically have been recruited from groups located at the margins of the labour market.[3] *Fraser* dealt with a constitutional challenge to an Ontario statute on the ground that it violated agricultural workers' freedom of association and right to equality by excluding them from the statutory protection that is available to virtually all other private sector workers

1 *Ontario (AG) v Fraser*, 2011 SCC 20 [*Fraser*].

2 *Health Services and Support—Facilities Subsector Bargaining Assn v British Columbia*, [2007] 2 SCR 391 [*Health Services*].

3 See Eric Tucker's chapter and Wayne Hanley's chapter in this collection for a history of the litigation and the attempt to organize farm workers in Ontario.

and by failing to provide them with alternative legislative support for meaningful and effective collective bargaining rights.

For the union that instigated the litigation, *Fraser* is a defeat. Eight of the nine judges agreed that the *Agricultural Employees Protection Act* (*AEPA*)[4] met the constitutional standard regarding freedom of association, although they did so for three very different sets of reasons. For the labour movement and its advocates, *Fraser* is ambiguous. The majority affirmed that "section 2(*d*), interpreted purposively and in light of Canada's values and commitments, protects associational collective activity in furtherance of workplace goals. The right is not merely a paper right, but a right to a process that permits meaningful pursuit of those goals."[5] On the other hand, *Fraser* marks the end of an emerging consensus among members of the Supreme Court that the types of collective activities by workers protected by the constitutional guarantee of freedom of association should be expanded incrementally. The Court is badly divided over the scope of protection that freedom of association provides to the traditional labour right to bargain collectively.

Two stories are intertwined in the four judgments that make up the Court's decision—the story of the farm workers and their union's attempt to obtain rights at work available to other working people in Ontario, and the tale of judicial discord over the meaning of freedom of association in the context of work. The first is more specific, and it focuses on the features of the actual dispute that drove the litigation, while the second is jurisprudential and institutional, and it concentrates on how the Supreme Court of Canada has interpreted freedom of association in the context of claims by unions for constitutional protection of the rights to bargain collectively and to strike. Appeal-level adjudication, especially of constitutional questions, requires courts to attend to the specific facts and context of a dispute, and at the same time, to articulate a consistent and principled approach to interpretation. The tension between these two levels of decision making in Supreme Court of Canada cases mirrors the tension between a just decision in the particular case and the need for legal certainty that is inherent in judicial decision making. In *Fraser*, what is remarkable is the extent to which, in three out of the four sets of reasons, the focus is almost exclusively jurisprudential and institutional; the distinctive legal treatment of agricultural workers is barely visible.

---

4 SO 2002, c 16 [*AEPA*].

5 *Fraser*, above note 1 at para 38.

This collection is designed to untangle the two stories that run throughout the decision, and our goal is to give greater emphasis to the social context out of which the decision emerged, while at the same time helping to illuminate *Fraser*'s broader jurisprudential and institutional implications. By bringing the social and legal contexts of the case together, we hope to reveal how legal processes, institutions, and tests tend to "screen out much of the messy reality of what may have catalyzed a legal dispute, and in this way the facts that are recited in legal decisions can obscure what actually happened as much as they can reveal it."[6] The law of evidence and the way in which legal questions are framed have a tendency to cloud the institutional and political processes that gave rise to conflicts that take the form of a legal dispute. The facts as reported in judgments are selected from the record, which is constructed (and contested) by the parties' lawyers as they attempt to prove material facts and to establish the background context relevant to resolving the legal questions before the court. By providing the history of the legal treatment of agricultural workers, of the litigation, and of the campaign to unionize agricultural workers in Ontario, as well as portraying the people who make up the agricultural workforce in Ontario, we hope that our multidimensional approach to *Fraser* reveals how the process of adjudication filters out evidence that is essential for understanding how law is involved in constructing and reproducing inequality.

Unravelling the second strand of *Fraser*, which is the broader discussion by the judges about the role of courts and the legal resources available to them in interpreting claims for constitutional protection of collective bargaining rights and the right to strike, is the second goal of the collection. The scope of freedom of association in the labour context has been deeply contested in Canada, and the jurisprudence has shifted. The UFCW's decades-long campaign to secure collective bargaining rights for agricultural workers is tightly interwoven with the Supreme Court of Canada's freedom of association jurisprudence. The union's challenge to the exclusion of agricultural workers from statutory protection of their right to join trade unions and make collective representations to their employer, which was upheld by the Supreme Court in 2001 in *Dunmore v Ontario (AG)*,[7] proved to be a tipping point in the Court's freedom of

6 Judy Fudge & Eric Tucker, "Introduction" in Judy Fudge & Eric Tucker, eds, *Work on Trial* (Toronto: Irwin, 2010) at 1.

7 [2001] 3 SCR 1016 [*Dunmore*].

association jurisprudence away from the individualistic and formal approach that prevailed.

Not only does *Dunmore* mark a shift in the Court's freedom of association jurisprudence towards a contextual approach, it also signalled a transition from discord towards greater consensus. In 1987, a divided Supreme Court of Canada ruled in the Labour Trilogy that the right to strike was not included in the freedom of association.[8] By 1991, the view that predominated on the court, which was still deeply split over the scope of s 2(d), was that freedom of association only protected what individuals could do lawfully, such that collective bargaining and strikes were outside the scope of constitutional protection.[9] In *Dunmore*, the Court relaxed its earlier ruling, when seven out of eight members decided that freedom of association included such collective rights as association in trade unions, although collective bargaining continued to be excluded.[10] In *Health Services* in 2007, the Court reversed the Labour Trilogy, and a unanimous seven-member Court held that freedom of association protected the right to bargain collectively, which included a duty to bargain in good faith.[11]

Fraser, however, suggests that another tipping point has been reached. It indicates a shift both in the tone of the judgment from consensus to conflict and the direction of the Court's freedom of association jurisprudence that began in *Dunmore*, which was incrementally to expand the scope of protection. Forty-eight paragraphs

---

8 The Labour Trilogy refers to three concurrently released appeals: *Reference re Public Service Employee Relations Act (Alta)*, [1987] 1 SCR 313 [*Alberta Reference*]; *PSAC v Canada*, [1987] 1 SCR 424; and *RWDSU v Saskatchewan*, [1987] 1 SCR 460. The main reasons were delivered in *Alberta Reference*, a case involving compulsory arbitration to resolve impasses in collective bargaining and a prohibition on strikes in the public sector. Of the six justices participating in the case, three held that collective bargaining was not protected by s 2(d), and four held that strike activity was not protected.

9 In *Professional Institute of the Public Service of Canada (PIPSC) v Northwest Territories (Commissioner)*, [1990] 2 SCR 367, 72 DLR (4th) 1, a close majority (4:3) confirmed that the freedom of association protected in the *Charter* did not include access to a statutory scheme of collective bargaining. The Court split 4:3, with five judges writing reasons. Justice Sopinka wrote substantive reasons dismissing the appeal, while Dickson CJ, La Forest J, and L'Heureux-Dubé J each wrote his or her own reasons, agreeing in the result with Sopinka J. Justice Cory's dissent was supported by Wilson and Gonthier JJ. As late as 1999, in *Delisle v Canada (Deputy AG)*, [1999] 2 SCR 989, 176 DLR (4th) 513, the Court was still divided over the scope of freedom of association; four of the seven judges held that only the establishment of an independent employee association and the exercise in association of the lawful rights of its members were protected under the freedom of association in the *Charter*.

10 *Dunmore*, above note 7.

11 *Health Services*, above note 2.

out of the 118-paragraph-long majority judgment in *Fraser* are taken up by a defense of the majority judgment in *Health Services* as a legally valid and binding precedent. This defensive posture is a response to Rothstein J's concurring judgment, which sought, without being asked by the parties or interveners, to overturn *Health Services*.[12] The disagreement among members of the Court suggests a brake on, and not a reversal of, the development of constitutional protection for collective bargaining. The implications of *Fraser* for cases currently before the courts and the trajectory of freedom of association jurisprudence are key questions that are taken up in this collection.

Accordingly, this collection takes a multidimensional approach to *Fraser* in order to attempt to portray the complex reality that led to the Supreme Court's decision and the broader context of attempts to obtain constitutional protection for labour rights, of which the decision is but a part. The chapters that follow focus on different dimensions of the case; some focus on the farm workers or the history of the litigation, while others concentrate on the jurisprudence and other attempts to recognize labour rights as a form of constitutionally protected human right. The goal with this collection is to intervene in the debate over the *Charter*'s application in the world of work rather than to provide a dispassionate reflection on it. The contributors to this collection are both interested and partisan, and it is precisely the nature of our interest and the reasons why we support the right of agricultural workers to bargain collectively that makes the collection so valuable for appreciating *Fraser*'s significance.

The contributors include trade unionists, lawyers, and academics, and several were involved in the *Fraser* case as witnesses, parties, lawyers, and interveners.[13] The perspective of the participants in liti-

---

12 Paul Cavalluzzo, in this collection [Cavalluzzo]; *Fraser*, above note 1 at paras 59 and 149.

13 For example, I was an expert witness in *Dunmore* and *Fraser* about the history of legal disadvantage experienced by agricultural workers and how their exclusion from labour relations legislation affects their capacity to associate. My interest in agricultural workers and their exclusion from basic labour rights was sparked and sustained by former students. In 1988, Irving Andre, then a student and now a judge at the Ontario Court of Justice, told me about the Seasonal Agricultural Workers Program when we discussed the collective bargaining exclusion of agricultural workers from Ontario's collective bargaining legislation in labour law class. He wrote a very fine paper on the topic, which became "The Genesis and Persistence of The Commonwealth Caribbean Season Agricultural Workers Program in Canada" (1990) 28 Osgoode Hall LJ 243. Martin Doane, a former student in a labour law class I taught, represented the UFCW Canada in *Dunmore*, and asked me to provide some evidence about who agricultural workers are, their terms and conditions of employment, the history of their exclusion from collective bargaining legislation,

gation helps to fill in part of the narrative that gets screened out by the legal process. It also helps to illuminate how legal rights are used as strategic resources in campaigns to empower precarious workers. The contributors are also partisan in that we all support constitutional protection for labour's core associational rights. Each believes that the state should provide effective legal support for collective bargaining rights for agricultural workers and that *Fraser* does not guarantee these rights. All of the contributors are committed to the principle that the state should guarantee freedom of association, which includes the right of workers to form trade unions, to bargain collectively, and to strike.

Our involvement in the case and commitment to the broader goal of obtaining fundamental labour rights for all workers, including agricultural workers, provides a nuanced perspective of the litigation and what was at stake. This familiarity with, and understanding of, the issues in dispute provide a helpful counterweight to more abstract analysis of the jurisprudence that is detached from the issues before the Court. One of the real limitations with the reasoning in *Fraser* is the fact that the Supreme Court became distracted with a debate over the validity and cogency of the reasoning in *Health Services*. What began as a case about whether a specific piece of legislation, the *AEPA*, provided a meaningful process of collective bargaining was transformed into one about the constitutionalization of the *Wagner Act*–model of collective bargaining.[14]

Seeing how *Fraser* progressed through the different levels of the courts helps to highlight the extent of this shift in judicial attention away from the agricultural workers. In the section that follows, I will briefly describe the decisions at each of the three levels of courts in *Fraser*. This overview of the judgments provides a jumping off point to show how the question the Supreme Court of Canada considered in *Fraser* was torn from its social and legal context and, in the process, profoundly transformed.

---

and the impact of the exclusion on their capacity to associate. Fay Faraday, who represented the UFCW Canada in *Fraser* and is a former labour law student, asked me to provide similar evidence in that case.

14 The three key elements of the *Wagner Act* model of labour legislation are: exclusive representation and bargaining rights for the union with the support of a majority of the employees; a duty on the employer to bargain with the union that has obtained exclusive representation rights; and the right to strike to settle negotiating disputes.

B. *Fraser* through the Courts[15]

At issue in *Fraser* was whether legislation designed by the Ontario government to provide agricultural workers with protection for their right to associate and the right to make collective representations to their employer, but that did not include other key elements of the collective bargaining regime available to the vast majority of workers in the private sector, was constitutional. The impugned legislation, the *AEPA*,[16] had an unusual history. It was enacted in response to the Court's 2001 decision in *Dunmore* in which the majority held that freedom of association imposes a positive obligation on the government to protect the rights of vulnerable workers (such as agricultural workers) to join and participate in unions and to make collective representations to their employers. According to Bastarache J on behalf of the majority, the Ontario government's failure to include agricultural workers in a legislative scheme to protect their collective bargaining rights impaired their ability to exercise their fundamental freedom.[17] However, the Court also specifically stated that collective bargaining was not protected under the scope of the *Charter*'s guarantee of freedom of association.[18] In 2002, the Ontario government enacted the *AEPA* in response to *Dunmore* and the legislation was carefully crafted to meet the narrowest interpretation of the constitutional requirements set out in the decision.[19] In fact, the

---

15 This summary of the *Fraser* litigation is based on Judy Fudge, "Constitutional Rights, Collective Bargaining and the Supreme Court of Canada: Retreat and Reversal in the *Fraser* Case" (2012) 41 Industrial Law Journal 1–29.

16 *AEPA*, above note 4.

17 *Dunmore*, above note 7 at paras 21–23.

18 *Ibid* at para 17.

19 The *AEPA* imposes a number of restrictions and obligations on employers in order to protect agricultural workers' right to organize and to make representations to their employer, including a prohibition on unfair labour practices. Unlike the Ontario *Labour Relations Act*, the *AEPA* does not provide a legal mechanism for unions or other employee representatives to obtain collective bargaining rights. In Canada, the *Wagner Act*-model of representations—in which unions that can demonstrate support of the majority of employees in a defined constituency obtain exclusive bargaining rights—prevails. Under the *AEPA*, while employees are permitted to join an employees' association, multiple employee associations can exist in a workplace and there is no process for determining the extent or authenticity of support for an association, let alone to provide exclusive bargaining rights for an association that can demonstrate majority support. Although the *AEPA* requires the employer to give an "employees'" association a reasonable opportunity to make representations respecting the terms and conditions of employment and to listen to oral representations or give a written acknowledgment that the employer has read the written representations, it does not impose a duty on the employer to bargain with

minister who sponsored the legislation specifically stated that it was not designed to provide collective bargaining.[20]

After the legislation came into effect, the UFCW attempted to organize agricultural workers.[21] After obtaining majority support of the employees at a mushroom factory, the union attempted to bargain with the employer. The employer refused. Instead of filing a complaint under the *AEPA*, which, in any event, did not impose an obligation on employers to bargain with employee representatives, the UFCW in *Fraser* sought a declaration that the exclusion of agricultural workers from the *Labour Relations Act* and the entire *AEPA* was unconstitutional. The UFCW argued that these laws breached section 2(d) of the *Charter* by failing to provide effective protection for the right to organize and bargain collectively and violated the equality rights protected in section 15 by excluding farm workers from the protections accorded to workers in other sectors.

Proceeding on the assumption that section 2(d) did not protect collective bargaining, the chambers judge, Farley J, dismissed the application on the ground that the *AEPA* met the minimum constitutional requirements necessary to protect the freedom to organize.[22] He began by adopting the comments made by Sharpe J at the trial level of *Dunmore*, finding that agricultural workers "are poorly paid, face difficult working conditions, have low levels of skills and education, low status and limited employment mobility," but he was of the view that the *AEPA* did not prevent them from attempting to form employee associations.[23] He noted that the *AEPA* provided protection of the freedom to organize employee associations and a right to make representations, which was required by *Dunmore*. Although Farley J mentioned that "perhaps unfortunately there is no specific requirement that the employer respond to the substance of the representations," he also noted that "this would then involve the parties in a form of collective bargaining," an activity that, according to *Dunmore*, the government is not required to protect.[24] He also allowed that it would

---

the employees' representative. Nor does it provide a dispute resolution mechanism to resolve bargaining impasses, although it did established a special roster on the Agriculture, Food and Rural Affairs Appeal Tribunal to deal with complaints.

20 Ontario, Legislative Assembly, *Official Report of Debates (Hansard)*, No 46A (22 October 2002) at 2339, quoted by Abella J in *Fraser*, above note 1 at para 332.

21 This description is drawn from the statement of facts in the majority (paras 8–12) and dissent (para 3) judgments.

22 *Fraser v Ontario (AG)* (2006), 79 OR (3d) 219 (SCJ).

23 *Ibid* at paras 23 and 33.

24 *Ibid* at paras 19 and 16.

have been preferable if the *AEPA* had mirrored the provisions of the *Labour Relations Act* more precisely when addressing possible employer interference with employee associations.[25] However, he advocated a "wait-and-see pragmatic approach," stating that these concerns should be brought to the Tribunal, which had not yet been asked to deal with the workers' complaints.[26] Justice Farley also dismissed the discrimination claim brought under section 15 of the *Charter*.[27]

However, by the time *Fraser* was before the Ontario Court of Appeal, the legal landscape was altered by the Supreme Court of Canada's decision in *Health Services*,[28] which, by overturning the Labour Trilogy, cleared the way for constitutional protection of a meaningful process of collective bargaining. On 17 November 2008, the Court of Appeal released a unanimous decision, which was written by Winkler CJ, granting the union's application that the specific legislation was unconstitutional. According to him, "the combined effect of *Dunmore* and *B.C. Health Services* is to recognize that section 2(*d*) protects the right of workers to organize and to engage in meaningful collective bargaining" and "may impose obligations on the government to enact legislation to protect the rights and freedoms of vulnerable groups."[29]

Although he noted that *Health Services* made it clear that the constitutional protection of collective bargaining did not mean that workers were entitled to a particular statutory model, Winkler CJ emphasized the need for meaningful collective bargaining. As a former senior labour-law practitioner on the employer side, he also had a very clear view of what was needed to make collective bargaining meaningful in the Canadian context. He adopted a contextual approach and looked to the dominant Canadian legislative model of collective bargaining in order to answer the question of what was needed to make collective bargaining meaningful. He stated that:

> At a minimum, the following statutory protections are required to enable agricultural workers to exercise their right to bargain collectively in a meaningful way: (1) a statutory duty to bargain in good faith; (2) statutory recognition of the principles of exclusivity and majoritarianism; and (3) a statutory mechanism for resolving bargaining impasses

25 *Ibid* at para 18.

26 *Ibid*. See also Hanley, above note 3.

27 *Ibid* at para 34.

28 *Fraser v Ontario (AG)* (2008), 92 OR (3d) 481 at para 3 (CA).

29 *Ibid* at para 52.

> and disputes regarding the interpretation or administration of collective agreements.[30]

He noted that the appellants did not ask to be covered by the *Labour Relations Act*, nor did they insist on the right to strike as the dispute resolution mechanism.[31] After reviewing the record, especially the union's attempt to organize and bargain on behalf of agricultural workers and the features of the *AEPA*, Winkler CJ held that the *AEPA* violated the agricultural workers' freedom of association, and that the Ontario government had failed to justify why the violation was necessary. He suspended the declaration of invalidity for twelve months to give the Ontario government an opportunity to develop legislation to provide agricultural workers with meaningful collective bargaining. In the meantime, the Ontario government appealed the decision to the Supreme Court.

The Supreme Court's decision in *Fraser* marks the end of an emerging consensus that began in *Dunmore* that the types of collective activities by workers protected by the constitutional guarantee of freedom of association should be expanded incrementally. The Court was badly divided over the scope of freedom of association and the fault line was *Health Services* and the extension of protection to a meaningful process of collective bargaining, which includes a duty to bargain. Chief Justice McLachlin and LeBel J, the authors of the majority decision in *Health Services*, wrote the majority decision in *Fraser* and Binnie and Fish JJ, who also formed part of the majority in the earlier case, joined them. Only one of the three judges in *Fraser* who had not participated in the *Health Services* decision, Cromwell J, joined with the majority. By contrast, the two other judges who did not take part in *Health Services*, Rothstein and Charron JJ, wanted to see it overturned. Justice Deschamps, who had agreed with the part of the majority judgment in *Health Services* that held the freedom of association included the duty to bargain in good faith, now wanted to narrow the decision and exclude the duty to bargain in good faith from the scope of constitutional protection. Only Abella J, who formed part of the majority in *Health Services*, would have upheld the Ontario Court of Appeal's decision.

This discord is likely to account not only for the defensive tone of the majority judgment, but also its focus. What is striking about the majority judgment is how little of it (about a third of the decision) is devoted to the *AEPA*, to the agricultural workers, or to the history

30 *Ibid* at para 80.

31 *Ibid* at para 57.

of the litigation. Instead, the majority's attention was diverted to defending *Health Services* as a precedent for the proposition that freedom of association includes the protection of collective bargaining rights.

Chief Justice McLachlin and LeBel J characterize *Dunmore* as marking a new stage in the development of section 2(d) jurisprudence in the field of labour relations; it "raised the question of whether section 2(*d*) requires the government to provide a legislative framework which enables employees to associate to obtain workplace goals in a meaningful process."[32] *Health Services* marked a second step as the Court began to "define the ambit of the right of association protected by section 2(*d*) in the context of collective bargaining."[33] They interpret *Health Services* as affirming "that bargaining activities protected by section 2(*d*) in the labour relations context include good faith bargaining on important workplace issues."[34]

However, they are quick to emphasize that *Health Services* did not require a particular model of collective bargaining. They characterize the Court of Appeal's decision that the *AEPA* violated section 2(d) as resting on an interpretation of *Health Services* that "constitutionalizes a full-blown Wagner system of collective bargaining," which they claim "overstates the ambit of the section 2 (*d*) right."[35] According to them, the appropriate question is "whether the legislative scheme (the *AEPA*) renders association in pursuit of workplace goals impossible."[36] The most controversial part of McLachlin CJ and LeBel J's judgment is their answer to this question. They had to ignore the record and stretch the meaning of the statute beyond what its words could bear in order to imply in an obligation on the employer to give consideration to employee representations and, on that basis, to conclude that the statute passed the constitutional standard.[37] The union's equality claim fared even worse. The majority dismissed the argument that the different and inferior collective bargaining rights for agricultural workers violated these workers' right to equal treatment under the law on the ground that it was premature and could not succeed on the record.[38]

By contrast, because he would have overruled *Health Services*, Rothstein J, with whom Charron J agreed, is able to uphold the

---

32 *Fraser*, above note 1 at para 26.

33 *Ibid* at para 34.

34 *Ibid* at para 40.

35 *Ibid* at paras 44 & 45.

36 *Ibid* at para 48.

37 *Ibid*. See for a discussion, Cavalluzzo, above note 12 and Tucker, above note 3.

38 *Ibid* at para 116.

constitutionality of the *AEPA* without having to offer a strained interpretation of the legislation. According to him, the impugned legislation meets the *Dunmore* standard. However, the bulk of Rothstein J's lengthy judgment (157 of 177 paragraphs) is devoted to overturning *Health Services*. Essentially, his judgment seeks to revitalize the approach to freedom of association offered in the Labour Trilogy—that freedom of association only protects what an individual can do lawfully.[39] Having reaffirmed his commitment to the approach to freedom of association articulated in the Court prior to *Health Services*, Rothstein J subjects the reasons offered in *Health Services* for overturning precedent to stinging criticism.[40] He also claims that *Health Services* results in an unworkable constitutionalization of the *Wagner* model of collective bargaining.[41] According to him, freedom of association does not protect either the right to bargain collectively or the duty to bargain in good faith.

Justice Deschamps agrees with Rothstein J that *Dunmore* is the standard and that the *AEPA* is constitutional.[42] However, she does not overrule *Health Services*, in which she formed part of the majority. Instead, she accepts that collective bargaining is a protected form of associational activity. What she does is narrow the scope of protected collective bargaining. She claims that the discussion of the duty to bargain in good faith in *Health Services* is *obiter*. Moreover, she argues that constitutional protection for such a duty should be rejected since the duty is to bargain in good faith is rooted in statute and not fundamental.[43]

Justice Abella is the only member of the Court who focused on the agricultural workers' stories. Although she endorses the Chief Justice and Justice LeBel's discussion of *Health Services*, and agrees that freedom of association protects a meaningful process of collective bargaining, which includes a duty to bargain in good faith, she has a more expansive view of what meaningful collective bargaining

39 *Ibid* at paras 159–65. See also Brian Langille, "The Freedom of Association Mess: How We Got into It and How We Can Get out of It" (2009) 54 McGill LJ 177 at 185–88 [Langille]. While Rothstein J accepts that *Dunmore* was correct that there are some collective activities for which there is no individual analogue, he disagrees with the majority that *Dunmore* "extends to *realization of collective*, as distinct from individual, *goals*." *Fraser*, above note 1 at para 165 [emphasis in the original]. For a similar discussion see Langille, at 178–204.

40 He refers in particular to articles by Langille, *ibid* at 157 & 158 and *Fraser*, above note 1 at paras 184, 228, and 248.

41 *Ibid* at para 256.

42 *Ibid* at para 308.

43 *Ibid* at para 300.

requires.[44] Justice Abella emphasizes the context of the case and the unique vulnerability of agricultural workers in deciding what meaningful collective bargaining requires. She explains that the system of statutory recognition of the exclusive bargaining right of a union that obtains the support of the majority of the relevant employees became the dominant model of collective bargaining in Canada because it prevented employers from promoting rivalry and discord among multiple employee representatives and, thus, promoted meaningful discussion. It is in this context that she mentions how in the instant case one of the mushroom operations that the UFCW tried to organize had sponsored its own "employee association" to compete against the union, which had the support of the majority of employees.[45] She agrees with the Court of Appeal that the absence of any statutory recognition of a majority union's exclusive bargaining rights undermines agricultural workers' rights to engage in meaningful collective bargaining.[46]

C. "Constitutionalizing" Labour Rights

What is clear from even this brief summary of *Fraser* is the extent to which in three of the four sets of reasons, the story of the agricultural workers and their attempts to obtain constitutional protection of a meaningful process of collective bargaining was subsumed within a much broader jurisprudential and institutional debate. The Court's preoccupation with the (ill-defined) question of "constitutionalizing" collective bargaining rights influenced how the issue was framed.[47] Instead of asking whether the *AEPA* provided support for effective collective bargaining, which was the question posed by the union that initiated the litigation, the majority stated that "the ultimate question is whether section 2(d), properly understood and applied, requires the Ontario legislature to provide a particular form of collective bargaining rights to agricultural workers, in order to secure the effective exercise of associational rights."[48] The Government of Ontario, citing Brian Langille's fear that the Court would

44 *Ibid* at para 327.

45 *Ibid* at para 347.

46 *Ibid* at para 335.

47 The question is ill-defined because it slips from the general question of what does freedom of association require in the labour relations context to the specific question of whether freedom of association requires the Ontario government to enact a specific model of collective bargaining law.

48 *Fraser*, above note 1 at para 18.

be required to construct "its own parallel labour code for Canadian workers," raised this question.[49] This question was picked up by Rothstein J, who rejected *Health Services* because it constitutionalized the *Wagner Act*.[50] This question about the constitutionalization of the *Wagner Act* served both to distract the Court's attention away from the record and whether the *AEPA* provided for meaningful collective bargaining for the agricultural workers who had attempted to organize trade unions and bargain collectively, and to draw it to whether or not the *Wagner Act* model of collective bargaining was constitutionally required.[51]

This question, which was initially raised in law review articles, encapsulates a number of distinct, but related, questions: Should judges be drafting detailed labour codes?[52] Do International Labour Organization (ILO) norms on collective bargaining require more than majority-based collective bargaining legislation?[53] Are all of the elements of *Wagner*-style collective bargaining regimes constitutionally protected?[54] Although important, these questions were not the ones that the applicants in *Fraser* were asking. What the farm workers and their union wanted to know was whether the *AEPA* provided a mean-

49 See the *Ontario (AG) v Fraser*, 2011 SCC 20 (Factum of the Appellant) at para 113, citing Langille, above note 39.

50 *Fraser*, above note 1 at para 145.

51 Cavalluzzo, above note 12.

52 Langille, above note 39.

53 Roy J Adams, "Prospects for Labour's Right to Bargain Collectively After *B.C. Health Services*" (2009) 59 UNBLJ 85; Roy J Adams, "*Fraser v. Ontario* and International Human Rights: A Comment" (2009) 14 CJLEL 377.

54 Brian Langille, "Why Are Canadian Judges Drafting Labour Codes and Constitutionalizing the Wagner Act Model?" (2009–2010) 15 CLELJ 101. For example, although Tim Bartikew concludes that "there was evidence to support the conclusion that the *AEPA* was an ineffective framework for protecting freedom of association," he also asserts that "it is difficult to accept that the evidentiary record in this case constituted a sufficient policy debate on the desirability of a general constitutional entrenchment of the exclusive-majoritariansim of our current regime." Tim Bartikew, "Proceed with Caution, or Stop Wherever Possible: Ongoing Paradoxes in Legalized Labour Politics" (2009) 15 CLELJ 77 at 81. However, the problem with this observation is that the applicants never made the claim that majoritarian exclusivity should be constitutionlized; in fact, it was the respondent who raised the spectre of the "constitutionalization of the *Wagner Act*" in what proved to be a successful attempt to overturn the Ontario Court of Appeal's decision. The applicants' claim was that, in light of the evidence of employer interference by promising employer-dominated unions, the *AEPA* did not provide for a meaningful process of collective bargaining and they pointed to the prevailing labour regime in Canada as embodying what has become accepted as a meaningful process of collective bargaining.

ingful process of collective bargaining. They did not ask to be covered by specific legislation. Instead, they drew the Court's attention to what existed in the *AEPA*, how it operated in practice, and how the *AEPA* revived legal schemes that historically were known to undermine freedom of association.[55] They also drew the Court's attention to the key elements in Canadian collective bargaining legislation in the private sector and to ILO standards in order to provide some benchmarks for determining what constitutes effective collective bargaining mechanisms, and they argued that the *AEPA* did not meet this standard.[56] However, the Supreme Court ignored the evidence before it about whether the *AEPA* provided a meaningful process of collective bargaining because it was answering a different question.

How the question is framed is at the heart of all litigation. By the time the Supreme Court of Canada heard the *Fraser* appeal in December 2009, it was clear the stakes were high. Over the two-day hearing, in addition to the parties and the original intervener, the Court heard from fourteen new interveners. Four provinces and the federal government were among the nine interveners supporting the appeal.[57] While it is essential for appellate courts to consider the broader implications of their decisions, it is also important to permit the party who initiates the litigation to frame the questions put to the court. In *Fraser*, the question about constitutionalizing the *Wagner Act*, although an important source of debate in the academic literature, was, in the context of the litigation, a distraction from the question of whether the *AEPA* provided for a meaningful process of collective bargaining.

Moreover, the bigger question, of which the litigation in *Fraser* is just a part, is not whether the *Wagner Act* model of collective bargaining should be constitutionalized, but what constitutional protection for labour rights means and why it is important. These questions are only legal questions in part since they also raise questions pertaining to the nature of democracy and the role of trade unions in contemporary societies such as Canada that are matters of history, philosophy, and political economy.

---

55 *Ontario (AG) v Fraser*, 2011 SCC 20 (Factum of the Respondent) at paras 106–22.

56 *Ibid.*

57 Four employer organizations argued that the appeal of Winkler CJ's decision should be granted, and three of them were represented by the law firm Heenan Blaikie, which also represented another intervener, the Mounted Police Members Legal Fund, that supported the appeal. By contrast, a group representing police officers, an organization representing migrant workers, the Civil Liberties Association, and the Canadian Labour Congress wanted the Court of Appeal's decision upheld.

D. Constitutional Rights at Work

What does the constitutional protection of labour rights mean and why is it important? This question is not straightforward because it can be pitched at different levels and posed in different contexts. There is a flourishing academic literature that looks at "constitutionalizing labour rights," and some of it has seeped into judicial decisions. Elsewhere, I have argued that the demand by unions for protection by constitutional courts of labour's key rights—to form unions, to bargain collectively, and to strike—under the freedom of association is part of a larger transformation in the nature of state, civil society, and market relations in the late twentieth- and early twenty-first century.[58] As the political and economic powers of unions have weakened, they have turned to the courts for protection. The project of embedding labour rights in constitutions is part of an attempt to swing the pendulum away from market expansion and neo-liberalism back towards social protection. The goal is to re-establish a balance between and among civil society organizations and the state by providing constitutional protections to ensure that unions and workers' organizations remain vibrant civil society actors.

Unions in Canada and Europe have sought to defend and entrench labour's traditional rights through litigation by arguing that they are protected under freedom of association.[59] To support these claims, unions have turned to international human rights instruments and institutions that specifically proclaim labour rights in order to provide courts with a principled basis for interpreting constitutional protections. The goal is to persuade constitutional courts that freedom of association includes basic labour rights. However, to be persuasive, unions have to do more than resort to international human and labour rights instruments; they have to demonstrate that the rights to join unions, to bargain collectively, and to strike, which are enshrined in these international human and labour rights instru-

---

58 Judy Fudge "Labour is Not a Commodity: The Supreme Court of Canada and the Freedom of Association" (2004) 67 Sask L Rev 25; Judy Fudge, "The New Discourse of Labour Rights: From Social to Fundamental Rights?" (2007) 29 Comp Lab L & Pol'y J 29; and Judy Fudge, "Constitutionalizing Labour Rights in Europe" in Tom Campbell, Keith Ewing, & Adam Tompkins, eds, *The Legal Protection of Human Rights: Sceptical Essays* (Oxford: Oxford University Press, 2011) [Fudge, "Constitutionalizing"].

59 Keith Ewing & John Hendy, "The Dramatic Implications of *Demir* and *Baykara*" (2010) 39 Indus LJ 2; Fudge, "Constitutionalizing," *ibid*. For a broader discussion of labour rights as human rights see Colin Fenwick & Tonia Novitz, eds, *Human Rights at Work: Perspectives on Law and Regulation* (Oxford & Portland: Hart Publishing, 2010).

ments, foster important social values, and it is because they cultivate these values that unions should be constitutionally protected.

The meaning of the rights enshrined in the *Charter*, like the values the *Charter* is designed to promote—democracy, dignity, equality, and personal autonomy—are essentially contested. Because these values have a range of different meanings, it is incumbent on courts to provide reasons for preferring one interpretation to another. Moreover, these reasons must connect to the context in which the right is invoked.

In *Health Services*, the Supreme Court of Canada identified human dignity, equality, liberty, respect for the autonomy of the person, and the enhancement of democracy as among the values that underlie the *Charter*.[60] Moreover, citing caselaw and referring to academic commentary, the Court asserted: "all of these values are complemented and indeed, promoted, by the protection of collective bargaining in s. 2(*d*) of the *Charter*."[61] It also said that collective bargaining should be protected under section 2(d) because "it emerges as the most significant collective activity through which freedom of association is expressed in the labour context."[62] The Court has begun to link the context of labour relations to the broader values that the *Charter* is designed to promote and to protect. However, it will need help to develop and to elaborate these linkages when deciding the cases that will inevitably come before it.

Why is collective bargaining valuable? Some commentators argue that collective bargaining is deserving of constitutional protection because it allows people to do collectively what they are free to do as individuals, which is to engage in individual contracting.[63] However, this is a thin approach to the values of collective bargaining and provides a correspondingly thin level of protection, which is confined to freedom from direct state interference in collective bargaining. The problem with the analogy between the individual right to contract and the right to bargain collectively is that it misses the distinctive nature of collective bargaining, that it is an exercise in solidarity in which individual interests are not simply aggregated but transformed in the process of democratic deliberation.[64] The formal "equal protection" approach to freedom of association elides

60 *Health Services*, above note 2 at para 81.

61 *Ibid.*

62 *Ibid.*

63 Langille, above note 39 at 188.

64 Alan Bogg, *The Democratic Aspects of Trade Union Recognition* (Oxford: Hart publishing, 2009) at 245–48 [Bogg]; Mark Barenberg, "Democracy and Domination in the

individual and collective bargaining by draining the latter of its social meaning.[65] It also ignores the distinctive historical role of trade unions as crucial institutions in civil society that cultivate greater social equality and expand collective representation. In fact, it is the formal equal protection approach to freedom of association that invites catchy, but facile, comparisons of trade unions with gun clubs, book clubs, or choirs.[66] Independent unions, which are free of em-

---

Law of Workplace Cooperation: From Bureaucratic to Flexible Production" (1994) 94 Colum L Rev 753.

65 See Barrett & Poskanzer, in this collection.

66 In the *Alberta Reference*, above note 8 at para 171, McIntyre J stated:

> The fifth approach rejects the individual nature of freedom of association. To accept it would be to accord an independent constitutional status to the aims, purposes, and activities of the association, and thereby confer greater constitutional rights upon members of the association than upon non-members. It would extend *Charter* protection to all the activities of an association which are essential to its lawful objects or goals, but, it would not extend an equivalent right to individuals. The *Charter* does not give, nor was it ever intended to give, constitutional protection to all the acts of an individual which are essential to his or her personal goals or objectives. If *Charter* protection is given to an association for its lawful acts and objects, then the *Charter*-protected rights of the association would exceed those of the individual merely by virtue of the fact of association. The unacceptability of such an approach is clearly demonstrated by Peter Gall in "Freedom of Association and Trade Unions: A Double-Edged Constitutional Sword" in *Litigating the Values of a Nation: The Canadian Charter of Rights and Freedoms* (1986), at p. 247:
>
>> A brief example illustrates this point. One of our levels of government may decide to ban the ownership of guns. This would not infringe any individual right under the *Charter*. But if some individuals have combined to form a gun club, does the *Charter*'s protection of freedom of association mean that the principal activity of the gun club, namely the ownership and use of guns, is now constitutionally protected? One is quickly forced to the conclusion that it does not. The *Charter* does not protect the right to bear arms, regardless of whether that activity is carried out by an individual or by an association. The mere fact that it is the principal activity of the gun club does not give it a constitutional status. I doubt whether there would be much, if any, disagreement on this point. Thus, by referring to this hypothetical situation we see that the principal activities of associations are not necessarily protected under the concept of freedom of association.

In *Fraser*, above note 1 at para 184, Rothstein J stated:

> that there may be qualitative differences between individuals acting alone and individuals acting in concert. Professor Langille refers to the example of a choir singing. See B. Langille, The Freedom of Association Mess: How We Got into It and How We Can Get out of It" (2009), 54 McGill L.J. 177 . . . at p. 185. While he ultimately believes that the choir metaphor should not apply to determine the scope of s. 2(d) rights, in my opinion the metaphor is apt

ployer and state control, have long been a bulwark against tyranny and are essential organizations in democratic societies. Unions and collective bargaining have played an important role in furthering core values such as freedom as non-domination and political equality in democratic societies.[67]

The need for constitutional protection of core labour rights is especially significant when trade unions are economically and politically weak.[68] Unions in Canada have not fared well in the new economy and density has declined.[69] In 2011, 29.7 percent of the workforce was unionized, and the majority of union members were found in

---

> in explaining the limited type of qualitatively different group activities that maybe protected by s. 2(d).

Later in *Fraser*, above note 1 at paras 211 & 212, Rothstein J went on to state that

> In an article critical of the Health Services decision, Professor Langille describes as "chilling" the suggestion that the Court should weig[h] the harm of banning book clubs as compared to banning collective bargaining and relegat[e] the former to a lower level of concern. Like Professor Langille, I question whether the approach advocated in *Health Services* accords with a purposive interpretation of *Charter* rights. In *Health Services*, the majority appeared to be inquiring into the purpose of an activity to see if it merits constitutional protection. This approach requires judges to select among a range of objects and activities on the basis of their general "importance" to society rather than their connection to the freedom to associate. It is inappropriate for the Court to engage in this sort of inquiry in defining the scope of a constitutional right.

67 Bogg, above note 64; Bob Hepple, *Labour Laws and Global Trade* (Oxford: Hart, 2004); Bob Hepple, "Rights at Work" in Dharam Ghai, ed, *Decent Work: Objectives and Strategies* (Geneva: ILO and IILS, 2006); Alan Fox, *History and Heritage: The Social Origins of the British Industrial Relations System* (London: George & Allen, 1985) at 436; and Desmond Morton, *Working People: An Illustrated History of the Canadian Labour Movement*, 4th ed (Montreal: McGill-Queen's Press, 1998).

68 Referring to recent decisions of the European Court of Justice, Hugh Collins concludes that "the lessons one draws from this history must be that collective labour law can only survive with strong laws that create a secure exception to the economic constitution that protects a market economy." Hugh Collins, "Theories of Rights as Justifications for Labour Law" in Guy Davidov & Brian Langille, eds, *The Idea of Labour Law* (Oxford: Oxford University Press, 2011) 137 at 139.

69 See Judy Fudge, "The New Workplace: Surveying the Landscape" (2009) 33 Man LJ 121 [Fudge, "The New Workplace"]; Michael Lynk, "Labour Law and the New Inequality" (2009) 59 UNBLJ 14 [Lynk]; Lane Kenworthy & Jonas Pontusson, "Inequality and the Politics of Redistribution in Affluent Countries" (2005) 3 Perspectives on Politics 449 [Kenworthy & Pontusson]. This decline is also the case for unions in advanced industrialized countries such as the United Kingdom and the United States with relatively deregulated labour markets.

the public sector, whereas, in 2010, 71.3 percent of the workers were union members, compared with 16 percent in the private sector.[70]

Moreover, since the economic crisis began in 2008, public sector unions have become a target for criticism and legislative restrictions. The *Economist* launched its opening salvo in a headline story published on 6 January 2011. It declared the need to do battle with public sector unions, not simply to reduce pubic spending in order to repay the huge debts caused by bailing out the banks, but in order to achieve productivity and wage parity between public sector and private sector workers.[71] According to the *Economist*, wages freezes are not enough; public sector unions and the institutions of collective bargaining need to be dismantled.

This solution was embraced by Republican politicians in some heavily indebted states in the United States. In Wisconsin, much-publicized and greatly contested legislation strips most public union workers of the right to collectively bargain over everything except wages, requires annual votes to recertify unions, and prohibits the deduction of union dues at source.[72] Ohio went even further in interfering with workers' rights by making it illegal for public sector workers to strike.[73]

---

70 Sharanjit Uppal, "Unionization" October 2011 *Perspectives on Labour and Income* (Statistics Canada Catalogue no 75-001-X) at 3 and 8.

71 "The Battle Ahead: Confronting the Public-Sector Unions" *The Economist* (6 January 2011) online: www.economist.com/blogs/multimedia/2011/01/confronting_public-sector_unions. Moreover, the *Economist* singled Canada out for attention, in its account of union decline in advanced liberal capitalist countries. According to it,

> There is one big exception to the story of union decline, however: the public sector. In the Canadian public sector union density has increased from 12 per cent in 1960 to more than 70 per cent today. Union density is now higher in the public sector than it was in the private sector in its glory days, in the 1950s.

"(Government) Workers of the World Unite!" *The Economist* (6 January 2011) online: www.economist.com/node/17849199.

72 Anne Marie Lofaso, "In Defense of Public- Sector Unions" (2011) 28 Hofstra Lab & Emp LJ 301. See also the special issue "Public Sector Collective Bargaining Under Challenge Symposium" (2011) 28 Hofstra Lab & Emp LJ 253; Paul M Secunda, "The Perceptible Disconnect between the Global Economic Crisis and the Wisconsin Public Sector Labor Dispute of 2011" (27 November 2011). Available at SSRN: http://ssrn.com/abstract_id=1963344.

73 Konrad Yakabuski, "Battle Rages Over Ohio's Union-Limiting Law" *The Globe and Mail* (29 October 2011) A8. In November 2011, Ohio voters resoundingly rejected this legislation. Sabrina Tavernise, "Ohio Turns Back a Law Limiting Unions' Rights" *New York Times*, online: www.nytimes.com/2011/11/09/us/politics/ohio-turns-back-a-law-limiting-unions-rights.html.

Such a full-scale attack on public sector unions has not yet occurred in Canada. However, the federal government has imposed wage restraints on its public sector workers and on two occasions in 2011 it has introduced legislation prohibiting workers employed by private sector airlines and the Crown-owned postal service from striking and imposed interest arbitration to settle the disputes.[74] While the union representing Canada's postal workers has challenged this interference with their members' rights to collective bargaining and to strike, at least one newspaper pundit is urging the federal government to eliminate public sector workers' right to strike or limit their right to bargain collectively to wages only as they do in Wisconsin.[75]

The new economy has produced distinctive patterns of winners and losers when it comes to labour market outcomes such as types of jobs, wages, benefits, and working hours.[76] Private sector unions are in retreat—fewer than one in five workers employed in the private sector are unionized. The consequences of a deregulated labour market accumulate along the ascriptive features of traditionally disadvantaged groups such as immigrants, especially those who are visibly different.[77] Moreover, one of the consequences of deregulation has been to downgrade the norm for new jobs for all labour market participants.[78] Precarious work and inequality undermine the sustainability of households and create fissures and tensions in so-

---

74 In June 2011, the federal government announced that it would legislate an end to a sixteen-hour private sector strike between Air Canada and its employees. The government introduced Bill C-5, *Continuing Air Services for Passengers Act*, for First Reading on 16 June 2011. However, the parties negotiated a settlement before the legislation was passed. Only four days later, it introduced legislation, Bill C-6, *Restoring Mail Delivery for Canadians Act*, SC 2011, c 17 forcing locked-out postal workers back to work for the Crown Corporation. Bill C-6 was introduced for First Reading on 20 June 2011 and Royal Assent was received on 26 June 2011. See the discussion in Derek Fudge's chapter in this collection.

75 Neil Reynolds, "Governments Don't Have to Surrender to Public Sector Unions" *The Globe and Mail* (24 October 2011) A11.

76 See Derek Fudge's chapter in this volume. See also OECD, *Divided We Stand: Why Inequality Keeps Rising* (Paris: OECD, 2011) at 21–45, for a discussion of rising inequality in Canada and other OECD countries.

77 Fudge, "The New Workplace," above note 69.

78 *Ibid.* Caterpillar's February 2012 shutdown of the Electro-Motive locomotive plant in London, Ontario, which put 700 people out of work (after a lock-out in which the company sought significant wage cuts) is but the most recent example of a multinational company moving to a "right-to-work" state (this time, Indiana) in order to avoid union wages and benefits. See Tavia Grant, "The Caterpillar Shutdown's Stark Warning for the Industrial Heartland" *Globe and Mail* (22 February 2012) A8–A9.

cial cohesion. The decline in union density is linked to increasing labour market inequality in Canada and other countries.[79] Our old labour laws do not fit the new reality of the private sector—small workplaces, different groups of workers, and a variety of different types of jobs.[80] Tinkering with the old model will not solve the problem, even if it postpones having to deal with it. If unions and collective bargaining are simply confined to the public sector and do not help the majority of working people, most of whom are employed in the private sector, the political support for public sector unions will continue to evaporate.

The challenges facing the labour movement and other civil society organizations that are concerned with justice and equality in the labour market are not easy. Constitutional protections for labour rights will not solve the problem of organized labour's slow decline. Nor will such legal rights revitalize its role as a vibrant social movement. Courts have neither the power nor the authority to create new institutions or influence economic conditions. However, constitutional protections could be interpreted by courts in ways that would give governments a reason to pause and consider whether there are less restrictive means of attaining legitimate political objectives than by interfering with or refusing to protect workers' constitutional rights. Constitutional review of legislation by judges could legitimately be used to foster democratic deliberation and to ensure that any restrictions on labour rights are proportionate to the goals and means that governments have chosen. It could also be used to ensure that governments live up to their international human rights commitments to protect collective bargaining rights for all workers, including those who, like agricultural workers, have historically been excluded from legislative rights at work.

---

79 Lynk, above note 69; Kenworthy & Pontusson, above note 69.

80 See Cynthia Cranford, Judy Fudge, Eric Tucker, & Leah Vosko, *Self-Employed Workers Organize: Law, Policy, and Unions* (Montreal-Kingston: McGill-Queens Press, 2005). I have discussed this problem in "Fragmenting Work and Fragmenting Organizations: The Contract of Employment and the Scope of Labour Regulation" (2006) 44 Osgoode Hall LJ 609; "After Industrial Citizenship: Market Citizenship or Citizenship at Work?" (2005) 60 RI 631; "Beyond Vulnerable Workers? Towards a New Standard Employment Relationship" (2005) 12 CLELJ 145; "Feminization and Fragmentation: The Challenge of Equity for Labour Market Policy" in Janine Brodie, ed, *Women and Public Policy in Canada* (Toronto: HBJ, 1995); "The Gendered Dimension of Labour Law: Why Women Need Inclusive Unionism and Broader-Based Bargaining" in Linda Briskin & Patricia McDermott, eds, *Women Challenging Unions* (Toronto: University of Toronto Press, 1993).

E. Putting *Fraser* in its Social and Legal Context

This collection begins by focusing on farm workers as an important antidote to their invisibility in three out of four of the Supreme Court's decisions in *Fraser*. The first four chapters detail the history of farm workers' exclusion from labour rights available to the vast majority of workers, their struggle to obtain collective bargaining rights in Ontario, Canada's heavy reliance on migrant workers in the agricultural sector and the treatment of these workers, and the social location of all agricultural workers, regardless of their migration status, in Ontario. In "Farm Worker Exceptionalism: Past, Present, and the post-*Fraser* Future," Eric Tucker restores history and social ballast to the Supreme Court of Canada's generally arid discussion of agricultural workers' collective rights in *Fraser*. He begins by providing the historical and social context for the UFCW's turn towards *Charter* litigation to obtain access for agricultural workers to employment and labour laws available to almost all other workers in the private sector in Canada. Tucker, who was an expert witness for the UFCW in its challenge to the exclusion of agricultural workers from Ontario's occupational health and safety legislation, reviews the historic roots of farm worker "exceptionalism" and the structural vulnerabilities that impede collective action at the workplace level and political action at the governmental level.[81] Having set the context, he then focuses on how *Charter* litigation on freedom of association was used to challenge farm worker exceptionalism. He concludes by exploring what it means to "end" farm workers exceptionalism, and he canvasses some possible directions for future action in the current chilly political and constitutional climate.

In "The Roots of Organizing Agriculture Workers in Canada", Wayne Hanley, the president of the United Food and Commercial Workers Union in Canada, recounts the decades-long struggle of agricultural workers to obtain legal protection for a meaningful process of collective bargaining. He shows how, despite hardship and setbacks, the UFCW found a willing constituency of union supporters and proponents of collective bargaining among farm workers in Ontario. Significantly, he details the union's attempt to use the *AEPA* to obtain a meaningful process of collective bargaining for agricultural workers. He also shows how across Canada, even in jurisdictions in which agricultural workers collective bargaining rights are legally protected, employers in this sector resist unionization and

81 See Tucker, in this collection.

collective bargaining. However, he concludes that despite the legal defeat, the political campaign to obtain collective bargaining rights for agricultural workers will continue, and refers to the success of the Agricultural Workers Alliance centres in providing farm workers with necessary collective support to pursue their rights at work.

Kerry Preibisch hones in on the tens of thousands of men and women from all over the world who enter Canada on temporary employment authorizations to work in the country's agri-food industries. In "Development as Remittances or Development as Freedom? Exploring Canada's Temporary Migration Programs from a Rights-Based Approach," she situates migrant workers in Canada's agricultural sector within the growing global trend towards temporary and seasonal migration, which has been supported by a policy discourse that portrays government-controlled temporary labour migration as delivering a "triple win" scenario for migrant-receiving countries, migrant workers, and migrant-sending countries. Focusing on migrant agricultural workers, she counters the depiction of Canada's temporary migration programs as delivering on economic development for migrants by providing a critical examination of Canada's temporary migration programs for the agriculture sector. She shows how migrants are placed in a very vulnerable position, even when compared with other workers within the country's agriculture and food system, owing to their position at the bottom of the occupational hierarchy, their precarious immigration status as temporary "foreign" workers, and their racialization as non-Whites from the global South. She also illustrates how changes to policies of temporary migration have made farm work an even more precarious form of employment for migrants in particular (and also Canadians), despite mounting research and greater public awareness of the exploitation of migrant agricultural workers over the past decades. Preibisch concludes by calling for greater attention to the rights, welfare, and dignity of migrants when designing temporary migration programs.

In "Envisioning Equality: Analogous Grounds and Farm Workers' Experience of Discrimination," Fay Faraday, who was counsel to UFCW Canada in four constitutional challenges, including *Fraser*, advocates for the rights of domestic and migrant agricultural workers and broadens her examination beyond the situation of migrant agricultural workers to consider agricultural workers more generally and how their claims for equality have been treated by the courts. She illustrates how the courts' failure to engage deeply with the equality argument raised by agricultural workers in *Dunmore* and *Fraser* yields an impoverished and decontextualized analysis which allows their differential and prejudicial treatment to persist. She argues that this failure has "created a disconnect or gap in which the court can express 'sympathy' for the 'vulnerable position' of agricultural workers without confronting how law has been used to construct that very vulnerability."[82] Faraday's goal is to close the gap between the courts' equality analysis and the social reality of agricultural workers. She begins by reviewing the breadth of evidence that was before the courts in *Fraser* before moving to a comparison of the substantive section 2(d) analysis of disadvantage in *Dunmore* with the cursory dismissal of the section 15 claim in *Fraser*. To conclude, Faraday analyzes the role of analogous grounds and how they help deepen the understanding of substantive equality by mapping how law operates to create and sustain relationships of power and powerlessness.

In "Harvest Pilgrims: Migrant Farm Workers in Ontario," Vincenzo Pietropaolo's photo essay portrays the dignity of the workers, the heartbreak of their separation from their families, and their toil. These photographs, which span a quarter of a century, depict the essential contribution that migrant workers make to Ontario's agricultural sector. They also document what too many judges on the Supreme Court of Canada ignored—the arduous and unequal working conditions of agricultural workers.

In "The *Fraser* Case: A Wrong Turn in a Fog of Judicial Deference," Paul JJ Cavalluzzo, who represented the farm workers throughout the proceedings up to and including the argument before the Supreme Court of Canada in *Fraser*, seeks to supplement academic analyses of *Charter* decisions. He notes that academic articles cited by courts often lack knowledge of the facts, and he argues that attention to what is at stake in the dispute can only be comprehensively presented by counsel. According to Cavalluzzo, the record, judicial history, arguments, and conduct of the hearing are important in terms of assessing the judgment of any Supreme Court. He begins his chapter by reviewing the record before the court and briefly surveying the judicial history of *Fraser* as a prelude to his criticism of considering the majority's finding that the constitutional claim of the farm workers was premature. He then turns to the doctrine of judicial deference and how it played a significant role in the analysis of the majority and the concurring decision of Rothstein J. Cavalluzzo also considers the role that the *Wagner* or North American model of labour relations and international human rights law played in the majority and Rothstein J's judgments. He concludes by sug-

82 See Faraday, in this collection.

gesting that all of the judges, except Abella J, participated in a larger political battle than the constitutional claim presented in the record before them.

In "What *Fraser* Means for Labour Rights in Canada," Steven Barrett and Ethan Poskanzer explore some of the implications of the Supreme Court of Canada decision in *Fraser* for the future of labour rights in Canada, from both a practical and doctrinal perspective. They draw upon their experience representing the Canadian Labour Congress in *Charter* cases—both were counsel for the Congress in its intervention in *Fraser*. They begin with an assessment of the Court's perpetuation of the distinction between legislative action and so-called legislative inaction (or exclusion), and the impact on existing and future constitutional challenges to legislation and government action in the collective bargaining sphere. In the second part, they shift to the doctrinal debate between the majority upholding *Health Services*, and Rothstein J, who advocated for the reversal of *Health Services* (and, in particular, against the extension of section 2(d) protection to collective bargaining), with a view to identifying and analyzing the differences between them in order to shed some light on the potential shape of labour rights litigation in the years to come. They focus on Rothstein J's criticism of the *Health Services* and *Fraser* majority, based on his view that the rest of the Court has inappropriately extended constitutional protection to associational objects and outcomes, recognized a uniquely collective dimension to freedom of association, and wrongly privileged worker and trade union associational activities. They suggest that Rothstein J's analysis of the underlying purpose of section 2(d) is inconsistent with its actual historical and philosophical origins, purpose, and rationale. Barrett and Poskanzer conclude by considering the extent to which Rothstein J's own approach to freedom of association doctrinally and practically supports some form of meaningful section 2(d) protection for both collective bargaining and the right to strike.

Taking a strong stance on the need to protect collective bargaining and other key labour rights, such as the right to strike, as part of the constitutional guarantee of freedom of association, Derek Fudge moves outside the confines of the court to look at the larger political battle over labour rights. He begins "Labour Rights: A Democratic Counterweight to Growing Income Inequality in Canada" by showing how governments and employer organizations from across Canada intervened in *Fraser* in order to launch an assault on the constitutional protection of collective bargaining rights. He also recounts how in the 1980s and 1990s, the *Charter* failed to serve as a shield against governments determined to roll back workers' hard won collective rights to bargain collectively and to strike. Fudge then turns to demonstrate the important contribution that unions make toward building a more just and equitable society. Given the significance of trade unions for providing greater income equality in Canada, Fudge argues that it is critical for the labour movement and its allies to launch a vigorous defense of labour rights. He concludes by describing some of the initiatives taken by National Union of Public and Government Employees (NUPGE) to demonstrate how important unions and labour rights are for a vibrant democracy and sustainable economy.

Two chapters move beyond the national confines of the case to specifically consider the role of international norms in court decisions. One, by Patrick Macklem, focuses on how the Supreme Court has used international law in general and in the labour context in particular, while the other, by Keith Ewing and John Hendy, contrasts how the European Court of Human Rights treats ILO supervisory body decisions with their treatment by the Supreme Court. In "The International Constitution," Patrick Macklem argues that as remarkable as the constitutional developments in the field of labour relations are, beneath their surface lies a more fundamental transformation that relates to Canada's engagement with the international legal order. He argues that the traditional dualist view of the domestic implications of international law, whereby an international treaty obligation does not become domestic law unless it has been implemented in domestic legislation, has gradually but steadily been replaced by a much more relational understanding of the boundary between the international and national legal spheres. According to him, nowhere is this shift more apparent than in its constitutional jurisprudence on freedom of association. Macklem's chapter locates current debates on the constitutional dimensions of labour market regulation in light of this transformation in Canada's constitutional relationship with international law. He argues that one of the consequences of this transformation is that the legal capacity of provincial legislatures to tailor labour market regulation to the interests of capital, engage in regulatory competition with other provinces, and experiment with new forms of regulating employment relations, is now curtailed by international standards that receive constitutional expression regardless of whether they have been implemented in domestic legislation. He then traces the Court's jurisprudential reversal of its stance toward freedom of association and situates it in light of dualism's demise, and addresses some of the implications of these twin developments in the context of contemporary debates over the merits of constitutional oversight of Canadian labour law.

In "Giving Life to the ILO—Two Cheers for the Supreme Court of Canada," Keith Ewing and John Hendy consider the relevant ILO Conventions relating to collective bargaining and trace the approach of the Canadian courts to international labour conventions. They trace how the approach of the Canadian courts to the importance of ILO Conventions gradually evolved through the 1980s Labour Trilogy to the new trilogy of *Dunmore, Health Services,* and *Fraser,* and consider the claim that it was inappropriate for the Supreme Court of Canada to rely on Convention 87 as an interpretive source for the proposition that the *Charter* right to freedom of association includes a right to bargain collectively. While they agree with that latter conclusion, they also explain why in their view the government of Canada is bound by membership of the ILO to promote collective bargaining, and why, as a result, the Supreme Court of Canada was fully entitled to rely on ILO principles relating to collective bargaining in construing the *Charter.* Drawing on recent decisions by the European Human Rights Court regarding freedom of association and ILO standards as a point of comparison, they explain why the Supreme Court's decision fails to implement these principles, and how this failure could have been avoided if the decision had been more deeply rooted in ILO standards.

Two goals have animated this collection. The first is to tell the story of the farm workers and their attempt to secure constitutional rights at work. This story was submerged at the Supreme Court by the bigger and amorphous debate over constitutionalizing labour rights. The second goal is to refocus the debate over the scope of the constitutional protection of freedom of association. The broader jurisprudential and institutional debate about how to interpret the freedom of association in the labour context has been sidetracked into a sterile debate that oscillates between a thin and formalistic approach to freedom of association and an enigmatic and misleading discussion of the "constitutionalization of the *Wagner Act.*"[83] We

---

83 Three weeks before *Fraser* was argued at the Supreme Court, the Court issued its ruling in *Plourde v Wal-Mart Canada Corp,* [2009] 3 SCR 465. Writing for the majority, Binnie J took a narrow and formalistic approach to a case involving the legality of Wal-Mart's closure of its first unionized store in Quebec after the United Food and Commercial Workers' Union's successful organizing drive. In justifying this approach, he noted that the right to collective bargaining recognized in the Canadian Constitution is a narrow right, commenting (at para 57): "Care must be taken not only to avoid upsetting the balance the legislature has struck in the Code taken as

believe that it is crucial for the Court to approach the process of interpreting constitutional rights and freedoms in a manner that is attentive to, and engages with, the social and historical context. It is important for courts to interpret the freedom of association to guarantee a democratic space for trade unions, one which requires governments to maintain, to protect, and to extend support for unions' core functions, which are expressing and representing people's rights in the world of work.[84]

---

a whole, but not to hand to one side (labour) a lopsided advantage because employees bargain through their union (and can thereby invoke freedom of association) whereas employers, for the most part, bargain individually." These remarks indicate little appreciation of the fact that in the instant case Wal-Mart is the world's largest public corporation by revenue and, with 2.1 million employees worldwide, the largest private employer in the United States and Mexico, and one of the largest in Canada.

84 Thus, we were heartened by the decision of Ball J of the Saskatchewan Court of Queen's Bench, released 6 February 2012, which interpreted the right to strike as a fundamental component of the freedom of association as guaranteed by s 2(d) of the *Charter.* See *Saskatchewan Federation of Labour v Saskatchewan*, 2012 SKQB 62. In his reasons, Ball J downplayed the Supreme Court's decision in *Fraser*, and, instead, emphasized the Court's decision in *Health Services*.

CHAPTER TWO
Farm Worker Exceptionalism: Past, Present, and the post-*Fraser* Future

*Eric Tucker**

A remarkable feature of the Supreme Court of Canada's majority judgment in the *Fraser*[1] case is the invisibility of Ontario's agricultural workers. Although the judgment makes clear that it is the constitutionality of the *Agricultural Employees Protection Act* (*AEPA*)[2] that is in question, the history of farm worker "exceptionalism under the law"[3] and their specific circumstances are only referred in passing in the recitation of the judicial history of case.[4] However, beyond that point, the reality of farm workers' lives, their legal exclusion from

* Research assistance of Alex Minkin is acknowledged.

1 *Ontario (AG) v Fraser*, 2011 SCC 20 [*Fraser*].

2 SO 2002, c 16 [*AEPA*].

3 The term "farm worker exceptionalism under the law" is borrowed from Greg Schell, "Farmworker Exceptionalism under the Law" in Charles D Thompson Jr & Melinda F Wiggins, eds, *The Human Cost of Food: Farmworkers' Lives, Labor, and Advocacy* (Austin, TX: University of Texas Press, 2002) at 139 [Schell]. The first part of the chapter draws from an earlier article, Eric Tucker, "Will the Vicious Circle of Precariousness be Unbroken? The Exclusion of Ontario Farm Workers from the *Occupational Health and Safety Act*" in Leah Vosko, ed, *Precarious Employment* (Montreal and Kingston: McGill-Queen's University Press, 2006) [Tucker, "Vicious Circle"].

4 The court quotes Farley J, the applications judge in *Fraser*, when he cites a finding of Sharpe J, the judge of first instance in *Dunmore*, that agricultural workers "are poorly paid, face difficult working conditions, have low levels of skills and education, low status and limited employment mobility." *Fraser*, above note 1 at para 13. Justice Sharpe's comments are from *Dunmore v Ontario (AG)* (1997), 155 DLR (4th) 193 (ON Gen Div).

protection, and the social effects of this exclusion play no role in the remainder of the judgment. The difference between the Supreme Court's judgments in *Fraser* and *Dunmore*[5] could not be more striking in this regard. In *Dunmore*, the Court was explicitly concerned with the inability of agricultural workers to enjoy freedom of association because of their vulnerability, which was exacerbated by their historical and present exclusion from a statutory labour relations scheme that protected freedom of association.[6] In contrast, the Court in *Fraser* neither discusses the deep history of farm worker exceptionalism nor acknowledges their specific vulnerabilities. In part, this difference in visibility is a function of the issue that was before the Court. In *Dunmore*, the Court needed to establish that farm workers were a vulnerable group in order to determine whether the state was under a positive constitutional duty to protect their freedom of association. In *Fraser*, their vulnerability was already a judicially recognized fact and the central issue was what the Government of Ontario was required to do in order to meet its constitutional obligation toward farm workers.

But this explanation of the difference in how the Court dealt with the social reality and legal treatment of agricultural workers is not sufficient; logically, the social and legal condition of agricultural workers ought to be as important to the "what protection is due" discussion as it was to the "whether protection is due" discussion. Indeed, the position of the Supreme Court of Canada in *Fraser* that the *Charter* does not require a uniform model of labour relations, but does require state action to enable vulnerable workers to meaningfully exercise their freedom of association,[7] would seem to demand that the Court put, at the core of its analysis, the specific conditions faced by vulnerable workers. The invisibility of agricultural workers from the majority's discussion of the *AEPA* is very peculiar. Surely, the judges needed to be attentive to the conditions of agricultural workers in Ontario generally, and to the situation of the particular group of workers who brought the case, if they were serious about inquiring into the adequacy of the *AEPA* as a vehicle that "provides agricultural workers with the protection necessary for them to exercise their constitutional freedom to form and maintain associations"[8] and more importantly, post-*Health Services*, whether it protects "the

5 *Dunmore v Ontario (AG)*, [2001] 3 SCR 1016 [*Dunmore* SCC].

6 *Ibid* at paras 39–48.

7 *Fraser*, above note 1 at para 47.

8 *Dunmore* SCC, above note 5 at para 67.

right of employees to associate for the purpose of advancing workplace goals through a process of collective bargaining."[9]

What explains this silence? Perhaps the Court's approach was necessitated by its decision to uphold the *AEPA* through a Herculean interpretative effort to tease a duty to bargain out of a statute that clearly intended not to provide one. The intrusion into this discussion of the history of exclusion and the social reality of agricultural labour would have made the Court's pretence that collective bargaining might occur under the auspices of the *AEPA* even less tenable. But this is pure speculation.

It is important, however, to restore history and social reality to the discussion of labour rights, whether in the context of litigation over the constitutional right to bargain collectively, or in discussions of strategy and tactics in the aftermath of the Court's disappointing judgment in *Fraser*.[10] This is the purpose of this chapter, which begins by providing the historical and social context for the turn towards *Charter* litigation to obtain access to employment and labour laws available to almost all other workers in the private sector in Canada. I will briefly review the historic roots of farm worker exceptionalism and the structural vulnerabilities that impeded collective action at the workplace level and political action at the governmental level. Having set the context, I will then focus on how *Charter* litigation on freedom of association was used to challenge to farm worker exceptionalism.[11] Finally, I will explore what it means to "end" farm workers exceptionalism, and I will canvass some possible directions for future action in the chilly political and constitutional climate of the post-*Fraser* world.

---

9 *Health Services and Support—Facilities Subsector Bargaining Association v British Columbia*, [2007] 2 SCR 391 at para 87 [*Health Services*].

10 In an earlier article, Eric Tucker, "The Constitutional Right to Bargain Collectively: The Ironies of Labour History in the Supreme Court of Canada" (2008) 61 Labour/Le Travail 151, I criticized the Court's use of history in the *Health Services* decision. The point of the article was not that Supreme Court of Canada judges were bad historians, but that because they used history instrumentally, they failed to learn from it. This failure is manifest in all the *Fraser* judgments, with the exception of Abella J's dissent. For a defence of the instrumental use of history in *Health Services*, see Thomas Kuttner, "Pondering *Health Services*: Some Reflections," online: http://www.cba.org/cba/cle/PDF/Constit09_Kuttner_paper_final.pdf (accessed 13 June 2011).

11 I do not address the equality rights line of argument, which is dealt with in greater detail in this volume by Fay Faraday.

A. The History of Farm Worker Exceptionalism and Vulnerability

The legal position of agricultural workers in mid-nineteenth century Ontario was not substantially different from that of other subordinate workers. All were subject to the master and servant regime that left the substantive terms and conditions of employment, including wages and hours, to be determined by agreement between the parties, but that criminalized employee breaches of contract while providing workers with summary procedures for wage recovery. As well, under this regime, it was ambiguous whether associational activities were lawful.[12] It was also a time when the overwhelming majority of Ontario's population was rural; farms were small, and agricultural labourers were often themselves smallholders or aspiring smallholders, seeking to sustain themselves while they made their farms. As a result, their interests were often closely aligned with their employers and collective action was more likely among agriculturalists generally than by farm workers as a distinct group.

Farm workers also did not receive special treatment when a liberal voluntarist regime superseded the master and servant regime. Under liberal voluntarism, all workers were left to fend for themselves in labour markets, but were not threatened with criminal sanctions for simple breaches of contract. They were also free to form unions without the threat of criminal prosecution for doing so, although their employers were also free to fire them if they did. Agricultural exceptionalism under the law emerged only with the development of a more protective regime of statutory labour law in the last quarter of the nineteenth century. Apart from wage protection laws, such as in the master and servant regime, the first strand of protective labour law addressed hazardous working conditions. The 1874 *Thrashing Machines Act* was one of the earliest such statutes and it aimed to protect agricultural workers from hazards associated with the growing use of steam-powered equipment. However, this protection of agricultural workers proved to be anomalous. Subsequent legislation protected workers on railways (1881) and in factories (1884), shops (1888), mines (1890), and construction (1911), but

12 Paul Craven, "Canada, 1670–1935: Symbolic and Instrumental Enforcement in Loyalist North America," in Douglas Hay & Paul Craven, eds, *Masters, Servants, and Magistrates in Britain and the Empire, 1562–1955* (Chapel Hill, NC: University of North Carolina Press, 2004) at 196–203; Eric Tucker, "'That Indefinite Zone of Toleration': Criminal Conspiracy and Trade Unions in Ontario, 1837–1877" (1991) 27 Labour/Le Travail 15.

no sector specific legislation was enacted to protect farm workers, despite the increasingly hazardous conditions they faced as mechanization and the use of chemicals expanded.[13] The enactment of omnibus occupational health and safety (OHS) legislation in 1978 did not change the situation. Despite protests from the New Democratic Party (NDP), farm workers were excluded from this legislation, although a provision was made for them to be brought under the Act by regulation. Their exclusion was supposed to be temporary, until it was determined what accommodations had to be made for the agricultural sector, but it took another twenty-five years and a *Charter* challenge to overcome the resistance of farm interests who had the ear of government, before the necessary regulation to extend coverage was finally promulgated.[14] However, even that action did not end exceptionalism for the protection of agricultural workers' health and safety. The regulation limited the general duty to establish joint health and safety committees and selectively applied generally applicable OHS regulations. Moreover, in the years since the extension of coverage, no OHS regulations specific to farming operations have been promulgated.[15]

Closely associated with the protection of workers from hazardous working conditions was the development of workers' compensation laws to protect the income of workers who were temporarily or permanently disabled by work. Here again, exceptionalism became inscribed in the law soon after legislation was enacted. The common law of employers' liability applied to all workers and severely limited their ability to recover damages for work injuries from their employers. In 1886, workers were given the option to sue their employers under a statutory scheme that limited their employers' common law defences and the size of workers' potential recovery. The scheme initially applied to all workers, but in 1893 farm interests successfully lobbied the Ontario legislature to have farm workers excluded

13 Eric Tucker, *Administering Danger in the Workplace* (Toronto: University of Toronto Press, 1990).

14 United Food and Commercial Workers' Union (UFCW) Canada filed a *Charter* challenge in the Ontario Superior Court of Justice in June 2003 alleging that farm workers' exclusion from the OHS Act violated both the s 7 rights to life and security of the person and the s 15 right to equality: *Fraser v Ontario (AG)*, Court File No 03-CV-250815CM3. The case did not proceed through litigation however, because in March 2004 the Ontario government announced that it would develop the regulation to bring farm workers within the OHS. This regulation, Ont Reg 414/05 was promulgated in June 2005 and took effect in June 2006.

15 The long struggle to bring farm workers into the *Occupational Health and Safety Act*, R.S.O. 1990, c. O.1 is discussed in Tucker, "Vicious Circle," above note 3.

on the basis that farm work was different than industrial work. The effect of their exclusion was to return farm workers to the tender mercies of the common law. By the time a no-fault workers' compensation system was enacted in 1914, farm worker exceptionalism was so well entrenched that Chief Justice of Ontario William Meredith, the author of the royal commission report that designed the scheme, doubted whether public opinion would support the inclusion of farm workers, and therefore did not recommend that they be covered, despite his belief that in principle they should. It was not until 1965 that workers' compensation coverage was made mandatory in two classes of farm operations.[16]

The next strand of protective labour law to develop was with respect to minimum wages and maximum hours of work. Legislation of this kind first began to be enacted in the early decades of the twentieth century and farm worker exceptionalism was the norm from the outset. The exclusion of agricultural workers remained the case as minimum standards laws were expanded in the post-World War II era and consolidated into the *Employment Standards Act* (*ESA*) in 1968.[17] In 1975, absolute exceptionalism gave way to partial exceptionalism, which remains the case today. A complete survey of the application of the *ESA* to agricultural workers is beyond the scope of this chapter, but it is notable that persons employed in growing mushrooms, as were the plaintiffs in *Fraser*, are exempt from the hours of work, eating periods, and overtime pay provisions of the *ESA*.[18]

The last strand of protective labour law addressed workers' collective action, and this is the area in Ontario where exceptionalism remains most entrenched—even after over a decade of *Charter* litigation. The earliest legislation created a regime Judy Fudge and I labelled "industrial voluntarism."[19] It did not directly protect or promote collective action by workers, but rather, aimed to facilitate the adjustment of disputes when they arose. Naturally, public interest in dispute resolution was limited to those areas where disputes were occurring, and so late nineteenth-century Ontario legislation targeted the skilled trades where workers had successfully organized craft unions. For example, the *Trades Arbitration Act* of 1873 provided a voluntary scheme of non-binding arbitration that could be used

16 Tucker, *ibid.*

17 On these developments, see Mark P Thomas, *Regulating Flexibility: the Political Economy of Employment Standards* (Montreal and Kingston: McGill-Queen's University Press, 2009) at 30–71.

18 O Reg 285/01, ss 4 and 8. Also see Thomas, *ibid* at 91–95.

19 Fudge & Tucker, below note 27.

by groups of masters and skilled labourers. The same was true for Ontario's 1894 *Trade Disputes Act*.[20] When the federal government first began enacting facilitative labour law at the beginning of the twentieth century, it too focused on dispute resolution, but in addition sought indirectly to promote norms that supported the development of collective bargaining relations between responsible unions and employers by putting each side's demands under public scrutiny. However, for both legal and pragmatic reasons, the federal government's signature legislation, the 1907 *Industrial Disputes Investigation Act*, which imposed compulsory conciliation prior to strikes or lockouts, was limited to mining and public utilities, like railways, where labour disruptions had a national impact.[21]

Workers in agriculture, like those in many other industries, were not covered by any of these pre-World War I collective bargaining statutes. Moreover, the structure of agriculture at the time was still not conducive to collective action by farm workers. Farming remained primarily a small-scale family operation that depended on a small number of hired hands and, in some sectors, larger pools of casual labourers at key periods of time. However, the structure of agriculture began to change during and after World War I as agricultural holdings expanded, the demand for farm labour grew, and the opportunity for farm hands to become farm operators diminished. The social distance between farmers and their hired hands grew, and their interests became more distinct. Collective action by farm workers to improve their conditions, however, remained exceptional. In part, this was a function of the geographic dispersion of hired hands. As well, despite the rapid growth in the number of farm workers, they were still greatly outnumbered by farm operators and unpaid family help. Farm workers were also a diverse group. In addition to being divided between permanent and seasonal workers, they were also ethnically diverse, as Canadian immigration agents increasingly turned their attention to central, eastern, and southern

---

20 SO 1873, c 26; SO 1894, c 42. See Margaret McCallum, "Labour and Arbitration in the Mowat Era" (1991) 6 CJLS 65.

21 SC 1907, c 20. An earlier statute, the *Conciliation Act*, could, in principle, apply to any dispute between employers and workers, although there is no record that the government ever initiated an investigation into a labour dispute involving farm workers or ever received from them an application to appoint conciliators or arbitrators. SC 1900, c 24.

Europe to fill the growing demand for agricultural workers.[22] Finding unity proved to be a difficult task.

Radical elements in the labour movement, such as the Industrial Workers of the World (IWW) and later the communists, evinced some interest in organizing farm workers, but faced enormous grower opposition and severe state repression, even when they tried. The larger labour movement did even less as its primary goal was to forge farmer-labour alliances against banks and processors.[23] The same was also true for the Co-operative Commonwealth Federation (Farmer-Labour-Socialist), formed in 1932, as its name makes explicit. Farmers who did not cast their lot with labour socialists, on the other hand, constituted a very powerful political lobby in support of farmer exceptionalism in the law. As a result, when the Canadian state began moving toward industrial pluralism or the *Wagner Act* model, involving protection for trade union activity against employer interference, mandatory employer recognition of majority unions, exclusive representations, and a duty to bargain in good faith, farm worker exceptionalism became entrenched.[24]

The first move in this direction in Ontario was the 1935 *Industrial Standards Act* that created a mechanism for the state to assist in the negotiation of wage and hours of work schedules that would apply to particular industries in a geographic area of the province. Notably, mining and agriculture were excluded from its operation.[25] In 1943, the province enacted a collective bargaining scheme that incorporated more elements of the *Wagner Act* model, but it too excluded agricultural workers.[26] Federal government legislative activity pre-dated World War II, through the enactment of an amendment to the *Criminal Code* in 1939 protecting freedom of association by making it a crime for an employer to refuse to employ a person for the sole reason

22 Donald Avery, *"Dangerous Foreigners": European Immigrant Workers and Labour Radicalism in Canada, 1896–1932* (Toronto: McClelland and Stewart, 1979) at 97.

23 Little has been written on the history of farm worker-farmer relations in Ontario. Therefore, much of the above has been extrapolated from studies of other Canadian jurisdictions. See Cecilia Danysk, *Hired Hands* (Toronto: McClellan & Stewart, 1995); John Herd Thompson & Allen Seager, "Workers, Growers and Monopolists: The 'Labour Problem' in the Alberta Beet Sugar Industry During the 1930s" (1978) 3 Labour/Le Travailleur 153.

24 It is notable that the American *Wagner Act* itself (formally the *National Labor Relations Act*) and the *Fair Labor Standards Act*, both passed in 1935, excluded agricultural workers. See Marc Linder, *Migrant Workers & Minimum Wages* (Boulder, CO: Westview Press, 1992) at 125–75, and Schell, above note 3.

25 SO 1935, c 28, s 2(e).

26 *Collective Bargaining Act*, SO 1943, c 4, s 24(a).

that the person was a member of a union. This law applied without restriction, but realists understood at the time that its significance was more symbolic than material. Indeed, the law is still on the books, but there is no record that an employer has ever been prosecuted for its violation.[27] The more important measure was the promulgation of PC 1003 under the government's expanded war powers, which established a national labour relations system that incorporated protection of organizing activity, compulsory recognition of unions with majority support, a duty to bargain in good faith, compulsory arbitration of grievances, and compulsory conciliation of bargaining disputes. Farm workers, however, were excluded from its operation, and this became the norm in the collective bargaining legislation that followed the end of the wartime emergency.[28] Thus, it was precisely at the moment that the state intervened most forcefully to promote collective bargaining through industrial pluralism that farm worker exceptionalism became most firmly entrenched, leaving farm workers to fend for themselves, essentially under a regime of liberal voluntarism, if they wished to act collectively in the post-war world.

Two significant post-war developments affected farm workers' opportunities to engage in collective bargaining, but they cut in opposite directions. The first was a continuation the pre-war trend toward the concentration of farming in fewer but more heavily capitalized operations that depended on higher levels of paid labour. From 1946 to 1971, the number of farms decreased from about 150,000 to about 95,000. By 2001, there were only about 60,000 farms. Over this same time frame, average capitalization increased from about $17,000, to $73,000, to $846,000. Weeks of paid labour also increased. Data is not available prior to 1971, but from 1971 to 2001, there was over a 50 percent increase from about 1.5 million to 2.3 million hours of paid labour in agriculture. More heavily capitalized farms hired a greater share of the farm labour.[29] Although there is great variation, clearly there is a capital-intensive sector where significant numbers of wage

27 Judy Fudge & Eric Tucker, *Labour Before the Law* (Toronto: Oxford University Press, 2001), 225–26 [Fudge & Tucker]. *Criminal Code*, RSC 1985, c C-46, s 425.

28 Farm workers were not exempted from post-war collective bargaining legislation in three jurisdictions: Saskatchewan, Manitoba, and Newfoundland. For Saskatchewan, see *The Freedom of Association Act*, SS 1938, c 87 and the *Trade Union Act*, SS 1944, c 69; for Manitoba, see the *Manitoba Labor Relations Act*, SM 1948, c 27; and for Newfoundland, see *Labour Relations Act*, SN 1952, c 258.

29 Data from 1951 to 1971 is calculated from *Historical Statistics of Canada*, online: www.statcan.gc.ca/pub/11-516-x/sectionm/4057754-eng.htm. Data from 1971 to 2001 comes from Tucker, "Vicious Circle," above note 3 at 263.

workers are drawn together, creating a more favourable structure for collective action. Mushroom farms are emblematic of this sector of agriculture, and so it is not surprising that trade union activity has been more concentrated here.[30] Other agricultural sectors that rely on large numbers of seasonal workers present a more challenging organizing environment.

The second significant post-war development was the turn to unfree labour,[31] to meet the demand for farm workers. Before the war, the demand for agricultural workers was met through the promotion of immigration and the mobilization of labour reserves within Canada. This policy continued in the aftermath of the war, although in 1946 and 1947 Polish ex-servicemen were recruited to work under contract for two years. In the mid-1950s, the government began to reduce its recruitment of relatively unskilled immigrants and this put more pressure on farm operators to mobilize Canadian labour reserves. For example, Aboriginal peoples on reserves in Alberta were subject to both positive incentives and the use of economic coercion by terminating welfare payments to those who remained in their communities rather than migrate to work in the sugar beet fields.[32] In general, the internal mobilization strategy did not meet farmers' demands for labour.

Significantly, the demand was not just for labour, but for *low-cost* labour. In the post-World War II period, farm operators found themselves increasingly caught in a cost-price squeeze in an environment in which their ability to control prices through marketing boards was diminishing. So too was their ability to control non-labour costs, thus making labour cost control an even greater imperative.[33] So

---

30 Unionization efforts among mushroom workers have given rise to the majority of challenges to farm worker exceptionalism. As well, mushroom workers were the source of most union certifications under the short-lived *Agricultural Labour Relations Act*. See below.

31 By unfree labour, I mean workers who face significant legal limits on their freedom to circulate in the labour market. For discussion of the free/unfree labour continuum, see Robert Miles, *Capitalism and Unfree Labour: Anomaly or Necessity?* (London: Tavistock, 1987) and Vic Satzewich, *Racism and the Incorporation of Foreign Labour: Farm Labour Migration to Canada Since 1945* (London: Routledge, 1945).

32 Ron LaLiberte & Vic Satzewich, "Native Migrant Labour in the Southern Alberta Sugar-beet Industry" (1999) 36 Canadian Review of Sociology and Anthropology 65; Vic Satzewich, *Racism and the Incorporation of Foreign Labour* (London: Routledge, 1991).

33 John Shields, "The Capitalist State and Class Struggle in the Fruit and Vegetable Industry in British Columbia" in GS Basran & David A Hay, eds, *The Political Economy of Agriculture in Western Farming* (Toronto: Garamond, 1988); Tom Murphy,

even though farm wages increased, they remained below the wages paid to relatively unskilled labour in other industries. Farm operators also generally resisted the end of farm worker exceptionalism, even though this might have made agricultural work more attractive, although, as we have seen, by the mid-1960s farm workers were gaining access to workers' compensation schemes. Not only did farm operators oppose the end of exceptionalism, but they also lobbied the federal government to permit the importation of temporary foreign workers, thereby more deeply entrenching it. Although the state initially resisted, the strength of the farm lobby, the state's interest in a cheap food policy, and the political weakness of farm workers ultimately led the Canadian government to establish the Seasonal Agricultural Workers Program (SAWP) in the mid-1960s. Over the years, the program expanded enormously, so that in 2009 it provided over 27,000 farm workers, of whom two-thirds were located in Ontario.[34] This program has been the object of numerous studies, which, in the words of Janet McLaughlin, creates a "system of exception within which workers' integration in Canada is defined by their structural vulnerability." Because their presence in Canada is tied to their employment with a particular farmer and farm workers are under the threat of repatriation, because farmers can designate which workers they will rehire for the next season, and because of the enormous poverty in their home countries, workers in this program are extremely reluctant to complain about violations of their rights under it, notwithstanding that various non-governmental groups, including unions, have attempted to provide support.[35]

More recently, the situation of farm workers has been made even more precarious by the creation of a low-skill temporary migrant program in 2002, which in 2009 provided nearly 8,000 temporary

---

"From Family Farming to Capitalist Agriculture: Food Production, Agribusiness, and the State" in Bryant Fairley, Colin Leys, & James Sacouman, eds, *Restructuring and Resistance from Atlantic Canada* (Toronto: Garamond, 1990).

34 Canada. Human Resources and Skills Development Canada (HRSDC), online: www.hrsdc.gc.ca/eng/workplaceskills/foreign_workers/stats/annual/table10a.shtml.

35 Janet McLaughlin, *Trouble in Our Fields: Heath and Human Rights among Mexican and Caribbean Migrant Farm Workers in Canada* (PhD, University of Toronto, 2009) at 102 [emphasis in original]. The literature is immense. For a small sample, see Tanya Basock, *Tortillas and Tomatoes* (Montreal: McGill-Queen's University Press, 2002); Kerry Preibisch, "Migrant Agricultural Workers and Processes of Social Inclusion and in Rural Canada: *Enciuentros* and *Desencuentros*" (2004) 29 Canadian Journal of Latin American and Caribbean Studies 203; Adrian A Smith, "Legal Consciousness and Resistance in Caribbean Seasonal Agricultural Workers" (2005) 20 CJLS 95.

farm workers, of whom some 1,300 were placed in Ontario.[36] These workers are even less protected than those who come under the SAWP, which is operated through bilateral agreements between Canada and a limited number of sending countries. Moreover, the new program provides expanded opportunities for farm operators to "pick their own" workers, thereby further exacerbating their vulnerability as well as the vulnerability of domestic farm workers.[37]

This program is of particular significance in the context of the *Fraser* decision, which arose out of unsuccessful efforts to organize mushroom and hothouse workers, who work year-round in an industrial environment. Because the work is not seasonal, their employers could not access the SAWP, and were dependent on new immigrants with secure status in Canada. Since 2002, however, these employers have been able to import temporary workers under the low-skill program, first by cutting pay rates to encourage domestic workers to quit, and then by getting the responsible government body to provide a labour market opinion that there was a shortage of workers.[38]

Even before unfree labour began to play a significant role in agriculture, there were sporadic attempts by the United Food and Commercial Workers' Union (UFCW) to organize Ontario farm workers employed year-round in industrial farm settings such as chick hatcheries and mushroom farms. The union attempted to bring these workers within the *Labour Relations Act* (*LRA*) by arguing that they were not employed in agriculture. In every case, the labour board rejected the claim.[39] As a result of legislative exclusion, adverse organizing conditions, and employers' refusal to voluntarily engage with unions, union density in Ontario agriculture was nil or virtually nil.[40]

---

36 HRSDC, online: www.hrsdc.gc.ca/eng/workplaceskills/foreign_workers/stats/annual/table4a.shtml.

37 Kerry Preibisch, "Pick-Your-Own Labor: Migrant Workers and Flexibility in Canadian Agriculture" (2010) 44 International Migration Review 404. More generally, see Judy Fudge & Fiona MacPhail, "The Temporary Foreign Worker Program in Canada: Low-Skilled Workers as an Extreme Form of Flexible Labor" (2009) 31 Comp Lab L & Pol'y J 101; Malcolm Sargeant & Eric Tucker, "Layers of Vulnerability in Occupational Health and Safety for Migrant Workers: Case Studies from Canada and the UK" (2009) 7:2 Policy and Practice in Health and Safety 51.

38 Preibisch, "Pick-Your-Own," *ibid* at 428–29.

39 *Spruceleigh Farms, A Division of Canada Packers Limited*, [1972] OLRB Rep October 860 (hatchery); *Wellington Mushroom Farm*, [1980] OLRB Rep May 813; *Cuddy Chicks*, [1988] OLRB Rep May 468.

40 Statistics Canada, CANSIM, v810459 279-0028 (covering 1976–1988, during which union density rose from 0.0 to 0.4 percent).

It was in this context that the UFCW first turned to the *Charter* to force an end to farm worker exceptionalism.

B. The *Charter* Rollercoaster

The first turn to the *Charter* came in 1988 in the *Cuddy Chicks* case, where the UFCW's alternative to the argument that hatchery workers did not work in agriculture was that, if they did, then their exclusion from the *LRA* violated the workers' constitutionally protected freedom of association. The Ontario Labour Relations Board (OLRB) never reached a substantive conclusion on that issue because its authority to entertain a *Charter* claim was disputed all the way to the Supreme Court of Canada, which ultimately held that the OLRB had the authority.[41] By then, however, there was an NDP government in Ontario that had initiated a process aimed at producing collective bargaining legislation for the province's agricultural workers. As a result, the parties agreed to adjourn the OLRB application.[42]

The NDP law, the *Agricultural Labour Relations Act* (*ALRA*), passed in 1994 over the objections of the Liberal and Conservative parties, extended the *LRA* to the agricultural sector subject to several modifications, the most important being that final offer selection was substituted for strikes and lockouts in the event the parties were unable to reach an agreement.[43] Under that law, the UFCW was certified as the bargaining agent of approximately 200 workers at the Highline mushroom factory. Two other certification applications were filed, one for Kingsville Mushroom Farm and the other for Fleming Chicks. However, before these applications could be heard, the NDP government was defeated by the Conservatives who promptly repealed the *ALRA* and terminated any agreements and certifications made under the *ALRA*.[44] This measure fully restored farm worker exceptionalism in the area of collective bargaining.

The immediate response of the UFCW was to challenge the repeal, arguing that it violated workers' freedom of association and equality rights. This was the *Dunmore* case. It is not necessary to go into detail about the Supreme Court of Canada's decision, which has

41 *Cuddy Chicks v Ontario (Labour Relations Board)*, [1991] 2 SCR 5 upholding [1988] OLRB Rep May 468.

42 *Cuddy Chicks Limited*, [1992] OLRD No 1170.

43 SO 1994, c 6.

44 *Labour Relations and Employment Statute Law Amendment Act, 1995*, SO 1995, c 1.

already been subject to voluminous commentary.[45] For my purposes here, the most important feature of the judgment is that the Court was attentive to the social reality of agricultural workers and the impact of legal exclusion on their ability to enjoy freedom of association in practice. This was necessary because, doctrinally, the Court required that for a case of under-inclusion to succeed, the plaintiff had to provide a proper evidentiary foundation that, absent positive state action, workers would be substantially incapable of exercising the freedom to associate. Farm workers could not be made to disappear from this litigation.

The major limitation of the case, however, was that although the court expanded upon the content of freedom of association from the narrow approach it had taken in the Labour Trilogy and the cases that followed, it still rejected the view that freedom of association extended to protect the associational activities like collective bargaining or striking.[46] Therefore, when it came to the question of how farm worker exclusion was to be remedied, the Court's options were limited, regardless of the social reality it described. In the result, the Court required the Ontario government "at minimum" to provide "the statutory freedom to organize in s. 5 of the LRA . . . along with protections judged essential to its meaningful exercise, such as freedom to assemble, to participate in the lawful activities of the association and to make representations, and the right to be free from interference, coercion and discrimination in the exercise of these freedoms."[47] To the extent that the Court was ordering the government to legislate freedoms or privileges, the legislation was redundant. Under the law at the time, farm workers were as free to assemble as any other workers, they were as free to form and participate in associations as any other workers, and they were as free to make representations to their employers as any other workers. Moreover, they also enjoyed a legal right not be interfered with in the exercise of associational activities, protected by the *Criminal Code*. What was new, therefore, was the legal *right*, guaranteed by provincial law, not to be interfered with in the exercise of associational activities. Pointedly, the Court did not require that the government impose on employers a *duty* to bargain with farm workers' associations, since such an obligation would have been inconsistent

---

45 For a sample, see Judy Fudge, "Labour is Not a Commodity: The Supreme Court of Canada and the Freedom of Association" (2004) 67 Sask L Rev 425, and the set of articles in (2003) 10 CLELJ.

46 *Dunmore* SCC, above note 5 at para 17.

47 *Ibid* at para 67.

with the Court's understanding of the parameters of freedom of association under the *Charter* at the time.

The same Conservative government that had repealed the *ALRA* was still in power when the *Dunmore* decision was released and it responded by enacting *AEPA*, which complied with, and in one respect exceeded, the letter of the Court's minimum requirements.[48] Section 1(2) of the Act listed the rights of agricultural employees virtually in the same language used by the Supreme Court of Canada. Section 5 elaborated on the right to make representations, largely for the purpose of limiting it with respect to timing and frequency. It did, however, go beyond what the court required by stipulating that employers had to listen to oral representation or read written representations, and where representations were made in writing, the employer had to give written acknowledgment that it had read them. There was no further duty to respond to oral or written representations. The message could not have been clearer. No duty to bargain was required by the Court and the legislature did not intend to provide one. This legislation left farm workers with a weak form of the industrial voluntarist regime that typified Canadian industrial legality in the era prior to World War II; farm workers had protection against employer interference with associational activities but could neither legally compel employers to bargain with their associations, nor did they have access to compulsory conciliation where public pressure might have been applied to encourage employers to recognize and bargain with responsible trade unions. In short, they had access to a *sui generis* regime that was exceedingly unlikely to promote collective bargaining.

Evidence to support this view was not long in coming. In the spring of 2003, the UFCW organized the workers at Rol-Land Farms, a large mushroom grower, attracting 70 percent of the workers as members. Rol-Land refused to voluntarily recognize the union as the employees' representative and so the UFCW applied to be certified under the *LRA*. Notwithstanding the employers' objection that the board lacked jurisdiction, it ordered that a vote be held and the ballots be counted pending a determination of the substantive issue. The union won the vote 132 to 45, but the parties agreed to put the proceeding on hold pending the outcome of the *Fraser* litigation, which had already commenced (as an application for a declaration). After the vote, the UFCW wrote to Rol-Land requesting a meeting, but Rol-Land did not respond. A second organizing drive took place

48 *AEPA*, above note 2.

at Platinum Produce, an industrial greenhouse operation. In this instance, Platinum agreed to meet with the union and a brief fifteen-minute session followed at which the employer expressed the view that it was not required to bargain with the union. The union subsequently submitted a draft collective agreement. A second meeting followed, which lasted five minutes. The employer refused any further meetings.

Of course, in principle, the UFCW could have filed a complaint with the Tribunal that was empowered to hear complaints that the *AEPA* had been violated, but at the time it seemed obvious that, at least in the case of Platinum Produce, no violation had occurred. Platinum Produce had given UFCW a reasonable opportunity to make representations and had heard or read its representations. Nothing more was required by the Act.

The *Charter* challenge launched in *Fraser* had little chance of success, insofar as it claimed that the *AEPA* failed to comply with *Dunmore*. In the first instance, Farley J emphasized that freedom of association after *Dunmore* protected the right to organize, but not to bargain collectively or strike. On that basis, the *AEPA* passed muster. Insofar as Farley J commented on the failure of the applicant to pursue a case through the Tribunal, it related to the question of whether the Tribunal would enforce the *AEPA*, not whether it would read the *AEPA* to require the employer to respond to representations. Indeed, while Farley J noted that it was perhaps unfortunate that the *AEPA* did not require a response, he also immediately observed that such a requirement would have involved the parties in a form of collective bargaining, something that *Dunmore* did not require.[49] Clearly, if the case was going to succeed, it depended on the Supreme Court of Canada revisiting *Dunmore* and finding that freedom of association did extend to collective bargaining.

That, of course, happened in *Health Services*, where the Supreme Court of Canada famously held that "s. 2(d) should be understood as protecting the right of employees to associate for the purposes of advancing workplace goals through a process of collective bargaining."[50] Moreover, the Court emphasized that the duty to bargain in good faith lies at the heart of collective bargaining and cited its own decision in *Royal Oak Mines* interpreting the duty in collective bargaining legislation, indicating that the constitutional duty to bargain collect-

49 *Fraser v Ontario (AG)* (2006), 79 OR (3d) 219 (SCJ).

50 [2007] 2 SCR 391 at para 87.

ively was in this respect aligned with the statutory duty to bargain in good faith as elaborated in the labour relations jurisprudence.[51]

It was against that changed jurisprudence that the Ontario Court of Appeal heard the appeal in *Fraser*. Other chapters in this collection address that decision in more detail, but for my purpose, the point to emphasize is that it would have ended farm worker exceptionalism in collective bargaining by requiring the Ontario government to bring farm workers into a regime that not only included a duty to bargain in good faith, but also a scheme for statutory recognition of exclusive bargaining agency based on majority support.[52] While that result does not address the question of the effectiveness of a *Wagner Act* model for farm workers in particular, or for private sector workers generally, at least it would have put them in a position that was not less favourable than that of most private sector workers. Whether more could or should be done to facilitate collective bargaining is a question to which I will return in the last section of this chapter.

The majority judgment of the Supreme Court of Canada in *Fraser* is both peculiar and troubling. It is a very defensive judgment. Nearly 50 of its 118 paragraphs are spent responding to the concurring judgments of Deschamps J, who would have narrowly interpreted *Health Services* into oblivion, and Rothstein J, who would have reversed its holding that freedom of association protects collective bargaining. Clearly, the near unanimity of opinion that supported *Health Services* no longer exists.

More troubling is that the Court perpetuates exceptionalism insofar as it deprives farm workers of access to a *Wagner Act* model of labour law without providing a suitable alternative. This legislation left farm workers with a weak form of the industrial voluntarist regime that typified Canadian industrial legality in the era prior to World War I. Farm workers were protected against employer interference with associational activities but could neither compel employers to recognize and bargain with their associations, nor to participate in conciliation where public pressure might have produced *de facto* recognition and bargaining. In *Health Services* the Supreme Court of Canada made it clear that the right to collective bargaining is not a right to a particular statutory scheme or model of labour relations.[53] However, at the same time, it also stated that in judging whether there was substantial interference with the right to collective bar-

51 *Ibid* at paras 97–107.

52 *Fraser v Ontario (AG)* (2008), 92 OR (3d) 481 (CA).

53 *Health Services*, above note 9 at para 91.

gaining, the Court would engage in a contextual and fact-specific inquiry to determine "whether the process of voluntary, good faith collective bargaining between employees and the employer has been, or is likely to be, significantly and adversely affected."[54] The meaning of the term "voluntary" in this passage is rather ambiguous, especially since the case arose out of public sector collective bargaining regime in which there was a duty to bargain in good faith, and it was clear from the rest of the Court's judgment that it viewed the *duty* to bargain in good faith as fundamental. For example, later in the judgment, where the Court elaborates upon the criteria for determining whether there had been substantial interference with the right to collective bargaining, it stipulates that there should be an inquiry into the question, "does the legislative measure or government conduct in issue respect the fundamental precept of collective bargaining—the duty to consult and negotiate in good faith?"[55]

In light of these passages, there are two troubling aspects of the majority's judgment in *Fraser*. The first is failure of the Court to engage in a contextual and fact-specific inquiry. As I stated at the beginning of this chapter, its approach in *Fraser* starkly contrasts with its approach in *Dunmore*, which did take the history and social reality of farm workers seriously. This discrepancy becomes most obvious at the point in the judgment where it should have had the greatest salience, the discussion of the *AEPA*. The Court asks itself whether "the *AEPA* process, viewed in terms of its effect, makes good faith resolution of workplace issues between employees and their employer effectively impossible."[56] In answering that question, however, the Court does not engage with social reality, but rather moves to an abstract and, frankly, tendentious exercise of statutory interpretation. For example, in addressing the absence of an express duty to respond to employee representations, the Court reasons, "[t]hey do not expressly refer to a requirement that the employer consider employee representations in good faith. Nor do they rule it out. By implication, they include such a requirement."[57] The considerations that support this implication, however, ignore reality. First, the Court says that statutes should be interpreted in a way that gives meaning and purpose to its provisions, and notes that "[n]o labour relations purpose is served merely by *pro forma* listening or reading."[58] But

54 *Ibid* at para 92.

55 *Ibid* at para 97.

56 *Fraser*, above note 1 at para 98.

57 *Ibid* at para 101.

58 *Ibid* at para 103.

anyone who pays any attention to reality knows the purpose of the *AEPA* was to comply with the minimum requirements of *Dunmore*, which stopped short of requiring collective bargaining of any kind. The provision had no labour relations purpose. The Court's second consideration is that legislatures are presumed to intend to comply with the *Charter*.[59] It is true that in enacting the *AEPA*, the government intended to and did successfully comply with the *Charter* as interpreted by the court in *Dunmore*. However, it obviously did not and could not intend to comply with the *Charter* as subsequently interpreted by the court in *Health Services*. Finally, the Court takes into consideration the expressed intent of the minister citing her statement in the legislative debates that the *AEPA* was meant to give employees the necessary protection to enjoy freedom of association.[60] But here again the Court ignores the context of the minister's statement. The legislation was intended to protect meaningful freedom of association as interpreted by *Dunmore*, not *Health Services*. In fact, the minister explicitly stated that the legislation was not designed to promote collective bargaining.[61]

In addition to ignoring reality in this very basic and fundamental way, the Court also ignored the social reality of farm workers. Does the Court really believe that meaningful collective bargaining of any sort will emerge out of the *AEPA*, even if it is interpreted to include a duty to "have those submissions considered in good faith by the employer"?[62] To answer this question, instead of engaging with the history and practice of farm worker exceptionalism, including the resistance of agricultural employers to every effort unions have made to establish collective bargaining relationships in agriculture, it limits its historical timeframe to the life of the *AEPA* and blames the union for not making "a significant effort to make it work."[63] In so doing, the majority ignores or denigrates the documented efforts of the UFCW to engage Rol-Land Farms and Platinum Produce in collective bargaining and the complete disinclination of these employers to participate in any meaningful way. It is only by dint of

59 *Ibid* at para 104.

60 *Ibid* at para 105.

61 Helen Johns, the Minister of Agriculture and Food, made this point clearly when she introduced the *AEPA*: "However, I need to make one thing very clear here. While an agricultural employee may join an association that is a union, the proposed legislation does not extend collective bargaining to agricultural workers." Legislative Assembly of Ontario, *Debates*, 22 October 2002, p 2339.

62 *Fraser*, above note 1 at para 107.

63 *Ibid* at para 109.

abstraction from history and social reality that the majority is able to claim that the *AEPA* regime passes constitutional muster.

Apart from its fantastic view that the *AEPA* regime, even "properly" interpreted, may, if given a chance, enable farm workers to engage in collective bargaining, there is also a second troubling aspect to the majority's decision that reinforces my view that it sustains exceptionalism in its most negative form. In *Health Services*, the Court used both the terms "duty to consult" and "duty to negotiate in good faith,"[64] but the emphasis was on the latter. For example, when the Court elaborated on the meaning of the right to bargain collectively, it delved into good faith bargaining as it had been discussed in statutory collective bargaining schemes containing such a duty. In *Fraser* the emphasis is different. Here the majority judgment minimizes its use of the term "duty to bargain in good faith" and instead deploys other, often circuitous, phrasing. Some examples include:

- "[A] process of engagement that permits employee associations to make representations to employers, which employers must consider and discuss in good faith." (para 3)
- "[T]he *AEPA*, correctly interpreted, protects not only the right of employees to make submissions to employers on workplace matters, but also the right to have those submissions considered in good faith by the employer." (para 107)

This does not sound like robust collective bargaining of the kind adverted to in *Health Services*, but a much paler right to "good faith consideration." What conduct will satisfy this duty? Would an employer response to an employee association representation for higher wages that it has considered the representation in good faith but is of the view that it would be uneconomical to grant it satisfy the judicially enriched duty under the *AEPA*? Moreover, as a practical matter, enforcing such a lesser duty will be exceedingly difficult. Labour relations boards already struggle to police the boundary between good faith bargaining and surface bargaining.[65] One can only imagine how difficult it will be for a tribunal that has no labour relations experience to differentiate between a good faith and a bad faith consideration and discussion.

So the problem is not just that a group of agricultural workers who might have actually benefited from the *Wagner Act* model has

---

64 See, for example, *Health Services*, above note 9 at para 97.

65 For example, see Brian Langille & Patrick Macklem, "Beyond Belief: Labour Law's Duty to Bargain in Good Faith" (1988) 13 Queen's LJ 62.

been excluded from it, but rather that the Supreme Court of Canada seems to be applying a lower standard and is ignoring history and social context when it considers whether alternative statutory schemes, like the *AEPA*, pass constitutional muster. As a result, the majority judgment does not encourage legislatures to develop innovative statutory schemes that might actually facilitate collective bargaining by the growing number workers who do not benefit from the *Wagner Act* model—either because they are excluded from it like farm workers, or because it does not fit the labour market realities they face like precarious workers. Rather, it sends a signal that statutory schemes that are even less likely than the dominant one to support freedom of association for vulnerable workers[66] meet minimum constitutional requirements. In sum, *Fraser* enables the continuation of farm worker exceptionalism in its ugliest form and fails to challenge governments to make freedom of association meaningful for those who need it most, but who are least able to enjoy it under current law.[67]

C. The Future of Farm Worker Exceptionalism

What can be done to end farm worker exceptionalism in the aftermath of *Fraser*? Before addressing this question, it is useful to briefly consider what ending farm worker exceptionalism might mean. As I noted earlier, bringing farm workers into the *LRA*, perhaps with modifications in regard to dispute resolution as in the NDP's *ALRA*, certainly would bring an end to formal legal exceptionalism, and given the chilly political climate in which we live, that is a worthy accomplishment. That leaves unanswered the question of whether ending formal exceptionalism would also help end substantive exceptionalism; in other words, would it enable farm workers to achieve the

66 For a discussion of the limits of the *Wagner Act* model and the need for a plurality of collective bargaining regimes that address the needs of precarious workers, see Cynthia J Cranford, Judy Fudge, Eric Tucker, & Leah F Vosko, *Self-Employed Workers Organize* (Montreal: McGill-Queen's University Press, 2005) at 172–92.

67 Adelle Blackett expressed the hope that the Supreme Court of Canada's insistence in *Health Services* that it was not constitutionalizing a particular model of labour relations keeps "the door open to the articulation of alternative systems that over time can become functional within the new economy of Canada." See Adelle Blackett, "Mutual Promise: International Labour Law and *B.C. Health Services*" (2009) 48 Sup Ct L Rev (2d) 365 at 400. The majority and concurring judgments in *Fraser* are not encouraging.

level of union density that prevails in the private sector generally?[68] The data in Table 1 indicate the likelihood that some amelioration would result, although a significant gap would still remain.

Table 1: Private and Agricultural Sector Union Densities Compared By Province, 2009

Jurisdiction	Private Sector Density	Agricultural Sector Density	Ratio Agricultural to Private	Year Covered
AB	12.37	1.8	14.55	N/A
NB	12.28	2.08	16.94	1971
ON	15	2.65	17.67	N/A*
MB	26.04	4.88	18.74	1948
Canada	17.77	5.25	29.54	N/A
SK	17.49	5.26	30.07	1944
QC	26.1	9.76	37.39	1964
BC	17.75	7.06	39.77	1975
PEI	8.95	4.35	43.72	1971
NS	13.71	7.14	52.08	1987
NF	21.05	14.3	67.93	1952

(Calculated from Statistics Canada, Cansim Table 282-0078)

* Agricultural workers were covered by a statutory scheme from 1993 to 1995 but the 1995 repeal law revoked any certification obtained under the 1993 statute.

In Canada, in 2009, the overall private sector union density was 17.77 percent, but in agriculture it was 5.25 percent, or about 30 percent of the "norm." However, there was considerable variation among provinces. The lowest ratio of agricultural to private sector union density was in Alberta, followed by New Brunswick, Ontario, and Manitoba. Notably, Alberta and Ontario maintain farm worker exceptionalism. Of the eight provinces that have abolished farm worker exceptionalism, six have higher ratios than the Canadian norm, with the highest in Newfoundland and Labrador. On the basis of this data, it is clear that the inclusion of farm workers in the private

68 One might argue private sector union density is not a good comparator because of the low and declining level of private sector union density. While the data point to the need for a more fundamental rethinking of Canadian labour law, it is arguably the most appropriate comparison for assessing the impact of farm worker exceptionalism and the potential benefit of ending it in Ontario and Alberta, the two provinces where it exists.

sector collective bargaining statute does not produce union densities equivalent to those that prevail in the private sector, but, in general, it has a positive effect. Therefore, while it is certainly necessary to think about innovation in Canadian labour law generally, and for the situation of agricultural and other vulnerable workers in particular, agricultural workers should not have to bear the burden of waiting until new models can be embedded in Canadian industrial relations.[69] Ending formal legal exceptionalism is more than a symbolic goal, it has some potential, albeit limited, to assist agricultural workers in establishing viable forms of collective representation and bargaining.[70]

With this in mind, we can return to the question of what might be done. Two crosscutting strategies present themselves. One is to abolish formal legal exceptionalism through constitutional litigation or political pressure either to bring agricultural workers under the *LRA* or to enact an alternative but effective collective bargaining law. The other is to organize outside the *LRA* framework, with the aim of overcoming legal exceptionalism without formally abolishing it and, perhaps, creating more favourable conditions for the enactment of an effective statutory framework in the future.

Starting with the abolitionist track, constitutional litigation seems to hold little promise in the short term for ending or even promoting the end of farm worker exceptionalism. In *Fraser*, three Supreme Court of Canada justices seemed ready to pull the plug on *Health Services* and five others were on the defensive, tending to reformulate the substance of constitutionally protected collective bargaining in narrower terms. So while in principle the majority in *Fraser* left the door open to re-litigate the constitutionality of the *AEPA* after it has been given more time to be "explored and tested," there are many obstacles that would have to be overcome in order to do so successfully. First, unions have to spend several years and substantial funds organizing farm worker associations. Then those associations would have to make representations to farm operators. Of course, it is possible that collective bargaining relationships might then be established, but there is no reason to expect farm operator opposition to collective bargaining to change. Assuming that no col-

69 A similar point is made by Abella J in her dissent in *Fraser*, above note 1 at para 351.

70 For example, a group of seasonal agricultural workers represented by the UFCW recently negotiated a collective agreement that was specific to them. See NUPGE, "Migrant Workers Win Historic Contract in Abbottsford" (17 November 2010) online: www.nupge.ca/content/3753/migrant-workers-win-historic-contract-abbotsford.

lective agreements emerged, even with minority but independent farm associations, the associations would have to make applications to the Tribunal alleging that farm operators failed to respond in good faith to their representations. Assuming that farm operators would be clever enough to meet their obligation to consult under the *AEPA* but not enter into collective agreements with farm worker associations, litigation challenging the constitutionality of the *AEPA* could then commence, and it would then take several years to get a case before the Supreme Court of Canada, and then an indeterminate length of time after that to get a judgment issued. It is possible that such an application would be successful, but it is a crapshoot with the odds seemingly tilted against the union. Unless another jurisprudential shift occurs on the labour rights front, this is not a strategy that has much to offer.[71]

A second alternative abolitionist strategy is to abandon the constitutional turn, at least for the near future, and return to normal politics and pressure the Ontario government either to bring agricultural workers into the *LRA* or to create an alternative, but effective, legal framework. Moral suasion has a role to play here, but it is doubtful that it will be sufficient. The fact that Ontario is an outlier in Canada, as one of only two jurisdictions that excludes farm workers from its basic private sector collective bargaining law does not seem to embarrass Liberal and Progressive Conservative politicians. It is also unlikely that the ILO's Committee of Freedom of Association recent finding that the *AEPA* fails to provide "appropriate machinery and procedures for the promotion of collective bargaining in the agricultural sector"[72] and thereby violates Canada's international obligations, will have much of a moral influence either.[73] Moreover, the fact that the Supreme Court of Canada has just endorsed the *AEPA* as *Charter* compliant will undercut the claim that the current scheme lacks legitimacy.

If farm workers' moral capital is insufficient to move the powers that be, their current political clout is even weaker. Notwithstanding the work of unions and social justice groups to advance the cause of farm workers, they have yet to establish a political organization

---

71 I do not address the equality rights angle of *Charter* litigation, which is considered in detail in this volume by Faraday.

72 ILO, Reports of the Committee on Freedom of Association, 358th Report (Nov 2010), Case 2704 (Interim Report) at para 361.

73 It obviously had no legal traction either since the Supreme Court of Canada conveniently chose to ignore this report in its judgment. See Ewing and Hendy, this volume.

capable of putting sufficient pressure on the Liberal and Progressive Conservative parties to end exceptionalism in the face of the well organized and effective farm lobby that supports its perpetuation. Additionally, despite the NDP's strong showing in the 2011 federal election, there is little likelihood of it forming the Ontario government or holding the balance of power in the province in the near future. The constellation of political forces that drove farm workers to take the constitutional turn seemingly remains entrenched.

The second track is to overcome legal exceptionalism by working to establish farm worker collective bargaining within the law as it now stands. Other chapters in this collection address in more detail the organizing efforts that have been undertaken by the UFCW and various social justice groups, such Justicia for Migrant Workers. The question they need to address is how to go forward on the assumption that legal exceptionalism will remain for the foreseeable future. In that regard, the experience of California farm workers, prior to the enactment of the California *Agricultural Labor Relations Act* in 1975 might be worth reflecting upon, without being naive about the difficulty of successfully replicating that strategy.[74] Essentially, in its early days, the union recognized that it lacked strength in the fields to win collective bargaining agreements from recalcitrant farm owners through traditional means of striking and picketing. Therefore, they supplemented organizing in the fields with a consumer boycott. Initially, the boycott targeted grapes from specific farm operators but later expanded to cover all California grapes. The disruption created by these tactics was so great that significant farm operators eventually backed the creation of a statutory collective bargaining scheme.[75]

The UFW's success is an extraordinary story of organizing by a large group of committed activists who were drawn to "*La Causa*," but it was assisted by a creative legal strategy that, *inter alia*, made use of whatever protective law there was and took advantage of

---

74 There is a large literature on Cesar Chavez and the United Farm Workers (UFW). For two helpful discussions of the implications of that experience for current union organizing, see Jennifer Gordon, "Law, Lawyers, and Labor: The United Farm Workers' Legal Strategy in the 1960s and 1970s and the Role of Law in Union Organizing Today" (2005–06) 8 U Pa J Lab & Employment 1, and Randy Shaw, *Beyond the Fields: Cesar Chavez, the UFW, and the Struggle for Justice in the 21st Century* (Berkeley: University of California Press, 2008).

75 The growers were hoping that within the framework of a statutory scheme they could enter into sweetheart contracts with the Teamsters. The UFW, however, was able to defeat the Teamsters, who eventually withdrew from the sector. For reasons largely unrelated to the California *ALRA*, the UFW subsequently imploded.

opportunities that arose precisely because farm workers were outside the collective bargaining statute. That experience might be helpful for lawyers in Ontario providing advice about how to operate outside the *Wagner Act* model in more of an industrial voluntarist regime.[76] For example, despite its weakness, the *AEPA* does protect the right to organize and provides a statutory tribunal with remedial powers to address violations by employers. Alternatively, a criminal prosecution could be launched, if only for its symbolic value, given the difficulty of securing a conviction.[77] Moreover, because agricultural workers are outside the *LRA*, they enjoy freedoms denied to covered workers. For example, the prohibition on recognition strikes does not apply, and a union representing farm workers can seek a collective agreement without having to establish majority support through an election or even a card check. Also, they are free to establish bargaining units of their own choosing. Alternatively, if they wish, agricultural worker unions can choose not to focus on the creation of formal collective bargaining relationships and may instead seek to improve working conditions through pressure tactics and direct action that might not be permitted to workers under the *LRA*.[78] In fact, the law regulating boycotts and picketing is now more permissive than it was at the time of the UFW's grape boycotts.[79] At the end of the day, the arrangements farm workers can establish will ultimately depend on the power they are able to muster.

In sum, the *Fraser* decision has dashed the hope that farm worker exceptionalism would be abolished by constitutional litigation. But even if farm workers had been brought within a *Wagner Act* model,

---

76 For a variety of reasons, often related to the poor fit between the *LRA* and the labour market realities faced by many workers, there has been an increase in non-traditional organizing activity taking place outside the statutory scheme. For an interesting reflection on the history and current manifestations of industrial voluntarism, see Sean Tucker & Alex Mucalov, "Industrial Voluntarism in Canada" (2010) 65 RI 215. Also, see Rosemary Warskett, "Remaking the Canadian Labour Movement: Transformed Work and Transformed Labour Strategies" in Vivian Shalla & Wallace Clement, eds, *Work in Tumultuous Times* (Montreal: McGill-Queen's University Press, 2007).

77 Fudge & Tucker, above note 27.

78 These kinds of tactics are being used by the Industrial Workers of the World's (IWW) Starbuck's Workers Union in New York City and has achieved some gains. For a recent discussion, see Daniel Gross & Staughton Lynd, "Solidarity Unionism at Starbucks: The IWW Uses Section 7," online: www.pmpress.org/content/article.php/20080722202202555.

79 For example, see *Pepsi Cola Canada (West) Ltd v RWDSU*, Local 558, [2002] SCR 156; *UFCW, Local 1518 v Kmart Canada Ltd*, [1999] 2 SCR 1083; and *Daishowa Inc v Friends of the Lubicon* (1998), 58 DLR (4th) 699 (Ont Ct Gen Div).

as the Ontario Court of Appeal's judgment required, the enormous challenge of actually organizing farm workers and establishing collective bargaining would have remained. Indeed, as noted earlier, the *Wagner Act* model does not work well for many groups of workers, and unions across North America are facing the need to develop creative approaches to organizing that often skirt around the law.[80] The question going forward for farm workers, at least for now, is how to meet that challenge without "the law."

80 For an insightful reflection upon the efforts of one union, UNITE-HERE, to meet this challenge, see Julius G Getman, *Restoring the Power of Unions: It Takes a Movement* (New Haven: Yale University Press, 2010).

CHAPTER THREE
The Roots of Organizing Agriculture Workers in Canada

Wayne Hanley

A. Farm Workers in Ontario Struggle to Organize

For eight years, as the battle for farm workers' rights in Ontario moved from court to court, Mindy Leng believed that Canada's *Charter of Rights and Freedoms* would finally provide her and tens of thousands of other farm workers in Ontario with the justice and equality she believed was at the heart of the law. But on 29 April 2011, the Supreme Court of Canada delivered a decision that left her almost speechless and all Ontario farm workers legally powerless and excluded from achieving effective collective bargaining with agribusiness employers.[1]

Mindy Leng and some of her family had worked at the Kingsville, Ontario, Rol-Land mushroom factory farm that was at the centre of the *Fraser* case. Mindy's job was to harvest mushrooms; clutching a knife in one hand while climbing up and down mushroom grow racks, set end-to-end like four-level bunk beds running the length of the industrial facility. She and hundreds of others did their work in almost total darkness, in a factory-sized sheet metal barn filled with

1 *Ontario (AG) v Fraser*, 2011 SCC 20 [*Fraser* (SCC)]. See also, UFCW Canada, News Release, "The Struggle Continues: Decision by Supreme Court Denies Ontario Farm Workers Right to Effective Collective Bargaining" (29 April 2011) online: UFCW Canada www.ufcw.ca/index.php?option=com_content&view=article&id=2340%3Arights-of-ontario-farm-workers-abandoned-by-supreme-court&catid=6%3Adirections-newsletter&Itemid=316&lang=en.

mould, high humidity, heat, chemicals, and harassment. Cuts and falls were very common, but compensation claims were not because of the fear of reprisals by the employer.

Mindy and her co-workers were paid by the total weight of the mushrooms they picked. Workers out of favour with the managers would be assigned to the barns with the smallest mushrooms, or just outright fired. Many of the workers were immigrants or recent refugees with limited English fluency like Mindy and her family, who had come to Canada as refugees from Cambodia. They would talk in their mother tongue while working, but that was banned by the owner, so they were forced to work in silence, except for the orders barked out in English by their managers.

In 2003, Mindy and other members of her family, along with an overwhelming majority of her other co-workers, voted to unionize with United Food and Commercial Workers Canada (UFCW),[2] in the face of Ontario legislation that denied farm workers in Ontario the right to unionize and engage in collective bargaining.

And so the fate of Mindy Leng, and ultimately all farm workers in Ontario, began to wind itself first through the labour board; then to a reversal in the lower courts; then to a successful appeal; and finally to the Supreme Court of Canada where, on 9 December 2009, Mindy Leng joined me, our legal counsel, and Stan Raper, the national co-ordinator of the UFCW Canada agriculture workers program, along with dozens of other lawyers and spectators.

Before departing for Ottawa, Mindy had been interviewed by the local TV station and told them, "We're human beings. We're not farm animals. We have human rights. We should be treated like other workers in Ontario and be allowed to unionize. We wanted a union. We needed a union. It is our right."

The Ontario Court of Appeal agreed with her.[3] That decision was appealed by the Government of Ontario to the Supreme Court of Canada. Joining Ontario in its fight to maintain the ban on farm unions was the Ontario Federation of Agriculture—the same collec-

2 UFCW Canada, News Release, "Farm Workers Vote Overwhelmingly to Join union" (19 September 2003) online: UFCW Canada www.ufcw.ca/index.php?option=com_content&view=article&id=462%3Afarm-workers-vote-overwhelmingly-to-join-union&catid=5%3Amedia-releases&Itemid=5&lang=en.

3 *Fraser v Ontario (AG)*, 2008 ONCA 760 [*Fraser* (Ont CA)]. See UFCW Canada, News Release, "Ontario Court Ruling Opens the Gate to Farm Unions" (17 November 2008) online: UFCW Canada www.ufcw.ca/index.php?option=com_content&view=article&id=619%3Aontario-court-ruling-opens-the-gate-to-farm-unions&catid=5%3Amedia-releases&Itemid=5&lang=en.

tion of agribusiness lobbyists who had helped elect Mike Harris in 1995. Harris's first act as premier was to revoke the short-lived *Agriculture Labour Relations Act* (*ALRA*)[4] that had, for the only time since 1940, allowed farm workers to unionize.

Almost two decades later, little had changed as the McGuinty Liberal Ontario government was just as recalcitrant and locked to the farm lobbyists, and working just as hard to keep the more than 80,000 workers in Ontario agriculture powerless to bargain with their employers. Their appeal to the Supreme Court was part of that. Their win was another blow against Ontario's farm workers.

From the perspective of UFCW officials and members, as well as many others, politics and corporate interests had without a doubt trumped equal rights and justice for Ontario farm workers. With one hand, the Supreme Court upheld the principle of freedom of association and the right to collective bargaining, but with the other hand the Court withheld those same rights from farm workers. The Court abandoned Ontario farm workers by telling them the Ontario farm union ban stood, and instead they would have to depend on their employer's "good faith" to enter into bargaining. Good luck or, more accurately, good riddance.

In our opinion, the Supreme Court decision cynically failed agricultural workers. It set them back. It was a decision that in our minds said to Ontario farm workers that "the *AEPA* is constitutional, so if you don't like it, then go change the government and the law."

It is somewhat ironic considering that many of these workers are migrant workers, like tens of thousands of other farm workers across Canada, and do not have the right to vote or change the government. And even though in most other provinces agriculture workers can form unions, because many of them are also migrant workers they face many of the same practical obstacles to organizing as Ontario farm workers, such as lack of English-language skills, and fear of being arbitrarily repatriated or blacklisted from returning to Canada the next season if they raise any workplace concerns or try to form a union.

These are not employers you can expect good faith from, and the historical evidence presented in the *Fraser* case was pretty clear about that, as it was to the dissenting Supreme Court judge on the *Fraser* case, Madame Abella J who had earlier chaired the Ontario Labour Relations Board (OLRB). It was just as clear to Winkler CJ of the Ontario Court of Appeal who, prior to becoming a judge, had

---

4 SO 1994, c 6 [*ALRA*].

decades of experience as a labour lawyer in the corporate sphere, and who sided with the Rol-Land workers.

But most of the members of the Supreme Court were not thinking about Mindy Leng or the thousands of vulnerable workers like her, so instead what happened was the continued marginalization of the rights of workers who put food on our tables. They are workers who do some of the most dangerous, hard, and important work there is, but they are out of sight and out of mind of the general public who do not have any idea how the food they buy at their local store gets there. This invisibility is very convenient for the corporate agribusiness and their lobbyists who continue to hide behind the archaic image of the family farm, in spite of the fact that the overwhelming output from the agriculture sector comes from multimillion-dollar, industrial-scale factory farms with work forces ranging from dozens to many hundreds of workers at these mega-sized operations.

That was the case at Rol-Land Farms, just like it was at two other Ontario corporate agriculture operations that UFCW Canada had organized prior to the Rol-Land campaign. To understand the history that led to the *Fraser* decision you have to go back to the 1980s.

You also have to understand who UFCW Canada is: Canada's largest private-sector union with hundreds of thousands of members working in food retailing, processing, warehousing, and distribution. In association with the Agriculture Workers Alliance (AWA), UFCW Canada also operates 10 AWA agriculture worker support centres across Canada, providing a variety of services to domestic and migrant agriculture workers. At locations in Quebec and British Columbia, the union also represents workers at a number of unionized agriculture operations.

UFCW Canada is also part of UFCW International. Together our roots reach back to the early twentieth century when we helped organize an earlier group of workers who were exploited because they were "foreigners," spoke a different language, and had no political clout. They were workers in packing houses across the United States and Canada, who, like Mindy Leng, stood together in the early 1900s and declared: "We are people, not animals."

Just like many farm workers today, workers back then in the packing houses faced discrimination, racism, and government and industry in partnership that together fought to suppress the rights of these marginalized workers. The struggle dragged on for decades, but ultimately the workers won.

So while the *Fraser* decision was a setback in a decades-long battle against the same players, we will continue to stand with total commitment to Mindy Leng and her co-workers and all agriculture workers across Ontario in their continuing struggle for full, effective, collective bargaining rights.

That struggle actually began with an organizing drive at another Ontario industrial-scale agriculture facility, Cuddy Chicks, which also hid behind Ontario's farm union ban at the OLRB. The year was 1987, by which point most of Ontario's family farms were starting to disappear because of factory farms. They are factories, which just happen to manufacture eggs, or tomatoes, or cucumbers, or countless other grown products on a multimillion-dollar industrial scale. In Cuddy Chicks' case, the product was fresh-hatched chicks ready to be shipped by the thousands to poultry-growing facilities.

The workers were doing assembly line work, just like car workers and meatpacking workers and bakery workers, and so on. But unlike those workers, the Cuddy workers were not able to form a union because they worked in the so-called agriculture sector which had been excluded from collective bargaining and the *Labour Relations Act* (*LRA*) right from its introduction in the 1940s.[5]

At the Labour Board, we argued that Ontario's exclusion of agriculture workers was discriminatory and contravened the *Charter*, but Cuddy argued that the Board did not have the jurisdiction to hear a constitutional challenge. That case, and the issue of the Board's jurisdiction, eventually arrived at the Supreme Court of Canada in 1990. The workers and UFCW Canada won. The Supreme Court ruled that labour boards did have the power to hear and rule on *Charter* challenges.[6]

With that opening, and with the election of a labour-friendly NDP Ontario government in 1990 that had pledged to address farm workers' labour rights, a new round of organizing began that mostly focused on large scale industrial factory farms. The Highline Produce mushroom growing facility in Leamington, Ontario, was one of them. Leamington is in the heart of Essex County—southwest Ontario's most intensive greenhouse and field crop production area. The working conditions at Highline were horrendous and the workers had been repeatedly frustrated in their attempts to get some positive action from their employer. Firings were a typical response to keep the workers and their concerns in line. While there were no farm unions in Leamington or anywhere in Ontario, workers at High-

---

5 Under the *Labour Relations Act*, RSO 1980, c 228, as it stood in 1987, s 2(b) stated that "This Act does not apply . . . to a person employed in agriculture."

6 *Cuddy Chicks Ltd v Ontario (Labour Relations Board)*, [1991] 2 SCR 5.

line were aware that unionizing had helped other workers throughout the region, and that it offered a solution to their mistreatment.

Highline was a factory farm that was just as industrial as any car factory, and just as dangerous and oppressive as car factories had been until they were unionized in the 1940s. Like those pre-union car factories, the Highline factory in the 1990s fully exploited marginalized workers; many of them recent immigrants, whose limited community network, employment skills, and English-language fluency drove them to take any work they could find.

One of these workers was Xin Yuan Lui who had come with his family as refugees from China. Along with a number of other refugee families, Xin and his family had settled in Essex County. They had expected that their human rights would be more respected than where they came from, so the brutality at Highline was a shock. But Xin and the workers desperately needed the work and their employer knew it. The owner of Highline was Dr. Murray O'Neil, a wealthy Ontario doctor who owned two other mushroom growing facilities in Ontario and another location in Quebec with the same kind of workforce.

But the doctor underestimated the courage and determination of Xin and his co-workers. With the support of UFCW Canada Local 1993, Xin and other union supporters spread the word clandestinely to fellow workers about the union campaign. Despite the possibility of dismissal or other reprisals, by 1994 Xin and the majority of his fellow Highline workers had signed enough cards to support an application for certification.

The application to certify the bargaining unit proceeded under new enabling legislation developed by the NDP provincial government under Premier Bob Rae, which had been elected with the support of organized labour including UFCW Canada. Following its election, Rae's government formed a tripartite cross-sector Task Force to create a legislative framework that would provide agricultural workers protection under labour relations laws.

For the next two years the Task Force consulted with workers, UFCW Canada, and other labour allies, and with the agriculture lobby on how to provide collective bargaining rights to farm workers while also addressing the needs of legitimate family farms, as well as the concern over work stoppages at harvest time. The Task Force released three background research studies and issued two consensus reports detailing how collective bargaining legislation could be tailored to the agricultural sector.[7]

Following this extensive study and consultation, the Ontario government introduced Bill 91, the *Agricultural Labour Relations Act, 1994* (*ALRA*).[8] Finally, in 1994, for the first time Ontario agriculture workers had the right to unionize and bargain collectively, a half-century after other Ontario workers were given that right.

In 1995, UFCW Local 1993 became the first ever *ALRA*-certified bargaining agent when the unit at Highline Produce was certified under the new Act. This breakthrough in organizing and political lobbying not only empowered the workers at Highline, but all Ontario agriculture workers. The *ALRA* established a legislative framework to provide for effective collective bargaining for agriculture workers, while also acknowledging the unique nature of the agriculture production system. The *ALRA* excluded the "family farm." Strikes were also prohibited. Instead, the Act provided expedited arbitration to resolve collective bargaining impasses.

The legislation addressed every concern the industry had, except one. The corporate agriculture industry no longer had the absolute, arbitrary, and sometimes ruthless power it previously had to hold down wages and impose working conditions that were unsafe and exploitative. In fact, the rate of workplace deaths and accidents in agribusiness has historically been higher than almost any other industry, accounting for more than one of every ten occupational fatalities in Canada.

But in 1995, in the midst of bargaining a first collective agreement at Highline, the newly gained rights of all Ontario agriculture workers were dashed with the Ontario election of the Mike Harris Tory government. The very first thing that Harris did as part of his Common Sense Revolution[9] was to plough the rights of Ontario farm workers straight back in the ground by repealing the *ALRA*, as well as revoking the certificate issued to the Highline workers.[10]

This attack on farm workers' rights certainly made a lot of "common sense" to Mike Harris and his supporters from the corporate

---

7 Task Force on Agricultural Labour Relations, *Report to the Minister of Labour* (June 1992) and *Background Studies* (Toronto: Task Force on Labour Relations, 1992); Task Force on Agricultural Labour Relations, *Second Report to the Minister of Labour* (Toronto: Task Force on Agricultural Relations, 1992).

8 Above note 4.

9 Harris's Progressive Conservative party campaigned and subsequently governed on a platform they called the "Common Sense Revolution."

10 *Labour Relations and Employment Statue Law Amendment Act, 1995*, SO 1995, c 1, s 80.

industrial farm lobby, who continued to talk about the threat to the family farm and the harvest, even though the *ALRA* protected both. Harris's move against farm workers also played well in rural, farm-owner communities which had traditionally been Tory strongholds. These were also communities where corporate farms, like Highline, had increasingly become dependent on new immigrants, refugees, and migrant workers, who, in spite of their work contribution, were often the targets of implicit and sometimes explicit racism as well as workplace exploitation. So the notion of granting them the same rights as every other worker in Ontario was not exactly a priority, but keeping them vulnerable and compliant was.

The same can be said today at corporate farms across Canada, which cycle more than 40,000 migrant and temporary foreign workers through their operations each season,[11] not just because it is cost-effective, but also because employers are free to deport guest workers, without appeal, if the workers complain of safety, workplace, or housing concerns. More than 70 percent of these temporary migrant workers are contracted to Ontario farms. The same was the case in 1995 when the Harris Tories made sure that neither foreign nor domestic farm workers could seek protection through collective bargaining.

Harris's ditching of the *ALRA* and the Highline certification, along with the exclusion of farm workers from the *Labour Relations Act, 1995*[12] led UFCW Canada to file the *Dunmore* case in 1995 against the Ontario government. Tom Dunmore was one of the workers at Highline. This litigation again argued that laws denying farm workers the right to unionize violated freedom of association and the right to equality. Five years later, the case became the second UFCW Canada *Charter* challenge to arrive at the Supreme Court.

---

11 Citizenship and Immigration Canada (CIC), *Canada Facts and Figures 2009—Immigration Overview: Permanent and Temporary Residents*, online: www.cic.gc.ca/english/pdf/research-stats/facts2009.pdf at 64 [2009 Facts and Figures]. Of the approximately 40,000 migrant agriculture workers in the 2009 season, 23,437 arrived in Canada under Canada's Seasonal Agricultural Workers Program (CSAWP). An additional 38,255 workers in 2009 arrived in Canada under the Low Skill Pilot Program with thousands of them destined for the agriculture industry. While CIC does not categorize the various work roles within this latter Low Skills group, based on our extensive observations and interviews, the number of workers from the Low Skills Program has grown to be about equal to the number of workers admitted under CSAWP each season, and the overall use of migrant agricultural workers continues to expand.

12 Section 3(b) of the *Labour Relations Act, 1995*, SO 1995, c 1, Sch A reads: "This Act does not apply . . . to a person employed in agriculture, hunting or trapping."

Once again, the Supreme Court ruled in favour of a UFCW Canada challenge.[13] In December 2001, the Court ruled that Ontario farm workers needed labour relations legislation to ensure they could effectively exercise their freedom of association rights guaranteed under the *Charter*. The Supreme Court ordered and directed the Government of Ontario to put in place such enabling legislation by June 2003.

In the meantime, UFCW Canada continued to expand efforts to reach out to farm workers in Ontario, as well as to raise public awareness about the Supreme Court ruling. At the same time, the provincial Tory government and the farm lobby continued to threaten in unison that in spite of the Supreme Court ruling, the new legislation demanded by the Court would not necessarily deliver the right to unionize.

Proactively, Michael Fraser, the leader of UFCW Canada at the time, argued that Highline and the agriculture industry should stop stalling and acknowledge farm worker collective bargaining rights in the wake of the Supreme Court ruling. In a press release Fraser stated, "Highline has no other moral choice but to implement the court's decision. Ultimately, they will have to do so anyway so why not show now that they respect the *Charter*?"

But the industry insisted that UFCW Canada had misinterpreted the decision. Dr. O'Neil, the owner, shot back that Ontario agriculture operators' companies were not under any obligation to recognize unions until the new Ontario legislation was presented. More than that, O'Neil and the farm lobby confidently predicted that legislation that respected freedom of association could meet the Supreme Court test without necessarily including the right to join unions to bargain collectively. It is probably no coincidence that what O'Neil and the lobby were predicting was exactly what the Harris-Eves government was already drafting with the guidance of the industry. The owner's statement was also an implicit warning to the workers that their efforts to organize would get them nowhere.

The workers were not scared off. Neither was UFCW Canada. It was always clear that as long as the Tories were in power, they and their corporate farm lobby backers would fight to maintain the exploitative *status quo* when it came to farm workers. That was a given, but it was not a deterrent. Even in advance of the *Dunmore* ruling, UFCW Canada helped to launch what would eventually become the paradigm for UFCW Canada's agriculture organizing efforts in Ontario, and eventually across Canada.

---

13 *Dunmore v Ontario (AG)*, 2001 SCC 94, [2001] 3 SCR 1016.

The components were, and continue to be, community building with workers and social justice allies; worker education and servicing; research; public awareness campaigns and political lobbying (here and abroad); and legal challenges.

The template was set in the spring of 2001, when UFCW Canada, along with the Canadian Labour Congress and two other unions, provided start-up funding to the Global Justice Caravan Project for a portable outreach office on wheels (a recreational vehicle) and expenses. The RV, its volunteer staff, and their coordinator, Stan Raper, spent the season travelling the back roads of rural southern Ontario speaking to workers at the farm gate, the local church or community centre, or while in town where workers did their weekly shopping. Many of the volunteers spoke Spanish and were members of a national collective that promoted literacy and provided English as a second language (ESL) training to hard-to-reach communities.

The goal of the Global Justice Caravan Project was to go straight to the source and document the plight and challenges facing the growing migrant workforce at Ontario agriculture operations. The research became the core of the first-ever *National Report on the Status of Migrant Workers in Canada* (which since then has been researched, updated, and published annually by UFCW Canada).[14]

The field research on which the report was based documented the appalling workplace safety, housing, and human rights violations that many of the workers faced, told in their own words, anonymously, out of fear of reprisal:

> If you get sick, the boss doesn't send you to the hospital. Or if you can't work because you are sick, they send you back to Mexico. They say "go die in your own country." They won't let you come back the next year.

Another worker recounted,

> I've been working at the farm since 1988. In 1995 I began to feel chest pains every hour. When the problem started my job was to spread pesticides to reduce and kill the flies. My employer took me to the doctor but he said there was nothing wrong with me, but every time I was told to use the pesticides, I would get the pain again and have trouble breathing.

The outreach workers also documented dozens of complaints about deplorable housing conditions: "In our living place the sewer

14 UFCW Canada and the Canadian Labour Congress, *National Report: Status of Migrant Farm Workers in Canada* (December 2002). This report and each of the later annual reports are available online: UFCW Canada www.ufca.ca.

is always plugged, so there is a terrible smell in the room we sleep. Sometimes we can't sleep at all. And on the farm I work we have forty men living in one small building with only four bathrooms, and only two of them work."

The abuse and exploitation were no surprise to the migrant workers. What did surprise them was that someone was actually listening, unlike their consular officials who appeared more concerned about protecting the interest of the employers (a persisting issue which this chapter will return to later). "It doesn't matter what we do. We aren't listened to anyways. If we raise a concern, the farmer tells the consul that he doesn't want us. Then the consul says the problem is that we're not working hard enough, and the next year you don't get to come back. They treat us like dogs. Worse than dogs."

The precarious immigration status of migrant workers made them particularly attractive to the corporate agriculture agenda. The workers and their problems were hidden away from the eye of the public. They often could not speak English. They were disconnected from the greater community. They were not aware of the labour laws. They were easy to control through threat of deportation. So in the 1990s, as corporate agriculture began to rapidly expand, it was mostly a migrant or recent immigrant workforce that grew along with it. That was the case in Essex County and across Ontario, and increasingly in other provinces.

Certainly there were also Canadian-born farm workers but if they had options they tended to avoid factory farms because they knew through the grapevine that along with low wages, danger and degrading treatment were often also part of the package.

Domestic or migrant, the safety and well-being of industrial agriculture workers in Ontario was absolutely not a priority for the industry or government (except during the short-lived period of the *ALRA*). The priority was maximizing revenue, which in 2000 alone saw the Ontario farm production industry yielding $7.8 billion in cash receipts.[15]

Taking on this mega-industry by helping workers organize was going to require more than just a travelling office, volunteers, and the recently favourable Supreme Court ruling. The campaign for justice needed a home base. We also needed a comprehensive strategy to address the challenge of serving and organizing not just domestic workers, but also migrant temporary workers.

---

15 Affidavit of George Brinkman (27 October 2004) filed by the Attorney General of Ontario in *Fraser v Ontario*, SCC Appeal Record, Vol II, Tab 24 at 31.

So a year after it started, UFCW Canada stepped up to become the sole funder and union behind what had started as the Global Justice Caravan Project, and in the spring of 2002, UFCW Canada opened its first-ever agriculture worker support centre in Leamington, Ontario. Today it is one of ten such centres, operated under the Agriculture Workers Alliance (AWA) banner in Ontario, Manitoba, Quebec, and British Columbia, where multilingual staff members help workers with legal, workplace, and health and employment insurance issues, to name just a few of the services.

From the get-go, the Leamington centre and the centres that followed it were created as a permanent base where workers could have access to service in their own language, available at a time convenient to them. Government and consular offices typically closed at 4 p.m., which is not much help if you do not finish work until sunset. So the Leamington centre was open from noon until 8 p.m., and also Sunday afternoons, which was the only time off most industrial farm workers ever got.

The centre offered ESL classes and also started to build alliances with community legal agencies to arrange bilingual legal services for the workers. Health and safety training were also offered because shamefully, at that time, Ontario agriculture operations were exempted from the *Occupational Health and Safety Act* and the training it required. Even if health and safety training had been required by law, many of the workers could not read English or French, so warning labels and fact sheets on hazardous products (like pesticides) would still not be effective. So what the centre did was translate the facts and publish them in an easy-to-read Spanish version.

In addition, while the new Ontario legislation as directed by the Supreme Court had yet to be introduced, the centre was an operating reality to the farming community that agriculture workers now had an advocate. We became the local watchdog and we were not going to be scared away. The industry, the government, and of course, the workers, were all aware that UFCW Canada had taken a stand in their neighbourhood to advocate, educate, empower, and promote the right to unionize.

The buzz the centre created that summer reverberated all the way back to Queen's Park, where in advance of tabling the new Act to cover farm workers, Conservative Premier Ernie Eves (carrying on the Mike Harris tradition) assured his supporters in the farm lobby that the forthcoming legislation would continue to protect the industry from the impact of the Supreme Court ruling.

On 7 October 2002, Minister of Agriculture Helen Johns confirmed what Dr. O'Neil, the farm lobby, and Premier Eves had been setting up for months: that while freedom of association would have to be acknowledged in the legislation, farm unions would not be part of that equation. Johns's introduction of Bill 187, the *Agricultural Employees Protection Act, 2002 (AEPA)*, delivered just the protection the corporate farm lobby wanted: legislation to protect the industry against the labour and organizing rights of agricultural employees.

The fact that the industry was so pleased with the *AEPA* was evidence of how hollow the legislation really was for agricultural workers. But Hector Delanghe, an industry lobbyist, insisted that the *AEPA* meant better times ahead for the workers because, "in the past there was no real voice for the farm worker. Now they can form an association."[16]

But associate to do what? Agricultural workers could form an association, but not a union to act as the exclusive bargaining agent like under other labour legislation across Canada. They could take their concerns to their employer, but the employer was not compelled to act on them. They could attempt collective bargaining, but only if the employer was willing to negotiate.

The *AEPA* fact sheet published by the ministry summed it up loud and clear:

> **What are an employer's obligations in relation to representations made by an employees' association?**
>
> The AEPA requires that an employer listen to the representations if made orally. If the representations are made in writing, the AEPA requires the employer to read them and give the employees' association written acknowledgement.[17]

The Act itself has a lot more words, but at the end of the day the message it sent to agriculture workers was that nothing substantial had changed. They would continue to be excluded from the same workplace rights and legislative protection for collective bargaining that other Ontario workers had enjoyed for over half a century.

---

16 "Farm Groups React Favourably to New Farm Labour Law" *Ontario Farmer* (15 October 2002).

17 See Ministry of Agriculture, Food and Rural Affairs, *Fact Sheet on the Agricultural Employees Protection Act, 2002* (June 2003) online: www.omafra.gov.on.ca/english/busdev/facts/03-045.htm#purpose.

The *AEPA* would not come into force for another eight months. While a legal challenge of the *AEPA* was not out of the question, the first priority was to continue reaching out to the workers. That included adding two new agricultural worker support centres in the spring of 2003, in Simcoe and Bradford, Ontario. Like the Leamington centre, the two new centres had a multilingual staff who offered a variety of support services at no cost to agriculture workers. The majority of these were migrant workers in Canada contracted to agricultural operations under the federal government's Canadian Seasonal Agriculture Workers Program (CSAWP).

Additionally, in the months leading up to the June 2003 Royal Assent of the *AEPA*, the UFCW Canada agriculture organizing staff began to conduct information and training sessions for domestic agriculture workers at various Ontario locations. The sessions would be held at local hotels. Despite having just finished a gruelling workday, dozens of workers would show up wanting to learn about their labour rights and how to organize. The sessions included explaining how Ontario law had historically banned farm workers from joining unions, and how UFCW Canada had successfully challenged the ban, including the 2001 Supreme Court decision. As for the *AEPA*, it was a new obstacle that could become the cause of a new *Charter* challenge if workers tried to form a union, but were stopped by the *AEPA*.

One of the workers who came to an information meeting in Windsor, Ontario, was Xin Yuan Lui; the same Xin Yuan Lui who a decade before had been a member of the short lived union at Highline. Now he was working at Rol-Land Farms, another mushroom factory farm in the Leamington area where working conditions were just as bad as Highline. He would later go on to become one of the key inside organizers of the Rol-Land campaign and one of the applicants named in the *Fraser* litigation. Mindy Leng also came out to the sessions with members of her family who also worked at Rol-Land. One of them, her father, would later be fired from Rol-Land for his union activities and would appear, in 2006, in front of the first-ever *AEPA* Tribunal seeking damages because of his dismissal.

Conditions at Rol-Land were so oppressive that the risk of being fired did not deter Xin, Mindy, or, in fact, most of the other workers from attending the information sessions and getting involved in the campaign. The sessions not only built up the courage that was already in the Rol-Land workers, but also provided them with training and tools to strategically talk about the union in their workplace and bring co-workers together in solidarity. And what was additionally exciting about these meetings was that the workers also brought members of their families who worked at other non-union jobs like Walmart, at call centres, and at other service sector jobs.

Like many domestic workers in the agriculture sector, the Rol-Land workers came from many cultures and homelands. They spoke different languages. But at these meetings, and in their workplaces, they started to become more than what labour relations acts define as a "community of interest." They became an actual community. Those who could speak English would translate for their fellow workers. They would babysit each other's children so they could attend the meetings. They would bring food for potluck dinners. They would exchange stories about what was going on at work. They always understood that they were at risk, but their shared hopes and commitment were stronger. They also understood that even if they voted to unionize, the *AEPA* might block their way unless the new Act was struck down on appeal. They were not looking for a legal battle but if that is what it took, so be it. As Xin said at one of the meetings, "if we do nothing, things will stay the same, or get worse."

On 27 June 2003, UFCW Canada filed an application with the Ontario Labour Relations Board (OLRB) on behalf of the workers at Rol-Land Farms to hold a certification vote. Well over 50 percent of the then 270 workers had signed cards.

That same week UFCW Canada also filed an application with the Ontario Superior Court charging that the Ontario government's exclusion of agricultural workers from the *Occupational Health and Safety Act* (*OHSA*) violated Canada's *Charter of Rights and Freedoms.*[18] Despite working in one of the most dangerous occupations, Ontario's agricultural workers were the only workers in the province that were excluded from the Act's health and safety rights and protections. (The UFCW Canada action directly resulted in the McGuinty Liberal government extending *OHSA* to cover farm workers in 2006).

The June 2003 *OHSA Charter* challenge and the Rol-Land application made headline news that alerted people in Ontario to just how serious the historic discrimination against Ontario farm workers was. Their plight was no longer invisible. The combined actions also made it very clear to the Ontario government and to the agriculture industry that UFCW Canada was not only committed to the Rol-Land workers, but to all agriculture workers in the province.

Not surprisingly the Rol-Land application was fiercely attacked by the company, including an injunction application in the lower

---

18 *Michael Fraser et al v Attorney General of Ontario*, Ontario Superior Court of Justice File No 03-CV-250815CM3.

courts that failed. On 7 July 2003, the OLRB proceeded to conduct the certification vote. The box was sealed pending preliminary arguments. Then, on 19 September 2003, the box was opened and the votes were counted. An overwhelming majority of the Rol-Land workers had voted to unionize.

The issue was heading back to the Labour Board, where challenges and arguments would be heard at a later date. In advance of those hearings, a week after the successful vote was conducted a letter was sent by UFCW Canada to Hank Vander Pol, the owner of Rol-Land. The letter proposed a co-operative, low-cost process of independently reaffirming the legitimacy of the Rol-Land employees' majority support to be represented by UFCW Canada. Once that was established, Rol-Land would grant voluntary recognition. In turn, UFCW Canada was prepared to agree in advance to the same collective bargaining regulations that had been incorporated in the *ALRA*. Vander Pol rejected the notion and refused to meet.

The determination hearings at the OLRB commenced some weeks later. The Board had two choices. It could dismiss certifying the Rol-Land bargaining unit on the grounds the *AEPA* excluded the workers from the *Labour Relations Act*. At that point, UFCW Canada would have appealed to the courts with a *Charter* challenge of the *AEPA*. The Board's other choice could have been to rule itself that the *AEPA* was unconstitutional, and to then certify the unit. If it had done so, the employer would have appealed the decision to the courts.

Either way, the case was likely on its way to court, so we, the Board, and Rol-Land agreed to temporarily adjourn the board hearings pending a decision by the courts on the legality of the *AEPA*, or Rol-Land's reconsideration of their decision not to recognize the will and rights of its workers through voluntary recognition.

To keep the heat on Rol-Land, an alliance of labour activists was formed across Ontario. A letter writing campaign was established to support the cause with allies including the Canadian Labour Congress, its affiliates, and other community groups who were ready to push a public campaign and boycott to support the cause of the Rol-Land workers. Hundreds of letters like the one below were faxed to the Rol-Land owner:

> Dear Hank Vander Pol,
>
> As a resident of Ontario and a consumer of mushrooms, I understand that you have refused to recognize your employees' basic rights to join a union of their choice and bargain collectively.

> I understand you are not prepared to recognize UFCW Canada based on the lack of Ontario legislation for agricultural workers. We find this decision appalling that in a democratic society, workers do not have the right to choose who and how they are represented. A large majority of your employees have freely made this decision and our union is in solidarity with Rol-Land farms employees and UFCW Canada.
>
> I will be continuing to follow your decision and I pledge my support to the Justice for Ontario Agriculture Workers Campaign. I can also assure you that I will be forwarding my concerns to other consumers and residents of Ontario to ensure you make the right decision.
>
> I will be personally contacting you to discuss this matter.
>
> Sincerely,
>
> J. Doe

B. Union Organizing and Community Building

Involving the community and labour allies was a key component to supporting the workers' morale, to pressure the employer, and also to raise public awareness that an attack on the labour rights of any group was an attack on the rights of all civil society. The engagement of public support through alliances, lobbying, media campaigns, and community outreach had supported the Rol-Land organizing campaign from the beginning. It was a strategy we would repeat and that evolved as we moved forward to organize both domestic and migrant agriculture workers in other locations, including Ontario.

Within months of the Rol-Land vote, two more certification applications were filed with the OLRB. One was for Platinum Produce, a greenhouse operation in Chatham, Ontario, where workers charged they were forced to continue to work while the greenhouse was being fogged with pesticides. An application for Stratford Chicks, a chick hatchery near Stratford, Ontario, was also filed. Both applications led to votes with the ballot box sealed pending the eventual legal outcome at Rol-Land. Like Rol-Land, the workers at both Stratford and Platinum were predominantly recent immigrants or temporary foreign workers delivered to the employer by independent job brokers.

Later that fall, in November 2003, UFCW Canada filed a new *Charter* challenge charging that the Employment Insurance (EI) program violated the *Charter* rights of migrant workers in Canada under the CSAWP because workers were forced to pay EI premiums but were excluded from collecting the unemployment insurance benefits. The federal attorney general filed a motion to strike out the claim, arguing that UFCW Canada did not have standing to represent migrant workers in the claim, in spite of the fact that we had been an advocate and supplied direct services to migrant workers for over a decade. The case would eventually be heard in the Ontario Superior Court of Justice.

While awaiting that court date, we advanced on another front when in April 2004, UFCW Canada filed a *Charter* challenge of the *AEPA*. The outcome of both the EI challenge and the *AEPA* challenge arrived within weeks of each other in December 2005 and January 2006.

The outcome of the EI challenge affirmed that UFCW Canada's history of advocacy and organizing were clear evidence of our status as a legitimate voice for migrant agricultural workers in Canada. In a well-reasoned decision, Ducharme J of the Ontario Superior Court of Justice denied the attorney general's motion to stop the union's EI challenge and awarded costs to UFCW Canada.[19]

In his decision, Ducharme J said that UFCW Canada had demonstrated in numerous ways over the course of several years that it had "a real and continuing interest in the well-being of foreign migrant agricultural workers," and "particular experience, expertise and success in representing the legal rights of agricultural workers, including SAWP workers, under the *Charter* and can bring that expertise to the presentation of legal issues in this case."[20]

It was the first time ever that any union had been granted status to challenge the federal government on behalf of unorganized workers. The decision was not just symbolic as later it would support our efforts to successfully challenge labour boards who initially questioned whether migrant workers could be organized in provinces which allowed domestic agriculture workers to unionize.

The court's recognition of our representative role also allowed us to advocate for parental leave for migrant workers, who had never claimed the benefit (which, unlike unemployment insurance benefits, could be paid to workers who qualified no matter where they lived in the off-season). With that in hand, the suit against the federal government was dropped, and in the subsequent years our staff at our AWA agriculture workers support centres across Canada have

19 *Fraser v Canada (Attorney General)*, 2005 CanLII 47783 (Ont SCJ).

20 *Ibid* at para 106.

to date helped CSAWP workers claim over $55 million in parental leave benefits.

The other decision, which came out in January 2006, was just as fateful; this time regarding the *Charter* challenge of the *AEPA*. In his judgment, Farley J of the Ontario Superior Court of Justice ruled that the *AEPA* likely met the minimum standard required by the 2001 Supreme Court *Dunmore* ruling.[21] As such, according to Farley J, the *AEPA* should stand until it was tested before the administrative tribunal that was established to enforce the *AEPA*.

Meanwhile, outside Ontario our organizing efforts were breaking through at large-scale agriculture operations in provinces where agriculture workers were included under the labour relations acts of those jurisdictions. In September 2006, certification applications for three locations in Quebec and one in Manitoba were filed with the labour boards in those provinces. The first to bargain a collective agreement was at Mayfair Farms in Portage la Prairie, which became the first-ever bargaining unit of any kind in Canada made up exclusively of migrant workers.

The organizing of the units had come through the same kind of community-based efforts that had been developed in Ontario. In Quebec and Manitoba, direct outreach, as well as servicing workers at the AWA support centres in those areas, were both keystones in building a community of confidence with workers. The workers were also aware of UFCW Canada's long-standing efforts on behalf of agriculture workers. They knew we were committed. They knew that we had gained EI benefits for them. They knew that we had proven we would stand with them until they were treated with the same respect and workplace rights as other workers in Canada.

As for the "test" that Farley J had called for, it commenced two months later in November 2006, when four men who had worked at Rol-Land Farms (including Mindy Leng's father) appeared before the first-ever Tribunal convened under the *AEPA*. A former manager at Rol-Land was prepared to give testimony that, as the men claimed, they had been fired because they were union sympathizers. The lawyer for the Tribunal was supplied by the Ontario attorney general.[22] Only one person on the Tribunal panel had any direct knowledge of the agriculture sector: a lobbyist who represented the Ontario

21 *Fraser v Ontario (AG)* (2006), 263 DLR (4th) 425 (Ont SCJ).

22 The history of these proceedings is summarized in *UFCW Canada et al v Rol-Land Farms et al*, 2008 CanLII 6652 (Ont Div Ct).

Cattlemen's Association. There was no labour representative on the Tribunal.

Quickly the *AEPA* Tribunal ground to a halt in a series of preliminary legal skirmishes that continued in spurts until the spring of 2007. No evidence was heard from the complainants and the hearings were eventually suspended when the employer declared bankruptcy. From the complainants' point of view, the *AEPA* had failed the test Farley J had called for. What followed was a series of court hearings and decisions that legal scholars have written much about, so I will not repeat their analysis. The collapse of the *AEPA* Tribunal hearings, which were followed shortly by the Supreme Court of Canada's June 2007 ruling in *BC Health Services*[23]—in which it ruled, citing *Dunmore*, that collective bargaining was a fundamental right protected by the guarantee of freedom of association in section 2(d) of the *Canadian Charter of Rights and Freedoms*—catalyzed the following series of events:

- In May 2008, the Ontario Court of Appeal heard the appeal of Farley J's decision, which had previously upheld the *AEPA* as constitutional.
- In November 2008, writing for a unanimous Court of Appeal, Winkler CJ found that the *AEPA* violated Ontario agriculture workers' right to collective bargaining and was unconstitutional.[24]
- In March 2009, UFCW Canada filed complaints with the United Nations International Labour Organization (ILO) that both Ontario and Canada were in violation of the ILO's Convention No 87—*Freedom of Association and Protection of the Right to Organize*, which declares the right to collective bargaining as a fundamental human right; the ILO Convention No 98—*Right to Organize and Collective Bargaining*; and the ILO's 1998 *Declaration on Fundamental Principles and Rights at Work*.
- In April 2009, the Ontario government's application seeking leave to appeal the Court of Appeal decision was allowed by the Supreme Court of Canada.
- In December 2009, the Supreme Court of Canada heard the appeal of the Winkler *AEPA* decision and reserved to consider its decision.
- On 15 November 2010, the ILO upheld the complaint filed by UFCW Canada (the Supreme Court of Canada had yet to render

23 *Health Services and Support—Facilities Subsector Bargaining Assn v British Columbia*, 2007 SCC 27, [2007] 2 SCR 391.

24 *Fraser* (Ont CA), above note 3.

its own decision). The ILO found both Canada and Ontario guilty of a discriminatory attack on the human and labour rights of farm workers in the province. The ILO decision was forwarded to the Supreme Court of Canada to add to the other evidence and submissions in front of it.

- Finally, on 29 April 2011, in spite of Ontario's violation of international human and labour rights standards, the Supreme Court upheld Ontario's appeal and judged the *AEPA* to be in keeping with the *Charter*. Despite the fact the *AEPA* Tribunal had been "tested" in 2006–2007 and found wanting, this was discounted by the Supreme Court.[25]

C. The Way Forward for Farm Workers in Canada

It had been eight years since Mindy Leng, her father, and most of their 270 co-workers had voted to unionize. Unfortunately, they were stopped in April 2011 by a powerful coalition of government and industry whose combined voice drowned out the call to give Ontario agriculture workers the same rights as those around them. Their struggle, and UFCW Canada's struggle alongside them, continues.

During those eight years, we could not wait for the courts and we continued to reach out to agriculture workers across Ontario and Canada with the same template and philosophy we had established through our founding efforts in Leamington. What we discovered was that the same oppressive and dangerous conditions that existed at Rol-Land were generally the norm, rather than the exception, at industrial-scale agriculture operations.

During the same decade, there was also a rapid expansion of the migrant and temporary foreign work force in Canadian corporate agriculture under federal programs that delivered migrant workers to employers, and then essentially abandoned them to fend for themselves. Many of these workers are forced to do life-threatening work without proper protective gear or training. They are crammed by the dozens into makeshift shanties and unsafe transport vans.

It is an employer-driven system, assisted by the government, where many workers must accept danger and exploitation if they want to work in Canada. If they raise concerns, they are typically deported without a hearing or right of appeal and blacklisted from ever returning.

---

25 *Fraser* (SCC), above note 1 at para 109.

Altogether, more than 40,000 migrant and temporary foreign workers toiled in Canadian agriculture in 2010.[26] They have become the backbone of Canada's agriculture production system. It is a system that in many ways is built on denying the human and labour rights of the workers, and is well documented in the *Status of Migrant Farm Workers in Canada Report, 2010–2011*.[27]

The report (updated annually since 2002) is based on UFCW Canada's direct experience with literally tens of thousands of agriculture workers every season through outreach efforts, and the operation of ten Agriculture Worker Alliance (AWA) worker support centres in Surrey, Kelowna, and Abbotsford, British Columbia; in Portage la Prairie, Manitoba; in Leamington, Virgil, Simcoe, and Bradford, Ontario; and in Saint-Rémi and Saint-Eustache, Quebec.

In 2010 alone, during the six month production season the AWA centres assisted with over 35,000 worker inquiries in their own language (inquires made at drop-in visits at the centres, during phone calls, and at outreach locations) across Canada regarding employer abuse; unsafe housing and working conditions; overcharging for rent or demanding recruitment fees; unilateral repatriations; and other threats or actions of employer reprisal.

Today, in association with UFCW Canada, the AWA has grown into the largest Canadian national organization for both foreign and domestic agriculture workers. Outside of Canada, UFCW Canada and the AWA have built an ongoing dialogue with sending governments, including Mexico, which is the largest source of workers in the CSAWP.

Mutual assistance pacts with three of Mexico's largest states are now in place to protect the rights of Mexican citizens working on Canadian farms. UFCW Canada and the AWA also continue to work closely with a number of major Mexican farm unions, public interest groups, and other Mexican civil organizations to protect the rights of Mexican migrant workers in Canada.

During that period we also established ongoing dialogue with other sending countries including Guatemala, Honduras, El Salvador, Thailand, and Jamaica. This international dialogue is part of a holistic approach to protecting and promoting the rights of all of those who work on Canadian farms, including migrant workers. It also reflects the reality that as globalization has created flows of migrant

---

26 *2009 Facts and Figures*, above note 11.

27 Available online: UFCW Canada www.ufcw.ca/templates/ufcwcanada/images/awa/publications/UFCW-Status_of_MF_Workers_2010-2011_EN.pdf.

labour between countries, the protection of the rights of migrant workers in Canada requires a trans-border strategy.

The strategy has had its success, with seventeen applications for certification filed, and a number of certificates issued for bargaining units with UFCW Canada collective agreements in place at a variety of locations in Quebec and British Columbia. Unique for Canada in some of these collective agreements is language regarding seniority and right of recall for migrant workers in the bargaining unit.

Unfortunately, but not surprisingly, some employers have attempted to circumvent collective agreements by blacklisting union supporters from returning, and then attempting a decertification campaign with the support of the workers they chose to call back. In two cases, applications regarding unfair labour practices were filed before the British Columbia Labour Relations Board in the spring of 2011, with allegations and evidence regarding such decertification attempts, pointing to collusion between local Mexico consular officials and two BC corporate agriculture employers where UFCW Canada collective agreements were in place. At the time of this publication, hearings into the allegations had yet to commence.[28]

Repatriation and blacklisting of some union supporters in other BC and Quebec locations has also been an issue. In all cases, the federal government, which administers migrant and temporary foreign worker programs, has declined to intercede (on behalf of the workers, that is).

As this story illustrates, even in provinces where the law provides the mechanism for agriculture workers to organize, it has been furiously undermined by the combined force of the industry, their lobby, and the implicit support of their political friends. In Ontario, the disregard for the rights of agriculture workers is even more blatant, with the power of the industry so strong that its exploitative agenda is incorporated into legislation.

How does one explain that to Mindy Leng, her father, Xin Yuan Lui, and the 80,000 other domestic and migrant agriculture workers in Ontario? And how does one explain to the 97 percent of people who are not in agriculture that much of the food that arrives on their table has come to them through the hands of those whose funda-

---

28 See letter from Brett Matthews (28 April 2011) online: http://www.ufcw.ca/templates/ufcwcanada/images/MexicoV_Consulate/ufcwcanada1518_floralia-complaint28apr2011.pdf; see also letter from Chris Buchanan (19 April 2011) online: http://www.ufcw.ca/templates/ufcwcanada/images/MexicoV_Consulate/ufcwcanada1518_sidhucomplaint19apr2011.pdf.

mental human and labour rights are violated every minute of their working day in the Ontario agriculture sector?

The only legitimate response is action: continuing to act on every front until the abusive regime that rules the corporate agriculture system is countered. The courts were one front—but for now the law is not a friend to the people, only to the corporate lobby. Additionally concerning, in 2011 the denial of effective collective bargaining for Ontario farm workers is slowly but surely expanding as labour laws in many jurisdictions are coming under attack from right-wing governments. So for now, in Ontario we are faced with playing by the rules of the *AEPA*. We will continue to organize. The cards that Ontario farm workers sign will be AWA cards (more than 6,000 have been signed to date), for even the *AEPA* allows unions or an alliance to be an "association" representative if workers choose it to be so.

But ultimately the rights of Ontario agriculture workers will require political action; the election of governments and leaders not tied to corporate interests, and who understand that workers' rights are human rights. The same can be said for the labour rights of all workers in Canada who face the threat of their labour rights being removed by right-wing, anti-labour governments unless they are stopped at the polls.

In 2011, the struggle for the rights of farm workers became a fight that could affect all workers. Together we can win it. To lose is not an option.

CHAPTER FOUR

Development as Remittances or Development as Freedom? Exploring Canada's Temporary Migration Programs from a Rights-based Approach

Kerry Preibisch

A. Introduction

Every year, some 40,000 men and women from more than seventy countries across the world enter Canada on temporary employment authorizations to work in the country's agri-food industries. This particular type of labour mobility is part of a growing global trend towards temporary and seasonal migration within immigration and citizenship policies. The re-emergence and rise of guest worker programs worldwide since the 1990s is supported by a policy discourse that portrays government-controlled temporary labour migration as delivering a "triple win" scenario: migrant-receiving countries can respond flexibly to labour demand using a regularized workforce while limiting permanent immigration; migrants can travel safely across borders to access higher wages and contribute to the well-being of their households; and sending countries benefit from the remittances their citizens send home and the skills they acquire abroad.[1] In particular, a consensus has emerged within policy circles

1 Xinying Chi, "Challenging Managed Temporary Labor Migration as a Model for Rights and Development for Labor-Sending Countries" (2008) 40 NYUJ Int'l L & Pol'y 49 [Chi]; Nicola Piper, "All Quiet on the Eastern Front?—Temporary Contract Migration in Asia Revisited From a Development Perspective" (2010) 29 Policy and Society 399; Martin Ruhs & Philip Martin, "Numbers vs. Rights: Trade-Offs and Guest Worker Programs" (2008) 42 International Migration Review 249 [Ruhs & Martin, "Numbers vs. Rights"].

that temporary migration programs contribute to economic development in sending countries.[2] Contributing to this discourse at the global level is the framing of Canada's guest worker arrangements as offering models or "tools" for fostering development and as part of Canada's foreign aid efforts, alongside continued references to the wage differentials between Canada and migrant-sending countries.[3] While Canada's temporary migration programs (TMPs) certainly provide workers in low-income countries access to the labour market of a high-income country and the potential to develop new skills, a growing body of scholarly literature suggests that the opportunities provided through labour migration to Canadian agriculture come at significant cost to migrants' freedom, security, and human dignity.[4] The academic literature, along with scores of policy-oriented documents, media reports, and other resources, has brought to light the

---

2 Chi, *ibid.*

3 Sedef Arat-Koc, "In the Privacy of Our Own Home: Foreign Domestic Workers as Solution to the Crisis in the Domestic Sphere in Canada" (1989) 28 Studies in Political Economy 33; Foreign Agriculture Resource Management Services, *Questions and Answers* (Mississauga: 2010) online: www.farmsontario.ca/pages.php?_ID=7; *Ontario (AG) v Fraser*, 2011 SCC 20 (Reply Factum of the Appellant—*Charter* s 15(1)).

4 Tanya Basok, *Tortillas and Tomatoes: Transmigrant Mexican Harvesters in Canada* (Montreal: McGill-Queens University Press, 2002) [Basok, *Tortillas and Tomatoes*]; Leigh Binford, "Contract Labor in Canada and the United States: A Critical Appreciation of Tanya Basok's Tortillas and Tomatoes: Transmigrant Mexican Harvesters in Canada" (2004) 29 Canadian Journal of Latin American and Caribbean Studies 289 [Binford, "Contract Labour"]; Kerry Preibisch & Evelyn Encalada Grez, "The Other Side of 'El Otro Lado': Mexican Migrant Women and Labor Flexibility in Canadian Agriculture" (2010) 35 Signs: Journal of Women in Culture and Society 289 [Preibisch & Encalada Grez, "The Other Side"]; Kerry Preibisch, "Migrant Agricultural Workers and Processes of Social Inclusion in Rural Canada: Encuentros and Desencuentros" (2004) 29 Canadian Journal of Latin American and Caribbean Studies 203 [Preibisch, "Migrant Agricultural Workers"]; Tanya Basok, "Mexican Seasonal Migration to Canada and Development: A Community-based Comparison" (2003) 41 International Migration 3 [Basok, "Mexican Seasonal Migration"]; Jenna Hennebry & Kerry Preibisch, "Deconstructing Managed Migration's Model: A Critical Look at Canada's Seasonal Agricultural Workers Program" (Paper delivered at the Annual Meeting of the Canadian Sociological Association (CSA), Vancouver, 2008); Janet McLaughlin, "Classifying the Ideal Migrant Worker: Mexican and Jamaican Transnational Farmworkers in Canada" (2010) Focaal 79 [McLaughlin, "Classifying"]; Jenna Hennebry, "Not Just a Few Bad Apples: Vulnerability, Health and Temporary Migration in Canada" (Spring 2010) Canadian Issues / Thèmes canadiens 73 [Hennebry, "Bad Apples"].

systemic exploitation of migrant farm workers and their exclusion from Canadian society.[5]

The contrast between the discourse surrounding the benefits of circular migration for development and growing awareness of the disentitlement and mistreatment of migrant workers highlights diverging definitions of development or, at the very least, the overemphasis on income poverty within migration policy circles. Development is now widely addressed in both study and practice from a rights-based approach that reconceptualizes development as a process that goes beyond meeting basic human needs to include expanding people's enjoyment of a range of freedoms, delineating the obligations of states and others to enhance the access of individuals to realize their rights, and empowering people to demand justice as opposed to being the passive recipients of charity.[6] With regards to mi-

---

5 Tanya Basok, "Canada's Temporary Migration Program: A Model Despite Flaws" *Migration Information Source* (Migration Policy Institute, November 2007); Gerardo Otero & Kerry Preibisch, *Farmworker Health and Safety: Challenges for British Columbia* (Vancouver: WorkSafe BC, 2010) [Otero & Preibisch]; David Fairey et al, *Cultivating Farmworker' Rights: Ending the Exploitation of Immigrant and Migrant Farmworkers in BC* (Vancouver: Canadian Centre for Policy Alternatives BC Office, Justicia for Migrant Workers; Progressive Intercultural Community Services and BC Federation of Labour, 2008) [Fairey]; United Food and Commercial Workers of Canada & Agriculture Workers Alliance, *The Status of Migrant Farm Workers in Canada 2010–2011* (Rexdale, ON: United Food and Commercial Workers of Canada, 2011) [UFCWC & AWA]; Standing Committee on Citizenship and Immigration, *Temporary Foreign Workers and Nonstatus Workers: Seventh Report of the Standing Committee on Citizenship and Immigration* (Ottawa: House of Commons Canada, 2009)[Standing Committee on Citizenship and Immigration]; Office of the Auditor General of Canada, "Chapter 2: Selecting Foreign Workers Under the Immigration Program" in *Report of the Auditor General of Canada to the House of Commons* (Ottawa: Office of the Auditor General of Canada, 2009) [Office of the Auditor General of Canada]; Evelyn Encalada Grez, "Harvesting Seeds of Justice: The Plight of Migrant Farm Workers in Ontario" (Fall/Winter 2005) *Women & Environments International Magazine* 16; Jenna Hennebry, *International Agricultural Migration and Public Health: Examining Migrant Farm Worker Health and the Public Health Implications of Agricultural Temporary Migration* (Public Health Agency of Canada, 2008) [Hennebry, *Examining*].

6 Jean Grugel & Nicola Piper, *Critical Perspectives on Global Governance: Rights and Regulations in Governing Regimes* (New York: Routledge, 2007) [Grugel & Piper]; Amartya Sen, *Development as Freedom* (Oxford: Oxford University Press, 1999). In 1999, the Nobel Prize-winning economist Amartya Sen published the book *Development as Freedom*, in which development is conceptualized as a process of expanding the substantive freedoms that people enjoy while removing sources of unfreedom. Sen argues that focusing on promoting human freedoms should be both the goal and means of development. The book, which contested previous held notions of development focused on income poverty and economic growth, is widely considered a foundational text of human development theory and rights-based approaches to development.

grants, the activism of non-governmental organizations (NGOs) and trade unions across the globe has been fundamental to pushing a rights-based approach to international labour migration.[7] As Nicola Piper has argued, such an approach provides the scope to consider the structural causes of migration as well as the social, political, and economic contexts in which it is embedded, thus opening the discussion to include other dimensions of migration-based livelihoods often excluded from analysis focused on economic betterment, such as the social and emotional costs for migrants and non-migrating members of their households.[8]

In this chapter, I counter the sanguinity characterizing the potential of guest worker programs to deliver on economic development for migrants by providing a critical examination of Canada's TMPs for agriculture. I show how migrants are positioned to be relatively more vulnerable than other workers within the country's agriculture and food system owing to their position at the bottom of the occupational hierarchy, their precarious immigration status as temporary "foreign" workers, and their racialization as non-Whites from the global South. Moreover, I illustrate how changes to policies of temporary migration have constituted farm work as an even more precarious form of employment for migrants in particular, but also Canadians, despite mounting research and greater public awareness of the exploitation of migrant agricultural workers over the past decade. Finally, while recognizing that temporary migration programs may contribute to aspects of economic development, enabling participants to access income and assets formerly out of their reach, I call for greater attention to the rights, welfare, and dignity of migrants when considering temporary migration programs.[9] Development defined in these terms unsettles the discourse surrounding temporary migration programs that can be characterized as optimistic, if not complacent, in its desire to suit political convenience.[10]

7 Grugel & Piper, *ibid*; Nicola Piper, "Temporary Economic Migration and Rights Activism: An Organizational Perspective" (2010) 33 Ethnic and Racial Studies 108.

8 Nicola Piper, "Feminisation of Migration and the Social Dimensions of Development: The Asian Case" (2008) 29 *Third World Quarterly* 1287 [Piper, "Feminisation"]; Grugel & Piper, *ibid*.

9 Piper, "Feminisation," *ibid*.

10 See Catherine Barber, Richard Black, & Paula Tenaglia, "Making Migration 'Development Friendly': Temporary Worker Schemes in the UK" (Sussex: Development Research Centre on Migration, Globalisation and Poverty, 2005 Working Paper).

B. Methods and Terminology

This chapter is based on a decade-long program of research on temporary labour migration to Canada's farm and food industries that has addressed a range of issues, including social exclusion and inclusion of migrant farm workers, the gendered and racialized character and experience of temporary labour migration, and the role of migrant labour in agricultural production. The analysis I present in this chapter draws on studies within this program of research that were based primarily on qualitative data derived from in-depth interviews with a diverse set of stakeholder participants in Ontario and British Columbia between 2002 and 2010, including thirty-nine civil servants in Canada and migrant-sending countries, thirty-nine employers and industry representatives, and 122 migrant workers.[11] My analysis is also informed by interviews and focus groups with Canadian farm workers and members of outreach or advocacy organizations. The chapter further relies on ethnographic observations from field research and my participation in various multi-stakeholder forums on migrant labour issues.

Throughout the chapter, I refer to those individuals who enter Canada to work under TMPs as migrant workers. The use of the word migrant is somewhat imprecise, as people with diverse citizenship statuses migrate to work in agriculture in Canada, including Canadian citizens and permanent residents who often reside in sub/urban areas and either drive to work or are transported by labour contractors. Some of these internal migrants cross provincial borders to find work, such as Quebec residents who seasonally harvest fruit in British Columbia. A unique group of Canadian citizens migrate transnationally to take up seasonal work in agriculture, as is the case of Low German-speaking Mennonites who live parts of the year in colonies in Mexico.[12] There are also a number of people migrating for work in agriculture, often from sub/urban locations, who do have permanent status and/or employment authorization, including individuals who were authorized to enter Canada but not to work (e.g. visitors), the formerly documented (people who overstayed their visas or whose refugee or sponsorship claim was unsuccessful), and those whose initial entry was undetected or undocument-

---

11 I am grateful to Aaráon Díaz, Evelyn Encalada Grez, Christina Hanson, Luz María Hermoso Santamaría, André Lyn, and Trish Scantlebury for their contributions to recruiting and interviewing migrants, and to Ana Lorena Leíja for her transcriptions.

12 Luann Good Gingrich & Kerry Preibisch, "Migration as Preservation and Loss: The Paradox of Transnational Living for Low German Mennonite Women" (2010) 36 Journal of Ethnic and Migration Studies 1499.

ed. Here, however, the term migrant refers solely to participants in TMPs, unless indicated otherwise, to avoid using official government discourse of "temporary foreign workers." Referring to migrants in TMPs as *temporary* obscures their long-term, structural importance to agricultural production and the decade-long tenure of some migrants; indeed, only their visa is temporary.[13] Further, labelling migrants as *foreign* is part of a nationalist discourse that contributes ideologically to their legal and social disentitlement within labour market and society.[14]

C. Policies of "Managed Migration" that Create Precarious Workers

Canada has three different managed migration schemes open to agri-food employers: the Seasonal Agricultural Worker Program (SAWP), the Pilot Project for Occupations Requiring Lower Levels of Formal Training, National Occupational Classification C and D (NOC C and D Pilot), and the Agriculture Stream of the aforementioned Pilot Project. The SAWP is Canada's longest-standing TMP for low-skilled workers. First implemented in 1966, the SAWP existed for many years as one of the only legalized channels for migrants classified as low skilled to enter the Canadian labour market[15] and the only mechanism for agri-food employers to legally employ migrants from abroad. Four decades later, when economic growth led to rising employer demand for a much broader range of low-skilled workers, particularly in the oil, gas, and construction industries, the federal government introduced the Low Skill Pilot Project in 2002 to expand the recruitment of migrants on temporary employment authorization. Renamed the Pilot Project for Occupations Requiring Lower Levels of Formal Training, National Occupational Classification C and D in 2007, the new guest worker program broadened access to the global pool for labour beyond primary agriculture to any employer that could demonstrate a labour shortage, primarily through proof of unsuccessful attempts

13 Kerry Preibisch, "Local Produce, Foreign Labor: Labor Mobility Programs and Global Trade Competitiveness in Canada" (2007) 72 Rural Sociology 418 [Preibisch, "Local Produce"].

14 Nandita Sharma, *Home Economics: Nationalism and the Making of Migrant Workers in Canada* (Toronto: University of Toronto Press, 2006) [Sharma].

15 The other channel was the Live-in Caregiver program, a mechanism for admitting mostly women as live-in domestics, that has its origins in the Caribbean Domestic Scheme (1955–1981).

to attract domestic workers through advertising.[16] For the ensuing eight years, employers of agricultural workers were open to hire migrants under the SAWP, under the new guest worker initiative, or both. In 2011, however, employers seeking to hire farm workers in those commodities eligible for the SAWP were obliged to follow new requirements tailored to the farm and food industry, referred to as the New Agricultural Stream under the Pilot Project NOC C and D. While all three initiatives share features common to most guest worker programs, including tied work permits, forced rotation, ineligibility for permanent residence, and restrictions that separate migrants from their families, they also have important differences that I discuss in this section.

The SAWP is very much a post-World War II guest worker program[17] characterized by heavy state involvement. The program is comprised of a set of bilateral agreements signed between Canada and participating migrant-sending countries to establish and operate an agricultural seasonal worker program. The first of these, the Commonwealth Caribbean Agreement, was signed in 1966 with Jamaica and subsequently included Trinidad and Tobago, Barbados, and members of the Organization of Eastern Caribbean States (OECS). In 1974, a similar agreement was signed with Mexico. These agreements, enshrined in Memoranda of Understanding (MOU), delineate the duties and obligations of workers, employers, and governments. The MOUs include operational guidelines and standard contracts that are subject to annual negotiation at meetings involving the Canadian federal government, select Canadian employer representatives,[18] and sending country governments. The administration of the program is restricted to specific parties: migrant-sending countries are charged with worker recruitment, selection, and documentation, as well as posting government agents within Canada to oversee the program's operation, including resolving employer-worker disputes. In addition, two industry organizations—Foreign Agricultural Resource Management Services (FARMS) in Ontario and Fondation des Entreprises en Recrutement de la Main-d' œuvre Agricole Étrangère (FERME) in Quebec—are designated to administrate employer applications. The degree of government involvement in the formal administration of the SAWP—including the authoriza-

16 In Alberta, polices implemented in 2007–2010 made some agri-food enterprises automatically eligible to recruit migrant workers.

17 Piotr Plewa, "The Rise and Fall of Temporary Foreign Worker Policies: Lessons for Poland" (2007) 45:2 International Migration 3–36.

18 Specifically, the Canadian Horticultural Council.

tion of private sector actors—distinguishes it among North American guest worker programs.[19]

Conversely, the NOC C and D Pilot and its Agricultural Stream represent a post-Cold War, neoliberal generation of guest worker programs that embody policies of labour market deregulation and expanded private sector involvement. They are not based on mutually negotiated bilateral agreements that commit the sending and receiving states to a set of shared responsibilities and authorize the involvement of specific private sector actors. Rather, they function as unilateral mechanisms of immigration policy that permit approved employers to hire workers from outside Canada within an operational framework that devolves much of the administration to market institutions. Specifically, employers can recruit from any country they wish; are not obliged to use the government-designated FARMS and FERME to place requests; and can do their own recruitment or pay a labour broker to assist them. In addition, the NOC C and D Pilot does not contain a standard contract, although the Canadian government has authored one for the Agricultural Stream. Under the new initiatives, migrant-sending countries have no formal role in managing the migration of their nationals to Canada or in negotiating the conditions of their employment abroad.

The scope and operation of the three programs also share similarities and differences. The SAWP is an industry-specific program designed to serve primary agriculture, although what this comprises has broadened over the past four decades to include animal production by 2011.[20] Designed as a seasonal program, however, SAWP employment contracts are a maximum of eight months long and are only permitted between 1 January and 15 December.[21] The NOC C and D Pilot provides more flexibility to businesses with non-seasonal production, issuing work permits at any time of the year and for up to two years in length, as does the Agricultural Stream for employers producing SAWP-eligible commodities. While the tenure of SAWP participants in the program is not specified—a policy that has

---

19 David Griffith, *The Canadian and United States Migrant Agricultural Workers Programs: Parallels and Divergences Between Two North American Seasonal Agricultural Labour Markets with Respect to "Best Practices"* (North-South Institute, 2003).

20 As of August 2011, SAWP-eligible commodities included fruit, vegetables (including canning and processing operations), greenhouses, nurseries, apiary products, Christmas trees, flowers, pedigreed canola seed, sod, tobacco, bovine, dairy, duck, horse, mink, poultry, and sheep.

21 The minimum time frame for an employment contract is no less than 240 hours in a period of six weeks or less.

led some migrants to accrue over thirty consecutive years of employment—since 2010, migrants participating in the new initiatives must leave Canada after four years of accumulated employment and are not eligible to return for another four years. The "4/4 Rule," while unpopular with both employers and migrants' rights activists, retains the ideological element of these new migration programs as temporary.

The responsibilities of employers and the costs they incur vary across the three TMPs. Employers are obliged to provide acceptable accommodation to migrants that they hire under the SAWP and the Agricultural Stream. While employers must do so without cost to SAWP workers,[22] the Agricultural Stream permits them to charge $30 per week.[23] Under the NOC C and D Pilot, a program open to all industry sectors, employers are only *expected to help* the worker find suitable, affordable accommodation.[24] Regarding transportation, employers hiring migrants under all programs must pay for migrants' return airfare, but those hiring under the SAWP can recover a portion of this through wage deductions.[25] Since many agri-food businesses prefer to provide housing for the migrants they hire in order to avoid the transportation problems linked to their location in rural or remote settings and benefit from other advantages of an on-site workforce, the NOC C and D Pilot was slightly more expensive than the SAWP for these employers. The 2011 introduction of the Agricultural Stream harmonizes the costs between programs by allowing employers to recoup their expenditures on airfare through rent.

Guidelines regarding wages also differ. Under the NOC C and D Pilot, employers are expected to offer wages that are equal to or higher than the prevailing rate paid to Canadians in the same occupation and region or, in a unionized environment, the same wage rate as established under the collective bargaining agreement. Under the SAWP, employers must pay migrants at rates equal to or greater than: (1) the legal wage for agricultural workers in the province of

---

22 British Columbia is an exception; in that province, employers can charge up to $505 a season in rent and must pay for migrants' entire airfare.

23 Human Resources and Skills Development Canada, *Agricultural Stream of the Pilot Project for Occupations Requiring Lower Levels of Formal Training (NOC C and D)* (Gatineau, QC: 2001) online: www.hrsdc.gc.ca/eng/workplaceskills/foreign_workers/Agricultural/directives.shtml.

24 Human Resources and Skills Development Canada, *Temporary Foreign Worker Program* (Gatineau, QC: 2011) online: www.hrsdc.gc.ca/eng/workplaceskills/foreign_workers/ lowskill.shtml.

25 In 2011, employers in every province but British Columbia hiring SAWP workers could recoup up to $632 in wage deductions from their employees from Mexico, and $505 from those from the Caribbean.

employment; (2) the rate determined by the Canadian government through the SAWP negotiations with migrant-sending countries to be the prevailing wage rate for the type of agricultural work performed in the province of employment; and (3) the rate being paid by the employer to his or her regular seasonal work force performing the same type of agricultural work. Since 2011, employers hiring workers under the NOC C and D Pilot in SAWP-eligible commodities must follow the guidelines of the Agricultural Stream that adopt the SAWP approach to determining wages, a policy adjustment that now encourages employers to pay migrants doing the same job (at times at the same worksite) equally.

Although the federal government contends that migrant workers have the same rights as Canadians[26] and recommends that farm employers treat migrants in "a fair and equitable manner,"[27] the structure and operation of Canada's TMPs within the context of global inequalities situates migrant agricultural workers as highly vulnerable workers. Legal analysts have argued that while migrant workers may share many of the same rights, they cannot exercise these in practice.[28] To begin, migrant farm workers enter a job considered one of the country's most precarious occupations.[29] Farm labour is near the bottom of the occupational hierarchy in Canada. Farm workers are also excluded from employment standards legislation covering workers in other industries. Historically, farm labour has also been excluded from minimum wage provisions in most provinces, including Ontario, where the majority of farm workers are employed.[30] A recent study found farm workers in British Columbia earning $8.23

26 Human Resources and Skills Development Canada, *Foreign Workers: Roles and Responsibilities* (Gatineau, QC: 2011), online: www.hrsdc.gc.ca/eng/workplaceskills/foreign_workers/ ei_tfw/rr_tfw.shtml.

27 Service Canada, *Service Canada Statement of Policy and Terms and Conditions for the 2007 Commonwealth Caribbean and Mexican Seasonal Agricultural Workers Program* (Ottawa: 2007) online: www.servicecanada.gc.ca/eng/on/epb/agri/policy.shtml.

28 Veena Verma, "Legal Analysis of the SAWP" (Presentation to members of the Mexican Congress delegation to Canada in Mississauga, ON: UFCW Local 175, 2007).

29 Precarious forms of employment involve atypical employment contracts, limited social benefits and statutory entitlements, job insecurity, low job tenure, low earnings, poor working conditions, and high risks of ill health: Leah Vosko, ed, *Precarious Employment: Understanding Labour Market Insecurity* (Montreal: McGill-Queen's University Press, 2006).

30 Human Resources and Skills Development Canada, *Minimum Wage Database* (Gatineau, QC: International and Intergovernmental Labour Affairs Labour Branch, 2005) online: srv116.services.gc.ca/dimt-wid/sm-mw/intro.aspx?lang=eng; Government of Ontario, *Employment Standards Fact Sheet: Agricultural Workers* (Toronto: Queen's Printer for Ontario, 2005) online: www.labour.gov.on.ca/english/es/pdf/fs_agri.pdf.

per hour, with those paid by piece rates regularly earning less than the minimum wage.[31] Hand harvesters have been subject to extreme forms of wage theft, including being underpaid for their work, not paid at all, and receiving bogus records of employment.[32] Although much agricultural work is year round, many jobs still involve high fluctuations in hours and employment periods. Additionally, researchers have documented routine violations of the laws that do protect farm workers.[33] In British Columbia, deregulation in the 2000s led to further erosion of the few protections covering farm workers.[34] Last but not least is the starting point for this volume, that farm workers in Ontario and Alberta do not enjoy the right of collective bargaining. Since these provinces together employ 67 percent of migrants employed under the SAWP and NOC C and D Pilot to work in agriculture, it can be said that two out of every three migrants to Canada do not have access to these fundamental labour rights.

Despite the fact that farm workers are among the lowest paid, least protected participants in the Canadian labour market, the work they perform is some of the most dangerous.[35] Agriculture remains among Canada's most hazardous occupations, ranking fourth in terms of incidence of workplace fatalities after mining, quarrying, and oil wells; logging and forestry; and fishing and trapping.[36] Workers' compensation statistics show a substantial claims and fatalities

---

31 Fairey, above note 5.

32 *Ibid*. Mark Thompson, *Rights and Responsibilities in a Changing Workplace: A Review of Employment Standards in British Columbia* (Victoria, BC: Ministry of Skills, Training and Labour, 1994) [Thompson]; Graeme Moore, *Hand-Harvesters of Fraser Valley Berry Crops: New Era Protection of Vulnerable Employees* (Vancouver, BC: Federation of Labour, 2004) [Moore].

33 Thompson, *ibid*; Moore, *ibid*; Singh Bolaria et al, "Farm Labour, Work Conditions, and Health Risks" in Ihor V Zielyk, David A Hay, & Gurcharn S Basran, eds, *Rural Sociology in Canada* (Toronto: Oxford University Press, 1992).

34 Fairey, above note 5; Thompson, *ibid*; David Fairey, *Eroding Worker Protections: British Columbia's New 'Flexible' Employment Standards* (Vancouver: Canadian Centre for Policy Alternatives, 2005); Moore, *ibid*. In 2002, British Columbia rolled back protections for agriculture workers by cutting enforcement measures, dropping employer requirements to keep records of wages paid to labour contractors; and reducing the minimum piece rates payable to farm workers for overtime pay and compensation for travelling to work: Fairey, above note 5.

35 Thompson, *ibid*.

36 William Pickett, "Fatal Work-related Farm Injuries in Canada, 1991–1995" (1999) 160 Canadian Medical Association Journal 1843; Andrew Sharpe & Jill Hardt, *Five Deaths a Day: Workplace Fatalities in Canada, 1993-2005*. (Ottawa: Centre for the Study of Living Standards, 2006).

picture compared to other industries.[37] Exposure to risks such as agrochemicals and climatic extremes is exacerbated by insufficient and inconsistent access to training.[38] Workplace health and safety in agriculture is further undermined by poorly maintained, inadequate farm equipment; deficient hygiene and sanitation at worksites; and lack of personal protective equipment.[39] In Ontario, agricultural workers were excluded from occupational health and safety laws until 2006 and still lack agriculture-specific regulations.[40]

While all agricultural workers face precarious employment, immigration and citizenship policies further weaken the position of migrants. First, Canadian immigration authorities issue closed work permits to migrant farm workers that are valid only with a single, designated employer. Such restrictions on their labour mobility sets them apart from citizens, permanent residents, and even unauthorized workers (who can "vote with their feet" to move to worksites offering better conditions), and severely limits their bargaining power. Indeed, it is this condition of their employment has led scholars to view them as a contemporary source of unfree labour.[41] While the Canadian government claims that migrant workers can request

---

37 WorkSafeBC, *Facts: Agriculture in BC* (Vancouver: WorkSafeBC Risk Management, 2007) online: www.worksafebc.com/news_room/news_releases/assets/nr_07_03_12/noi_summaries .pdf; WorkSafeBC, *Statistics* (Vancouver: WorkSafeBC Enterprise Data Warehouse, 2009) online: www2.worksafebc.com/Portals/Agriculture/Statistics.asp.

38 Hennebry, *Examining*, above note 5; Janet McLaughlin, *Trouble in our Fields: Health and Human Rights among Mexican and Caribbean Migrant Farm Workers in Canada* (PhD Doctoral Thesis, University of Toronto, 2009) [unpublished] [McLaughlin, *Trouble in our Fields*]; Otero & Preibisch, above note 5; Hennebry, "Bad Apples," above note 4; Jenna Hennebry, Kerry Preibisch, & Janet McLaughlin, *Health Across Borders—Health Status, Risks and Care among Transnational Migrant Farm Workers in Ontario* (Toronto: CERIS Ontario Metropolis Centre, 2010) [Hennebry, Preibisch, & McLaughlin].

39 *Ibid* to all of the above sources.

40 Eric Tucker, "Will the Vicious Circle of Precariousness be Unbroken? The Exclusion of Ontario Farm Workers from the Occupational Health and Safety Act" in Leah Vosko, ed, *Precarious Employment: Understanding Labour Market Insecurity* (Montreal: McGill-Queen's University Press, 2006); Malcolm Sargeant & Eric Tucker, "Layers of Vulnerability in Occupational Safety and Health for Migrant Workers: Case Studies from Canada and the UK" (2009) 7 Policy and Practice in Health and Safety 51.

41 Basok, *Tortillas and Tomatoes*, above note 4; Vic Satzewich, *Racism and the Incorporation of Foreign Labour: Farm Labour Migration to Canada* (New York: Routledge, 1991) [Satzewich]; Ricardo Trumper & Lloyd Wong, "Racialization and Genderization: The Canadian State, Immigration, and Temporary Workers" in B Singh Bolaria & Rosemary Bolaria, eds, *International Labour Migrations* (Delhi: Oxford University Press, 1997) [Trumper & Wong]; Sharma, above note 14; Binford, "Contract Labour," above note 4.

to change employers, in practice it is almost impossible to do so.[42] When the Alberta Federation of Labour (AFL) created a Temporary Foreign Worker Advocate in 2007 to provide free services to migrant workers, ninety-three of the 123 case files seen in the first six months involved migrant workers "desperately seeking alternate or even any employment,"[43] a sharp illustration of the problematic nature of closed work permits.

Moreover, like prototypical TMPs that seek to "import labour, not people,"[44] there are no provisions to allow the dependents of participants to accompany them in Canada. While the new initiatives do not bar family members from accompanying migrants, they certainly impose barriers around this occurring.[45] To underline this policy stance, farm workers under all three guest worker initiatives have been excluded from a new pilot project to allow the spouses, common-law partners, and dependent children of temporary migrant workers to receive open work permits that would authorize them to accept any job with any employer.[46] Mechanisms common in guest worker programs to separate productive from reproductive labour[47] produce a highly flexible workforce as migrant farm workers are more likely to accede to employer requests to work long, anti-social hours and less likely to be pulled from their work owing to reproductive

---

42 Jenna Hennebry & Kerry Preibisch, "A Model for Managed Migration? Re-Examining Best Practices in Canada's Seasonal Agricultural Worker Program" (2010) International Migration, early view; *Alberta Federation of Labour, Temporary Foreign Workers: Alberta's Disposable Workforce (The Six-Month Report of the AFL's Temporary Foreign Worker Advocate)* (Edmonton: 2007) [Alberta Federation of Labour].

43 Alberta Federation of Labour, *ibid* at 9.

44 Stephen Castles, "Guestworkers in Europe: A Resurrection? (2006) 40 International Migration Review 741.

45 NOC C and D Pilot participants are obliged to demonstrate to an immigration officer that they have the financial resources to cover their family's travel cost and potentially, international fees for their children to attend school: Judy Fudge & Fiona McPhail, "The Temporary Foreign Worker Program in Canada: Low-Skilled Workers as an Extreme Form of Flexible Labour" (2009) 31 Comp Lab L & Pol'y J 101 [Fudge & McPhail]. Moreover, the immigration ministry —Citizenship and Immigration Canada—considers a migrant's request to have his family accompany him as having the potential to raise legitimate concerns regarding any intention by the foreign national to become a permanent resident (Fudge & McPhail, *ibid*).

46 Citizenship and Immigration Canada, *Backgrounder: British Columbia Pilot Project for Spouses, Common-Law Partners and Working-Age Dependent Children of Temporary Foreign Workers* (Ottawa: Citizenship and Immigration Canada, 2011) online: www.cic.gc.ca/english/ department/media/backgrounders/2011/2011-08-12.asp.

47 Michael Burawoy, "The Functions and Reproduction of Migrant Labor: Comparative Material from Southern Africa and the United States" (1976) 81 The American Journal of Sociology 1050.

responsibilities. The separation of migrants from their families also produces a particularly vulnerable workforce, as excessive hours and lack of family support exacerbate workplace risks. Furthermore, the TMPs serving agri-food industries do not include a process of earned residency that would allow migrants to transfer from temporary to permanent migration status after a period of accumulated employment. This is despite policies allowing migrants in other jobs designated as low skilled to do so; caregivers, for example, can apply for permanent residency after contributing at least twenty-four months within four years of their arrival in Canada. Such restrictive citizenship policies applied specifically to farm workers thus constitute these migrants as "permanently temporary."[48] Moreover, as non-citizens, they are ineligible for the range of services and protections associated with citizenship or permanent residency that facilitate integration, such as government-funded English classes.[49] While they pay into Employment Insurance, most migrants are ineligible for most of this benefit. They also lack the right to vote and, as such, are placed at a social and political disadvantage in Canadian society.[50]

The TMPs available to agri-food industries contain other coercive mechanisms that constrain migrant workers in exercising the rights they do have. Migrant workers constitute a highly disposable workforce, as dismissal almost always results in deportation. There is no independent appeal mechanism that allows migrants to contest the reasons for being let go or to sanction employers who act unfairly.[51] The SAWP actually contains provisions within the employment agreement that allow employers to dismiss and, therefore, repatriate workers for "non-compliance, refusal to work, or any other sufficient reason."[52] Although forced rates of repatriation in the SAWP are low, the threat of repatriation acts as a powerful tool of labour control regardless of its actual exercise, even more so for workers who have witnessed the firing of their co-workers for having suffered an injury or

48 Hennebry, *Examining*, above note 5.

49 Basok, "Mexican Seasonal Migration," above note 4.

50 Veena Verma, *The Regulatory and Policy Framework of the Caribbean Seasonal Agricultural Workers Program* (Ottawa: The North-South Institute, 2007); Singh Bolaria, Gurcharn S Basran, & David A Hay, "The Health Effects of Powerlessness: The Case of Immigrant Farm Labour" in Gurcharn S Barsan, Ihor V. Zielyk, & David A Hay, eds, *The Political Economy of Agriculture in Western Canada* (Toronto: Garamond Press, 1988).

51 Veena Verma, *The Mexican and Caribbean Seasonal Agricultural Workers Program: Regulatory and Policy Framework, Farm Industry-Level Employment Practices and the Future of the Program Under Unionization* (Ottawa: The North-South Institute, 2003).

52 *Ibid.*

illness, refusing unsafe work, or becoming pregnant.[53] As one Jamaican worker stated: "When you working for a white man and you can work, it is the greatest thing. But if you sick, even with your teeth, it seems as if you're finished."[54] Alberta's Temporary Foreign Worker Advocate found that the threat of deportation was used against NOC C and D Pilot workers to discourage them from filing for workers compensation benefits or complaining about wages and working conditions.[55]

Housing arrangements common to farm work, whereby on-site accommodation is often provided by the employer, further shape labour relations. Although good quality, low-cost housing is scarce in rural Canada, the benefits of employer-provided housing are often compromised by its tendency to extend employers' control beyond the sphere of work and foster paternalistic labour relations.[56] In terms of the former, migrants living at their worksites become hyper-accessible to their employers who often value a migrant labour force precisely because they are available 24/7. Migrants' privacy is regularly violated by employers who take liberties accessing migrants' quarters. These housing arrangements pose particular risks of sexual harassment and violence for migrant women. In the SAWP, employers' control is reinforced through contractually permitted housing guidelines that, while intended to cover care of the property, have also been used to limit the mobility of workers through curfews or restrictions on visitors.

Housing for migrant workers is often inadequately serviced, crowded, and dilapidated.[57] A further abuse has been the overcharging of rent.[58] The scope for such abuses to occur is reinforced through inconsistent use, monitoring, and enforcement of rental agreements, as well as the exemption from provincial tenancy legislation of some housing arrangements. Further, since the agri-food operations employing foreign workers are located in rural settings, often at great distances from population settlements, migrants tend to be isolat-

---

53 Kerry Preibisch, "Pick-Your-Own Labor: Migrant Workers and Flexibility in Canadian Agriculture" (2010) 44 International Migration Review 404 [Preibisch, "Pick-Your-Own Labor"].

54 Preibisch, "Local Produce," above note 13.

55 Alberta Federation of Labour, above note 42.

56 Ellen Wall, "Personal Labour Relations and Ethnicity in Ontario Agriculture" in Vic Satzewuch, ed, *Deconstructing a Nation: Immigration, Multiculturalism and Racism in '90s Canada.* (Halifax, NS: Fernwood Publishing, 1992) [Wall].

57 Standing Committee on Citizenship and Immigration, above note 5; Alberta Federation of Labour, above note 42.

58 Standing Committee on Citizenship and Immigration, above note 5; UFCWC & AWA, above note 5.

ed.[59] Employer-provided housing arrangements, combined with the rural location of migrant farm workers' jobs, thus contribute spatially to migrants' social exclusion.[60] In addition, migrants can come to depend heavily on their employer for transportation or to access services, including healthcare. Migrants' dependence on their employers has been found to foster paternalistic labour relations.[61]

With the exception of a handful of unionized workplaces in British Columbia and Quebec,[62] migrant workers do not have recall rights and thus subsequent contracts depend on their employer requesting them by name through the SAWP or on their application for migrants under the new initiatives. The SAWP's policy of nominative recruitment has resulted in a widely held perception among Mexican workers that failure to be recalled could jeopardize their tenure in the program.[63] Self-discipline and acquiescence is reinforced among Mexican workers who are subject to virtual evaluations by their employers that are considered each year by Mexican authorities when deciding placements, a practice that can also discourage migrants from reporting violations while in Canada.[64] One migrant, when describing the high degree of compliance fostered by the evaluation, characterized it metaphorically as "a passport that allows you to return the following year." Sending countries exercise additional practices that constrain workers' freedom. For example, Mexican authorities formerly required SAWP participants to remain with the same employer for three years before considering transfer requests.[65] Although this rule is no longer enforced, workers with multiple placements in their employment records are assessed negatively for future jobs.

In addition to the terms and conditions of their immigration status, migrant farm workers' social location within the global political economy impacts their vulnerability. Structural inequalities between migrant-sending and receiving states produce migrants whose

59 In 2002, only 7 percent of the Jamaican workers surveyed in the NSI country-level study lived within two kilometres of the nearest town, while 21 percent were located more than twenty-one kilometres away: Roy Russell, *Jamaican Workers' Participation in CSAWP and Development Consequences in the Workers' Rural Home Communities* (Ottawa: North-South Institute, 2003).

60 Preibisch, "Migrant Agricultural Workers," above note 4.

61 Wall, above note 56.

62 At the time of writing, there were three certified agricultural bargaining units in BC and six in Quebec.

63 Basok, *Tortillas and Tomatoes*, above note 4.

64 Fairey, above note 5.

65 Binford, "Contract Labour," above note 4.

economic need and lack of opportunities at home reflects heavily in their on-the-job performance and acceptance of substandard working and living conditions. Moreover, sending countries' reliance on labour migration reduces their incentive and ability to protect migrants' rights,[66] despite having a formal commitment to do so (as in the SAWP) or as a result of their commitments to international conventions.[67] The remittances sent home by migrants result in much-needed foreign exchange, improve the well-being of the households and communities that receive them, and ease the political pressures created by unemployment and uneven regional development. It is not in the interest of sending states for migrants to permanently settle abroad and reduce the amount of remittances directed homewards. Sending countries thus also have a stake in ensuring migrants' return or "circularity," as it is referred to in policy circles. Indeed, when government is involved in recruitment, as is the case for all SAWP workers, policies tend to align with interests of host country authorities to target those migrants most likely to engage in circular migration, favouring candidates from marginalized regions who are land-poor or landless, who have minimal education, and who are married and/or have dependents. The Caribbean countries also exercise a compulsory savings scheme, whereby migrants must return home to recoup 19 percent of their wages. Beyond sending-states' interest in capturing remittances, ensuring circularity, and preventing irregular settlement, maintaining diplomatic harmony with Canada, an important trading partner, is also of consequence.[68] Additionally, sending countries have limited institutional capacity to protect their citizen migrant workers, particularly those states that are poor and poorly governed.[69]

While global disparities may reduce migrant sending-states' incentives to defend migrant rights, their ability to do so is also constrained by the very architecture of Canada's TMPs that has been designed to encourage competition between countries. For example, the application for SAWP migrants asks employers to indicate the country that will supply them with labour, rather than simply indicating the number of workers required. Concomitantly, sending country representatives that press employers or industry associations too

---

66 Chi, above note 1.

67 Countries that send large numbers of migrant agricultural workers to Canada, Mexico, Jamaica, and Guatemala have all ratified the International Convention on the Protection of the Rights of All Migrant Workers and Members of their Families.

68 The class (and often ethnic) gulf between consular staff posted in Canada and program participants further undermines the protection of migrant rights.

69 Chi, above note 1.

aggressively jeopardize losing employment of their own citizens to a competitor country.[70] Sending countries also compete to obtain and retain employment for their nationals in Canada by selecting candidates with the skill sets and experience desired by employers.[71] More egregiously, sending-state officials, in their bid to ensure the smooth operation of the program, have assisted employers in repatriating injured or ill workers and blacklisting union organizers.[72]

The introduction of the NOC C and D Pilot and its Agricultural Stream only upped the ante of competition by broadening the pool of labour beyond the SAWP bilateral partners to the global market. This resulted in the rapid diversification of the non-citizen agricultural labour force beyond the fourteen SAWP nationalities to include migrants from some seventy-five different countries by 2008.[73] The degree of competition between countries in their bid to secure remittances is reflected in an advertisement that the Honduran Consulate in Toronto placed in a farming magazine to promote their nationals.[74] With the headline "Hire Me" in bold lettering, the image depicts sombrero-clad Hispanic men hand-hoeing a patch of particularly dry-looking earth. All of the men have their heads bent towards the ground and away from the viewer's gaze, emphasizing their submission to the manual labour in which they are engaged. One younger-looking man is without shoes or a shirt, exposing a muscled chest and arms, thus indicating both strength and presumable willingness to labour in hot conditions. The caption reads "Workers from Hon-

---

70 Kerry Preibisch & Leigh Binford, "Interrogating Racialized Global Labour Supply: An Exploration of the Ethnic Replacement of Foreign Agricultural Workers in Canada" (2007) 44 Canadian Review of Sociology and Anthropology 5 [Preibisch & Binford, "Interrogating"].

71 McLaughlin, "Classifying," above note 4; Kerry Preibisch & Luz Maria Hermoso Santamaria, "Engendering Labour Migration: The Case of Foreign Workers in Canadian Agriculture" in Evangelia Tastsoglou & Alexandra Z Dobrowolsky, eds, *Women, Migration, and Citizenship: Making Local, National, and Transnational Connections* (Aldershot and Burlington: Ashgate, 2006) [Preibisch & Santamaria, "Engendering"].

72 McLaughlin, *Trouble in our Fields*, above note 38; United Food and Commercial Workers of Canada, *Charges Allege Mexico Consulate Blacklisted Unionized Mexican Migrant Workers in B.C.* (United Food and Commerical Workers of Canada, 2011) online: www.ufcw.ca/index.php?option=com_content&view=article&id=2353%3Acharges-allege-mexico-consulate-blacklisted-unionized-mexican-migrant-workers-in-bc&catid=6%3Adirections-newsletter&Itemid=6&lang=en.

73 Kerry Preibisch, "Migrant Workers and Changing Workplace Regimes in Contemporary Agricultural Production in Canada" (2012) 19:1 International Journal of the Sociology of Agriculture and Food, Special Issue on "Migrants in the Global Food System" 62–82: [Preibisch, "Migrant Workers"].

74 Advertisement. Workers from Honduras, "Hire Me" (March 2011) 61 *The Grower* 37.

duras. 100% motivated to do what is needed, focussed on quality [and with] experience in hard work." The advertisement includes a toll-free number and web address where farmers can report problems with workers twenty-four hours a day, seven days a week, 365 days a year. It pledges to cover the costs of replacing a worker who defaults on his contract with funds through the country's 2011 budget, while promising that workers will be subject to "constant monitoring of performance." The website further extols the Honduran government's recruitment and pre-migration procedures: "Although we don't expect problems with our carefully selected workers, that have been briefed on their obligations and conduct with their bosses, the Government of Honduras has implemented this page, to help in case of grievances against Honduras workers."[75] The imagery and the text of the advertisement powerfully reflect how sending states compete for work placements in Canada by appealing to employers' perceived desires. The threat of competition is real: labour replacement of one nationality of migrant workers by another has a long history in Canadian agriculture.[76] Most recently, the introduction of the NOC C and D Pilot has resulted in labour displacement that has assumed provincial proportions: in Quebec, Guatemalans under the NOC C and D Pilot replaced Mexicans under the SAWP as the preferred farm labour force within six years, growing from 215 workers in 2003 to some 3,458 in 2009.[77] According to trade unions, this shift is a direct result of the successful organizing of Mexican workers in that province by the United Food and Commercial Workers of Canada (UFCW Canada) throughout the 2000s.

Apart from fostering competition between migrant-sending countries for employment placements in Canada, employers use discriminatory hiring practices in order to differentiate their workforce along various axes of social difference—nationality/race, ethnicity, gender, citizenship status—as part of their labour arrangements. Work teams may be differentiated from one another on these bases in order to provoke competition in order to raise productivity levels, for example, by pitting migrants against non-migrants, or non-indigenous Mexican men under the SAWP against indigenous Guatemalans

---

75 Online: Workers from Honduras www.workersfromhonduras.org/denuncias.html.

76 Lloyd Wong, *Migrant Seasonal Agricultural Labour: Race and Ethnic Relations in the Okanagan Valley* (PhD Dissertation/Thesis, York University, 1988) [unpublished]; Preibisch & Binford, "Interrogating," above note 70.

77 Preibisch, "Migrant Workers," above note 73.

under the NOC C and D Pilot, or women against men.[78] Additionally, employers may hire linguistically, culturally, and gender-differentiated groups to minimize worker interaction on the shop floor or assign tasks according to nationality.[79] Segmenting the labour force is also a strategy aimed at reducing worker solidarity.[80] These divisions are often promoted outside the worksite, with separate dormitories and kitchens for migrants of distinct nationalities, including Canadians.

That guest worker programs foster discriminatory hiring practices reflects the historical role of race and gender in the social organization of workers in Canada.[81] Race and gender have played fundamental roles in shaping immigration and citizenship policies historically.[82] In terms of race, although overtly discriminatory criteria were removed from immigration policy in the 1960s, racist beliefs have informed the use of guest worker programs as a means of importing the labour of people of colour from the global South while preventing their settlement.[83] Currently, the majority of migrants on temporary employment authorizations are non-White from developing countries in Asia, Latin America, and Africa.[84] How racism and racialization contributes to the precarious labour market experiences of migrants has not figured prominently in the academic literature.[85] Researchers have noted, however, that Canadians and permanent residents in rural areas in areas of high employment of temporary visa workers perceive their migrant neighbours in highly racialized terms[86] and that this contributes to their social exclusion.[87] Language barriers, lack of knowledge about their rights, and limited access to agencies further positions migrants from the global South

78 Preibisch & Encalada Grez, "The Other Side," above note 4; Binford, "Contract Labour," above note 4.
79 Preibisch, "Local Produce," above note 13.
80 Binford, "Contract Labour," above note 4.
81 Sharma, above note 14; Trumper & Wong, above note 41.
82 Daiva Stasiulis & Abigail Bakan, *Negotiating Citizenship: Migrant Women in Canada and the Global System* (Houndsmill: Palgrave-Macmillan, 2003); Trumper & Wong, *ibid*; Sharma, *ibid*; Satzewich, above note 41; Grace-Edward Galabuzi, *Canada's Economic Apartheid: The Social Exclusion of Racialized Groups in the New Century* (Toronto: Canadian Scholars' Press, 2006).
83 *Ibid* to all sources.
84 Sharma, above note 14; Fudge & McPhail, above note 45.
85 Adam Perry, "Barely Legal: Racism and Migrant Farm Labour in the Context of Canadian Multiculturalism" 16:2 Citizenship Studies [forthcoming in 2012].
86 Harald Bauder, "Landscape and Scale in Media Representations: The Construction of Offshore Farm Labour in Ontario, Canada" (2005) 12 Cultural Geographies 41; Preibisch & Binford, "Interrogating," above note 70.
87 Preibisch, "Migrant Agricultural Workers," above note 4.

as highly vulnerable workers.[88] More generally, nationalist policies and discourse that position migrant workers as temporary foreigners contribute to their ideological disentitlement to the rights and treatment afforded Canadians.[89]

Gender has played a similar organizing role to race in labour migration to Canada. With respect to agri-food production, a recruitment bias for male workers has resulted in a largely male workforce. Only 3 percent of the SAWP workforce and 15 percent of the agricultural NOC C and D workforce in 2008 were women. Women's scant representation among the farm worker population strongly influences their migratory experiences. Women tend to face greater restrictions on their mobility than men and face unique barriers in meeting their gender-specific health needs.[90] Contrary to the profile of male participants, most women tend to be lone parents and, as such, separation from their children implies unique stressors on their mental health.[91]

Canada's temporary migration programs have also been designed to curtail independent migrant representation. In the SAWP's bilateral model, civil society organizations, trade unions, and migrants themselves have been excluded from the program's operation and monitoring, an arena open only to governments and industry. Although migrant-sending governments were never an ideal proxy to represent migrant interests in the SAWP, even this level of representation is excised from the unilateral framework of the NOC C and D Pilot, which has no formal role for migrant-sending states in negotiating and managing labour migration. The Canadian government justified the move away from bilateral migration policies due to the SAWP's resource-intensiveness and ill fit with the country's commitments to the World Trade Organization (WTO) regarding the General Agreement on Trade in Services (GATS).[92] The latter of these is less plausible than the former in light of the GATS focus on high-skilled migrants[93] and the global emergence of bilateral, managed migration agreements across the high income world. In terms of resource-intensiveness, however, the SAWP is clearly the flared trousers within the Canadian state's policy wardrobe next to the NOC C and D Pilot

88 Naomi Alboim, *Discussion Paper 2: The "Pilot" for Recruiting Temporary Foreign Workers for Low-skilled Jobs Should be Abolished* (Toronto: The Maytree Foundation, 2011) [Alboim].

89 Sharma, above note 14.

90 Preibisch & Santamaria, "Engendering," above note 71; Preibisch & Encalada Grez, "The Other Side," above note 4.

91 Preibisch & Encalada Grez, *ibid*; Preibisch & Santamaria, *ibid*.

92 Preibisch, "Pick-Your-Own Labor," above note 53.

93 Grugel & Piper, above note 6.

and its Agricultural Stream. Yet downloading the operation of the management of migration to market institutions has infused greater precariousness into farm work. Crucially, the new initiatives were implemented without the appropriate regulatory framework to protect migrant workers and prevent fraud in relation to work permit applications.[94]

A principal issue has been recruitment, as the Canadian government allowed private labour brokers to link workers to employers while failing to draft and implement corresponding regulation. Although some measures to regulate this migration industry have been put in place within the last few years, particularly by provincial authorities, the regulatory void has resulted in a range of exploitative situations for migrants.[95] One of the most problematic issues has been brokers charging migrants excessive recruitment fees for their placements in Canada. Of the 123 cases handled by the Temporary Foreign Labour Advocate in the first half of her term, eighty-nine were brought to Canada by labour brokers who charged fees ranging from $3,000 to $10,000.[96] Recruitment fees have been so disproportionate to migrants' expected earnings over their visa length that throughout in the mid 2000s, a number of cases emerged whereby NOC C and D migrants sought to extend their stay in Canada and recoup the costs of their migration by claiming refugee status or absconding from their designated employers to find unauthorized work elsewhere.[97] Additional abuses by recruiters have included collecting recruitment fees for non-existent jobs; charging excessively for providing extra services to migrants; and misrepresenting migrants' expected earnings, opportunities for permanent residence, or family reunification.[98] The lack of regulation has also resulted in abuses by employers, including unfair dismissal, underemployment, and hiring migrants without authorization to do so, thus placing both parties in a situation of illegality.[99]

---

94 Office of the Auditor General of Canada, above note 5.

95 Standing Committee on Citizenship and Immigration, above note 5; Alberta Federation of Labour, above note 42; Kerry Preibisch & Jenna Hennebry, "Buy Local, Hire Global: Temporary Migration in Canadian Agriculture" in Patti Lenard & Christine Straehle, eds, *Legislated Inequality: Temporary Migrant Workers in Canada* (Montreal: McGill-Queen's University Press, forthcoming).

96 Alberta Federation of Labour, *ibid.*

97 Standing Committee on Citizenship and Immigration, above note 5.

98 Standing Committee on Citizenship and Immigration, *ibid*; Alberta Federation of Labour, above note 42.

99 Standing Committee on Citizenship and Immigration, *ibid*; Alberta Federation of Labour, *ibid.*

Canada's shifting policies with regards to temporary labour migration to agri-food jobs, such as the introduction of the NOC C and D Pilot, reflects a move towards increasing use of workers on temporary employment authorization as a strategy of labour market policy. Within the last fifteen years, the country's TMPs have experienced considerable growth. The SAWP was extended to all but one Canadian province (Newfoundland and Labrador) by 2004 and now authorizes close to 30,000 placements for international migrants, up from some 12,598 in 1990. The precipitous growth of the NOC C and D Pilot has received significant attention, expanding from some 1,580 workers in its first year of implementation, 2002, to 38,255 by 2009, a twenty four-fold increase over seven years.[100] While these figures include all low-skill occupations filled by migrant workers, a considerable portion is in agriculture. In 2009, 10,359 of the temporary foreign worker (TFW) positions approved and confirmed under the NOC C and D Pilot were in agriculture-related fields.[101] The expansion of the NOC C and D Pilot indicates that this guest worker arrangement has grown beyond a pilot initiative. Among its various shortcomings, analysts have noted that the program may discourage employers from improving wages and working conditions, making investments in research and development, and employing permanent residents and citizens[102]—processes observed in other high-income countries.[103]

In sum, migrant workers are accorded fewer rights and are greatly constrained in claiming the rights they do have, owing fundamentally to both their employment in a sector characterized by reduced labour standards, protections, and rights, but also immigration and citizenship policies that exacerbate their labour market experience and heighten their vulnerability. As Luin Goldring and her colleagues have argued, participants in TMPs experience precarious status resulting from the insecurities derived from less than full legal citizenship rights, including temporary work authorization, no right to permanently remain in the country of employment, dependence on

100 Alboim, above note 88.

101 These include harvesting labourers; general farm workers; labourers in food, beverage, and tobacco processing; nursery and greenhouse workers; landscaping and grounds maintenance labourers; farm supervisors and specialized livestock workers; farmers and farm managers; landscape and horticulture supervisors; agricultural and related service contractors and managers; landscaping and grounds maintenance contractors and managers; aquaculture and marine harvest labourers; and nursery and greenhouse operators and managers.

102 Alboim, above note 88.

103 Martin Ruhs & Bridget Anderson, eds, *Who Needs Migrant Workers? Labour Shortages, Immigration, and Public Policy* (Oxford: Oxford University Press, 2011).

a third party for one's right to be in the country, ineligibility for the range of public goods available to residents, and denial of the right to sponsor family members within the country's existing family reunification policies.[104] Thus discriminatory immigration and citizenship policies, along with migrant farm workers' position within the occupational hierarchy, serve to cheapen and weaken them within the labour market. Further, the government has implemented policies over the past decade that have made farm work and temporary labour migration even more precarious.

D. From Meeting Needs to Expanding Freedoms

There is little question the majority of men and women participating in Canada's TMPs for employment in farm and food industry jobs are able to accrue economic benefits from these transnational livelihoods. Surveys carried out in the late 1990s and early 2000s found that on average, Mexican workers in the SAWP could earn around CAD$1,000 per month while in Canada.[105] Corroborating these findings, a survey of 257 Mexican farm workers carried out in 2006 found that the average migrant to Ontario had a contract of just under six months, worked some 64 hours per week, and remitted $6,657 to their households over that period.[106] It is this difference in wages that motivates most migrants. As one migrant related:

> The economic situation in which you find yourself makes you leave your family to go far away, because if it was not for the situation you face in Mexico—if all the families were fed—there would not be this problem of being alone [in Canada], of leaving your children with your wife. All the families would be together (Interview, 2003).

---

104 Luin Golding, "Temporary Worker Programs as Precarious Status: Implications for Citizenship, Inclusion and Nation-building in Canada" (Spring 2010) Canadian Issues/Themes Canadiens 50; Luin Goldring, Carolina Berinstein, & Judith Bernhard, "Institutionalizing Precarious Immigration Status in Canada" *CERIS Working Paper* (Toronto: CERIS, The Ontario Metropolis Centre, 2007).

105 Leigh Binford, "The Seasonal Agricultural Workers Program and Mexican Development" *FOCAL Policy Paper* (Ottawa: Canadian Foundation for the Americas, 2006) [Binford, "Seasonal Agricultural Workers Program"]; Basok, *Tortillas and Tomatoes*, above note 4.

106 Lidia Carvajal, *The Farm-level Impacts in Mexico of the Participation in Canada's Seasonal Agricultural Workers Program (CSAWP)* (PhD Thesis, University of Guelph, 2008) [unpublished] [Carvajal]. However, migrants' earnings depend on the length of their contract; Binford's survey of 187 Mexican migrants found that half returned less than CAD$4,900 to their households over the season they were in Canada.

Indeed, the SAWP is highly valued for the economic opportunity it presents; for most participants, they have virtually no alternative source of income that would allow them to earn as much.[107] According to one study, over 90 percent of migrants surveyed believed that participation in the SAWP had enabled them to improve their well-being and that of their families.[108] At the macro level, Carvajal found that remittances sent home by Mexican SAWP workers in 2005 represented more than 75 percent of the US$89 million in remittances Mexico received from Canada that year. While this figure pales in comparison to the amount of remittances sent from the United States, it still constitutes a significant household income flow that sustains more than 10,000 families in Mexico.[109]

Contrary to the notion of circular migration as temporary, analysis of the SAWP shows that "participants in the Canadian program become locked into a cycle of transmigration" whereby they have to renew their seasonal visas year after year in order to keep up with the rising reproduction costs of their households.[110] For Mexican migrants, most require five work seasons in Canada in order to meet their households' most immediate needs such as debt repayment, clothing, construction, and other prime necessities.[111] Following this initial period, however, many continue to work in Canada in subsequent seasons because their earnings do not allow them to accumulate a substantial amount of capital;[112] because the needs of their households often increase over time, including with investments in children's education; and finally because the expectations of their households tend to rise with an improved standard of living.[113] The investments in education are particularly noteworthy; one study noted that the children of SAWP migrants who had left school and entered the labour market had on average 9.8 years of schooling, some

---

107 McLaughlin, *Trouble in our Fields*, above note 38; Binford, "Seasonal Agricultural Workers Program," above note 105; Basok, *Tortillas and Tomatoes*, above note 4.

108 Gustavo Verduzco, "The Impact of Canadian Labour Experience on the Households of Mexicans: A Seminal View on Best Practices" *FOCAL Policy Paper* (Ottawa: Canadian Foundation for the Americas, 2007) [Verduzco].

109 Carvajal, above note 106.

110 Basok, *Tortillas and Tomatoes*, above note 4; Binford, "Seasonal Agricultural Workers Program," above note 105.

111 Binford, "Seasonal Agricultural Workers Program," *ibid.*

112 Unions have charged that SAWP wage levels are artificially low. In addition, migrants' earnings are subject to program-specific and federal deductions and a portion must go to financing their living costs in Canada.

113 Binford, "Seasonal Agricultural Workers Program," above note 105; Basok, *Tortillas and Tomatoes*, above note 4.

2.2 years more than their parents.[114] Furthermore, studies of how temporary agricultural migrants spend their Canadian earnings have found that once household needs are met, very little income is left to make capital investment that could enhance their livelihoods at home and reduce their dependence on international migration, in part because the bulk of participants are drawn from marginalized communities that have few opportunities to leverage their remittances productively.[115] One study that tracked on-farm investments found that while 35 percent of migrants invested heavily in farming or purchasing land (between CAD$10,000 and $20,000), most of this was geared towards subsistence, rather than commercial production.[116] Indeed, Binford suggests that Canada's SAWP is best conceived as contributing to poverty alleviation as opposed to development.[117]

A focus on remittances and productive investment, however, continues to narrowly define development in economic terms. Piper and Grugel note that a fundamental difference between needs-based and rights-based approaches to development is an emphasis in the latter on people and their ability to claim rights and entitlements.[118] As I have sought to make clear in this chapter, migrant agricultural workers are not granted the same rights as Canadian citizens and permanent residents and are highly constrained in their ability to claim the rights they are accorded. Moreover, Canada's TMPs routinely subject migrants to violations of core labour rights enshrined in international law that protect migrant workers and members of their families, as well as some of their universal human rights.[119] This wider view of development from a rights-based approach encompasses how TMPs restrict migrants' rights and increase the social costs to migrants and their households. While it is beyond the scope of the paper to rigorously examine the outcomes of migrants' structural vulnerabilities in social terms, the scholarship on temporary labour migration to agriculture emphasizes the following. Firstly, the structure and operation of Canada's TMPs for agricultural work

---

114 Verduzco, above note 108.

115 Tanya Basok, "Migration of Mexican Seasonal Farm Workers to Canada and Development: Obstacles to Productive Investment" (2000) 34 International Migration Review 79; Basok, *Tortillas and Tomatoes*, above note 4; Binford, "Seasonal Agricultural Workers Program," above note 105.

116 Carvajal, above note 106.

117 Binford, "Seasonal Agricultural Workers Program," above note 105.

118 Jean Grugel & Nicola Piper, *Critical Perspectives on Global Governance: Rights and Regulations in Governing Regimes* (New York, Routledge, 2007) at 50.

119 International Labor Organization, *International Labour Migration: A Rights-based Approach* (Geveva: International Labour Office, 2010).

poses threats to migrants' welfare. An emerging group of studies has shown how migrants are exposed to greater risks to their mental and physical health than the general farm worker population, while facing considerable obstacles to accessing quality healthcare.[120] Janet McLaughlin has profiled migrants who have been incapacitated or died in Canada, highlighting how in most cases, injured or ill workers are deported before receiving appropriate medical care.[121] Secondly, as this chapter has shown, migrants face a number of employment-related grievances, most significantly as a result of their unfreedom and disposability. Thirdly, the social relations that characterize Canada's TMPs for agriculture—between migrants and their employers, migrants and the broader society, and migrants themselves—have given rise to multiple assaults on migrants' dignity and personhood. For migrant women in particular, these have involved pre-migration pregnancy tests, pregnancy as grounds for dismissal and deportation, and sexual harassment and assault.[122] Migrants commonly refer to their experiences in Canada as a sacrifice and many speak of the "humiliations" they endure in order to maintain the approval of their employer and, thus, their access to the Canadian labour market. Illustrative of this point, when migrant farm workers launched a migrant-led organization in 2010, the name reflected a fundamental demand: *Dignidad Obrera Agrícola Migrante*, which translates as Migrant Agricultural Worker Dignity. Finally, the separation of migrants from their households for lengthy and recurrent periods comes at significant costs to family relationships. Marital strain and breakdown, often as a result of real or perceived infidelity, affects many families. In addition, lengthy separation of parents and children often breeds estrangement and tension in their relationships.[123] While the consequences for non-migrating families are under-studied, there are indications that the social costs and experiences of non-migrating members of households merit special attention.

---

120 McLaughlin, *Trouble in our Fields*, above note 38; Hennebry, "Bad Apples," above note 4; Hennebry, Preibisch, & McLaughlin, above note 38; Otero & Preibisch, above note 5; Kerry Preibisch & Henna Henneby, "Temporary Migration, Chronic Effects: The Health of International Migrant Workers in Canada" (2011) 183 Canadian Medical Association Journal 1033.

121 McLaughlin, *Trouble in our Fields, ibid.*

122 Preibisch & Encalada Grez, "The Other Side," above note 4.

123 Kerry Preibisch & Evelyn Encalada, "Transnational Homemaking: Between Hearts and Pockets" (Research report prepared for the Programa Inter-institucional de Estudios Sobre la Región de América del Norte (PIERAN), forthcoming).

E. Conclusion

The expansion of temporary migration programs across the high-income world is often defended by referencing their benefits for enhancing development within migrant-sending countries. These arguments taken to their extreme in the Canadian context depict guest worker arrangements as part of the country's foreign aid contributions. Portraying TMPs as delivering a "win" to migrants in terms of development focuses on the potential of labour migration to address income poverty, harness remittances, and build productive investment within migrant-sending regions. Development defined in these terms is at odds with a rights-based approach that is now the dominant paradigm within development policy and increasingly, informing migration policy on a global stage. Examining TMPs from this approach yields a less rosy picture, bringing to light how the economic opportunities provided by employment abroad also expose migrants to new vulnerabilities owing to precarious legal status, discrimination in the labour market and society, and exploitative working and living conditions. As I have tried to highlight in this chapter, the sources of migrant farm workers' vulnerability, precariousness, and cheapness are multiple and intersecting. Host country policies, through mechanisms such as the expansion of guest worker arrangements and the introduction of less regulated models, play no small part in generating and reinforcing the inequality and exploitation of migrants. Indeed, the NOC C and D Pilot and its Agricultural Stream have infused even more precariousness into the agricultural labour market. Finally, while a rights-based approach often leads to conclusions that all guest worker arrangements are inherently exploitative[124] or involve "trading off" the rights of participants for labour market access,[125] they also raise difficult yet pertinent questions that demand our careful attention, including the ideological positioning of migrants as less deserving of rights than citizens, how economic development built on migrant labour may hinder development in countries that export labour, or the role of borders in creating and maintaining global inequalities.

---

124 David Griffith, *American Guestworkers: Jamaicans and Mexicans in the U.S. Labor Market* (University Park: Penn State University Press, 2006).

125 Ruhs & Martin, "Numbers vs. Rights," above note 1.

CHAPTER FIVE
Envisioning Equality: Analogous Grounds and Farm Workers' Experience of Discrimination

Fay Faraday

> Legislative equality for agricultural employees is overdue. In a society that is becoming highly conscious of civil rights and equality before the law it seems unlikely that the right to minimum protection on the job will continue to be denied to farm workers, particularly in view of the increasingly industrial nature of farming.
>
> —Kathryn Nelson and Innis Christie (1975)[1]

A. Introduction

Since well before the *Canadian Charter of Rights and Freedoms* was enacted, respected scholars have criticized the web of laws that deny Ontario farm workers the core rights, including the right to bargain collectively, that virtually all other workers enjoy. They argue that this legal exclusion cannot be reconciled with principles of equality and fairness. Building on this criticism, farm workers have long been described as "among the most economically exploited and politically neutralized individuals in our society."[2] Even the Supreme Court of Canada has accepted that agricultural workers are a particularly dis-

1 Kathryn Nelson & Innis Christie, "The Agricultural Labourer in Canada: A Legal Point of View" (1975) 2 Dal LJ 330 at 365.

2 David M Beatty, *Putting the Charter to Work: Designing a Constitutional Labour Code* (Montreal: McGill-Queen's Press, 1987) at 89 [Beatty, *Putting the Charter to Work*].

empowered group in Canadian society. Writing in *Dunmore v Ontario (AG)* in 2001, the majority of the Court found:

> Distinguishing features of agricultural workers are their political impotence, their lack of resources to associate without state protection and their vulnerability to reprisal by their employers; . . . agricultural workers are "poorly paid, face difficult working conditions, have low levels of skill and education, low status and limited employment mobility."[3]

From the earliest days under the *Charter* it was predicted that farm workers' exile from core labour protections would be ended by the new equality guarantee.[4] And yet, four decades after Nelson and Christie's analysis, legislative equality remains overdue and courts have failed to engage seriously with farm workers' claims to equality before and under the law and to equal protection and equal benefit of the law.[5]

Through *Cuddy Chicks*,[6] *Dunmore*,[7] and *Fraser*,[8] courts and commentators have analysed agricultural workers' struggle for collective bargaining rights almost exclusively through the lens of freedom of association. However, the workers' legal claims have always simultaneously asserted their fundamental right to equality under section 15 of the *Charter*. Most recently in *Fraser*, the workers argued that by excluding them from the wide range of protections for collective bargaining under the *Labour Relations Act, 1995* and by relegating them to separate and unequal treatment under the *Agricultural Employees Protection Act* (AEPA), the government denied agricultural workers equal benefit and protection of the law.[9] In summary, they

---

3 *Dunmore v Ontario (AG)*, [2001] 3 SCR 1016 at para 41 [*Dunmore*].

4 Beatty, *Putting the Charter to Work*, above note 2 at 93.

5 Section 15(1) of the *Charter* guarantees as follows: "Every individual is equal before and under the law and has the right to the equal protection and equal benefit of the law without discrimination and, in particular, without discrimination based on race, national or ethnic origin, colour, religion, sex, age or mental or physical disability."

6 *Cuddy Chicks Ltd v Ontario (Labour Relations Board)*, [1991] 2 SCR 5.

7 Above note 3.

8 *Fraser v Ontario (AG)*, 2011 SCC 20 [*Fraser* (SCC)], reversing 2008 ONCA 760 [*Fraser* (Ont CA)], which in turn had reversed (2006), 263 DLR (4th) 425 (Ont SCJ) [*Fraser* (Ont SCJ)].

9 See the chapters by Wayne Hanley and Paul Cavalluzzo in this collection for a more detailed discussion of farm workers' exclusion from the *Labour Relations Act, 1995* and the nature of rights under the *Agricultural Employees Protection Act, 2002*, SO 2002, c 16. Briefly, the *AEPA* provides truncated rights to form employee associations which can make representations to an employer. Multiple employee associations are permitted in each workplace with no mechanism to monitor

argued that the impugned laws violate section 15 by substantively discriminating on the analogous ground of the claimants' status as agricultural workers. The long history of agricultural workers' exclusion from basic labour standards, combined with the federal and provincial governments' long-term involvement in recruiting disadvantaged populations (both domestic and migrant) to work in agriculture have been instrumental in constructing the agricultural workforce as a distinctly marginalized group. In turn, denying that marginalized population access to the tools of self-organization and self-empowerment that are guaranteed for other workers perpetuates and reinforces their disadvantage.

The agricultural workers' freedom of association and equality claims are distinct: neither claim depends on the other for success. Instead, each legal claim shines a light on a distinct aspect of farm workers' experience of the law. While the section 2(d) analysis highlights the injury to farm workers' freedom of association, the section 15 analysis provides the more complete context that illuminates why *this* particular group of workers has been singled out for such exceptional treatment. The section 15 analysis, then, addresses most directly the political and socio-economic dynamics of disempowerment that sustain farm workers' "exceptionalism" in law.[10]

The courts' failure to engage deeply with the equality argument yields an impoverished and decontextualized analysis which allows the differential and prejudicial treatment to persist. This failure has created a disconnect or gap in which the court can express "sympathy"[11] for the "vulnerable position"[12] of agricultural workers without confronting how law has been used to construct that very vulnerability. In this way, the courts confer an unhealthy "privileged

---

their authenticity or the extent of employee support. Employee associations may make representations orally or in writing that employers must either listen to or read. The Supreme Court in *Fraser* found that under these provisions the employer must "consider" the representations in good faith. The *AEPA*, however, contains no institutional support for collective bargaining, and no support in the form of conciliation or mediation services and no access to a dispute resolution mechanism in the event of a bargaining impasse. It also provides no right to grievance arbitration and no access to a regulatory and adjudicative tribunal that has experience with and expertise in labour relations.

10 See Eric Tucker's chapter in this collection.

11 *Fraser* (SCC), above note 8 at para 115.

12 *Ibid*. Similarly, the Ontario Court of Appeal agreed that "the AEPA perpetuates and reinforces the pre-existing disadvantage of agricultural workers," but determined that their claim could not be recognized under s 15: *Fraser* (Ont CA), above note 8 at para 111.

innocence"[13] on the law by rendering known systemic marginalization *through law* effectively non-justiciable.

This chapter seeks to bridge that disconnect, to mind the gap. First, it begins by reviewing the breadth of evidence that was before the Court. The Supreme Court of Canada found that the section 15 claim "cannot succeed on the record before us."[14] However the record before the Court totalled forty volumes of evidence, a significant portion of which examined the history and present day practice of systemic marginalization experienced by agricultural workers. None of that evidence was referred to by the Court. Second, it compares the substantive section 2(d) analysis of disadvantage in *Dunmore* with the cursory dismissal of the section 15 claim in *Fraser.* Third, it analyses the role of analogous grounds and how they help deepen the understanding of substantive equality.

B. Constructing Agricultural Workers on the Margins

1) Rendering Evidence Invisible

In *Law v Canada,* after reformulating the legal test for proving discrimination under the *Charter,* Iacobucci J expressed the optimistic view that:

> None of the foregoing discussion implies that the claimant must adduce data, or other social science evidence not generally available, in order to show a violation of the claimant's dignity or freedom. Such materials may be adduced by the parties, and may be of great assistance to a court in determining whether a claimant has demonstrated that the legislation in question is discriminatory. However, they are not required. A court may often, where appropriate, determine on the basis of judicial notice and logical reasoning alone whether the impugned legislation infringes s. 15(1).[15]

The reality of constitutional litigation is quite different. *Charter* claimants regularly file extensive evidence—including both experiential and expert evidence—in support of their allegations of discrimina-

13 See Sheila McIntyre, "Answering the Siren Call of Abstract Formalism with the Subjects and Verbs of Domination" in Fay Faraday, Margaret Denike, & M Kate Stephenson, eds, *Making Equality Rights Real: Securing Substantive Equality Under the Charter* (Toronto: Irwin Law, 2006) at 100.

14 *Fraser* (SCC), above note 8 at para 116.

15 *Law v Canada,* [1999] 1 SCR 497 at para 77 [*Law*].

tion. The *Fraser* case was no exception. The Union filed affidavits from Michael Fraser (then the Canadian Director of UFCW Canada) and Stan Raper (the Union's key organizer and coordinator of its migrant worker support centres) outlining the history and experience of organizing farm workers in Ontario and the precariousness of the workers' employment circumstances. The Union record also included experiential evidence from four mushroom factory workers about their treatment in the workplace, the concerns that lead them to seek unionization, and the demographics of their workforce. The Union record presented extensive expert evidence accompanied by the many background studies, reports, archival material, and academic literature referred to in each of the experts' affidavits. Three lengthy expert affidavits from Judy Fudge (the expert witness relied upon by the Court in *Dunmore*) set out the history of legal disadvantage experienced by agricultural workers and how their exclusion from labour relations legislation affected their capacity to associate. A significant part of her evidence addressed Canada's and Ontario's history of consciously recruiting vulnerable populations to work in agriculture and how these workers' exclusion from law contributed to their ongoing marginalization. Expert evidence from sociologist Victor Satzewich, based on extensive archival research, addressed the history and policy reasons behind Canada's recruitment of unfree migrant labour to work in agriculture from the 1940s through to the creation of the Seasonal Agricultural Workers Program (SAWP) in the 1960s and 1970s. Expert evidence from sociologist Tanya Basok addressed the practical experience of migrant workers under the SAWP. Finally, expert evidence from agrologist James White (also accepted as an expert in *Dunmore*), set out a range of data from Statistics Canada on the structure of farm businesses and their use of farm labour, and the demographics of farm labour.[16]

In its cursory dismissal of the section 15 claim, the Court rendered invisible this entire record. While the Court's ruling that the claim was "premature" does not foreclose a future section 15 claim, one must ask whether that opening provides more than a theoretical access to justice. It is not a trivial investment in time and resources—on the part of both the Union and the expert witnesses—to develop the thorough multi-dimensional record that is needed to support *Charter*

16 The attorney general of Ontario also filed extensive evidence including expert evidence from George Brinkman on agricultural economics; expert evidence from Richard Chaykowski on labour economics and labour relations policy; and evidence from four managers within the Ontario Ministry of Agriculture and Food. The Intervener Ontario Federation of Agriculture filed evidence from two farmers.

litigation and to support an appropriately nuanced legal analysis of fundamental rights. *Charter* claimants can ill risk making a claim on limited evidence. While courts may, in theory, take judicial notice of whether discrimination exists, the perspectives and experiences of marginalized groups are typically not reflected in mainstream assumptions and "logical reasoning" about how the world works. Expert and experiential evidence is needed to shift the legal gaze onto the uncomfortable truths about the real experiences of those who are "vulnerable to having their interests overlooked and their rights to equal concern and respect violated."[17] Where such evidence has been marshalled, the Court's decision to pass over it in silence reinforces an official public narrative in which farm workers' perspectives remain absent. This not-seeing sustains their marginalization.

2) Bringing Agricultural Workers' Reality into Focus

As the facts underlying the agricultural workers' equality claim are not articulated in any of the *Fraser* judgments, this section of the chapter aims to make that evidence visible. It sets out a brief overview of the themes raised in the Union's evidence that provide the context from which to examine a legal claim for equality.[18] The first part reviews farm workers' treatment under the law and the impact that exclusion has had on shaping the domestic labour market. The second part examines the rise of migrant labour and the construction of an increasingly precarious, increasingly "flexible," international labour source for Ontario farms.

a) The Legal Web of Exclusion: Creating Marginalization Domestically

Securing an adequate supply of farm labour has been a problem in Ontario since before Confederation. The nature of the work is physically arduous and has many aspects that are resistant to mechanization. It is dangerous work performed under difficult working conditions.[19] In addition, because some 40 percent of agricultural jobs are seasonal, job security is low. Since the early twentieth-century,

17 *Andrews v Law Society of British Columbia*, [1989] 1 SCR 143, Wilson J at 152 [*Andrews*].

18 This part of the chapter draws, in particular, on the expert evidence of Judy Fudge, especially her affidavit of 5 August 2004, and the expert evidence of Vic Satzewich.

19 See, for example, William Picket et al, "Fatal work-related Farm Injuries in Canada 1991–1995" (1995) 160 CMAJ 1843 which found that in the 1990s, agriculture had the fourth highest fatality rate of all industries in Canada.

as the capital investments required to become a farm operator rose and alternatives to farm work became more attractive, farm families and workers left rural communities and agricultural labour was increasingly provided by hired, landless labourers.[20] In addition, as farms grew larger and required more workers to operate, the demand for labour outstripped the local supply. The expansion of industry and availability of better-paying jobs in other economic sectors caused farmers continuing difficulties in finding and retaining workers. It is the long-term government response to this need for labour that has both created and perpetuated a distinct history of marginalization that is constitutionally significant.

The creation, through law, of a low rights, low wage sector of the economy has a direct impact on constructing *who* supplies the workforce for that sector. Government policy and legislative choices over the course of more than a century have built a framework that predictably ensures that the agricultural workforce is dominated by workers from the economic margins. Two key choices have driven this dynamic. First, Ontario excluded farm workers from many of the legislative protections that are available to virtually all other workers in the province. Second, since the early 1900s, the federal and provincial governments have institutionalized international migrant labour as the keystone of Ontario's agricultural workforce. Unpacking these two choices is important both to understanding how law operates systemically to create a constituency that is marginalized and to understanding the impact of agricultural workers' particular exclusion from collective bargaining laws.

Agricultural workers were constructed as a uniquely marginalized group through laws which expressly excluded them from almost all of the statutory rights and benefits that protect almost all other workers in Ontario.[21] Historically farm workers were excluded from the *Workmen's Compensation Act*, 1914; the *Minimum Wage Act*, 1920; the *Collective Bargaining Act*, 1943; the *Hours of Work and Vacations with Pay Act*, 1944; the *Employment Standards Act*, 1968; and the *Occupational Health and Safety Act*, 1978.[22] Where agricultural workers are now covered by law, this has only come many decades after other workers won the same rights. They gained coverage under

20 Joy Parr, "Hired Men: Ontario Agricultural Wage Labour in Historical Perspective" (1985) 15 *Labour/Le Travail* 91 at 92.

21 I summarize these exclusions only briefly here. Farm workers' exclusion from labour and employment laws is addressed in more detail in Eric Tucker's chapter in this collection.

22 Affidavit of Judy Fudge (5 August 2004) at para 33.

the *Workmen's Compensation Act* in 1965 (fifty-one years after other workers). They gained coverage under the *Occupational Health and Safety Act* only in 2006 (thirty-eight years after other workers) and only after UFCW Canada filed a *Charter* challenge to their exclusion from the statute.[23] While some fruit, vegetable, and tobacco harvesters became entitled to minimum wage, annual vacation entitlements, and public holidays under the *Employment Standards Act* in 1975,[24] agricultural workers generally remain excluded from employment standards protections for minimum wages, overtime, vacation pay, public holiday pay, maximum hours worked in a day, maximum hours worked in a week, minimum prescribed rest periods between shifts, minimum rest periods in a week or two-week period, and minimum rest periods for meals.[25]

The result of these legislative exclusions is that agricultural wages are low and hours of work are long and unpredictable. Agricultural workers who work full-time for a full year earn about half the overall average wage in Ontario. In 2000, male full-time farm workers earned between $22,681 and $25,366 which was only 47 percent of the average male income in Ontario. Female full-time farm workers earned between $19,161 and $20,602 which was only 51 percent of the average female income.[26] Farm workers also work longer hours than other Ontario workers. They work an average of 44.7 hours per week, with 40 percent regularly working 50 hours or more each week. By contrast, Ontario employees other than agricultural workers average only 32.3 hours per week.[27] Migrant farm workers usually work seven days a week (six full days plus a half-day on Sunday). While they average 10 hours per day for most of the year, it is not unusual for them to work up to 16 hours per day during the harvest.[28]

---

23 While the notice of application and the Union's evidence in the case were served in June 2003 (*Fraser v Ontario (AG)* Ontario Superior Court of Justice file number 03-CV-250815CM3), the litigation did not proceed because in March 2004 the government announced that it would pass the necessary regulation to bring farm workers within the legislation.

24 Fruit, vegetable, and tobacco harvesters are entitled to annual vacation and public holidays only if they have been employed as harvesters for thirteen weeks: O Reg 285/01 made under the *Employment Standards Act 2000*, s 2(2), 8, 9, and 24–27.

25 *Employment Standards Act 2000*, SO 2000, c 41, Parts VII, VIII, IX, X, XI; O Reg 285/01 made under the *Employment Standards Act 2000*, sections 2(2), 4(3), 8, 9, and 24–27

26 James White, *A Profile of Ontario Farms and Farm Labour* (September 2003) at 51–52 [White].

27 *Ibid* at 4–5.

28 Affidavit of Tanya Basok (26 March 2004); Kerry Preibisch, *Social Relations Practices Between Seasonal Agricultural Workers, Their Employers and the Residents of Rural Ontario* (North-South Institute, 2003) at 18–19; Gustavo Verduzco & Maria Isabel

By exempting farm work from basic labour protections, the state constructed agriculture as a low rights, low wage sector, which in turn fundamentally shaped who works in the sector. Workers who have other options will take other work over agricultural work if it is available. As a result, since the 1950s, the agricultural labour force has been made up of workers who have difficulties finding employment elsewhere and it has been well-recognized that supplies of labour for agriculture "have depended heavily upon defects in society—unemployment, underemployment, illiteracy and discrimination."[29]

Today Ontario's agricultural work force continues to reflect this vulnerability. Domestic agricultural workers are overwhelmingly those who are significantly restricted in their occupational mobility due to their limited job skills, low levels of education, and limited English language capability. Agricultural workers as a group have lower levels of education than the general population. Three-quarters of Ontario's domestic agricultural workers (74.9 percent) have at most a high school education compared to 35.6 percent in the general population. Nearly a fifth of agricultural workers (17.3 percent) have less than a grade nine education, compared to only 3.3 percent of the general population.[30]

While there are no precise figures on the racial composition of the domestic agricultural workforce, agricultural workers are heavily recruited from non-white recent immigrant and migrant communities. In the *Fraser* case, 80 percent of the workers in the mushroom factory the union organized were recent immigrants from Vietnam, China, Sudan, Cambodia, South and Central America, Portugal, and the Middle East. Many of them spoke little or no English.

Recent immigrants are also actively recruited for the most precarious forms of domestic farm labour. Labour contractors have increasingly been used to recruit immigrant workers, predominantly from South Asian and South East Asian communities in urban centres, to work in the greenhouse industry in southern Ontario. Hundreds of these "jobbers" are bussed in to farms daily for as many as eight months at a stretch. They are normally paid in cash by the contractor, without the usual statutory deductions, placing them in

---

Lozano, *Mexican Farm Workers' Participation in Canada's Seasonal Agricultural Labor Market and Development Consequences in their Rural Home Communities* (North-South Institute, 2003) at 86–87.

29 Varden Fuller & Calvin Beale, "Impact of Socio-Economic Factors on Farm Labor Supply" (1967) 15 Can J Agr Eco 1237 at 1238; Ellen Wall, "Farm Labour Markets and the Structure of Agriculture" (1994) 31 Canad Rev Soc & Anth 65 at 69–70.

30 White, above note 26 at 51.

an extremely vulnerable position because they are essentially undocumented workers.[31]

Finally, since the 1940s, the federal and provincial governments have actively intervened to recruit domestic labour to work in agriculture from regions of the country that consistently have high unemployment.[32]

b) Institutionalizing Unfree Migrant Work

Alongside this construction of a marginalized domestic agricultural labour force, since the early 1900s the federal and provincial governments have also actively recruited international sources of "unfree" labour to work in agriculture.[33] Unfree labour refers to workers who face legal restrictions on their right to be in Canada and their ability to change jobs.

The governments recruited two categories of unfree workers who could be deported if they left agricultural work. First, they recruited unfree immigrant labour. In exchange for the right to apply for permanent residency in Canada, these workers were required to work in agriculture for a defined period of years. If the workers left the agricultural employment to which they were allotted before their mandatory term expired, they could be subject to deportation or prosecution under provincial law. Following World War II, over 1,900 Polish war veterans and over 7,000 Displaced Persons from Eastern Europe were recruited as unfree immigrants specifically to work on Ontario farms.[34] These sources of labour did not provide long-term stability in agriculture as the immigrants could and did leave agriculture after their restriction period was completed.

Second, the government recruited unfree seasonal migrant labour. These are workers who have no right of permanent residence in Canada. They are permitted to enter Canada for a limited time period, are restricted to working in particular agricultural operations, have no

---

31 Affidavit of Stan Raper (28 March 2004); Cross-examination of Stan Raper, Q 44–45, 60–64, and 269–70.

32 Vic Satzewich, *Racism and the Incorporation of Foreign Labour: Farm Labour Migration to Canada since 1945* (New York: Routledge, 1991) at 73–77 [Satzewich, *Racism*]. During World War II, German prisoners of war, Japanese-Canadian internees, and Canadian conscientious objectors were also used as farm labour. See also, Ron Laliberte & Vic Satzewich, "Native Migrant Labour in the Southern Alberta Sugar-beet Industry: Coercion and Paternalism in the Recruitment of Labour" (1999) 36 Canad Rev Soc & Anth 65.

33 The discussion of the categories of unfree labour draws on Satzewich, *Racism, ibid*, and his affidavit of 18 March 2004.

34 Satzewich, *Racism, ibid* at 85–98.

right to circulate in the labour market, and must return to their country of origin promptly once their authorized work term is completed.

Through these interventions, the government has institutionalized migrant labour as a key element of Ontario's agricultural workforce. In particular, they have institutionalized a system that recruits vulnerable workers under employment structures that heighten their vulnerability.

It is the second category of unfree migrant labour that since the 1960s has grown to become the core of Ontario's seasonal agricultural labour force. In response to lobbying from Ontario fruit and vegetable growers, in 1966 the federal government implemented the Commonwealth Caribbean Seasonal Agricultural Workers Program (SAWP) which admitted workers from Jamaica to enter Canada on a seasonal basis for agricultural work. The countries participating in the SAWP have since expanded to include Mexico, Barbados, Grenada, Trinidad and Tobago, Antigua and Barbuda, Saint Christopher-Nevis, Dominica, Montserrat, Saint Lucia and Saint Vincent, and the Grenadines.[35]

Under the SAWP, migrant workers enter Canada for a defined period each year to perform agricultural work. An individual worker can work for a maximum of eight months between 1 January and 15 December of each year. While in Canada, these workers are governed by the laws of the province in which they work.[36] As a result, like domestic agricultural workers, SAWP workers in Ontario are equally excluded from collective bargaining and a range of employment standards rights.

Workers who come to Canada under the SAWP fall into the category of "unfree" migrant workers because they are admitted to Canada on strict conditions of entry. Even though many of them have returned to Canada for many years—some returning every year for decades—they have no right of permanent settlement in Canada. They must "return promptly" to their home country when their work

---

35 The SAWP is given effect through the *Immigration and Refugee Protection Act*, SC 2001, c 227 and *Immigration Regulations* which permit foreign workers to enter Canada in accordance with administrative arrangements between Canada and other countries. Canada and the countries participating in the SAWP negotiated administrative arrangements which are set out in signed Memoranda of Understanding, including Operating Guidelines and a standard Agreement for Employment which must be signed by the worker, employer, and government agent of the sending country.

36 *Agreement for the Employment in Canada of Commonwealth Caribbean Seasonal Agricultural Workers—2011* and *Agreement for the Employment in Canada of Seasonal Agricultural Workers from Mexico—2011*, both available on the Human Resources and Skills Development Canada website online: www.hrsdc.gc.ca/eng/workplaceskills/ foreign_workers/sawp_ contracts.shtml.

period expires. They can work only for SAWP employers. They are prohibited from seeking or taking any other jobs while in Canada. They can only transfer from one SAWP employer to another with the prior written approval of the Canadian government, their home government, and both the transferring and receiving farms.[37] They face deportation and possible expulsion from the SAWP without any right of appeal if they breach any of these conditions.

The employment relationship under the SAWP leaves migrant workers particularly vulnerable.[38] The employer has the power to select by name which employees the employer wants to return the following season. The SAWP also gives employers and governments wide discretion to exclude workers from the program or to repatriate them—including repatriating them at their own cost—without right of appeal.[39] Because of these institutional structures, SAWP workers have a real and widespread fear that they will suffer some form of reprisal or be repatriated if they complain about their treatment under the SAWP, if they complain about their living or working conditions, or even if they try to enforce their existing legal rights such as taking time off when they are injured. The migrant workers who come to Canada under the SAWP have low job skills, very little formal education, and come from positions of extreme poverty. They come from rural areas in developing countries where work is scarce, insecure, and badly paid. Their income from the SAWP is their primary source of income for the year.[40]

SAWP workers' vulnerability is deepened by the institutionalized competition between Mexico and the Caribbean countries. In expanding the SAWP to include Mexico and other countries in the 1970s, the Canadian government expressly noted that this was a "useful development" because the inter-country competition dampened pressure from sending governments to improve conditions for their workers.[41]

---

37 Caribbean and Mexican SAWP employment contracts, *ibid.*

38 The circumstances of migrant workers are addressed in more detail in Kerry Preibisch's chapter in this collection.

39 See Part X, Premature Repatriation, in the Caribbean and Mexican SAWP employment contracts, above note 36.

40 Affidavit of Tanya Basok (26 March 2004).

41 Affidavit of Vic Satzewich (18 March 2004). This statement is supported in archival documents as follows: Brief for Meeting on Sept 23 Between External Affairs and Manpower and Immigration, 20 September 1974, RG 118, vol 81, accession 85-86/071, file 3315-5-1, pt 8; and Memo from the Acting Director, Manpower and Employer Services Branch to the Director, Programs and Procedures Branch, 17 September 1974, National Archives of Canada, RG118, accession 85-86/071, file 3314-5-1, pt 8.

This competition has intensified over the last decade as the Canadian government has opened up even more sources for unfree migrant agricultural labour with the introduction and expansion of the Temporary Foreign Worker Program (TFWP).[42] As promoted on the Human Resources and Skills Development Canada website, employers are now "free to choose" between the SAWP and the Pilot Project for Occupations Requiring Lower Levels of Formal Training.[43] Introduced as the Low-Skilled Pilot Project in 2002 and expanded in 2007, this program allows employers to hire migrant workers on work visas that can be issued for a period of two years. Work visas are issued with reference to the specific employer thereby tying the worker to the employer. Unlike the SAWP, which is restricted to workers from Mexico and the Caribbean countries whose governments have signed Memoranda of Understanding with Canada, the TFWP is open to workers from any source country. Unlike the SAWP, there are no government-to-government negotiations that give shape to or provide oversight of the program and governments are not involved in selecting employees. Recruiting happens privately, often through recruitment agencies based either in Canada or abroad.[44] While HRSDC provides a sample contract to help ensure that terms of employment comply with provincial minimum standards, the government has no authority to ensure contract compliance. The instructions on the sample contract warn that "it is the responsibility of the employer and the temporary foreign worker to

---

42 Evidence about the Temporary Foreign Worker Program was not before the Court in *Fraser*. This program only expanded after the litigation was commenced. The information is included in this chapter for purposes of providing a complete picture of the current context of unfree migrant labour. See also Kerry Preibisch's chapter in this collection.

43 Employees coming into Canada under the Agricultural Stream to work in on-farm primary agriculture deal with the following commodities: fruits, vegetables (includes canning/processing), greenhouses, and nurseries; apiary products; tobacco; sod; flowers; Christmas trees; pedigreed canola seed; swine; dairy; bovine; poultry; duck; sheep; horse; and mink. Employees doing agricultural work for an occupation or in a commodity that is not classified in the agricultural stream above can be recruited through the Regular Stream. See: www.hrsdc.gc.ca/eng/workplaceskills/foreign_workers/Agricultural/directives.shtml

44 See Judy Fudge & Fiona MacPhail, "The Temporary Foreign Worker Program in Canada: Low-Skilled Workers as an Extreme Form of Flexible Labor" (2009) 31 Comp Lab L & Pol'y J 101; Kerry Preibisch, "Pick-Your-Own-Labor: Migrant Workers and Flexibility in Canadian Agriculture" (2010) 44 International Migration Review 404.

familiarize themselves with laws that apply to them and to look after their own interests."[45]

Migrant workers now constitute a very significant percentage of those who work in agriculture in Ontario. Statistics Canada figures for 2002 estimated that 76,600 people were employed in primary agriculture in the province.[46] In 2001, 15,979 SAWP workers came to Ontario, making up roughly a fifth of Ontario's agricultural workforce. In 2010, 15,435 SAWP workers came to Ontario, filling 17,766 positions.[47] In the same year, a further 1,695 positions in Ontario were filled through the TFWP.[48]

In summary, the interweaving of these two legal and policy tracks—legal exclusion domestically and recruitment of unfree migrant labour internationally—combine to create an agricultural workforce that is characterized by its disempowerment within frameworks that have been created and sustained by government. While their faces change over time, what has remained consistent through the decades is that farm workers—both domestic and migrant—come from those populations in society with the fewest options and with the greatest difficulty finding employment elsewhere.

C. Different Ways of Seeing: *Dunmore*'s Substantive Disadvantage versus *Fraser*'s Vulnerability

How, then, do courts look at this evidence? The challenge is whether the legal process allows us to see the fullness of this dynamic of disempowerment. *Dunmore* and *Fraser*, arising as they do from very similar circumstances, demonstrate that different ways of looking

45 Agricultural Stream of the Pilot Project for Occupations Requiring Lower Levels of Formal Training (NOC C and D), Employment Contract, available online at: catalogue.servicecanada.gc.ca/iforms-iformulaires/.

46 White, above note 26 at 3. Of this figure, 44,500 were either self-employed or farm managers. The remaining 32,100 were employees (non-family hired labour). These figures, however, do not include all seasonal workers, foreign worker, and workers supplied by labour contractors.

47 Foreign Agricultural Resource Management Services (FARMS), "Statistics: 2009/2010 2 Year Activity Comparison," online: www.farmsontario.ca/pages.php?_ID=5. The 15,435 workers were able to cover 17,766 positions because there were 2,331 cases in which workers transferred to a position at a second or subsequent SAWP employer.

48 Human Resources and Skills Development Canada, *Temporary Foreign Worker Program: Labour Market Opinion (LMO) Statistics Annual Statistics 2007–2010*, Table 4 (Annual), online: www.hrsdc.gc.ca/eng/workplaceskills/foreign_workers/stats/annual/table4a.shtml.

produce very different degrees of seeing—and very different legal results. Again, while the discussion of the evidence in *Dunmore* arose in the context of section 2(d), it is the way of looking at the evidence that is significant here.

In *Dunmore*, the Supreme Court engaged in a broad and deep historically sensitive analysis of the evidence and articulately identified a number of dynamics by which the law operated to create and sustain a constitutionally significant disadvantage for agricultural workers. The substantive analysis of disadvantage in *Dunmore* thus provides an instructive contrast with the cursory description of "vulnerability" in *Fraser*. This section reviews what *Dunmore* identified and accepted about the law's role in constructing relationships of power/powerlessness between different groups in society. It is a reminder that what we know to be true about the operation of law and power under section 2(d) should not become less true when we turn to section 15.

Dunmore was not decided on the basis of section 15. Having engaged in a detailed analysis which concluded that farm workers' exclusion from the *Labour Relations Act* violated section 2(d), the majority of the Court found it unnecessary to consider the status of agricultural workers under section 15. The majority held that "assuming without deciding the existence of a s. 15(1) violation, such a violation would not alter the remedy" that was ordered.[49] The Court observed that where a group is denied a statutory benefit accorded to others, the claim is normally reviewed under section 15. However, because the particular denial at issue affected the claimants' capacity to exercise a specific constitutional right (freedom of association), it could also be analysed under section 2(d).[50] While section 2(d) and section 15 provide different lenses which bring into focus different constitutional values, the Court's analysis of the underlying facts illuminated more general truths about the relationship between law and power that are valid and relevant to both analyses.

Three aspects of the Court's analysis of the evidence in *Dunmore* are significant. These aspects relate to the length, breadth, and depth of the context that was considered constitutionally relevant.

First, the Court took a long-term view of what evidence was relevant to the constitutional inquiry. It looked at the "decades-long exclusion of agricultural workers from the labour relations regime" beginning with their exclusion from the first *Collective Bargaining*

49 *Dunmore*, above note 3 at para. 2.

50 *Ibid* at paras 22, 28, and 30.

Act, 1943 and continuing to their exclusion in 1995 that provoked the *Charter* challenge in *Dunmore*. The Court found that the impugned 1995 legislation "occupies only a small space in this history; it ought not prove decisive in this appeal."[51] Instead, the Court found that the impact of the 1995 statute had to be understood in the context of that much longer history.

This long-term view took in not only farm workers' unique experience of deprivation under labour laws, but also examined what is known about the relationship between legal protection and workers' capacity to organize generally. In this way, *Dunmore* looked at the nature and practice of the right at stake. The Court found that "the history of labour relations in Canada illustrates the profound connection between legislative protection and the freedom to organize."[52] The long view of the evidence revealed the "widespread consensus" that generally, for workers without certain minimum statutory protections, the freedom to organize would be a hollow freedom.[53] Thus, the 1995 law was not viewed in isolation, but rather within the context in which "it must be presumed that the legislature understood the history of labour relations" and understood the relationship between legislative protection and the capacity to organize.[54]

Second, the Court took a broad view of what evidence was relevant to the constitutional inquiry. In this respect, the Court situated farm workers' exclusion from the labour relations law in the broader context of farm worker exceptionalism. The Court found that the harms of the particular legal exclusion were even more profound for farm workers because they "already possess a limited sense of entitlement as a result of their exclusion from other protective legislation related to employment standards and occupational health and safety."[55] In this context, their exclusion from labour relations laws not only perpetuated their inability to organize without legislative support but also exerted a chilling effect on their efforts at self-organization.

The Court also took a broad view of the practical significance of unionization and its denial for farm workers. The Court accepted the union's framing of the legal problem in which the denial of unionization implicated a range of collective activities that were not related narrowly to collective bargaining. Following the union's characterization of the dispute, the impugned legislation was seen to restrict

51 *Ibid* at para 40.

52 *Ibid* at para 35.

53 *Ibid* at para 42.

54 *Ibid* at para 41.

55 *Ibid* at para 45.

the "wider ambit of union purposes and activities" relating to workers' "empowerment and participation in both the workplace and society at large," including promoting workplace democracy, protecting workers from abuses of managerial power, pooling resources, expressing collective views cogently and forcefully, and enhancing workers' social and political capacity to access courts and engage in political education and action.[56]

Third, the Court looked deeper into an analysis of power. The Court took a nuanced view of the *practice* of rights—the degree to which individuals can or cannot have a real *experience* of rights because of their relative power in society. The Court expressly drew the connection between farm workers' inability to organize without legislative support and their social location of powerlessness. The Court found that "it is possible to draw a distinction between groups who are 'strong enough to look after [their] interests without collective bargaining legislation' and those 'who have no recourse to protect their interests aside from the right to quit.'"[57] The Court found that RCMP officers could organize without legislative support on the strength of their "relative status, their financial resources and their access to constitutional protection" directly under the *Charter* because they are employed by government. That power was in sharp contrast to agricultural workers' political impotence, lack of resources, vulnerability to employer reprisal, and lack of direct access to the *Charter* to hold their employers constitutionally accountable. When viewed in this context—looking at the reality of power—the Court stated that "it is no wonder . . . that agricultural workers have failed to associate in any meaningful way in Ontario," while RCMP officers had organized in several provinces.[58]

What is important is how these three strands of the Court's analysis in *Dunmore* separately and together draw out the dynamics by which law was responsible for shaping agricultural workers' unique social location of powerlessness. The Court found that there was a correlation between the state's legislative choices and the material and normative effects of those laws. Those effects combine to create and perpetuate disadvantage. One can draw out of *Dunmore*'s reasoning the following patterns by which law operates in practice to shape relationships:

---

56 *Ibid* at para 12.

57 *Ibid* at para 41.

58 *Ibid* at paras 41, 39, and 45.

a) There is a "profound connection" between the law and a group's practical capacity to act in society.[59]
b) The law shapes a group's sense of its social location.[60]
c) The law influences, in a material way, how a marginalized group is treated by others.[61]
d) The law has didactic effects which shape society's normative sense of a group's appropriate social location.[62]

Ultimately, the Court recognized that by its differential treatment in law, "the government is *creating conditions* which in effect substantially interfere" with a group's capacity to participate in society. The Court recognized that the law can operate in a way that "*substantially orchestrates, encourages and sustains*" a group's disempowerment. Recognizing these dynamics, the Court in *Dunmore* held that it was "inappropriate for the Ontario Legislature to distance itself from the effects" of the impugned law.[63]

While in *Dunmore* the Supreme Court engaged with the evidence in a way that identified law as a dynamic agent that shaped farm workers' relative position in society, the courts in *Fraser* made only very brief, glancing reference to the evidence and treated farm workers' "vulnerability" as a static condition that exists outside of law. In *Fraser* the Court's view was pulled into very tight focus—out of history and out of breadth and depth—onto the *AEPA* itself and the "scant" history under that Act.[64] At the Ontario Superior Court, Farley J's reasons did not analyze the evidence but merely adopted Sharpe J's assessment from the Superior Court in *Dunmore* that farm

---

59 *Ibid* at para 35. The Court found that farm workers' selective exclusion from laws that generally protect others impaired the group's capacity to develop social, political, and economic relationships which are important to their empowerment in both the workplace and in society at large.

60 *Ibid* at para 45. Farm workers' exclusion from legislative protection created a "limited sense of entitlement." This diminished sense of entitlement in turn exerted a "chilling effect" on their capacity to organize.

61 *Ibid* at paras 22, 26, 44, and 46. The Court recognized that failure to include farm workers within a sphere of legislative protection exposed them to unfair labour practices, may "affirmatively permit restraints" on their activities, and, in a practical sense, "can only be viewed as a stimulus to interfere with organizing activity."

62 *Ibid* at para 46. The Court found that this didactic effect "must not be underestimated." Legal exclusion promoted the normative sense that "workplace democracy has no place in the agricultural sector" and that "agricultural workers' efforts to associate are illegitimate."

63 *Ibid* at paras 22, 26, and 47 [emphasis added].

64 *Fraser* (SCC), above note 8 at para 109. The Ontario Court of Appeal did take a more contextual view of the evidence with respect to s 2(d) but did not do so under s 15.

workers were historically, and continued in the present to be, a "disadvantaged group."[65] The Ontario Court of Appeal took a broader view of the evidence under section 2(d). However under section 15, the Court very briefly referred to farm workers' "pre-existing disadvantage" and stated the conclusion that they "remain a vulnerable group with low skills, low education, low job mobility and low incomes."[66] The majority of the Supreme Court simply referred, without comment and without analysis of the evidence, to the Superior Court's finding that "the situation of farm workers had not changed appreciably since *Dunmore* . . . where this Court wrote with sympathy of the vulnerable position of these workers."[67]

Adopting this shorthand which, however sympathetically, labels farm workers as "vulnerable," obfuscates more than it enlightens. While the Court's multi-dimensional approach to the evidence in *Dunmore* was analytical, looked for causation, and identified accountability for disadvantage, the approach in *Fraser* was descriptive and naturalized the "vulnerability" in a way that was ahistorical and decontextualized. *Fraser* located that vulnerability in the workers themselves rather than understanding it as the end product of a regulatory response to the social relationship of farm labour.

The contrasting approaches to the evidence in *Dunmore* and *Fraser* feed into and support very different kinds of legal analysis. I suggest that an appropriately attentive legal discourse on equality must—with respect to both the evidence and the law—pause long enough to unpack the specific and mutually reinforcing ways in which a claimant group can be *made* vulnerable by the law. In the final section of this chapter, then, I turn to examine how a nuanced analysis of the relationship between law and power as applied under section 2(d) in *Dunmore* could, on the facts in *Fraser*, provide an enriched understanding of analogous grounds and the meaning of substantive discrimination under section 15. While the opportunity was missed in *Fraser*, the analysis may yet be instructive in moving forward into a deeper understanding of substantive equality.

---

65 *Fraser* (Ont SCJ), above note 8 at paras 31 and 33.

66 *Fraser* (Ont CA), above note 8 at paras 67–70 and 111.

67 *Fraser* (SCC), above note 8 at para 115.

D. Seeing Real Experiences of Discrimination: Giving Meaning to Analogous Grounds

One of the enduring difficulties in legal reasoning, especially in judicial decision making, is to translate a conceptual and analytical approach to interpreting and applying a constitutional guarantee into a legal test that does not simply become a rote and mechanical analysis. This difficulty has plagued the Supreme Court of Canada's approach to equality.

Beginning with *Andrews*, the Supreme Court of Canada has repeatedly confirmed that section 15 of the *Charter* protects substantive, not formal, equality. Substantive equality is not about "treating likes alike" at the front end. It is instead concerned with acknowledging and accommodating the real differences between people to ensure that the law secures equality in its effect.[68] Discrimination was defined in *Andrews* as

> a distinction, whether intentional or not but based on grounds relating to personal characteristics of the individual or group, which has the effect of imposing burdens, obligations, or disadvantages on such individual or group not imposed upon others, or which withholds or limits access to opportunities, benefits, and advantages available to other members of society.[69]

Most recently, in *Withler*, the Supreme Court confirmed that the "animating norm of s. 15" is substantive equality. The Court wrote:

> To determine whether the law violates this norm, the matter must be considered in the *full context* of the case, including the law's *real impact* on the claimants and the members of the group to which they belong . . . .

---

68 Fay Faraday, Margaret Denike, & M Kate Stephenson, "In Pursuit of Substantive Equality" in *Making Equality Rights Real*, above note 13. As stated by McIntyre J in *Andrews*, above note 17 at 165:

> To approach the ideal of full equality before and under the law—and in human affairs an approach is all that can be expected—the main consideration must be the impact of the law on the individual or the group concerned. Recognizing that there will always be an infinite variety of personal characteristics, capacities, entitlements and merits among those subject to a law, there must be accorded, as nearly as may be possible, an equality of benefit and protection and no more of the restrictions, penalties or burdens imposed upon one than another. In other words, the admittedly unattainable ideal should be that a law expressed to bind all should not because of irrelevant personal differences have a more burdensome or less beneficial impact on one than another.

69 *Ibid* at 174–75.

> At the end of the day there is only one question: Does the challenged law violate the norm of substantive equality in s. 15(1) of the *Charter*?[70]

Despite its commitment to substantive equality, the Court's treatment of farm workers under section 15 fails to consider both the "full context" of the case and the "real impact" of the law. Instead it gets trapped in a mechanical application of the legal test. That collapse tracks both parts of the legal test that is used to prove discrimination under section 15.

According to *R v Kapp*, the test under section 15 pursues two inquiries.[71] First, it asks whether the impugned law creates a distinction based on an enumerated or analogous ground. In its application, however, the concept of "analogous grounds" tends to collapse into the narrower question of whether the differential treatment is based on a "personal characteristic." Rather than fully engaging with the record, the courts' findings on this point tend to be brief, unadorned statements of the conclusion that the proposed ground is not a personal characteristic. They miss the full context and real impact of the law by failing to remember why *any* ground is constitutionally significant and by failing to analyze how grounds operate in the real world. In this way, they diminish the understanding of why any ground may be recognized as analogous and what it may tell us about discrimination.[72]

Second, the legal test asks whether the impugned distinction creates a disadvantage by perpetuating prejudice and stereotyping. In the statement of the test itself, the concept of "substantive discrimination" collapses down from the broad definition in *Andrews* into a narrower question of "stereotype" or "prejudice," taking the focus off the multitude of different ways in which discrimination imposes serious *material* harms on marginalized groups.[73]

In this way, the concepts that were originally intended to help deepen our critical thinking about discrimination—analytic tools that would help uncover how discrimination operates—become instead static objects that stand as hurdles that a claimant must overcome.[74] They deflect analysis away from the only real question,

---

70 *Withler v Canada (AG)*, 2011 SCC 12 at para 2 [emphasis added].

71 *R v Kapp*, 2008 SCC 41 at para 17.

72 See *Fraser* (Ont SCJ), above note 8 at paras 33–34; *Fraser* (Ont CA), above note 8 at para 114.

73 See *Fraser* (SCC), above note 8 at para 116.

74 See, for example, Bruce Ryder, Cidalia Faria, & Emily Lawrence, "What's *Law* Good For? An Empirical Overview of Charter Equality Rights Decisions" (2004) 24 Sup Ct L Rev (2d) 1.

which is whether the impugned law violates the norm of substantive equality. This chapter now goes back to the basics to reclaim our critical perspective on those analytic tools.

1) Grounding the Analysis of Discrimination

As the section 15 jurisprudence focuses ever more minutely on the "legal test," it draws further away from the language of section 15 and from what section 15 of the *Charter* actually guarantees. Section 15 guarantees four different experiences of equality in relation to the law without discrimination: "Every individual is equal before and under the law and has the right to the equal protection and equal benefit of the law *without discrimination* . . ." This is the fundamental right. Section 15 guarantees these rights "in particular, without discrimination based on race, national or ethnic origin, colour, religion, sex, age or mental or physical disability." While the enumerated grounds identify those that historically were most commonly employed to perpetrate discrimination, the grounds on which discrimination can arise are not closed. Justice Wilson reminded us in *Andrews* that section 15's application must remain alive to the evolving ways in which harms are imposed and harms are recognized:

> [I]t is important to note that the range of discrete and insular minorities has changed and will continue to change with changing political and social circumstances . . . It can be anticipated that the discrete and insular minorities of tomorrow will include groups not recognized as such today. It is consistent with the constitutional status of s. 15 that it be interpreted with sufficient flexibility to ensure the 'unremitting protection' of equality rights in the years to come.[75]

There is nothing inherent in any "ground" that makes it an engine of discrimination. What makes any ground significant—socially, politically, economically, or legally—is whether the ground is employed by those with power, through design or effect, as a mechanism or lever to distribute or withhold rights in a discriminatory way. Grounds mark the boundary of inclusion/exclusion. As Dianne Poth-

---

75 *Andrews*, Wilson J, above note 17 at 152–53. At para 175 in *Andrews*, McIntyre J wrote that the enumerated grounds were those that "reflect the most common and probably most socially destructive and historically practiced bases of discrimination," but agreed that claims could be brought on grounds beyond these.

ier writes, "It is the grounds of discrimination that separate people who experience discrimination from those who do not."[76]

The utility of a ground, then, lies in whether it can illuminate the social, political, economic, or legal dynamics of exclusion, disempowerment, and marginalization. Grounds do not describe a static condition. Grounds are functional. What matters is not so much what they *are* but *how they work*. In this way, grounds are the important means of providing the necessary history and context of discrimination.[77]

Often the discussion of analogous grounds collapses into the question of whether the proposed ground is a "personal characteristic" or is "constructively immutable." However, this shorthand tells us nothing about how or why a ground becomes a vehicle for oppression and why its operation should be recognized as unconstitutional. A richer and more informative approach to analogous grounds can, however, be gleaned from the caselaw to reanimate grounds in a meaningful way.

The Court has unanimously accepted that to constitute an analogous ground, the claimant is "not required to establish membership in a sociologically recognized group."[78] This approach enables section 15 to be flexible and responsive to the evolving practice of discrimination. Instead, the touchstone to determine if a ground is analogous is whether its recognition would "serve to advance the fundamental purpose of s. 15(1)." This assessment is made "on the basis of a complete analysis of the purpose of s. 15(1), the nature and situation of the individual or group at issue, and the social, political and legal history of Canadian society's treatment of the group."[79] Analogous grounds are based on "characteristics that we cannot change or that the government has no legitimate interest in expecting us to change to receive equal treatment under the law."[80] They will often encompass those "lacking in political power," "vulnerable to having their interests overlooked and their rights to equal concern and respect violated," and "vulnerable to becoming a disadvantaged group."[81]

---

76 Dianne Pothier, "Connecting Grounds of Discrimination to Real People's Real Experiences" (2001) 13 CJWL 37 at 41.

77 *Ibid.*

78 *Law*, above note 15 at para 66.

79 *Ibid* at paras 93–94.

80 *Corbière v Canada (Minister of Indian and Northern Affairs)*, [1999] 2 SCR 203 at paras 11–13 [*Corbière*].

81 *Andrews*, Wilson J, above note 17 at 152–53; *R v Turpin*, [1989] 1 SCR 1296 at 1331–332; *Law*, above note 15 at para 26.

The Supreme Court has already accepted that the world of work and labour relations cannot be a judicial "no go" zone under section 2(d) of the *Charter*. Similarly, it should not be immune to real *Charter* scrutiny under section 15.[82] Following the textured, purposive approach above, recognizing an occupational status as an analogous ground can—on particular facts—serve to advance the purpose of section 15 and uncover a real history of discrimination. The unique history of government involvement in constructing agricultural work as a low-rights zone and in recruiting marginalized populations to fill that social niche is one that warrants deeper examination under the lens of analogous grounds. This analysis has two parts. The first is conceptual and addresses the notion that work is a fundamental aspect of personal identity. The second is evidentiary and addresses the ways in which being an agricultural worker represents a particular form of disempowerment in Canadian society.

a) Work is Personal

Early *Charter* cases in lower courts mechanically rejected occupational status as an analogous ground on the basis that one's occupation was not a personal characteristic and that the particular groups raising the claims (such as doctors, nurses, teachers, municipal employees, and even employers) were not disadvantaged in society. However, the jurisprudence has evolved to openly question the assumption that work is outside the scope of section 15 and to affirmatively find that work shares many of the markers of other analogous grounds.

Many Supreme Court cases, arising both under the *Charter* and in the employment/labour context, have passionately repeated that work is an important defining personal characteristic. It is now an oft-repeated mantra that work is "one of the most fundamental aspects in a person's life,"[83] and is the means by which most individuals "lay claim to an equal right of respect and of concern from others."[84] Work is an "essential component" of, and "fundamental to[,] a person's identity."[85] Work is both one's calling card and a key mechanism for distributing social, economic, and legal power. To say that "I am

82 *Health Services and Support—Facilities Subsector Bargaining Assn v British Columbia*, 2007 SCC 27 at para 26.

83 *Reference re Public Service Employees Relations Act (Alberta)*, [1987] 1 SCR 313, Dickson CJC at 368–69 [*Alberta Labour Reference*].

84 David M Beatty, "Labour is not a Commodity" in BJ Reiter & J Swan, eds, *Studies in Contract Law* (Toronto: Butterworths, 1980) at 323–24; *Slaight Communications Ltd v Davidson*, [1989] 1 SCR 1038, Dickson CJC at 1054–55 [*Slaight Communications*].

85 *Slaight Communications*, Dickson CJC, *ibid* at 1054–55.

a lawyer" is to identify a very particular location in society with its accompanying privileges and entitlements. To say that "I am an agricultural worker" or "I am unemployed" is to occupy a very different social location with a very different and tattered set of entitlements.

It is also well-established that the work relationship is inherently one of unequal power in which the employee is subordinate. Because of this power imbalance, the Court has recognized that workers in general are vulnerable and that their vulnerability is underscored by the importance that our society attaches to the employment relationship. The Court has also recognized that specific groups of workers are subject to particular disadvantage, are particularly vulnerable to having their interests overlooked by the state, and may have a unique need for state protection under legislation.[86]

While the Supreme Court has in the past denied section 15 claims by particular groups of workers, it has done so in view of their particular status in society.[87] It has specifically left it open to find that a group of workers could constitute an analogous ground on appropriate facts.[88] That door remains open following *Fraser*, as the section 15 claim was dismissed not on the basis of analogous grounds, but on the basis that it was premature. Meanwhile, in Quebec the court has found the occupational status of home childcare workers to be an analogous ground under section 15 of the Canadian *Charter*.[89] In addition, the Quebec Human Rights Tribunal has found the precarious non-standard employment status of freelancer and of casual employee to be prohibited bases of discrimination under the enumerated ground of "social condition" under the Quebec *Charter*.[90]

---

86 *Alberta Labour Reference*, above note 83 at 368–69; *Slaight Communications*, *ibid* at 1051–52; *Wallace v United Grain Growers Ltd*, [1997] 3 SCR 701 at paras 91–94; *Dunmore*, Bastarache J, above note 3 at paras 20–22 and 45–46, and L'Heureux-Dubé J at para 167, ; *Delisle v Canada (Deputy AG)*, [1999] 2 SCR 989, Bastarache J at paras 44–45 [*Delisle*].

87 *Delisle*, Bastarache J, *ibid* at paras 44–45. .

88 *R v Généreux*, [1992] 1 SCR 259 at 310–11; *Delisle*, Bastarache J, *ibid* at paras 44–45, L'Heureux-Dubé J at para 8; *Baier v Alberta*, [2007] 2 SCR 673 at paras 65–66. Justice L'Heureux-Dubé in *Dunmore*, writing for herself, found that agricultural workers did meet the threshold for an analogous ground: *Dunmore*, above note 3 at para 167.

89 *Confédération des syndicat nationaux v Québec (Procurer general)*, 2008 QCCS 5076.

90 See Stéphanie Bernstein, "Sector-Based Collective Bargaining Regimes and Gender Segregation: A Case Study of Self-Employed Home Childcare Workers in Quebec," in Judy Fudge, Kamala Sankaran, & Shae McCrystal, eds, *Challenging the Legal Boundaries of Work Regulation* (Oxford: Hart, forthcoming in 2012); *Commission des droits de la personne et des droits de la jeunesse v Sinatra* [1999] CanLII 52 (Tribunal des droits de la personne); *Commission des droits de la personne et des droits de la jeunesse v Syndicat des constables spéciaux* [2010] CanLII 3 (Tribunal des droits de la personne).

So, conceptually, the door is open to considering how work and occupation function in a way that is analogous to other grounds that signify that social processes of marginalization are operating. Work and occupation are personal: they are a core part of personal identity; they are vehicles for marking and distributing status; they are axes for empowerment/disempowerment; and they bear similarity with the human rights ground of social condition. How then does this ground function for agricultural workers?

b) Applying the Lessons from *Dunmore*: Integrating Knowledge About Farm Workers' Marginalization

Ultimately, whether a particular occupational status is an analogous ground must be determined on a case-by-case basis, taking into account the history of the claimant group's treatment in society and in law, and the patterns of discrimination that create them as a specific group. The occupational status of agricultural workers does have real functional utility under section 15. Recognizing the status of agricultural workers serves section 15's remedial purposes of rectifying and preventing discrimination and ameliorating the conditions of disadvantaged persons. Recognizing the status as an analogous ground also usefully illuminates the very distinct pattern of marginalization that agricultural workers have experienced and in which government choices and actions have been implicated. This status helps draw out an understanding of the full context and real impact of the law. It is at this point, of recognizing how the status of "agricultural worker" functions in Canadian society, that the lessons from *Dunmore* can be applied.

Dunmore's analysis of substantive disadvantage under section 2(d) in fact maps the same considerations that are relevant to identifying analogous grounds. *Dunmore* taught us that, for some groups, vulnerability is socially constructed through law. As set out above, *Dunmore* accepted how law can construct a part of the population *as a group* in a way that restricts its members' practical capacity to act; that affects their material well-being; that affects their sense of social security; that affects others' material treatment of them; and that communicates normatively about their appropriate status in society. In the same way, taking the long and broad view of the evidence available in *Fraser* highlights the complete history of differential treatment in law that created "agriculture worker" as a unique legal and social status with diminished rights. It enables us to view a century of farm workers' exclusion from basic labour protections as an enduring pattern in which "agricultural worker" has been a constant marker of "suspect distinctions."[91]

The ground of "agricultural worker" also sheds light on the full history and context of agricultural workers' location in Canadian society and the social, political, and legal history of their treatment. It sheds light on the unique way in which legislative exclusion was accompanied by government initiatives to recruit unfree labour from marginalized populations and created a uniquely disempowered and discrete segment of society. It illuminates how state regulation that denies equal protection and equal benefit of the law to a group of workers can create a subclass of workers that is populated by workers from the margins. With farm workers, this differential regulation created, built on, or reinforced those workers' particular experience of marginalization—including experiences of intersecting systemic discrimination based on race, national origin, and insecure citizenship status—to construct a particular group of workers as a social and legally disadvantaged group. That socially constructed disadvantage, in turn, continues to facilitate the enactment of laws that sustain or reinforce their marginalization. This is particularly so when the migrant workers who form the core of the seasonal labour force have no right to participate in the political process that produces the laws that construct their experience. In these unique circumstances, one's work—and the state's regulation of that work—depend upon, coincide with, and reinforce a distinctive form of social exclusion.

Finally, the analogous ground sheds light on the nature of the interest at stake. As with other "personal characteristics," the government has no legitimate interest in asking agricultural workers to change their jobs in order to receive equal treatment in law. These workers hold mainstream jobs in Ontario's second largest industry. Even if individual farm workers change jobs, that still leaves agricultural workers as a group with second class status. To require workers to quit their jobs to get equal rights reinforces the very vulnerability at issue. It reinforces the reality which was recognized by the 1968 Woods Task Force and in *Dunmore* that agricultural workers are so marginalized and their interests so disregarded by the state that they "have no recourse to protect their interests aside from the right to quit."[92]

---

91 *Corbière*, above note 80 at para 11.

92 *Canadian Industrial Relations: The Report of the Task Force on Labour Relations* (Ottawa: Privy Council Office, 1968) at paras 253–54; *Dunmore*, above note 3 at para 41.

2) Substantive Discrimination

Uncovering the full context of agricultural workers' construction in law as a disadvantaged group enables one to see more clearly the "real impact" of their exclusion from collective bargaining laws. It allows one to see how that differential treatment violates the norm of substantive equality. Excluding farm workers from this core labour right perpetuates their long history of exclusion from basic labour protections available to other workers. As in *Dunmore,* it reinforces their "limited sense of entitlement" as members of Canadian society. It denies them equal protection and benefit of the law in a way that fails to correspond to farm workers' needs, capacities, and circumstances. Farm workers have been actively seeking to unionize and pursue collective bargaining for decades. And since 1980, the Ontario Labour Relations Board has agreed that "there is no 'industrial relations basis'" for denying them the right to bargain collectively.[93]

Most importantly, in denying farm workers true protection for the right to bargain collectively, the laws continue to deny them access to the very collective process by which disempowered workers can act together to rectify their disadvantage. The nature of the right at stake is critical. Collective bargaining is the fundamental mechanism of self-organization, representation, and rights-enforcement that empowers workers to remedy their disadvantage and to bring democracy and the rule of law into the workplace. Collective bargaining is specifically about creating a participatory forum that moderates the imbalance of power at work and facilitates workers' self-determination. In contrast to minimum standards legislation and other individual rights legislation, Wilson J described unionization and collective bargaining as securing "the promotion of the self-advancement of working people."[94] Excluding farm workers from this forum of engagement excludes them from a fundamental social institution that is open to other workers. Denying farm workers these rights dispossesses them of their stake in workplace democracy, devalues their interest in participating in shaping the terms and conditions of their work, and deprives them of a remedy for their pre-existing disadvantage.

The most compelling factor in finding discrimination is when differential and prejudicial treatment is visited upon those experiencing pre-existing disadvantage. As has been recognized since the 1970s, farm workers have been subjected to prejudicial burdens not

93 *Wellington Mushroom Farm,* [1980] OLRB Rep May 813 at para 29 and paras 6–18.

94 *Lavigne v Ontario Public Service Employees Union,* [1991] 2 SCR 211, Wilson J.

experienced by other workers. They have faced more limitations and been denied more opportunities than others. Their continued exclusion from true labour relations protections means that the legal processes that enable much of the rest of our workforce to be involved in decision making at the workplace in a realistic way are unavailable to farm workers. Thus a group of workers who are already among the least powerful are given even less opportunity than the rest of us to participate in the formulation and application of the rules governing their working conditions.[95]

E. Conclusion

The failure to engage with analogous grounds in a functional way permits an unacceptable privileged innocence to prevail about the real impacts of an impugned law. By failing to use analogous grounds critically in order to map how the law operates to create and sustain relationships of power and powerlessness, the section 15 jurisprudence sterilizes the legal and the public debate about discrimination. Instead of analyzing who is disempowered under the law and, just as importantly, who benefits from that disempowerment, it obscures a real examination of and challenge to the hierarchies that the law reflects and embodies. This turning away from grounds is one of the mechanisms, or habits of thought, that enables section 15 to fall short of the promise of substantive equality. In *Fraser*, rote reliance on abstract tests and a disengagement from the evidence ignored how the law operates to create, sustain, and normalize the real harms of impoverishment, disenfranchisement, and precariousness experienced by a largely racialized, increasingly migrant workforce. They equally operated to obscure the benefits that accrue on the other side of the power ledger by overlooking the coerciveness of laws and policies that encourage and mandate a compliant and ever more "flexible" work force.[96] This benefit, extracted at the cost of what is widely acknowledged to be among the most disempowered groups in our society, is not a vision of substantive equality.

In the end, what farm workers are seeking is not radical. They have simply been seeking the right to bargain collectively, in a meaningful and effective way. These rights have long been available to virtually all other workers in Canada, including farm workers in all provinces other than Ontario and Alberta. The harms that accrue

95 Beatty, *Putting the Charter to Work*, above note 2 at 144.

96 *Dunmore*, above note 3 at paras 54–55.

from and the disempowerment that is perpetuated by their legal exclusion are well documented. What was true in 1975 is even more true today: farm workers' legislative equality is long overdue. In the end, the legal principles needed to make the links to recognize the discrimination are also not radical. The connections between law and power, between work and social location, have already been made, particularly in *Dunmore*. It is simply time to stop looking away.

CHAPTER SEVEN
The *Fraser* Case: A Wrong Turn in a Fog of Judicial Deference

Paul JJ Cavalluzzo

A. Introduction

At the outset let me advise that in *Fraser* I represented the farm workers throughout the proceedings up to and including the argument before the Supreme Court of Canada. I make this pronouncement not only to disclose my perspective and experience but also to encourage other lawyers to comment on cases in which they have participated. No person knows the case like the counsel who argued it. Counsel's comments are particularly important in the area of *Charter* law where fundamental freedoms are at stake. Our law libraries are filled with scholarly texts and articles on *Charter* jurisprudence. In *Fraser*, the majority and Rothstein J debated about the extent of the scholarly criticism of *BC Health Services*.[1] Indeed, Rothstein J relied

1 Throughout this paper I will be referring to six crucial s 2(d) decisions of the Supreme Court of Canada which culminated in *Ontario (AG) v Fraser*, 2011 SCC 20 [*Fraser*]. The Labour Trilogy included *Reference Re Public Service Employee Relations Act (Alberta)*, [1987] 1 SCR 313 [*Alberta Reference*] (challenge to compulsory arbitration provisions in legislation); *PSAC v Canada*, [1987] 1 SCR 242 (challenge to federal compensation restraint legislation) [*PSAC*]; *RWDSU v Saskatchewan*, [1987] 1 SCR 460 [*Saskatchewan Dairy Workers*] (challenge to back-to-work legislation applicable to dairy workers). The trilogy was important in that the majority ruled that s 2(d) does not protect the right to strike but was evenly split on whether s 2(d) protects the right to collective bargaining. The next case, *Professional Institute of the Public Service of Canada v Northwest Territories*, [1990] 2 SCR 367 [PIPSC], is important because, for the first time, a majority of the Court concluded that s 2(d) does not

upon the academic criticism in rejecting the scope of protection for section 2(d) as found by the Court in *BC Health Services*. He found that the extent of academic criticism of *BC Health Services* was a reason for overturning it.[2]

Frequently, academic articles cited by courts lack knowledge of the facts and attention to what is at stake in the dispute that can only be comprehensively presented by counsel. Since *Charter* cases are necessarily contextual, it is important that systemic "on the ground" considerations become part of the general discussion. The record, judicial history, arguments, and conduct of the hearing are important in terms of assessing the judgment of any court. Moreover, an analytical critique of the impact of the judicial decision on the parties who must live with it is of crucial importance to ensure that the "consumers" are heard. In my view, counsel on the case can make an important and invaluable contribution to the development and evolution of the *Canadian Charter of Rights and Freedoms*. Counsel are accountable to clients who have important interests and rights at stake and who also finance the litigation, whereas academic commentators are accountable to their peers and students, as well as to the principles of academic integrity and freedom. *Charter* law is far too important to be left to the academics alone!

This chapter has been divided in five parts. First, there is a review of the record before the court and a brief survey of the judicial history. The second part focuses on the finding of the majority that the constitutional claim of the farm workers was premature. In the third part, I focus on the doctrine of judicial deference and how the doctrine played a significant role in the analysis of the majority and the concurring decision of Rothstein J. In the fourth part, I

---

protect the right to collective bargaining. The next case is *Dunmore v Ontario (AG)*, [2002] 3 SCR 1016 [*Dunmore*]. *Dunmore* is the farm workers case which gave rise to the *Agricultural Employees Protection Act*, which is the Act at issue in *Fraser*. It is important because it held that s 2(d) protects some collective or group activities, which strayed from the view of the majority in the Labour Trilogy and *PIPSC* that the focus of s 2(d) is on individual rights alone. However, importantly, *Dunmore* upheld the existing precedent made in *PIPSC* that s 2(d) does not protect the right to bargain collectively. It did hold that s 2(d) does protect the right to organize. The final case preceding *Fraser* is *Health Services and Support—Facilities Subsector Bargaining Assn v British Columbia*, [2007] 2 SCR 391 [*BC Health Services*]. *BC Health Services* is crucial because it overruled *PIPSC* and the Labour Trilogy to hold that s 2(d) protects the right to bargain collectively. It also followed *Dunmore*'s holding that s 2(d) protects more than individual rights and activities.

2 The use and role of academic commentary in judicial decisions is inevitable but controversial.

deal with the Wagner or North American model of labour relations upon which, in my view, the majority and Rothstein J spent undue time discussing and placed undue emphasis. The final part describes the role that international human rights law played in the decision. In my conclusion, I suggest that all of the judges, except Abella J, participated in a larger political battle than the constitutional claim presented in the record before them. As a result, the plight of farm workers in Ontario was given inadequate focus and attention and, accordingly, their discriminatory treatment by the legislature of Ontario continues. One can think of few other more vulnerable workers who have required the intervention of the *Charter* in order to eliminate this historic discrimination.

B. The Record

Farm workers in Ontario are one of the most economically vulnerable and politically powerless groups of workers. Since the inception of labour and other employment-related laws, the legislature of Ontario has discriminated against farm workers by failing to give them the same statutory benefits and protections given to other employees. This legislative discrimination was a clear result of their political and economic vulnerability in comparison to the political and economic power of the farmers' lobby. Unfortunately, in *Fraser*, the Supreme Court of Canada failed to address this extraordinary imbalance of power.

In the 1940s when Ontario introduced collective bargaining legislation, farm workers were excluded from its application. At that time, the sole justification for the exclusion was that unionization and collective bargaining would be inappropriate on the family farm. Whether or not the "family farm exception" was a legitimate excuse to deny farm workers the right to organize and bargain collectively, its legitimacy wore thin as the nature of agricultural production changed from the family farm to the corporate farm or "agribusiness."

It can reasonably be argued that the exclusion of farm workers from the collective bargaining law has a more nefarious genesis than the family farm exception. Like most collective bargaining laws in Canada, the Ontario legislation was taken from the Wagner Act passed by Congress in 1935 as part of FDR's "New Deal." The Wagner Act, like Ontario's law, excluded agricultural workers and domestics. The political rationale for the exclusion was based in racism as is described by Chris Hedges in his recent book, *Death of the Liberal Class*[3]:

> The Wagner Act, known as "the labor bill of rights," had created the NLRB, it forbade employers from engaging in unfair labor practices. Although the gains by workers were made primarily in the North, since southern whites sought to block union organizing among blacks, the NLRB represented a major achievement for working men and women. To get it in place, Roosevelt had permitted the NLRB to exclude agricultural and domestic workers, a coded way to exclude blacks and keep southern politicians, who were mostly Democrats, behind him.

Little did we know that Ontario farm workers were likely excluded from our collective bargaining law as a result of an unholy concession made to the Southern Dixiecrats by FDR in 1935, an exclusion that exists to this day. In light of this historic anomaly, the discriminatory legislative exclusion of farm workers in Ontario is even more irrational than we previously believed.

In the 1970s, the United Food and Commercial Workers Union (UFCW) began to organize farm workers even though they continued to be excluded by the *Labour Relations Act* (*LRA*).[4] A seminal case before the Ontario Labour Relations Board (OLRB) in 1980 showed the unfairness and absurdity of the legislative exclusion when applied to a corporate farm. In *Wellington Mushroom Farm, A Division of Campbell Soup Co Ltd*,[5] UFCW applied to be certified for a unit of employees at a mushroom growing operation of Campbell Soup. The facility had a floor space of some 136,000 square feet and resembled a factory or warehouse. The building was purchased for and was used only for mushroom growing and packaging. The OLRB found that the working conditions and internal organization resembled those of an industrial plant. In fact, the OLRB made the following finding:

> We are satisfied that there is no material difference between the employer-employee relationship in the respondent's mushroom operation, and that of Campbell's manufacturing employees. We are further satisfied that the respondent's production process closely resembles that of a manufacturing operation, and that the economic position of the respondent's employees is similar to that of an industrial worker.

---

3 Chris Hedges, *Death of the Liberal Class* (Toronto: Vintage Canada Editions, 2011) at 107.

4 See chapters by Hanley and Tucker, who discuss the context of *Fraser* and the history of litigation in support of union attempts to organize farm workers.

5 [1980] OLRB Rep May 813 [*Wellington Mushroom Farm*].

In spite of its findings, the OLRB was forced to dismiss the union's application because persons who are "employed in agriculture" are expressly excluded from the *LRA*.[6] Ironically, what gave rise to the *Fraser* case was the UFCW's attempt to organize farm workers at a similar mushroom growing operation with the same exclusion in the labour law. The only difference was the introduction of the *Charter* in 1982.

The *Wellington Mushroom Farm* decision brought on a great deal of criticism from the labour relations community and academia. Indeed, there was much criticism about the discriminatory treatment of farm workers years before this decision. For example, in 1968, the Woods Task Force Report questioned the justification of this legislative exclusion:

> We wish to express concern about the lack of accessibility of collective bargaining legislation to agricultural workers and domestic servants. We make no recommendation in this respect because, except in the Yukon and Northwest Territories, these classes fall almost exclusively under provincial jurisdiction. Their exclusion as employees from collective bargaining does not, however, seem to us to be justified.[7]

With the enactment of the *Charter*, farm workers were given hope that this legislative discrimination would cease through the intervention of the courts. As a result, a constitutional challenge was brought by the UFCW in the 1980s alleging that the legislative exclusion from the *LRA* was contrary to section 2(d) of the *Charter*. This was the *Cuddy Chicks* case,[8] which reached the Supreme Court of Canada on the question of whether the OLRB had jurisdiction to examine the constitutionality of its enabling legislation. The court ruled that the OLRB has jurisdiction to apply the *Charter* and the matter was remitted to the OLRB to address the merits of the application for certification. However, before the OLRB resolved the application, a new government was elected that promised to confer collective bargaining rights on farm workers, and the parties decided to delay. After a broad two-year consultation, a tripartite task force reached a consensus report finding that unionization and collective bargaining could work in the agricultural sector.[9] In 1994, drawing

6 Section 2(b) of the *LRA* provided that "This Act does not apply . . . to a person employed in agriculture."

7 *Canadian Industrial Relations: The Report of the Task Force on Labour Relations* (Ottawa: Queens Printer, 1968).

8 *Cuddy Chicks Ltd v Ontario (Labour Relations Board)*, [1991] 2 SCR 5.

9 *Report of the Task Force on Agricultural Labour Relations: Report to the Minister of Labour* (June 1992) and the three research studies that were prepared for the Task

on the recommendations in these reports, the legislature of Ontario enacted the *Agricultural Labour Relations Act*, SO 1994, c 6 (*ALRA*).

The *ALRA* incorporated much of the *LRA* including exclusive representation for a union with majority support, the duty to bargain in good faith, and the right to grievance arbitration. It included special provisions to address the situation of the family farm members working on farms. However, final offer selection was the required method to resolve bargaining impasses rather than strikes and lockouts.

The *ALRA* was in effect from June 1994 to November 1995 when a new government repealed it[10] and amended the *LRA* to, once again, deny farm workers the right to unionize and bargain collectively.[11] The repeal of the *ALRA* was not preceded by any consultation or studies on the operation of the *ALRA*.

The union challenged the repeal of the *ALRA* and exclusion from the *LRA* in *Dunmore* arguing that they violated section 2(d) by denying farm workers the right to unionize. In *Dunmore* the Supreme Court ruled for the first time that section 2(d) protects certain collective or group activities such as "making majority representations to one's employer."[12] The Court ruled that the protection of such activities, which are part of the right to organize, are guaranteed by the purpose of section 2(d) and by international human rights law. The Court also made another significant finding. It ruled that because of the vulnerability of farm workers, the government has a positive obligation to provide statutory support to ensure that farm workers can meaningfully exercise their freedom of association in the workplace.

In making this finding, the Court relied upon the vulnerability of farm workers and the "didactic effect" of section 3(b), the legislative exclusion:

Force that are collected in a document entitled *Background Studies* (June 1992); Task Force on Agricultural Labour Relations, *Second Report to the Minister of Labour* (November 1992).

10 *Labour Relations and Employment Statue Law Amendment Act, 1995*, SO 1995, c 1, s 80. This legislation repealed the *ALRA*, nullified any collective agreements under the *ALRA*, nullified all certifications and voluntary recognitions that existed under the *ALRA*, and terminated all proceedings that had been commenced under that Act. The effect was to statutorily terminate the only union certifications that had ever been achieved in Ontario agriculture and to terminate collective bargaining that had been in process at the time.

11 *The Labour Relations Act, 1995*, SO 1995, c 1, Schedule A, s 3(b) provided: "This Act does not apply . . . to a person employed in agriculture, hunting or trapping."

12 *Dunmore*, above note 1 at paras 16 and 30.

> Distinguishing features of agricultural workers are their political impotence, their lack of resources to associate without state protection and their vulnerability to reprisal by their employers; as noted by Sharpe J., agricultural workers are "poorly paid, face difficult working conditions, have low levels of skill and education, low status and limited employment mobility."
>
> The inherent difficulties of organizing farm workers, combined with the threats of economic reprisal from employers, form only part of the reason why association is all but impossible in the agricultural sector in Ontario. Equally important is the message sent by s. 3(b) of the *LRA*, which delegitimizes associational activity and thereby ensures its ultimate failure. Given these known foreseeable effects of s. 3(b), I conclude that the provision infringes the freedom to organize and thus violates s. 2(d) of the *Charter*.[13]

However, the Court did not change the prevailing law that section 2(d) does not protect the right to collective bargaining: *PIPSC v Northwest Territories (Commissioner)*.[14] The Court suspended its declaration of unconstitutionality for eighteen months to give the government time to draft appropriate legislation. The Court directed the legislature to enact a statutory framework including protections for the freedom to organize:

> I conclude that at minimum the statutory freedom to organize in s. 5 of the *LRA* ought to be extended to agricultural workers, along with protections judged essential to its meaningful exercise, such as freedom to assemble, to participate in the lawful activities of the association and to make representations, and the right to be free from interference, coercion and discrimination in the exercise of these freedoms.[15]

In response to *Dunmore*, the government enacted the *Agricultural Employees Protection Act*, 2002 (*AEPA*). Prior to its enactment, no government studies, papers, or reports were commissioned or prepared that refuted the recommendations of the tripartite task force referred to above, which led to the *ALRA*. The minister's statements in introducing the legislation clearly showed that the government did not intend to confer collective bargaining rights on farm workers.

---

13 *Ibid* at paras 41, 46, and 48.

14 Above note 1. In *Dunmore*, the claim was framed specifically with reference to the "right to unionize" and not with reference to the extent to which "collective bargaining" *per se* was protected under s 2(d): *ibid* at para 12.

15 *Ibid* at para 67.

This is not surprising for a government that was not "labour friendly" and that constructed the *AEPA* around an extremely narrow reading of the remedy ordered in *Dunmore*. There was no evidence that the government even considered collective bargaining as a possible option.[16]

The *AEPA* does provide a right to make representations. However, the only duty on the employer is to listen to the representations, if made orally, and to acknowledge that the representations were read if they were made in writing. There is no right to make representations that reflect majority positions, nor an exclusive right of representation for an association selected by the majority of the employees. There is no dispute settlement mechanism to resolve bargaining impasses or collective agreement disputes. This "labour legislation" was unique in Canada for its failure to provide these protections, which are safeguarded in labour statutes virtually uniformly across the country.

Finally, the *AEPA* is administered by the Agricultural, Food and Rural Affairs Appeal Tribunal which typically deals with issues relating to crop insurance, product marketing commissions and boards, tax assessment on farm land, and environmental negotiation. It is not a tripartite board like the OLRB. It has no expertise or experience in labour relations. It does not have a trained staff or labour relations officers who can inquire into a complaint, attempt to settle it, and report to the Tribunal. The Tribunal reports to the Minister of Agriculture rather than the Minister of Labour.

As will be described later in the chapter, no association of farm workers has ever been successful in organizing and engaging in collective bargaining with any employer under the *AEPA*. This was true at the time *Fraser* was initiated and is true today nearly a decade after its enactment. As was argued before the Supreme Court, this legislation is unique in many ways including the fact that this must be the only "labour legislation" in history under which no bargaining has ever occurred. I presume that one's perspective will determine whether the law was a success!

To this day, the government has never explained why these vulnerable workers should be denied the kind of legislative protection to which other employees in Ontario are entitled. It was an accepted

16 See, for example, Ontario Ministry of Agriculture and Food, "Rights of Association for Agricultural Workers: A Response to *Dunmore v. Ontario*" (September 2002) [unpublished], which does not include collective bargaining among the options for the government response to the ruling.

fact in both *Dunmore* and *Fraser* that farm workers are a vulnerable and disadvantaged group who need legislative support in order to ensure they can meaningfully exercise their freedom of association in the workplace. Needless to say, the *AEPA* led to another constitutional claim: the *Fraser* case.

In *Fraser*, the application judge dismissed the application because he was satisfied that the government met its positive obligation to provide the required legislative support with the *AEPA*, in light of his ruling "that nothing in *Dunmore* suggests that the Supreme Court was backing away from its view that collective bargaining has been excluded from the protective ambit of s.2(d)."[17] In short, he held that in the labour context, section 2(d) protects the right to organize, but not the right to bargain collectively. In regard to the employer's obligation to listen to or read the employees' representations, he said that the employer is not obliged to respond to the representations as "this would then involve the parties in a form of collective bargaining."[18]

Prior to the appeal of *Fraser* being heard in the Court of Appeal, the Supreme Court rendered its judgment in *BC Health Services* in which it overruled the Labour Trilogy and the restrictive analysis that had prevailed under it and found that collective bargaining is protected as an exercise of freedom of association under section 2(d) of the *Charter*. The Court ruled that "historically [collective bargaining] emerges as the most significant collective activity through which freedom of association is expressed in the labour context." It also held that "s.2(d) should be understood as protecting the right of employees to associate for the purposes of advancing workplace goals through a process of collective bargaining." In other words, it protects "the right of employees to associate in a process of collective action to achieve workplace goals." The Court went on to hold that section 2(d) protects a "procedural right to collective bargaining" which is described as "the right of employees to join together in a union to negotiate with employers on workplace issues or terms of employment." Very importantly, the Court ruled that "the fundamental precept of collective bargaining" is the duty to consult and negotiate in good faith. The Court admonished that section 2(d) requires that legislation respect and protect the duty to bargain in good faith:

> It follows that the state must not substantially interfere with the ability of a union to *exert meaningful influence* over working conditions *through*

---

17 *Fraser v Ontario (AG)* (2006), 79 OR (3d) 219; 263 DLR (4th) 425; [2006] OJ No 45 (Ont SCJ) at para 16 [*Fraser* (Ont SCJ)].

18 *Ibid* at para 19.

> *a process of collective bargaining conducted in accordance with the duty to bargain in good faith.* Thus the employees' right to collective bargaining imposes corresponding duties on the employer. It requires both employer and employees to meet and to bargain in good faith, in the pursuit of a common goal of peaceful and productive accommodation.[19]

Whatever one thinks of the legislation in the *Fraser* case, one thing seems clear: the *AEPA* does not respect and protect the process of collective bargaining, which includes the duty to bargain in good faith. This effect was the clear intent of the legislature that enacted the law. The application judge and the Court of Appeal ruled that the *AEPA* does not protect the collective bargaining process. Not surprisingly, not one of the seventeen parties at the Supreme Court made such an argument. Indeed, the Government of Ontario argued that the *Charter* could not impose a duty to bargain on an agricultural employer because the employer is in the private sector. The *Fraser* case was argued on the basis that the *AEPA* does not impose a duty to bargain. Needless to say, the majority decision was a complete surprise to all in that the majority decided that, "correctly interpreted," the *AEPA* imposes a duty to bargain on agricultural employers[20]—a decision based on a position not argued by any party.

The record in the *Fraser* case was comprehensive. It consisted of forty volumes of evidence. The Supreme Court granted intervener status to six governments, five business lobby groups, and four labour/human rights groups. The case was argued on 17 December 2009. Despite the fact that the legality of the *AEPA* was the issue, most of the oral and written argument dealt with the meaning and scope of *BC Health Services*. The plight of farm workers in Ontario was overtaken by larger events. The decision of the Court was rendered on 29 April 2011. After struggling to achieve meaningful collective bargaining rights for close to forty years, farm workers in Ontario were told by the majority of the Court that their application was premature.

C. Prematurity

One of the cruellest ironies of the majority's decision in *Fraser* is the finding that the farm workers' *Charter* application was premature

---

19 *BC Health Services*, above note 1 at paras 19, 41, 68, 87, 89, 90, and 97 [emphasis added].

20 *Fraser*, above note 1 at para 107.

after over forty years of struggling for meaningful collective bargaining rights. Of course, this would not have been an issue if the majority had interpreted the *AEPA* as the parties and lower courts did, that is, that it did not impose a duty on the employer to bargain.

In making its finding of prematurity, the majority described the historical record under the *AEPA* as "scant." It also found that the union "had not made a significant attempt to make it work."[21] With respect, this finding fails to appreciate the context of organizing farm workers in Ontario with such limited statutory support as provided by the *AEPA*. There was as much evidence before the Court on this point as there was in *Dunmore*, if not more. Moreover, the majority failed to refer to the complete history under the *AEPA* that there was not one instance of any bargaining, let alone any labour agreement bargained anywhere in the province under the *AEPA*. Indeed, in 2010 the International Labour Organization (ILO) Committee on Freedom of Association relied on this fact in making its finding that the *AEPA* infringed freedom of association.[22] This expert tribunal appreciated the significance of this fact. The failure to have one successful association-employer bargaining relationship continues to this day, nearly a decade after the law's enactment.

The majority also relied upon the application judge, Farley J, who noted that "[t]he *AEPA* . . . contemplates a meaningful exercise of the right of association, and provides a Tribunal for the resolution of disputes."[23] What this reference fails to point out is that Farley J found that "a meaningful exercise of the right of association" did not include any duty on the employer to bargain.[24] Moreover, Farley J's reference to the Tribunal did not relate to a dispute concerning a complaint that an employer refused to bargain because he had ruled that there was no such legal duty. His reference to the Tribunal related to other aspects of the *Charter* claim relating to the right to organize.[25]

Finally, the majority determined that the *AEPA* could be workable if it was "correctly interpreted" so as to impose a duty on the employer to consider in good faith the representations of the farm workers. As a result, the *AEPA* complied with section 2(d) of the *Charter* in that it met the requirements laid down by *BC Health Services*. In short,

21 *Ibid* at para 109.

22 ILO Freedom of Association Committee, *Complaint against the Government of Canada (Ontario) presented by the United Food and Commercial Workers Union Canada (UFCW Canada)* Report No 368, Case No 2704.

23 *Fraser*, above note 1 at para 109.

24 *Fraser* (Ont SCJ), above note 17 at paras 16 and 19–22.

25 *Ibid* at para 18.

the legislation provided the necessary statutory support to make the freedom of association of farm workers meaningful in their workplace.

Once again, with respect, this finding fails to apply basic principles of collective bargaining and labour relations. The majority's hope that the Tribunal created under the *AEPA* could provide effective relief under the statute is naive and unrealistic. What would happen if an employer advises the farm workers that it considered their submissions in good faith and that it cannot afford to meet their demands? Upon a complaint by the farm workers, the Tribunal could do nothing because the employer complied with the majority's interpretation of the *AEPA*, that is, it considered their representations in good faith. What do the farm workers do then to break the bargaining impasse? There is no more legislative support for them in the *AEPA*. Perhaps the Ontario Court of Appeal was correct in its determination that farm workers in Ontario need statutory support that provides a dispute settlement mechanism to resolve bargaining impasses. Unfortunately, as Rothstein J stated, the majority never assessed whether Winkler CJ was correct in this aspect of his ruling. Whether he was right or wrong, I can think of no other labour legislation in Canada that does not provide for such a dispute settlement mechanism, whether it be a right to strike or a right to final and binding arbitration. Without such mechanisms, the right to bargain collectively is ineffective and therefore not meaningful. This fact is one of the fundamental rules of Canadian labour law which was recognized by Dickson CJ in his eloquent dissent in the *Alberta Reference*:

> Closely related to collective bargaining, at least in our existing industrial relations context, is the freedom to strike. Professor Carrothers, *Collective Bargaining Law in Canada* (Toronto, Butterworths, 1965), describes the requisites of an effective system of collective bargaining as follows at pp. 3-4:
>
>> What are the requirements of an effective system of collective bargaining? From the point of view of employees, such a system requires that they be free to engage in three kinds of activity: to form themselves into associations, to engage employers in bargaining with the associations, and to invoke meaningful economic sanctions in support of the bargaining.
>
> The Woods Task Force Report at p. 129 identifies the work stoppage as the essential ingredient in collective bargaining:

> Strikes and lockouts are an indispensable part of the Canadian industrial relations system and are likely to remain so in our present socio-economic-political society.
>
> At p. 138 the Report continues:
>
>> Collective bargaining is the mechanism through which labour and management seek to accommodate their differences, frequently without strife, sometimes through it, and occasionally without success. As imperfect an instrument as it may be, there is no viable substitute in a free society.
>
> At p. 175 the Report notes that the acceptance of collective bargaining carries with it a recognition of the right to invoke the economic sanction of the strike. And at p. 176, it is said, "the strike has become a part of the whole democratic system."
>
> The importance to collective bargaining of the ultimate threat of a strike has also been recognized in the cases. Lord Wright noted in *Crofter and Hand Woven Harris Tweed Co. Ltd. v. Veitch*, [1942] 1 All E.R. 142 (H.L.) at pp. 158-9, "The right of workmen to strike is an essential element in the principle of collective bargaining."
>
> As the editors of *Khan-Freund's Labour and the Law*, 3rd ed. (London, Stevens & Sons, 1983), point out in respect of this comment: "If the workers could not, in the last resort, collectively refuse to work, they could not bargain collectively" (at p. 292). See also *Broadway Manor; Dairy Workers* case; *Blount, per* Wright, J. The necessity and lawfulness of strikes has also been acknowledged by this court: *Perrault v. Gauthier* (1898), 28 S.C.R. 241 at p.56; *C.P.R. Co. v. Zambri* (1962), 34 D.L.R. (2d) 654 at pp. 657 and 664, [1962] S.C.R. 609 at pp. 618 and 621.[26]

It seems clear that even if the *AEPA* can be interpreted to imply a duty to bargain, it still does not provide adequate support for farm workers to have a meaningful freedom of association in the workplace. Without a statutory mechanism to resolve bargaining impasses, their right to bargain collectively is meaningless. This is a fundamental rule of the collective bargaining process—the process that *BC Health Services* clearly holds is protected by section 2(d). It is not surprising that Winkler CJ, with his extensive experience in collective bargaining and labour law, recognized this fundamental rule in determining what level of statutory support farm workers require in Ontario to ensure that their freedom of association is meaning-

---

26 *Alberta Reference*, above note 1 at 369–70.

ful. In short, the constitutional claim that the *AEPA* does not provide the necessary statutory support in light of the government's positive obligations under section 2(d) was very ripe for judicial resolution.

D. Judicial Deference and Labour Law

1) The General Rationale for Judicial Deference

Judicial deference to the legislature has played a significant role in the *Charter* review of labour laws. There are two basic reasons why Canadian courts have deferred to the legislature in respect of law making in the area of labour relations and collective bargaining.

The first reason relates to an institutional concern. Some commentators suggest that judges and courts do not have the expertise and experience to competently deal with labour relations problems. It is argued that legally trained judges are not necessarily equipped to deal with the social and economic problems raised in labour disputes. Moreover, adjudication is not an appropriate process to resolve labour issues that may present polycentric problems with impacts far beyond the parties before the court. Legislatures, however, are equipped to deal with these pressing social and economic problems. Moreover, legislatures should be permitted to experiment in labour policy making without having to justify the policy before a court on a *Charter* application.

The second reason relied upon in calling for judicial deference to the legislature in labour law making is a political one. Labour laws represent a delicate and dynamic balancing of interests between labour and management. Any tinkering with this balance of interests could prejudicially upset the balance of bargaining power between these two powerful forces in Canadian society. The choice to be made is a political one that should be made by the legislature that is accountable to the public through the electoral process. In short, the courts should not get involved in the "politics of labour relations."

2) The Limits of Judicial Deference

In my view, judicial deference is a very problematic doctrine because of its ambiguous meaning and elastic nature. It is not clear when the doctrine of judicial deference is invoked whether the claim is that the court must defer to an expert tribunal, to the legislature, or to the record established in the case. Nor is it obvious that the terms "judicial activism" and "judicial deference" map nicely onto liberal or conservative political views. Moreover, from a doctrinal perspective, although the jurisprudence gives some indications of when the court may defer to the legislative choice, there appear to be no firm principles upon which the court can rely in determining whether to defer. This failure to be precise about the type of deference involved and the principles upon which a court should defer is particularly problematic when a fundamental freedom is at stake and section 52 of the *Charter* directs that it is the supreme law of the land.

The history of the *Charter*'s application to labour laws is probably the best example of where deference has been used in a manner which frustrated the protection of fundamental freedoms in the working lives of Canadians. The root of the problem stems back to the Labour Trilogy when, in the early stages of the *Charter*, the Supreme Court was faced with the crucial issues of whether section 2(d) protects the right to collectively bargain and the right to strike in the context of public sector essential service legislation, wage restraint legislation, and a "back to work" law. In the Labour Trilogy, there was a very rigorous debate between McIntyre J and Dickson CJ on the scope of section 2(d). These were very difficult issues for the Court and probably demonstrated an imprudent approach to *Charter* litigation by trade unions in the early days of the *Charter*. Other progressive groups chose a more incremental approach to *Charter* litigation and were far more successful in the results they achieved.

The limits of adjudication are apparent and have shaped how our administrative law has evolved since *CUPE v NB Liquor Corporation*[27] was decided in 1979. In that case, Dickson CJ initiated the courts' approach (which was much lauded by administrative law scholars and practitioners) of deferring to expert statutory tribunals when it comes to reviewing decisions that fall within the scope of their expertise. However, there are serious questions of whether this approach can be readily transported to *Charter* law as McIntyre J did in the *Alberta Reference*.

I would suggest that there are several reasons why judicial deference is a much more difficult fit in *Charter* law as opposed to administrative law. Not only is the nature of the judicial endeavour different in the two cases, this easy transposition of the doctrine of deference from the administrative law realm ignores the status of the *Charter* as the primary law of Canada, which protects the fundamental freedoms of Canadians. A court should not defer to the legislature since the Constitution has conferred upon the court the

---

27 [1979] 2 SCR 227 [*NB Liquor Corporation*].

power and duty to review laws in order to ensure that they are consistent with the *Charter*. The court is the final arbiter as to the scope of the fundamental freedom at issue. Deferring to the legislature in its determination of the scope of the fundamental freedom is an abdication of this responsibility.

The process of decision making in judicially reviewing an expert statutory tribunal is qualitatively different than the judicial review of legislation to ensure that the law is consistent with the *Charter*. Judicial review in an administrative law context ensures that the rule of law is followed by ensuring that the tribunal acts within its statutory limits and in accordance with the rules of fairness or natural justice. The focus of the review is on procedural fairness and jurisdictional limits. It is important to note that judicial deference is only applied in ensuring that the tribunal has acted in accordance with the mandate granted to it by the legislature. In this regard, judicial deference is owed to the tribunal because of its expertise and experience in dealing with the activity it was established to regulate. However, no deference is owed in respect of procedural rights issues because the court is the guardian of these common law rights.

The judicial review of legislation to ensure *Charter* compliance is a wholly different process. In this regard there is no expert tribunal over which the court exercises supervisory jurisdiction. The legislature has the democratic authority to pass laws. In doing so, it is accountable to the electorate. However, under our system of government, this democratic authority is not unlimited. There is no rationale for judicial deference to the legislature because of the court's constitutional role in ultimately determining the scope of Canadians' fundamental freedom. As a result, administrative law principles of deference are not easily transportable to *Charter* review. If anything, the most apt analogy is the court's role in ensuring that the citizen's constitutional, procedural, and common law rights are respected by the statutory tribunal. In regard to this role, no deference is given to the tribunal. Similarly, in determining whether legislation respects the fundamental freedoms guaranteed to citizens by the *Charter*, no judicial deference is owed to the legislature.

In this regard, I believe that the majority in *Fraser* is correct in determining that judicial deference should be applied at the section 1 stage and not in assessing the scope of the fundamental freedom. Unfortunately, this was not the approach taken for the first twenty-five years of the life of the *Charter* in the context of the review of labour laws. As described by the majority in *BC Health Services* and in *Fraser*, this approach led to a "judicial no-go zone." This is where

Rothstein J wishes to retreat, as is evidenced in his concurring judgment in *Fraser.*

From a constitutional perspective, there is justification for deference to be applied at the section 1 stage. Under our *Charter*, fundamental freedoms are not absolute. The state may limit the freedom so long as the limit is reasonably justifiable in a free and democratic society. Reasonableness necessarily connotes deference in that it assumes that there is not only one correct solution to the problem. In respect of legislatures, this means that where there is a legitimate legislative objective, there may be more than one way to achieve this objective. As Hogg states in his text, *Constitutional Law of Canada*:

> But the court was willing to defer to the legislative choice on the basis that the choice was within a margin of appreciation, a zone of discretion in which reasonable legislators could disagree while respecting the *Charter* right.[28]

However, if there is some legitimacy in applying judicial deference at the section 1 stage, there are two serious considerations which must be assessed in applying this doctrine. First, the court is not dealing with an expert and specialized tribunal, which deals with these problems on a daily basis. The legislature is not an expert statutory tribunal. It is a generalist body, like a court, which deals with numerous and various problems every day. In labour relations matters, there is no reason to suggest that a legislator is more experienced than a judge in respect of the rights and duties created by labour legislation even though the legislation may have been drafted by ministry bureaucrats. For example, Winkler CJ, who wrote the unanimous judgment of the Ontario Court of Appeal in *Fraser*, has far more expertise and experience in collective bargaining and labour relations than any legislator sitting in the legislature when the *AEPA* was enacted in 2002. Moreover, in *Fraser*, like most constitutional cases, the court has more information and evidence before it than the legislature. Indeed, in *Fraser*, given the paucity of evidence and information relied upon in enacting the legislation, the Court likely had far more information (forty volumes of record) than the bureaucrats. In terms of the issue before the court in *Fraser*, that is, what statutory support was needed in order to ensure meaningful collective bargaining rights for Ontario farm workers, judicial deference to the legislature would be a triumph of form over substance. Finally,

---

28 Peter Hogg, *Constitutional Law of Canada*, 5th ed supp (Scarborough, ON: Thomson Carswell, 2006) vol 2 at 38:43 [Hogg].

international law and the laws of other democratic states are appropriate sources to turn to in determining the legitimacy of restrictions on Canadians' fundamental freedoms. No doubt, a court of law is at least as expert and competent as the legislature in reviewing these laws for the purpose of determining the reasonableness of any restrictions. Of course, I am not saying that courts should not defer to the legislature. However, the application of judicial deference should be very nuanced and contextual depending on the rights at issue, the evidence and submissions before the court, and the legislation under review.

The other serious consideration in applying judicial deference in labour matters is a political one. Some judges and commentators are concerned that the court should not interfere in the delicate balance of interests which is reflected in labour legislation. In McIntyre J's view, labour laws represent a political balancing of the interests between management and unions made by a legislature which is accountable to the electorate.[29] In my view, this consideration should not be addressed in a political and legal vacuum. To some, the word "political" instinctively means that the court should not be involved. Surely this is an unrealistic response. *Charter* review deals with acts of government which inevitably lead to a political decision. This is not a situation in which the court is being political; the court's role is mandated by the *Charter.* Moreover, although this concern has some legitimacy, there are real limitations to these concerns when fundamental freedoms are at stake. In most instances, political choices should be respected because the electorate will have the opportunity to "adjudicate" upon these choices in the next election. However, in light of the fundamental freedom in issue, the court has a duty to ensure that the government has demonstrated that any restrictions on it are reasonable limits justified in a free and democratic society. This requires a very contextual approach in the review of labour policy because labour rights are human rights and are an instantiation of freedom of association. As Dickson CJ pointed out in the Labour Trilogy, labour and collective bargaining rights protect far more than economic interests. Labour laws enhance employee dignity and self-worth, and bring the rule of law to the workplace.[30]

Labour laws in Canada enhance other values underlying the *Charter,* such as liberty and autonomy of workers, equality, and dem-

---

29 *Alberta Reference,* above note 1 at 416–19.

30 *Ibid* at 367–69.

ocracy.[31] The judgment in *BC Health Services* is an eloquent testament to how the right to bargain collectively is consistent with the values underlying the *Charter*.[32] As well, labour laws in Canada are legally required to be consistent with international human rights laws which are binding on Canada.[33]

As a result, in determining whether to defer to the legislature, the court must assess such matters as the impact of the law under review on the equality of the bargaining power between labour and management, as well as the economic and political vulnerability of the workers making a constitutional claim. These matters are directly relevant to the purpose of freedom of association in the workplace. If the law prejudices any *Charter* values that the collective bargaining process advances, the law should be reviewed with the strictest of scrutiny. In short, the mantra of government counsel that the labour law before the court represents a political choice made by the legislature should be the beginning of the section 1 analysis rather than the end.

3) The Fog of Judicial Deference in *Fraser*

In assessing how the Supreme Court of Canada applies the *Charter of Rights and Freedoms*, we normally associate judicial deference with judicial restraint. The doctrine of judicial restraint in constitutional theory probably originates with Frankfurter J of the Supreme Court of the United States.[34] In his view, a court should generally defer to the democratically elected legislature, which is accountable to the electorate. Even in a system with a clear separation of powers in which judicial review of legislation is legitimate, the court should respect the political choices made by the legislature in the laws it enacts. If an incorrect choice is made, the electorate will have the opportunity to correct it in the next election. In a democracy, the electorate is the ultimate authority. Justice McIntyre implicitly accepted this analysis in the *Alberta Reference*.

Contrary to this analysis, I suggest that judicial deference to the legislature in *Fraser* resulted in judicial activism rather than judicial restraint both in the majority judgment and the concurring

---

31 See Derek Fudge's chapter in this book.

32 *BC Health Services*, above note 1 at paras 80–86.

33 *Ibid* at paras 69–71; *Alberta Reference*, above note 1 at 349.

34 Noah Feldman, *Scorpians: The Battles and Triumphs of FDR's Great Supreme Court Justices* (New York: Twelve Hachette Book Group, 2010) at 182, 231–34, 251–52, 347–48, 383–84, 418–19, and 429 [Feldman].

judgment of Rothstein J, although the precise nature of their activism differed. Dealing first with Rothstein J's judgment, he was prepared to overrule *BC Health Services*, a decision which was less than two-and-a-half years old at the time of the argument in *Fraser*. His judgment is surprising not only because *BC Health Services* was only a few years old, but also because *BC Health Services* had overruled twenty years of jurisprudence. Of further concern is that this move to overrule *BC Health Services* was done on Rothstein J's own motion, as not one of the numerous parties before the Court argued that it should be overruled. Curiously, one of his justifications for overruling *BC Health Services* was that it explicitly rejected judicial deference—the judicial "no go zone"—in matters of labour relations. In his view, this was a clear error because, as McIntyre J said in the *Alberta Reference*, courts are not equipped to carry out the requisite balancing of interests in the labour relations context.[35] However, if we consider the issue before the Court, that is whether section 2(d) protects the right to bargain collectively, his comments in terms of judicial deference are questionable and problematic.

Curiously, in relying on McIntyre J's comments on judicial deference in the *Alberta Reference*, Rothstein J did not advert to the fact that McIntyre J's comments were made in respect of constitutionalizing the right to strike in 1987 in the very early stages of the *Charter*. His comments were not directed to the right to bargain collectively. Indeed, in the companion case of *PSAC*, the second case of the trilogy, McIntyre J explicitly said that his finding in the *Alberta Reference* in relation to the right to strike "does not preclude the possibility that other aspects of collective bargaining may receive *Charter* protection under the guarantee of freedom of association."[36] He found no violation in the case before him because the wage restraint legislation did not restrict the role of the trade union as the exclusive agent of the employees and the law required the employer to continue bargaining and deal with the unionized employees through the union. Interestingly, Rothstein J does not refer to the judgments of Dickson CJ in the trilogy, who expressed no concerns about giving labour relations legislation rigorous scrutiny under the *Charter* in determining the scope of the fundamental freedom. The irony is that it was Dickson CJ who formulated the concept of judicial deference in labour relations matters in *NB Liquor Corporation*. Of course, he developed this doctrine in the context of administrative law at a time

35 *Fraser*, above note 1 at para 223.

36 *PSAC*, above note 1 at 269.

when courts were only too eager to intervene in labour relations matters. He created this doctrine to ensure that courts recognized their institutional limits in reviewing the decisions of labour relations and labour arbitration boards, which were established by the legislature to expeditiously and expertly deal with labour disputes. If one reads his *Charter* judgments, one will see that Dickson CJ never intended that judicial deference be applied in a constitutional context whereby the courts would abdicate their responsibility as the final arbiters of the scope of our fundamental freedoms. Prior to *BC Health Services*, the application of this doctrine led to a "judicial no-go zone" under which labour legislation became virtually immune from *Charter* scrutiny. Of course, this was the reason why the Court rejected the application of judicial deference in defining the scope of the fundamental freedom in *BC Health Services*.

When we move to the majority judgment in *Fraser*, we discern very mixed messages on judicial deference. On its face, the judgment says the right things about judicial deference. The majority judges say that in *BC Health Services* the Court rejected a "judicial no-go zone" for an entire right on the ground that it may involve the court in policy matters. The majority ruled that the pre-*BC Health Services* jurisprudence pushed deference too far. The other positive aspect of the majority ruling is that deference should not be considered in determining the scope of section 2(d). It should be applied in the section 1 analysis. In their view, deference to the legislature properly plays a part, not in defining the constitutional right, but within the margin of appreciation that the *Oakes* test acknowledges, particularly at the minimal impairment stage.

In my view, this analysis (which was implicitly made in *Dunmore*), is eminently reasonable and correct. However, in the case before them in *Fraser*, the majority became so deferential to the legislature that it became activist regarding the record and arguments raised by the parties in defending the legislation under review. Some commentators refer to this as conservative judicial activism, that is when the court goes to extreme lengths in refusing to interfere with government action or inaction. I conclude that the majority's ruling is a graphic example of judicial activism because even though it upheld *BC Health Services*, it refused to rule that the legislation before it was unconstitutional on the questionable basis of implying a duty to bargain in the law. As Rothstein and Abella JJ stated, upholding *BC Health Services* inevitably leads to a finding that the *AEPA* is unconstitutional.

Anyone familiar with the record and submissions in the *Fraser* case would be surprised at the majority's conclusion that the *AEPA* contains an implicit duty to bargain for a number of separate and distinct reasons.

First, nobody argued that there was such a duty. Up to and including the argument before the Supreme Court of Canada, all parties and the lower courts operated on the understanding that the law did not impose a duty to bargain. Not only did the government not argue this, but it argued against such a duty in defending the legislation.

In the United States, Douglas J also disposed of an appeal on a basis not argued before the Supreme Court of the United States. In *Terminiello v Chicago*,[37] Frankfurter J, in his dissent, was very critical of Douglas J because of his strong views that judges should exercise judicial restraint in dealing with the record and parties' arguments in constitutional cases. In his recent book, *Scorpions*, Professor Noah Feldman described Frankfurter J's reaction:

> Frankfurter saw the opinion as an abdication of judicial restraint. In his dissent, he criticized Douglas for ignoring what every lawyer and judge who had been involved in the case from the outset had thought the case was about. Ordinarily, appellate courts rule only on arguments that the parties make in court. Never before in the 150-year history of the Supreme Court, Frankfurter claimed, had the Court completely ignored the parties' arguments to overturn a state-court judgment on grounds it had invented out of whole cloth. Whether Douglas's decision was entirely unprecedented or not, Frankfurter was on to something. Douglas had a constitutional objective to promote. He could not care less what the rest of the world thought about it—and that certainly included the lawyers and the judges in the state courts who had dealt with Terminiello's conviction.[38]

The majority engaged in the type of activism criticized by Frankfurter J by providing an interpretation of the *AEPA* that none of the parties advocated and that the record does not support. Moreover, this critique by Frankfurter J, the patron saint of judicial restraint, would also apply to the decision of Rothstein J, who was prepared to overrule *BC Health Services* on his own motion without any party calling for the overruling of this recent precedent.

Second, the language of the *AEPA* could not be construed so as to imply a duty to bargain in good faith. The only obligation on the agricultural employer is to provide employees with an opportunity

37 337 US 1 (1949).

38 Feldman, above note 34 at 327.

to make representations, to listen if the representations are oral, and to give the employees a written acknowledgement that the employer has read them if the representations are in writing. To imply a duty to bargain in good faith in the absence of the express language universally used by Canadian legislatures to impose such a duty is questionable at best.

Third, the legislative intent was clear that the legislature did not intend to confer collective bargaining rights on agricultural employees. Indeed, Minister of Agriculture Helen Johns, explicitly said so in introducing the legislation:

> I'd like to say that the Supreme Court was very clear . . . They did not say that [agricultural workers] had the right to collectively bargain.[39]

> However, I need to make one thing very clear here. While an agricultural employee may join an association that is a union, the proposed legislation does not extend collective bargaining to agricultural workers.[40]

All of the background and written material echoed this clear intent. Of course, the reason for this is that the Conservative government was only strictly complying with what the *Dunmore* case expressly required. *Dunmore* did not impose the duty to bargain because it did not reconsider the Labour Trilogy, which was then the governing law.

In implying a duty to bargain or consider the employee representations in good faith, the majority relied upon three considerations that do not stand up to scrutiny. First, they said that in order to give meaning to the right of agricultural employees to make representations and the duty of the employer to listen or read the representations, the employer must do so in good faith. Second, the legislature is presumed to intend to comply with the *Charter*. Since *BC Health Services*, an employer must consider employee representations in good faith. Any ambiguity should be resolved accordingly. Finally, the majority relied on the express intention of the minister in introducing the legislation when she said that the Government of Ontario would meet its obligations to guarantee that agricultural employees have the protections necessary to ensure that their freedom of association is meaningful.

---

39 Ontario, Legislative Assembly, *Official Report of Debates (Hansard)*, No 93A (16 October 2002) at 2128 (Hon Helen Johns).

40 Ontario, Legislative Assembly, *Official Report of Debates (Hansard)*, No 46B (22 October 2002) at 2339 (Hon Helen Johns).

The holding of the majority flies in the face of the record before the Court. It was clear that in enacting the *AEPA*, the Government of Ontario was acting under the pre-*BC Health Services* law in which there was no obligation to provide a duty to bargain however that duty is framed. There was no ambiguity as to the government's intention. No presumption of constitutionality should be permitted to override the clear and unequivocal evidence. As the three other judgments clearly point out, the majority's decision fails to account for the fact that the scope of protection under section 2(d) changed after the *AEPA* was enacted.

When the minister said that the government wanted to ensure that freedom of association was meaningful, she was referring to the scope of the freedom as defined in *Dunmore*, which expressly ruled that section 2(d) does not protect a duty to bargain. In a very graphic description, Rothstein J referred to the majority's interpretation as stretching the interpretive exercise beyond its breaking point.[41]

The question arises as to why the majority would go to this length in upholding the *AEPA*. Most observers would agree that a declaration of unconstitutionality inevitably results from a ruling which upheld *BC Health Services*. Indeed, Rothstein J described the majority's ruling as "entirely novel and unprecedented."[42]

In my view, the answer to the question of why the majority engaged in such an implausible interpretation probably relates to a misguided application of judicial deference, an application which, in my opinion, on its face, may have deferred to the legislature but which in fact disregarded the record and submissions, the legislation before them, and the legislative intent. One can speculate that the majority wanted to show that, despite Rothstein J's admonitions to the contrary, the majority was prepared to defer to the legislature on questions of labour policy. Unfortunately, if judicial deference is the rationale for its holding, the majority acted contrary to its own judgment in that it applied deference at the threshold stage rather than at the section 1 stage. Another possible rationale might be that the majority also wanted to show that the Wagner model is not the only model which the legislature might adopt in regulating labour relations. I will deal with this possible rationale in the next section. Finally, there is the possibility of the "second look" effect as described by Professor Hogg in his text, *Constitutional Law of Canada*.[43] In es-

41 *Fraser*, above note 1 at para 283.

42 *Ibid* at para 290.

43 Hogg, above note 28 at 36-33.

sence, Professor Hogg concludes that the Supreme Court is more likely to defer to a legislature that has enacted a statute in response to a court ruling that its previous legislation was unconstitutional. Of course, the *AEPA* was enacted in response to the *Dunmore* case. Professor Hogg describes this effect as part of the supposed ongoing dialogue between the courts and the legislatures in the application of the *Charter*.

Whatever the explanation, one thing is clear: if the majority had really deferred to the will of the legislature, it would have found that there was no legislative intent to impose a duty to bargain on agricultural employers. In my view, the majority disregarded what the legislature intended and found the law constitutional retroactively. As Abella J points out in her dissent, the majority failed to assess the legislative intent in light of the prevailing law in 2002 when the *AEPA* was enacted. As a result, it implied a duty to bargain in the law that was never intended by the government that enacted it. One could say that the majority turned judicial deference on its head and as a result could be accused of the judicial activism which judicial deference was intended to curb. Unfortunately, the plight of the farm workers was lost in this curious dialogue between the court and the legislature.

E. The Wagner Model

Normally, a court's framing of the issue will give an indication of the result it will reach in its judgment. The *Fraser* case is no exception. In the very first paragraph of its judgment, the majority framed the issue as follows:

> This appeal raises anew the issue of the constitutionality of the labour relations regime that applies to farm workers in Ontario. Most Canadian provinces have brought the farming sector under their general labour relations laws, with some exceptions and restrictions. Except for a very short period of time, Ontario has always excluded farms and farm workers from the application of its *Labour Relations Act* (currently *Labour Relations Act, 1995*, S.O. 1995, c.1, Sched. A) ("*LRA*"). In the present appeal, our Court must determine whether Ontario's latest attempt to frame a separate labour relations regime for the farming sector respects the constitutional guarantee of freedom of association, or violates it by failing to safeguard the exercise of collective bargaining rights. The *Agricultural Employees Protection Act, 2002*, S.O. 2002, c.16 ("*AEPA*") or ("Act"), was a response to this Court's decision in *Dunmore v. Ontario (Attorney General)*,

2001 SCC 94. [2001] 3 S.C.R. 1016, which found that the previous legislative scheme violated s.2(*d*) of the *Canadian Charter of Rights and Freedoms*.

Later, in paragraph 44 of its judgment, the majority framed the issue in more particularized language:

> Against this background, we return to the issue in this case. The Court of Appeal held that *Health Services* constitutionalizes a full-blown Wagner system of collective bargaining, and concluded that since the *AEPA* did not provide such a model, absent s.1 justification, it is unconstitutional. The court appears to have understood the affirmation of the right to collective bargaining in *Health Services* as an affirmation of a particular type of collective bargaining, the Wagner model which is dominant in Canada.

Throughout its judgment, the majority characterizes the ruling of the Ontario Court of Appeal as deciding that section 2(d) protects "a particular kind of collective bargaining," that is, the Wagner or North American model. The focus of its attention was whether the Government of Ontario acted in accordance with the *Charter* by adopting a non-Wagner model to regulate the labour relations of agricultural employees.

With respect, this mischaracterizes the issue before the court. The question is not whether the government can adopt a non-Wagner model to regulate labour relations. The agricultural workers conceded that the government could. The Court of Appeal never ruled that the government could not legislate such a model. However, the real question in relation to the *AEPA* is what minimum statutory protections are required in order to ensure that farm workers in Ontario have an effective collective bargaining process which will advance their common workplace goals. A related question is why the government chose a non-Wagner model for these most vulnerable of workers when the Wagner model is the model chosen for virtually every other employee in the Province of Ontario or elsewhere in Canada. Moreover, the Wagner model is used to regulate the labour relations of farm workers in every other Canadian jurisdiction except Alberta, which is the only other province where farm workers have no collective bargaining rights. The record was replete with examples of where the Ontario government discriminated against agricultural workers by not giving them the same level of legislative protection given to other employees in respect of other employment matters such as health and safety and employment standards.

The question of the power of a legislature to adopt a non-Wagner model was an *ex post facto* rationalization raised by the Government of Ontario in defence to the constitutional claim of the agricultural workers. Before the enactment of the *AEPA*, the government conducted no study and commissioned no reports on why agricultural workers should be treated differently than other employees in the province. The expert witness of the government who justified the model adopted in the *AEPA* was only retained *after* the litigation was commenced, was not consulted prior to the enactment of the *AEPA*, and has no expertise in regard to farm workers. The record also showed that the government never considered enacting a regime that conferred collective bargaining rights on farm workers. The only apparent policy rationale was that the government was strictly complying with *Dunmore*, which did not expressly require the government to extend the right to bargain collectively to farm workers. As these employees were so vulnerable and the farmers' lobby comparatively powerful politically, the government did not go beyond the narrowest requirements of *Dunmore*.

What the government did not foresee was that five years later in *BC Health Services*, the Supreme Court of Canada would rule that section 2(d) protects the right to collective bargaining. Faced with the legislative intent underlying the *AEPA* and the record before it, the Ontario Court of Appeal applied the holding in *BC Health Services* to agricultural workers in Ontario. The Court of Appeal, like the parties before it, including the Government of Ontario, acted on the basis that the *AEPA* did not impose a duty to bargain on employers. It concluded that the *AEPA* substantially interferes with the ability of agricultural workers to bargain collectively. The government was unable to show that under the *AEPA* there was any instance of where a union or employees' association had successfully organized and engaged in good faith bargaining on behalf of agricultural workers in Ontario. The UFCW had organized two units at a mushroom factory and a greenhouse operation. In one instance, the response of the employer was to create a "company-dominated" union in order to avoid dealing with the union chosen by the majority of the employees. In the other instance, the employer did not have the courtesy to respond to the union's proposal because of its position that the law did not require it to bargain with the union.[44] The Court of Appeal concluded that when these employers refused to bargain with the

44 See the *Ontario (AG) v Fraser*, 2011 SCC 20 (Factum of the Respondent) at paras 59–60 and Hanley's chapter in this book.

UFCW, the union and the employees were left without any remedy under the *AEPA*, as the employers were under no statutory duty to bargain in good faith with the employees' representative.

Applying the analyses of *BC Health Services* and *Dunmore*, the Court of Appeal concluded that if the legislation is to provide for meaningful collective bargaining, it must go further than simply stating the principle and must include provisions that ensure that the right can be realized. It went on to conclude that at a minimum, the following statutory protections are required to enable workers to exercise their rights to bargain collectively and, hence, their freedom of association, in a meaningful way:

1) a statutory duty to bargain in good faith;
2) statutory recognition of the principles of exclusivity and majoritarianism; and
3) a statutory mechanism for resolving bargaining impasses and disputes regarding the interpretation and application of collective agreements.[45]

The statutory duty to bargain is the inevitable result of *BC Health Services*. If section 2(d) protects the right to bargain collectively and, in light of *Dunmore*, farm workers need statutory support in order to ensure the effective exercise of their freedom of association, a statutory duty to bargain must be imposed upon the employer. In Canada this is not a revolutionary concept. As early as 1944, Bora Laskin identified the failure to statutorily enforce "upon employers a duty to bargain collectively with the trade union representing the majority of their employees" as the principal defect that undermined unions' ability to make collective representations.[46] To rectify this defect, the rights of collective bargaining—specifically including a duty to bargain in good faith—have been affirmatively protected in Canadian labour laws since PC1003 in 1944 and have remained cornerstones of contemporary Canadian labour legislation to this day.

The requirement of a dispute settlement mechanism for bargaining and collective agreement disputes is eminently reasonable. As Rothstein J said:

> Indeed, when a duty is imposed on a party by law, it must be accompanied by sanctions or means of enforcement if there is non-compliance with the duty. Without sanctions or means of enforcement, compliance

---

45 *Fraser v Ontario (AG)*, 2008 ONCA 760 at para 80.

46 Bora Laskin, "Union Representation and Collective Bargaining" (1944) 8 Public Affairs 48.

> with the duty would be, to all intents and purposes, voluntary. This would hardly meet the requirement, according to the Chief Justice and LeBel J., that collective bargaining be mandatory.[47]

Moreover, a dispute settlement mechanism to enforce statutory or contractual rights is hardly unique to the Wagner model. As Rothstein J points out, a purposive and liberal approach to remedies under the *Charter* "give[s] modern vitality to the ancient maxim"[48] where there is a right, there must be a remedy. Needless to say, this ancient maxim finds fruition in other labour relations models. As was referred to above and recognized by Dickson CJ in the *Alberta Reference*, one of the fundamental rules of Canadian labour law is that without a dispute settlement mechanism, the right to bargain collectively is ineffective and therefore not meaningful.

Finally, in determining that majoritarian exclusivity is necessary in order to ensure that collective bargaining is meaningful, the Court of Appeal relied upon the history, policy, and practice of Canadian labour relations. The court referred to the following statement of Professor Carter in his co-authored text, *Labour Law in Canada*, which described that history, policy, and practice:

> A fundamental principle of Canadian collective bargaining law is that, once a trade union has acquired bargaining rights for a particular bargaining unit, it enjoys exclusive rights to bargain collectively on behalf of the employees in that bargaining constituency . . . The trade union's exclusive right to bargain imposes a corresponding obligation on the employer to recognize the trade union as bargaining agent for all employees in the bargaining unit, regardless of whether all of these employees are members of that trade union . . . These twin principles of "majoritarianism" and "exclusivity" are common threads running through all Canadian collective bargaining legislation.[49]

The evidence before the court also established that, since the 1930s, Canadian labour relations policy and law have recognized that allowing multiple employee representatives, without regard to whether an association has majority support, is conducive to employer influence over employee associations and undermines, rather than promotes, workers' effective exercise of freedom of associa-

---

47 *Fraser*, above note 1 at para 259.

48 *Ibid* at para 261.

49 Donald Carter et al, *Labour Law in Canada*, 5th ed (The Hague: Kluwer Law International, 2002) at 286–87.

tion.[50] Bora Laskin stated that the failure of Ontario's early labour laws to certify employees' majority choice of representative allowed employers to "make a mockery of freedom of association" by ignoring employees' choice and by fostering employee representation committees and company unions at the expense of independent trade unions. The principle of exclusive representation has been a cornerstone of all Canadian labour legislation since 1944 because in its absence employers were free to, and did, actively subvert employees' freedom of association.[51] If this phenomenon looks familiar, it is. As stated above, in the record before the court this very thing happened at the mushroom factory where the UFCW represented 70 percent of the employees and the employer's response was to create a "company dominated" association with only a handful of employees rather than dealing with the UFCW.[52] This conduct is considered lawful under the *AEPA*.

The Court of Appeal also ruled that exclusivity is consistent with *Charter* values in that it provides employees with a unified and thus more effective voice from which to promote their collective objectives. As such, it mitigates the historical inequality between employers and employees, which, in turn, enhances equality values recognized in *BC Health Services* as an important *Charter* value promoted through collective bargaining. Finally, the Court ruled that Canadian labour relations practice demonstrates beyond question that, in Canada, majoritarian exclusivity is required to make collective bargaining workable.

Unfortunately, the majority of the Supreme Court viewed the Court of Appeal's approach as a misunderstanding that *BC Health Services* affirmed the Wagner model as the only constitutional way to regulate labour relations in Canada. With respect, this is a clear misreading of the Court of Appeal's judgment.[53] Although it is apparent that majoritarian exclusivity is a feature of the Wagner or North American model, it is also a fundamental feature of the Canada labour relations system for obvious reasons. The Wagner model is the virtual unanimous labour relations regime in every jurisdiction in North America. This model is how Canadian governments gave life to freedom of association over sixty years ago. In effect, the *Labour Relations Act* instantiates freedom of association in Ontario.

---

50 Respondent's Factum, above note 44 at para 43.

51 Bora Laskin, "Recent Labour Legislation in Canada" (1944) 22 Can Bar Rev 776.

52 Respondent's Factum, above note 44 at para 59.

53 *Ibid* at para 131.

As Dickson CJ said in the *Alberta Reference*: "Freedom of association is the cornerstone of modern labour relations."[54] To suggest that features of the Wagner model should not be used to inform the meaning of freedom of association in the workplace is questionable at best.

Not surprisingly, the majority's preoccupation with the Wagner model seems to have diverted its attention from the real issue before it. It never assessed whether the Court of Appeal was correct in ruling that a statutory bargaining duty, majoritarian exclusivity, and dispute settlement mechanisms were necessary in order to ensure that freedom of association is meaningful in the Ontario agricultural workplace. Moreover, the majority never questioned why the Government of Ontario chose a non-Wagner model for this most vulnerable group of employees without any study or report supporting this novel and unique approach for labour relations in Canada. The union did not argue that a legislature could not regulate labour relations by a regime other than the Wagner model. The union conceded that Canadian legislatures could experiment and innovate with labour relations systems other than the Wagner model. However, as noted by Abella J in response to the argument that the courts should give the legislatures room to innovate in the area of labour relations, "to innovate by eliminating a fundamental protection for the most vulnerable workers is nullification, not innovation."[55] This was the lesson that the majority and Rothstein J missed.

F. International Law

One of Rothstein J's grounds for concluding that *BC Health Services* was wrongly decided is that, in his view, the majority was in error when it decided that international law "pointed to" compulsory bargaining. His argument is that the majority in *BC Health Services* erred in conflating ILO Convention No 87 and ILO Convention No 98 because Canada has not ratified Convention No 98. He also suggested that in any event, Convention No 98 does not contemplate the imposition of a duty to bargain in good faith in that it only protects voluntary bargaining. In defence of the position they took in *BC Health Services*, McLachlin CJ and Lebel J referred to their reliance on the decision rendered by the ILO Committee on Freedom of Association (CFA) in the conflict between the employees in *BC Health Services* and the Government of British Columbia. They noted that the deci-

54 *Alberta Reference*, above note 1 at 334.

55 *Fraser*, above note 1 at para 351.

sion concerned the very conflict that formed the factual background of the decision in *BC Health Services*. The majority pointed out that "[a]fter applying Convention No. 87 and noting that Canada had not ratified Convention No. 98, the CFA concluded that the action of the government of British Columbia violated the employees' freedom of association."[56]

While I agree with the majority's defence and reference to the CFA decision in the *BC Health Services* dispute, what is troubling is that they make no mention of the counterpart CFA decisions in the *AEPA* dispute. On two occasions the CFA had the opportunity to review the *AEPA*.[57] On each occasion, it ruled that the *AEPA* violates Canada's obligations under international human rights law by failing to provide agricultural workers with the right to bargain collectively.

I will only refer to the latest decision as it confirmed the earlier decision. In November 2010, the CFA released its decision in a complaint against the Government of Canada presented by the UFCW and supported by the Canadian Labour Congress and the UNI Global Union.[58] This decision was released after the oral arguments were made before the Supreme Court in December 2009 but before the judgment was released in April 2011. Upon motion by the UFCW, the Court agreed to admit the decision into evidence.

In the decision, the CFA noted that Ontario made a similar argument in regard to Canada not ratifying Convention No 98:

> While taking due note of the Provincial Government's reminder that Canada has not ratified Convention No. 98, the Committee recalls that the purpose of the procedure on freedom of association is to promote respect for trade union rights in law and practice, therefore complaints lodged with the Committee can be submitted whether or not the country concerned has ratified the freedom of association Conventions (see Digest, op. cit., para. 5).[59]

In response to the UFCW's assertion that under the *AEPA* employers are not under any obligation to bargain with any employee association, Ontario submitted that the *AEPA* complied with international law because of "the principle of the *voluntary* nature of collective bargaining as an essential aspect of freedom of association

56 *Ibid* at para 94.

57 ILO Freedom of Association Committee, *Complaint against the Government of Canada (Ontario) presented by the Canadian Labour Congress (CLC)* Report No 308, Case No 1900; ILO Case No 2704, above note 22.

58 ILO Case No 2704, *ibid.*

59 *Ibid.*

established by the Committee on numerous occasions."[60] In regard to this submission, the CFA stated:

> The Committee recalls that it had already examined a case concerning the denial of the right to collective bargaining to certain categories of workers in the Province of Ontario, including agricultural and horticultural workers (see Case No. 1900, 308th Report, paragraphs 139 194). In this regard, the Committee referred to the preliminary work for the adoption of Convention No. 87 which clearly indicated that one of the main objects of the guarantee of freedom of association is to enable employers and workers to form organizations independent of the public authorities and capable of determining wages and other conditions of work by means of freely concluded collective agreements (see Digest, op. cit., para. 882). It consequently requested the Government to take the necessary measures to ensure that these workers enjoy the protection necessary, either through the OLRA or by means of occupationally specific regulations, to establish and join organizations of their own choosing, and to take the necessary measures to guarantee for them access to machinery and procedures which facilitate collective bargaining.[61]

In concluding that the *AEPA* infringed freedom of association, the CFA noted the failure of the *AEPA* to facilitate any negotiated agreements or good faith negotiations at all:

> The Committee, observing in particular that neither the Government nor the complainant have referred to any successfully negotiated agreement since the Act's adoption in 2002, nor even to any good faith negotiations engaged in, continues to consider that the absence of any machinery for the promotion of collective bargaining of agricultural workers constitutes an impediment to one of the principle objectives of the guarantee of freedom of association—the forming of independent organizations explicitly capable of concluding collective agreements. It requests the Government to take the necessary measures to ensure that the Provincial Government puts in place appropriate machinery and procedures for the promotion of collective bargaining in the agricultural sector and requests it to keep it informed of the progress made in this respect. Appropriate machinery can be adapted to national circumstances provided the principles reflected above are fully respected.[62]

---

60 *Ibid* [emphasis added].

61 *Ibid.*

62 *Ibid.*

It is of serious concern that this decision was not referred to, let alone relied upon, in determining whether the *AEPA* violated freedom of association. From Dickson CJ's dissent in the *Alberta Reference*, through *Dunmore* and *BC Health Services*, international human rights law has played an important role in informing the interpretation of section 2(d) in a labour context. Needless to say, the majority reached another conclusion because of its interpretation that the *AEPA* imposed a legal duty to bargain. However, that should not excuse a court from dealing with and, perhaps "wrestling with" the applicable international law particularly when the decision deals with the very legislation before the court.

However, there is one positive note for those who support the use of international law as an aid in interpreting the *Charter*. In the decision, the CFA disposes of Rothstein J's two concerns about the "conflation" of Convention No 87 and Convention No 98 and the "voluntary" nature of collective bargaining in international law. Hopefully, the Supreme Court will refer to this decision in the future.

G. Conclusion

The majority's decision and the concurring decisions of Rothstein and Deschamps JJ demonstrate what can happen when a court addresses a broader problem than that raised in the record before it. A primary rule of adjudication is that a court should not make a decision beyond the facts and issues presented to it in the case it has to decide. The Ontario Court of Appeal was not making a broad pronouncement that section 2(d) requires majoritarian exclusivity and dispute settlement mechanisms. What it was saying was that in order for freedom of association, including the right to collective bargaining, to be meaningful for farm workers in Ontario, the workers require more legislative support than was provided in the *AEPA*. In determining the requisite level of support, the Court drew upon Canadian labour relations history, policy, and practice. As it should have been, the Court of Appeal was focused on the record before it, that is, the plight of farm workers in Ontario. As directed by *Charter* jurisprudence, the Court gave a very contextual interpretation of the *Charter* in light of the workers making the constitutional claim, *Charter* values, and Canadian labour history and practices. Indeed, it was what the Supreme Court of Canada did in *BC Health Services*.

Unfortunately, in *Fraser*, the Supreme Court was diverted by the larger battle presented to it by all of the intervening governments and business lobby groups. The focus became the legitimacy of *BC Health Services* rather than whether the *AEPA* provided farm workers with meaningful associational rights consistent with the government's positive obligations under section 2(d). A cursory review of the majority and Rothstein J's judgments shows that more time is spent on debating the merits and implications of *BC Health Services* than on the legality of the *AEPA*. The plight of the farm workers was lost in this larger event. Although the meandering and esoteric debate over *BC Health Services* sheds light on the Supreme Court of Canada's ambivalence over the interpretation of freedom of association in the labour context, it had little to do with whether the *AEPA* provided farm workers in Ontario with the opportunity to join together and associate in order to pursue common objectives that would improve their working conditions and lives and enhance their respect, dignity, and worth in the workplace. After all, that is what the *Charter* was intended to do.

CHAPTER EIGHT
What *Fraser* Means For Labour Rights in Canada

*Steven Barrett and Ethan Poskanzer**

This chapter explores some of the implications of the Supreme Court of Canada decision in *Fraser*[1] for the future of labour rights in Canada (or at least for litigating labour rights in the courts), from both a practical and doctrinal perspective.

The judgments in *Fraser* have already been summarized in previous chapters, as has the Supreme Court of Canada's earlier freedom of association jurisprudence. Therefore, rather than repeat this discussion, we begin this chapter in Part A with an analysis of the potential short- and medium-term impacts of *Fraser* on litigation strategy and outcomes. This part begins with an assessment of the Court's perpetuation of the distinction between legislative action and so-called legislative inaction (or exclusion), and then turns to a review of the practical impact of the *Fraser* decision on existing and future constitutional challenges to legislation and government action in the collective bargaining sphere.

In Part B, we shift to the doctrinal debate between the majority's reasons upholding *Health Services*,[2] and Rothstein J's reasons advo-

* A caveat is in order. We both appeared as counsel for the Canadian Labour Congress as intervener in the Supreme Court of Canada in *Delisle, Dunmore, Health Services*, and *Fraser*. As with everyone else, while we come at these issues with a perspective, our analysis should be assessed on its merits.

1 *Ontario (AG) v Fraser*, 2011 SCC 20 [*Fraser*].

2 *Health Services and Support—Facilities Subsector Bargaining Association v British Columbia*, [2007] 2 SCR 391 [*Health Services*].

cating for the reversal of *Health Services* (and, in particular, against the extension of section 2(d) protection to collective bargaining). By identifying and analyzing the differences between them, we hope to shed some light on the potential shape and contour of labour rights litigation in the years to come. Our discussion includes an assessment of Rothstein J's criticism of the *Health Services* decision (and so too of the *Fraser* majority's reasons), based on his contention that the rest of the Court has inappropriately extended constitutional protection to associational objects and outcomes, has incorrectly recognized a uniquely collective dimension to freedom of association, and has wrongly privileged worker and trade union associational activities. In so doing, we also assess the extent to which his analysis of the underlying purpose of section 2(d) is inconsistent with its actual historical and philosophical origins, and purpose and rationale. Part B also considers the extent to which Rothstein J's own approach to freedom of association logically, doctrinally, and practically supports some form of meaningful section 2(d) protection for both collective bargaining and the right to strike.

A. The Doctrinal and Practical Implications of the Fraser Majority's Reasons

1) Perpetuating a Rigid Distinction Between Legislative Action and "Inaction"

From a doctrinal perspective, the *Fraser* decision would seem to perpetuate a somewhat artificial and rigid distinction between legislative action and inaction (a distinction which, as discussed below, seems particularly inappropriate in the labour relations context). More specifically, in its reasons, the *Fraser* majority upheld the *Agricultural Employees Protection Act* (*AEPA*)[3] regime based on its characterization of the constitutional challenge to the legislative exclusion of agricultural workers from the normative collective bargaining regime applicable to virtually all other workers as merely involving a challenge to the failure to affirmatively extend legislative protection. On this basis, the majority upheld the *AEPA* by asserting that legislatures are not

3 *Agricultural Employees Protection Act*, SO 2002, c 16 [*AEPA*].

> constitutionally required, in all cases and for all industries, to enact laws that set up a uniform model of labour relations imposing a statutory duty to bargain in good faith, statutory recognition of the principles of exclusive majority representation and a statutory mechanism for resolving bargaining impasses and disputes regarding the interpretation or administration of collective agreements.[4]

As it turns out, the majority would seem particularly susceptible to the criticism that it wrongly focused its approach on a concern with imposing positive obligations on legislatures to "constitutionalize" the Wagner Act model, given that elsewhere in its reasons, the majority recognized the inappropriateness and impossibility of maintaining a rigid distinction between positive rights and negative freedoms upon which that concern is premised. As the *Fraser* majority wrote:

> [67] . . . This bright line between freedoms and rights, seems to us impossible to maintain. Just as freedom of expression implies correlative rights, so may freedom of association. The freedom to do a thing, when guaranteed by the Constitution interpreted purposively, implies a right to do it. The Charter cannot be subdivided into two kinds of guarantees—freedoms and rights.
>
> [70] . . . A purposive protection of freedom of association may require the state to act positively to protect the ability of individuals to engage in fundamentally important collective activities, just as a purposive interpretation of freedom of expression may require the state to disclose documents to permit meaningful discussion.[5]

Nonetheless, despite questioning the rationale for a rigid distinction between positive rights and negative freedoms in general terms, the majority seemingly conceives and determines the *Fraser* case as if it primarily if not exclusively involves a claim for legislative protection of positive rights.

Moreover, even if one were to accept the traditional distinction between positive rights and negative freedoms in the abstract, it would seem to be somewhat unrealistic, given the labour relations context in which the case arose, to conceptualize the issue in *Fraser* as not, at the very least, also implicating a negative freedom, namely, freedom from the deliberate and overt legislative exclusion of agricultural workers from the general normative collective bargaining

---

4 *Fraser*, above note 1 at para 47 of the majority's reasons.

5 *Ibid.*

regime applicable to virtually all other workers (the effect, if not purpose, of which, the union argued, was to impair the capacity of agricultural workers to engage in meaningful collective bargaining). This view is reinforced by the deep and extensive involvement of the state and legislation in regulating—both by protecting, and by tightly circumscribing and restricting—the rights and freedoms of workers in the collective bargaining and labour relations context.[6] Thus, to treat the legislative exclusion from the normative collective bargaining regime as only or primarily an instance of legislative inaction is to ignore the extent to which the Canadian collective bargaining system has, over the past seventy years of deep and extensive state regulation, become synonymous with the normative legal labour relations regime embodied in and instantiated by the *Labour Relations Act* (*LRA*) (particularly for more vulnerable workers).

Indeed, the long history in Canada of extensive legislative intervention if not occupation of the collective bargaining sphere, coupled with the targeted nature of the farm workers' exclusion, combine to make it especially difficult to view the exclusion in *Fraser* as in substance being simply an instance of a failure to act; rather, it is more in the nature of a deliberate and conscious legislative action and decision to exclude. As the majority itself accepted (citing Bastarache J in *Dunmore*): "[H]istory has shown, and Canada's legislatures have uniformly recognized, that a posture of government restraint in the area of labour relations will expose most workers not only to a range of unfair labour practices, but potentially to legal liability under common law inhibitions on combinations and restraint of trade."[7] It would seem to follow, at least in the labour relations context, that when "restraint" takes the form of "exclusion," treating the exclusion for constitutional purposes as an instance of government "inaction" misses the mark altogether. When viewed in the full historical and legislative context of the normative Canadian labour relations and collective bargaining regime, the exclusion of agricultural workers hardly reflects a typical form of legislative inaction.

However, as a result of the majority's approach in *Fraser*, and the outcome of the appeal, we can expect a difficult road ahead for any future constitutional challenges in the collective bargaining sphere,

---

6 *Ibid*. In her concurring reasons, Deschamps J also questions the utility of a distinction between positive and negative rights, or between positive acts and omissions, given the extent to which, in her view, "in our society, government activity is pervasive and unavoidable" (see paras 316–17). This pervasive impact of legislative intervention is particularly prevalent in the labour relations sphere.

7 *Ibid* at para 68; see also text following note 70 below.

to the extent that the courts view the claim as involving a challenge to so-called legislative inaction, and to the extent that the legislative scheme, either expressly or by implication, mandates some form of good faith bargaining. This not only includes section 2(d) challenges to collective bargaining legislation excluding workers altogether from the normative collective bargaining regime (at least where it provides for some form of bargaining duty), but also challenges to the absence of other statutory provisions viewed in other Canadian jurisdictions as required to ensure meaningful collective bargaining, such as first contract arbitration, card-based certification, or anti-strikebreaker restrictions.

2) Impact on Litigation Discourse and Strategy

Fraser will also likely have a significant impact on future litigation strategy, including the discourse that contending parties may be forced to adopt. For example, those challenging a particular statutory scheme may feel compelled to emphasize and demonstrate how the legislation is inconsistent with a good faith bargaining obligation. At the same time, those seeking to uphold legislation or government action will seek to characterize the challenge as wrongly seeking to "constitutionalize," in one way or another, an incidental feature of the statutory collective bargaining scheme. Being forced to engage in this exercise would seem to be rather removed from the more relevant inquiry as to whether a legislative or governmental exclusion, restriction, or prohibition substantially interferes with the constitutionally protected process of meaningful collective bargaining.

These competing approaches flowing from the uncertain impact of the *Fraser* decision are illustrated by the *Independent Electricity System Operator v Canadian Union of Skilled Workers* case.[8] In that case, the Ontario Divisional Court reversed the Ontario Labour Relation Board's (OLRB) ruling that the non-construction employer provisions of the *LRA*, which invalidated certain construction collective agreements and stripped employees of union representation where the OLRB declares an employer to be a non-construction employer, infringed section 2(d).[9] On the one hand, now that *Fraser* has been decided, the unions are arguing, and the OLRB held, that the termin-

---

8 *Independent Electricity System Operator v Canadian Union of Skilled Workers*, 2011 ONSC 81, released 18 February 2011, leave to appeal granted (7 July 2011), M39810 (Ont CA) [*IESO*].

9 As of this writing, leave to appeal has been granted to the Ontario Court of Appeal.

ation and overriding of collective agreements, coupled with loss of representational or bargaining rights, undermines the requirement that legislatures respect a process of good faith bargaining, which necessarily includes respect for longstanding bargaining rights and negotiated collective agreements. On the other hand, the employers are arguing, and the divisional court accepted, that the unions are merely seeking to constitutionalize a particular statutory bargaining structure, and that there is no infringement of section 2(d) since employees are free to attempt to organize again under the non-construction provisions of the Act.

Paradoxically, driven by a dissatisfaction with a conception of freedom of association as being anchored primarily or even solely in a duty of good faith bargaining, unions may choose to shift emphasis from the duty to bargain in good faith to the right or freedom to strike, by arguing both that the right to strike is a necessary precondition for meaningful collective bargaining, and a vital and independent component of the section 2(d) guarantee itself. Until now, unions litigating *Charter* challenges have not directly raised, and so the courts have not had to directly address, whether the right to strike itself is protected by section 2(d) of the *Charter*. Indeed, in *Fraser* itself, the union emphasized the need for some form of independent dispute resolution, rather than directly raising the right to strike or arguing that the right to strike is a necessary component of freedom of association.

While the *Fraser* majority's reasons may be viewed as having ruled out the "constitutionalization" of a positive obligation on legislatures to affirmatively provide, at least in all cases, for a statutory dispute resolution mechanism, the *Fraser* Court was neither asked to, nor did it, address the prior and fundamental question of whether freedom of association protects, against legislative interference or prohibition, the right of workers to collectively withdraw their services. Indeed, not only did nothing in the *AEPA* itself directly prohibit agricultural workers from exercising a common law or even constitutional freedom to strike, but as noted above, the *Fraser* case was regarded by the majority, and in fact by the courts throughout, as a positive rights case (that is, one in which the applicants were seeking legislative protection), but not as a negative freedom case (that is, one involving the right to be free of legislative or governmental interference in the exercise of a fundamental freedom).[10]

---

10 This difference is reflected in a distinction Brian Langille has recently described as the difference between a "taking a bat to/respect" case, and a "going to bat for/

As also discussed above, it is difficult to accept this stark dichotomy between positive rights and negative freedoms as reflecting labour relations reality in Canada, particularly given the extensive involvement of the state in regulating and channelling collective bargaining activity.[11] Nonetheless, it seems clear that the *Fraser* majority was uncomfortable with what it perceived to be the Court of Appeal's decision to impose positive obligations on the legislature (which the majority regarded as "constitutionalizing" the Wagner Act for all time[12]), and with its perception that it was being asked to determine which components of the legislative scheme merited some form of positive or affirmative constitutional protection.

By contrast, where the challenge manifestly involves a claim to be free of legislative interference in or prohibition of the exercise of constitutionally-protected associational activity (as was the case in *Health Services*), not only may the Court's approach and analysis

---

promote" case (see Langille, "What is Going on in *Fraser*," unpublished (15 July 2011) [Langille]). While this is a colourful and useful distinction, we part company with Langille when he insists that *Fraser* can only be conceptualized as a "going to bat for" case. In our view, in excluding agricultural workers, the Ontario legislature was, in substance, and both in purpose and effect, "taking a bat to" their collective bargaining freedom.

11 As recognized by the Court itself in *Dunmore v Ontario (AG)*, [2001] 3 SCR 1016 [*Dunmore*], there is now an inextricable historical and practical link in Canada between legislation and collective bargaining:

> [H]istory has shown, and Canada's legislatures have uniformly recognized, that a posture of government restraint in the area of labour relations will expose most workers not only to a range of unfair labour practices, but potentially to legal liability under common law inhibitions on combinations and restraints of trade . . . it may be asked whether the distinction between positive and negative state obligations ought to be nuanced in the context of labour relations, in the sense that excluding agricultural workers from a protective regime substantially contributes to the violation of protected freedoms" (para 20)

The Court also recognized that "legislative protection is so tightly woven into the fabric of labour relations that, while there is no constitutional right to protective legislation *per se*, the selective exclusion of a group from such legislation may substantially impact the exercise of a fundamental freedom" (para 35).

12 Notably, the unions were not, in fact, arguing that the Wagner Act model of labour relations was constitutionally required "in all cases and for all industries" (as the majority asserts in para 47); rather, the unions position was that both the deliberate intent, and practical effect, of singling out agricultural workers for exclusion from the legislative model applicable to virtually all other workers, and relegating them to a singularly inadequate and restrictive statutory model, was to exclude them from any meaningful capacity to engage in the process of collective bargaining. See Cavalluzzo in this volume.

be less constrained, but where the right to strike is the target of the legislative prohibition, the Court will be required to determine whether it falls within the ambit of section 2(d) protection.

In this respect, there are certainly strong doctrinal and practical arguments to be made that a right to strike is a fundamental component of freedom of association, and vital to make collective bargaining meaningful. This has been recognized by labour relations practitioners and scholars, and under international law.[13] While we can expect government and employer counsel to argue that the majority's emphasis on good faith bargaining implies that the imposition of a duty to bargain in good faith is sufficient to ensure meaningful collective bargaining, this argument would run contrary to the knowledge of any experienced labour practitioner and lawyer on both the union and employer side of the bargaining table.

It seems that the question of whether the right to strike in itself falls within the section 2(d) guarantee will likely end up before the courts in the relatively near future. Perhaps emboldened by their perception of the bottom line result in *Fraser*, governments may view the decision as an invitation to resume their legislative assault on the collective bargaining rights of Canadian workers in general, and the right to strike in particular. Indeed, this may well underlie the federal government's recent introduction of back to work legislation for Air Canada workers, and enactment of back to work legislation for postal workers, which not only prohibited existing strike activity but also imposed a lopsided dispute resolution mechanism.[14] Given that this legislation has now been challenged by the Canadian Union

---

13 See Dickson CJ's explanation for why the right to strike forms an integral component of freedom of association in *Reference re Public Service Employee Relations Act (Alta)*, [1987] 1 SCR 313 at 369–70 [*Alberta Reference*] (including the references cited therein), as well as his review of international law recognition that the right to strike forms part of freedom of association and is protected by International Labour Organization (ILO) Convention No 87 (to which Canada is signatory) at 348–59. Most recently, see the European Court of Human Rights decision in *Affaire enerji yapi-yol sen c Turquie* [CEDH], Requête no 68959/01, 21 avril 2009 (right to strike protected by the freedom of association guarantee in Article 11 of the *Convention for the Protection of Human Rights and Fundamental Freedoms*), discussed in this volume by Ewing and Hendy. See also the various papers presented at an international symposium on the right to strike, collected together in (2010) 15:2 CLELJ, and the discussion in Barrett, "The Supreme Court of Canada Decision in *Fraser*: Stepping Forward, Backward or Sideways?" in Canadian Labour and Employment Law Journal [forthcoming].

14 Bill C-5, *Continuing Air Service for Passengers Act*, 41st Parl, 1st Sess, First Reading, 16 June 2011; Bill C-6, *Restoring Mail Delivery for Canadians Act*, SC 2011, c 17.

of Postal Workers (CUPW), and given the pending challenge to essential services legislation in Saskatchewan, the issue of whether section 2(d) includes the right to strike will likely be thrust upon the judicial agenda.

Separate and apart from the right to strike, when it comes to challenges to statutory restrictions on negotiating or reaching agreement on important terms and conditions of employment, or challenges to legislation which has overridden key collective agreement terms (including, for example, wage control legislation), *Fraser* would appear to support the view that such restrictions are *prima facie* inconsistent with the section 2(d) guarantee. Without the capacity to negotiate and enter into a binding agreement, it is difficult to conceive of there being the potential for good faith bargaining.[15] This is the view already taken by one judge of the Federal Court who, in the *Meredith* decision reached subsequent to *Fraser*, found that federal legislative wage control restrictions infringed section 2(d), on the basis that the legislative reversal of negotiated wage increases made it effectively impossible to make collective representations and to have those representations considered in good faith.[16] A similar result was reached by the Ontario Superior Court in the *AJC* decision, holding that the same wage control legislation infringed section 2(d) by preventing bargaining over a key term and condition of employment, and that these wage controls could not be justified under section 1 to the extent they reached back to prevent arbitration over salary matters that were of significant importance to the union during a year prior to the onset of the recession.[17] At the same time, in *Federal Government Dockyard Trades and Labour Council v The Attorney General*,[18] a judge of the BC Supreme Court found that the same federal wage control legislation did not infringe section 2(d) when it overrode wage increases awarded at interest arbitration, but on the basis that a collective agreement wage term awarded at interest arbitration did not result from a constitutionally protected

---

15 This point was recognized in the (pre-*Fraser*) BC Supreme Court decision striking down restrictions on the ability of teachers to bargain over such matters as class size: *British Columbia Teachers' Federation v British Columbia*, 2011 BCSC 469.

16 *Meredith et al v Canada (AG)*, 2011 FC 735, released 21 June 2011 [*Meredith*].

17 *Association of Justice Counsel v AG Canada*, 2011 ONSC 6435, released 1 November 2011 [*AJC*].

18 *Federal Government Dockyard Trades and Labour Council v The Attorney General*, 2011 BCSC 1210, released 8 September 2011 [*Dockyards*].

process of collective bargaining,[19] and on the basis that even if it did, the government's good faith efforts as an employer to negotiate and consult with the union over its intention to alter the wage increase awarded at arbitration prior to doing so by imposing wage controls meant that there was no interference with section 2(d).[20]

Turning to the practical implications of *Fraser* in the context of challenges to legislative attempts to alter bargaining unit structures, the prospect for success may be more difficult, particularly given the *Fraser* majority's emphasis that no particular bargaining processes or structures are constitutionally required. This is reflected in the Quebec Court of Appeal's decision, released after *Fraser*, which reversed the pre-*Fraser* Quebec Superior Court's finding that the restructuring of bargaining units in the health care sector infringed section 2(d).[21]

---

19 Certainly, the *Dockyards* decision can be criticized for taking an unduly narrow and unrealistic view in excluding from the scope of constitutional protection those terms of collective agreements that are the product of a process of collective bargaining, culminating in a legislatively mandated or permitted interest arbitration process. Far from involving a failure of collective bargaining, a collective agreement is no less a result of the constitutionally protected process of collective bargaining when it is arrived at following a strike or lockout or following arbitration where arbitration has been substituted for the right to strike or lockout, than it is when it is arrived out prior to reaching that stage of the collective bargaining process. Indeed, as recognized in the *AJC* decision, and as we point out in Section B, far from being separate from and somehow lying outside of the collective bargaining process, the right to strike (or to arbitrate where the right to strike has been replaced) is an essential element of the collective bargaining process, in the absence of which there can be no meaningful collective bargaining.

20 In reaching this conclusion, the Court appears to have ignored the absence of any suggestion in the *Fraser* majority's reasons that would support the notion that so long as government negotiates or consults in good faith prior to overriding key collective agreement protections, there is no infringement of section 2(d). Indeed, it is difficult to conceive of a court accepting that, so long as the government negotiates or consults in good faith prior to interfering with another fundamental freedom (for example, freedom of expression or freedom of religion), there would be no infringement. In our view, the Court in the *AJC* decision correctly held that it is the very act of legislatively imposing wage controls, regardless of any prior discussions, that prevents any meaningful collective bargaining from taking place, and therefore infringes section 2(d).

21 *Confederation des syndicates nationaux v Attorney General of Quebec et al* (31 October 2008), No. 500017-018968-043, rev'd (*sub nom Quebec (AG) v Confédération des syndicats nationaux*), 2011 QCCA 1247. See also a similar result in an earlier Alberta Queens Bench judicial review decision: *Alberta Union of Provincial Employees v Alberta Health Services*, 2010 ABQB 344.

There also remain a number of existing and potential challenges to legislation that, as was the case in *Fraser*, excludes workers from access to normative collective bargaining legislation.[22] Despite the result in *Fraser*, there is still a strong basis for arguing that the complete exclusion from the statutory labour relations regime interferes with freedom of association, particularly where there is neither an express duty to bargain nor any legitimate basis for implying one. Thus, for example, in the Quebec challenge to the exclusion of certain agricultural workers, and in the Ontario challenge to the exclusion of RCMP officers, the legislation neither provides for an alternative *AEPA*-like regime nor provides for any process of bargaining, in good faith or otherwise. Moreover, in the case of the RCMP (as with other government employers), the government is directly bound by the *Charter* to comply with the freedom of association guarantee, and so, at the very least, to bargain in good faith with an organization chosen by workers (and not one imposed upon them by statute or regulation).

At the same time, the unfortunate effect of the *Fraser* decision may be that such excluded workers will, even if successful under section 2(d) and section 1, be subjected to inferior regimes, since at the remedial level, governments will argue that section 2(d) does not obligate legislatures to include such excluded workers in the normative labour relations regime as opposed to an *AEPA*-like statutory structure.

Another doctrinal aspect of the *Fraser* decision that may also influence future litigation discourse is the Court's use of the word "impossible" to describe the standard or threshold that must be met in order to make out interference with freedom of association, whatever its scope and content. Thus, the majority vacillates among a number of different tests, including suggesting that substantial interference in the exercise of the freedom is the test for infringement, or that the test is one of substantial impossibility (at least when it comes to imposing positive obligations on government to legislate), or that rendering the exercise of the freedom impossible is an instance of substantial interference, or that impossibility is the test itself, or that the test for impossibility (if that were the test) is itself substantial interference, or that the test is "substantial impairment"

---

22 This includes Quebec. *Travailleurs et travailleuses unis de l'alimentation et du commerce, Section locale 501 v Johanne L'Écuyer & Pierre Locas*, 2010 QCCRT 0191, and *Mounted Police Association of Ontario v Canada (AG)*, 2009 CanLII 15149 (Ont SCJ).

of which rendering the exercise of the freedom "effectively useless" is an illustration.[23]

No doubt, given the ambiguity of the Court's various formulations, we will see government and employer counsel argue that, despite the fact that in the case of alleged interference with any other *Charter* right or freedom, the threshold has never been set as high as "impossibility," nonetheless when it comes to freedom of association there is no breach unless it is established that legislative or government action makes it impossible for workers to exercise their section 2(d) freedoms.[24]

B. The Majority v Rothstein Debate: Where Does it Leave and Lead Us?

While the majority reasons in *Fraser* can be criticized for taking an overly formal and narrow approach to determining the extent to which the *AEPA* provides for meaningful collective bargaining for agricultural workers, at the same time, they do provide strong reaffirmation of the principle recognized in *Health Services* that, at least at some fundamental level, collective bargaining is protected

---

23 *Fraser*, above note 1 at respectively, paras 2 and 64, para 32, paras 33 and 47, para 34, paras 46 and 48, para 47, and paras 54 and 98. As Langille, above note 10, has pointed out, while the impossibility standard may play some role in a pure "going to bat for"/promote challenge, it has no place in a "taking a bat to"/respect case:

> The idea that there is a stringent test of impossibility to be deployed here is . . . inconsistent with our basic understanding of the *Charter*. If the government interferes with my freedom of speech—or religion—or any other freedom—the test is not, has not been, and should not be, has the state made it impossible to exercise the freedom? The test is whether they have interfered with the freedom in a way that cannot pass s. 1 muster. B.C. Health was not a case in which the claimants were asking the Court to find a constitutional obligation on the state to create rights against other private entities—it was simply a case where provincial legislation directly impinged on a fundamental freedom.

24 This argument has already been rejected by the Federal Court in *Meredith*, above note 16, which concluded that any reference to "impossibility" in *Fraser* was not to be taken as a "paramount consideration or threshold" but rather that "the word 'impossible' must be taken in the context of other words such as 'meaningfully' and 'effectively,' and the phrase 'good faith.' If legislation makes it possible for employees to make collective representations that are ineffective or not meaningful, or if representations are possible but government action demonstrates a lack of good faith, a breach of subsection 2(d) of the *Charter* will still have occurred." See also Langille, *ibid*.

by section 2(d),[25] and for the conclusion that legislatively overriding important collective agreement protections, and precluding future bargaining over such terms, infringes section 2(d).[26]

However, the fact that two members of the Court (Rothstein J joined by Charron J), strenuously took issue with the reasoning and holding in *Health Services*, and have urged its reversal just four years after its unanimous adoption, has been taken by some observers, at least in the management bar,[27] to suggest or signal the ultimate demise of section 2(d) protection for collective bargaining. As a result, it can be safely predicted that Rothstein J's unsuccessful effort to resurrect the 1987 Labour Trilogy[28] will likely lead to future attempts to challenge the ongoing legitimacy of *Health Services*, and, therefore, to continuing debate over the guiding principles underlying section 2(d), particularly in the labour relations context. For this reason, it is important to any assessment of the future implications of *Fraser* for labour rights in Canada to consider the difference in approach and reasoning between the *Fraser* majority and Rothstein J, and to critically analyze and assess both perspectives.

As a result, in this section of this chapter, we focus on what we believe to be some of the key aspects of the differences between the approach taken by the majority and by Rothstein J, in the course of which we also attempt to articulate, or at least stumble towards, a principled and sustainable approach to the protection of labour rights under section 2(d) of the *Charter*.

We begin in Section 1 with a critique of Rothstein J's most restrictive conception of freedom of association, namely, that it is restricted to protecting "formative activities." This section includes a discussion of the extent to which his criticism of the majority for affirming section 2(d) protection for collective bargaining, and for finding that good faith bargaining is a derivative component of freedom of association, is rooted in and dependent upon this overly restrictive approach to the content of freedom of association.

---

25 *Fraser*, above note 1 at paras 37, 40, 42, 43 51, and 54 of the majority's reasons.

26 *Ibid* at paras 34, 37, 38, 50, and 76 of the majority's reasons.

27 See for example John Craig, "Reflections on the Fraser Decision: Six Weeks Later," online: www.workplacewire.ca/labour/reflections-on-the-fraser-decision-six-weeks-later/ and Heenan Blaikie, "*Ontario v. Fraser*—The Supreme Court of Canada Significantly Narrows the Scope of the Constitutional Protection of Collective Bargaining," online: http://www.heenanblaikie.com/en/media/BioXML_PublicationsHB/pdf_file/ENEWS_Labour_2011-04-30_Tor_EN_email.pdf.

28 *Alberta Reference*, above note 13; *PSAC v Canada*, [1987] 1 SCR 424; *RWDSU v Saskatchewan*, [1987] 1 SCR 460.

In Section 2, we contrast Rothstein J's alternative conception of freedom of association (namely, that it extends to protecting the right of individuals to do together what they can otherwise lawfully do on their own) with the view taken in *Dunmore*, and by the *Fraser* majority, that freedom of association also has an additional and important collective dimension reflecting the need to encompass uniquely or inherently associational activity.

In Section 3, we review the extent to which even Rothstein J's alternative conception of freedom of association (what we call the "equal protection" approach) logically and practically compels constitutional recognition of a freedom (of a different kind than found by the majority) to engage in collective bargaining, and to strike.

In Section 4, we contrast the differing approaches taken in *Fraser*—not only by the majority and Rothstein J, but also by the Court of Appeal and by Abella J in dissent—to assessing the constitutionality of legislation that is alleged to substantially interfere with those activities or processes which are essential to ensuring meaningful section 2(d) protection.

Finally, in Section 5, we examine the extent to which the various approaches to freedom of association taken by the majority and by Rothstein J are rooted in very different understandings of the underlying purposes for the protection of freedom of association, in turn resulting in competing perspectives on the use and relevance of Canadian labour history, the international human rights protection of trade union and worker freedoms, and *Charter* values. This includes a discussion of the extent to which Rothstein J's restrictive view of the ambit of freedom of association (at its highest as being a form of "equal protection" clause of some kind for group and individual activities) does not accord with the philosophical underpinnings and historical purposes of the guarantee. We also critically assess his complaint that the majority's approach somehow "privileges" workers and trade unions.

1) Justice Rothstein's Attempt to Restrict Freedom of Association to Formative Activities

At various passages in his reasons in *Fraser* where he criticizes the majority's approach to freedom of association, Rothstein J articulates and relies upon the most restrictive conception of freedom of association that has been articulated in the caselaw, namely, that freedom of association only protects joining and forming activity ("formative activity").

By narrowly casting the scope of section 2(d) protection as being limited to formative activity, Rothstein J is then able to proceed to brand protection of anything more, including the process of collective bargaining, as going beyond protected formative activity and as therefore resulting in unwarranted protection or enhancement of the goals or objects of workers or trade unions. However, once it is recognized that freedom of association must protect more than merely formative activity, this aspect of his attack on section 2(d) protection for collective bargaining is left without any doctrinal foundation.

Justice Rothstein's restrictive formative activity approach is first identified in the following passage from his reasons, where he suggests that section 2(d) protects the right of individuals to form associations, but nothing more:

> [153] In *Dunmore*, the requirement that government provide legislation to protect workers was anchored in the proposition that certain workers could not associate without government intervention. This concept was embodied by the idea that the lack of legislation was a "substantial interference" to *the ability to form an association* (para. 25). Deschamps J. describes *Dunmore* as holding that agricultural workers "were substantially unable to exercise their constitutional right [to associate] without the support of a legislative framework" (para. 307 (emphasis added)). This characterization is in line with the words of Bastarache J. who himself noted *the distinction between forming an association and enhancing and facilitating the goals of that association*:
>
> . . . a group that proves capable of associating despite its exclusion from a protective regime will be unable to meet the evidentiary burden required of a *Charter* claim. In such a case, inclusion in a statutory regime cannot be said to safeguard, but rather to enhance, the exercise of a fundamental freedom. [para. 39]
>
> [154] *Health Services*, in contrast, was not focussed on ensuring that government did not interfere with *the right of individuals to form an association*. Indeed the action was brought by existing associations. Instead, the decision in *Health Services* centred on the purported need to constitutionalize collective bargaining in order for the association to be "meaningful". The majority concluded that without a legislated right to collective bargaining, and without constitutional protection of terms

> of the collective agreement in that case, *the formation of an association was meaningless.*[29]

According to Rothstein J, by focusing on "enhancing" the "goals" of an association, that is, associational activity beyond forming or joining, *Health Services* was a radical departure from the *Dunmore* decision:

> [155] This sentiment was an express break from *Dunmore* because the majority in *Health Services* focussed on the goals of an association and the *enhancement* of those goals, rather than the ability of the claimants to associate (*which they already had done*). Constitutionalizing collective bargaining therefore cannot be said to safeguard the ability to associate, but instead is concerned with "enhanc[ing] the exercise of a fundamental freedom," which cannot form the basis of a *Charter* claim (*Dunmore*, at para. 39).
>
> [156] It is this shift *from protecting what is necessary to exercise the freedom to associate, to constitutionalizing the goals of an association—that is, negotiating a collective agreement*—which results in *Health Services* being inconsistent with the ruling in *Dunmore*. The majority in *Health Services* found that the freedom of association is meaningless unless the government also imposes a duty on employers to bargain in good faith, and protects the fruits of that bargaining process. *The focus shifted in Health Services from protecting the right to associate to enhancing the goals of the association. This was an express break from Dunmore.*
>
> [171] . . . as I have discussed above, this *conflates two arguments*. The first is that *restrictions on the ability to associate, either directly or because the government interfered with an activity because of its "associational nature", are unconstitutional*, which *was* the finding in *Dunmore*. The second is that *governments are required to provide legislation which enhances the ability of an existing association to pursue its goal of negotiating a collective agreement, which was the finding in Health Services, but was contrary to Dunmore*. As noted above, an application of the actual holding in *Dunmore* would have asked only if the government substantially interfered with the ability to associate.[30]

Now, there are many difficulties with Rothstein J's characterization of the holding in *Health Services* in these passages, and with the restrictive conception of freedom of association upon which his

29 *Fraser*, above note 1 [emphasis added].
30 *Ibid* [emphasis added].

characterization rests, including the suggestion that *Health Services* had anything to do with obligating governments to enhance the goals of unions, or the ability of workers to negotiate a collective agreement. Rather, the case challenged legislation that extinguished a collective agreement that had already been negotiated by workers in the exercise of their associational freedoms.

Admittedly, it may well follow—as a matter of logic or definition—that if freedom of association is restricted to the narrow activities of forming and joining, then recognizing any other associational activities that extend beyond mere formative activity is liable to the charge of "constitutionalizing" or "enhancing" the goals of the association.

However, while this narrow view of freedom of association was taken by the majority in the initial 1987 labour freedom of association trilogy, it was rightly rejected in *Dunmore*, which explicitly recognized that limiting freedom of association solely to formative activity is an unjustifiably narrow doctrinal approach inconsistent with principles of *Charter* interpretation, the purpose and history of freedom of association, and its understanding at international law and in other jurisdictions. As a result, Rothstein J's repeated protestations that it is the majority in *Fraser* and not his own reasons that depart from *Dunmore* are untenable.

As has been recognized since even before the *Dunmore* decision,[31] freedom of association would be vacuous and devoid of meaningful content if all that individuals are free to do is form and join an association that is unable to engage in any activities. This is not to say that any and all collective or group activities should be constitutionally protected; the challenge for constitutional lawyers and judges is to develop a principled basis for determining the scope of associational activities. However, the fact that this may not be an easy

---

31 As Sopinka J held in *Professional Institute of the Public Service of Canada v Northwest Territories (Commissioner)*, [1990] 2 SCR 367 at para 77 [*PIPSC*]:

> [I]f the freedom to establish, belong to and maintain an association is to have any meaning, it must include the freedom of individuals to join together in pursuit of objects they could lawfully pursue as individuals. A restriction on the collective exercise of an activity legally permitted to individuals is essentially an attack on the ability of individuals to establish an association for that purpose.

Indeed, Dickson CJ's dissent in the *Alberta Reference* case aptly characterized what he termed the "purely constitutive definition" of freedom of association, entailing "only a freedom to belong to or form an association," as "legalistic, ungenerous, indeed vapid": above note 13 at 362–63.

or obvious task does not justify narrowly restricting the freedom to formative activity alone.

Thus, by repeatedly labelling any activities beyond forming and joining as unprotected objectives or as unprotected outcomes, Rothstein J incorrectly collapses an important distinction between protection of the process of collective bargaining (even if understood as a process without any attached or derivative bargaining duty), and protection of the objective or outcome of collective bargaining (either conceived, in Rothstein J's view, in the form of the majority's implied duty of bargaining in good faith, or as a guarantee that the process of bargaining will result in a collective agreement or in particular terms of a collective agreement). In so doing, he wrongly characterizes the process of collective bargaining as the ultimate goal of trade unions, rather than the very process or means through which employees seek to achieve their collective goal, that is, arriving at a collective agreement, including attempting to negotiate particular terms and conditions of employment to be included in a collective agreement.[32] As a result, his criticism of *Health Services* as a break with *Dunmore* (in particular, by extending section 2(d) protection to "*collective goals* which an association was formed to pursue, rather than protecting the freedom of association itself"[33]) depends not only on narrowly defining freedom of association to protect only formative activities, but also on artificially predefining the process of collective bargaining as a goal or outcome in and of itself, rather than the process through which workers seek to achieve workplace goals.[34]

---

32 As the Court recognized in *Health Services*, above note 2 at para 29, citing Bora Laskin, collective bargaining is not the end result or objective, but rather the means: it is "the procedure through which the views of the workers are made known, expressed through representatives chosen by them . . . . [and] through which terms and conditions of employment may be settled by negotiations between an employer and his employees on the basis of a comparative equality of bargaining strength."

33 *Fraser*, above note 1 at para 152 [emphasis added].

34 If there is a "break" with *Dunmore* in *Health Services*, it is only in concluding that collective bargaining cannot be excluded from s 2(d) protection given the doctrinal implications of *Dunmore*. In other words, *Health Services* took seriously the doctrinal approach outlined in *Dunmore*, and applied it to conclude that the *Alberta Reference* holding that collective bargaining was not protected could no longer be sustained. For a discussion and prediction that s 2(d) protection for collective bargaining was the logical doctrinal implication of *Dunmore*, see Barrett, "*Dunmore v. Ontario (Attorney General)*: Freedom of Association at the Crossroads" (2004) 10 CLELJ 83. It is in this sense that *Health Services* created what Abella J described in dissent (at para 325) as a "a completely different jurisprudential universe," that is, in the sense of recognizing s 2(d) protection for collective bargaining, but not in the sense

Furthermore, while Rothstein J suggests that collective bargaining is more substantive outcome or goal than process, because—as he writes, "collective bargaining itself is an outcome for which parties organize"[35]—it is difficult to see how the trite observation that workers form and join unions so that they can collectively bargain with their employer would automatically disqualify the process of collective bargaining from constitutional protection. If anything, one might ask whether workers would even bother to form and join unions without any capacity to engage in collective bargaining of any kind. Workers join trade unions not for the sake of belonging itself, and trade unions engage in organizing activities not for the sake of the organizing campaign itself; rather, this joining and organizing activity would not take place if the *raison d'être* was not to be able to at least attempt to deal with employers on a more equal footing through collective bargaining and all it entails.[36] Thus, his critique turns out be an attempt to preemptively attach the label of "outcome" to the process of bargaining in order to deny bargaining any section 2(d) protection.

To some extent, Rothstein J's criticism of the majority's approach to section 2(d) protection of collective bargaining would seem to be directed at the majority's conclusion that section 2(d) protects collective bargaining in the sense that it includes the derivative obligation to bargain in good faith. He may be suggesting that merely because workers have successfully organized, this accomplishment should not, as a constitutional matter, automatically result in those same workers achieving the "objective" of requiring their employer to bargain in good faith. As Rothstein J points out, a good faith bargaining duty not only precludes an employer from refusing to recognize and bargain with a trade union, but also from taking certain substantive issues to impasse, and also includes at least the possibility in exceptional circumstances of terms being imposed by a labour board.[37]

However, the notion that good faith bargaining is the substantive or primary goal of trade unions fails to recognize the extent to

---

asserted by Bastarache J of *Health Services* departing from *Dunmore* on doctrinal grounds.

35 *Fraser*, above note 1 at para 269.

36 This is not to say that collective bargaining is automatically entitled to constitutional protection just because formative activity is protected; rather, whether or not collective bargaining is protected must be determined on its own merits in accordance with conventional principles of constitutional interpretation: see the discussion in Section 5.

37 *Fraser*, above note 1 at paras 265–68.

which the good faith bargaining duty alone will rarely, if ever, result in a collective agreement. Rather, in the real world of labour relations, a collective agreement results from the process of collective bargaining (which, as discussed elsewhere in this chapter, necessarily includes the right to strike or where it is curtailed a process of independent and binding arbitration as an integral component). The duty to bargain on its own does not and cannot dictate or guarantee that workers will be successful in negotiating a collective agreement, nor in general does it dictate specific terms of a collective agreement. Indeed, the primary purpose of the duty to bargain is to support and ensure an informed and rational bargaining process, including disclosure of relevant information. While, as Rothstein J observes, the duty to bargain can, in very limited circumstances, result in the imposition of substantive contract terms, the possibility of this rare and exceptional remedial response hardly converts the duty to bargain in good faith from what is primarily a procedural protection into a broader guarantee that unions will achieve substantive bargaining outcomes.[38]

Moreover, it is this same inability to distinguish between process and substance, or associational activities and objectives, which leads Rothstein J to object to the validity of the broader holding in *Health Services*, confirmed by the majority in *Fraser*, that overriding important collective agreement protections, or prohibiting future negotiations over important matters by precluding their inclusion in collective agreements, infringes section 2(d). He contends that this would extend constitutional protection to the result, substance, or fruits of collective bargaining.[39] However, this criticism fundamen-

---

38 While Rothstein J relies on Hon George W Adams, *Canadian Labour Law*, 2d ed, loose-leaf (Aurora, ON: Canada Law Book, 1993), for his assertion that the duty to bargain is substantive in nature (para 267), the fact is that Adams emphasizes the extent to which the "underlying philosophy of the duty also embraces 'a freedom of contract rationale,' that the parties are best able to determine the content of their agreement and, failing agreement, each has recourse to economic sanctions." As Adams points out, labour boards have consistently ruled that "the duty is not to be used to redress imbalances of economic power between the parties" (see 10.1710). He also observes that because labour boards are so "reluctant to interfere with free collective bargaining by assessing the substance of fairness of bargaining proposals," several jurisdictions were forced to enact first contract arbitration (see 10.1850). Thus, Rothstein J's depiction of the bargaining duty as achieving the objective of negotiating a collective agreement or specific terms of an agreement would seem to be significantly overstated.

39 *Fraser*, above note 1. See, for example, paras 156, 216, 256, and 264 of Rothstein J's reasons.

tally misunderstands the nature of constitutional protection and adjudication. Protecting the integrity of a constitutionally guaranteed process (in this case, the process of collective bargaining) will often, if not invariably, require the constitutional invalidation of the legislative or governmental measure, that failed to respect that constitutionally protected process.

Even in the administrative law context, where procedural fairness has not been accorded, the courts may invalidate the results of the flawed process, thereby restoring the parties to the position they were in prior to the breach.[40] Similarly, in the constitutional criminal law context, violations of various procedural protections (for example, the right to a fair trial or to counsel) may result in the overturning of a conviction. This congruence does not mean that the court is protecting any particular result (for example, a right of the accused to commit an offense). Rather, in order to protect the integrity of the constitutionally guaranteed process, the substantive outcome resulting from the unconstitutional conduct must be reversed. It follows that if constitutionally protected processes are to be protected, legislatively reversing the results, or predetermining future results, can only be understood as undermining the integrity of the process.[41]

Finally, it can hardly be suggested that where respecting or protecting a constitutional right or freedom results, at the remedial level, in a particular substantive outcome, it is the substantive outcome that is receiving constitutional protection. Indeed, the Court recognized this fundamental distinction in *Dunmore* itself, when it concluded that that "while the inevitable *effect* of allowing this appeal may be to extend a statutory regime to agricultural workers, depending on the legislative response to this decision, the appellants are not seeking a constitutional 'right' to inclusion in the *LRA*."[42] Similarly, while the effect of a court finding that legislation that overrides freely negotiated collective agreement protections will be that the legislation is invalid, with the result that the negotiated provisions are reinstated, this effect does not mean that the reason for that remedial result is that there is a constitutional right to negotiated provisions, but rather that there is a constitutional right to

40 See, for example, the Supreme Court of Canada's decisions in *Cardinal v Director of Kent Institution*, [1985] 2 SCR 643, and in *Newfoundland Telephone Co v Newfoundland (Board of Commissioners of Public Utilities)*, [1992] 1 SCR 623.

41 By way of analogy, it would be hard to say that a judicial process would be fair if the judge had a closed mind or had predetermined the result.

42 *Dunmore*, above note 11 at para 36 [emphasis in the original].

be free of legislative or governmental action that undermines the process of collective bargaining.

Similarly, Rothstein J's contention that the result in *Health Services* improperly elevates contracts above legislation[43] fails to recognize the necessary consequences of extending protection to a constitutionally guaranteed process (in this case, collective bargaining). Consistent with the relationship between legislation and constitutionally protected rights and freedoms, *Health Services* elevates or gives priority to protecting the integrity of the constitutionally protected process of collective bargaining over legislation that fails to respect and undermines that process. Moreover, as discussed more fully in Section 5, Rothstein J fails to recognize that, to the extent one regards protection for the process of collective bargaining as being a core and integral purpose of freedom of association, there is something different about the collective agreements that result from the process of collective bargaining, as compared to other contracts that result from ordinary, unprotected negotiating activity.[44]

2) Differing Approaches of the Majority and Justice Rothstein to the Collective Dimension of Freedom of Association

As discussed previously in Section 1, in some passages in his reasons, Rothstein J adopts a very narrow formative activity theory of freedom of association, which in turn forms the basis for his attempt to characterize constitutional recognition of collective bargaining as falling outside of the activities protected by section 2(d). However, if this restrictive formative activities theory of freedom of association is rejected (as it has been by the Supreme Court of Canada itself since at least the *PIPSC* decision[45]), then his criticism loses its foundation.

---

43 *Fraser*, above note 1 at paras 216–18 of Rothstein J's reasons.

44 As discussed more fully in Section 5, collective agreements should be seen as having been negotiated through a unique process of constitutionally-protected associational activity—collective bargaining—and as resulting from and as reflecting the unique function served by collective bargaining in securing and promoting the core purpose of s 2(d), as well as fundamental *Charter* values. As a result, while interference with ordinary contracts does not infringe s 2(d) of the Charter, interference with collective agreements must be seen as doing so because of their unique attributes. Indeed, if collective agreements were to be treated for constitutional purposes like any other contract, the very purpose of constitutional protection for collective bargaining would be eviscerated.

45 Above note 31.

Indeed, Rothstein J himself recognizes in his reasons in *Fraser* that the formative activity theory of freedom of association is insufficient, and he instead adopts an alternative or additional theory of freedom of association. Under this approach, he accepts that, at the very least, *Dunmore* stands for the proposition that protected associational activities extend to those activities engaged in by individuals acting "side by side" together, but doing exactly and only that which "each may do apart."[46] Resorting to a choir analogy as illustrating the outer boundaries of freedom of association, he accepts the section 2(d) protection to the right of individuals to sing together in a choir, and contends that the breakthrough in *Dunmore* was to recognize that while a choir may produce qualitatively different musical effects than would or can an individual singing alone, section 2(d) nonetheless protects singing together in concert.

While Rothstein J accepts this "equal protection" approach to freedom of association as flowing from *Dunmore*, he claims that *Health Services* wrongly went beyond *Dunmore* when it reinterpreted section 2(d) "as giving rise to collective rights with no individual rights foundation," an interpretation "not justified by the purpose of the *Charter* guarantee," which he asserts is "to prevent the government from interfering with associations by treating groups differently than it treats individuals."[47]

However, despite Rothstein J's claim that his critique of both the *Fraser* majority and the *Health Services* decision is faithful to the *Dunmore* principles, his "equal protection" conception of freedom of association—requiring that a protected associational activity be rooted in and constrained by the type of activity which individuals can engage in when acting alone—was squarely rejected by Bastarache J in *Dunmore*. Justice Rothstein's critique misses the fundamental holding of *Dunmore* that freedom of association must extend to associational activities which, "for one reason or another, [cannot] be understood as the lawful activities of individuals . . . . [S]uch activities may be collective in nature, in that they cannot be performed by individuals acting alone." This is because, according to Bastarache J:

> [16] . . . the collective is "qualitatively" distinct from the individual: *individuals associate not simply because there is strength in numbers, but because communities can embody objectives that individuals cannot.* For example, a "majority view" cannot be expressed by a lone individual, but a group of individuals can form a constituency and distill their views

46 *Fraser*, above note 1. See, for example, paras 184–86 of Rothstein J's reasons.

47 *Ibid* at para 178.

> into a single platform. Indeed, this is the essential purpose of joining a political party, participating in a class action or certifying a trade union. *To limit s. 2(d) to activities that are performable by individuals would, in my view, render futile these fundamental initiatives* . . . . The collective dimension of s. 2(*d*) is also consistent with developments in international human rights law . . .
>
> [17] As I see it, the very notion of "association" recognizes the qualitative differences between individuals and collectivities . . . . [t]he law must recognize that certain union activities -- making collective representations to an employer, adopting a majority political platform, federating with other unions—may be central to freedom of association *even though they are inconceivable on the individual level.* This is not to say that all such activities are protected by s. 2(*d*), nor that all collectivities are worthy of constitutional protection . . . . *It is to say, simply, that certain collective activities must be recognized if the freedom to form and maintain an association is to have any meaning.* As one author puts it, the *per se* exclusion of collective action reduces employee collectives to mere "aggregate[s] of economically self-interested individuals" rather than "co-operative undertakings where individual flourishing can be encouraged through membership in and co-operation with the community of fellow workers" . . . . This would surely undermine the purpose of s. 2(*d*), which is to allow the achievement of individual potential through interpersonal relationships and collective action . . .[48]

Thus, *Dunmore* explicitly recognized, as a core purpose of freedom of association, not only the protection of individuals and the equal protection of groups and individuals, but also the protection of individuals acting together through groups that undertake activities and pursue objectives that are uniquely collective in nature or which have an inherently collective component.

While Rothstein J criticizes the result in *Health Services*, based on his view that it wrongly extends protection to certain collective activities that are entirely unconnected with individual rights (and thereby accords greater rights to the group than to the individual), he fails to come to grips with *Dunmore's* central understanding that certain collective or group activities may well have no individual counterpart, but nonetheless must be constitutionally protected if

48 *Fraser*, above note 1 [emphasis added].

reedom of association is to fulfill the purpose of allowing individuals to form and act through associations.[49]

Indeed, Rothstein J recognizes that some *Charter* rights and freedoms, such as minority language and aboriginal protections, have an inherently collective dimension and are predicated upon the existence of a group. However, he insists that because "everyone" has freedom of association, this somehow makes it solely an individual right.[50] Apart from the fact that both minority language rights[51] and aboriginal and treaty rights[52] also are granted to individuals, his reasons ignore the fact that the right that "everyone" has is freedom of "association," and it is no less the case for section 2(d) than for section 23 or section 35 that by singling out protection for "association," section 2(d) necessarily, and by definition, is predicated on the existence of a group, and the exercise by that group (of individuals and through individuals acting together) of collective activities. On this basis, he can be criticized for insisting on maintaining a false dichotomy between the individual and the collective; even accepting that freedom of association inheres in and is for the benefit of the individual, this premise does not detract from the conclusion that, in some circumstances, it can only be exercised by or through a group, or that the associational activity may be distinct from the actions of the individuals who make up the group—whether it be a meeting,

49 In his reasons, Rothstein J criticizes (in para 181) the majority's reliance on Dickson CJ's view in the *Alberta Reference* that freedom of association has this "collective dimension," on the basis that the chief justice's view was not adopted by the majority in the *Alberta Reference*. However, Rothstein J ignores the fact that in *Dunmore*, Bastarache J expressly relied upon and adopted Dickson CJ's emphasis on the need for s 2(d) to extend to "occasions when no analogy involving individuals can be found for associational activity, or when a comparison between groups and individuals fails to capture the essence of a possible violation of associational rights." Indeed, immediately after doing so, Bastarache J emphasized that "[t]his passage [from Chief Justice Dickson], *which was not explicitly rejected by the majority in the Alberta Reference or in PIPSC*, recognizes that the collective is 'qualitatively' distinct from the individual: individuals associate not simply because there is strength in numbers, but because communities can embody objectives that individuals cannot": *Dunmore*, above note 11 at para 16 [emphasis added].

50 *Fraser*, above note 1 at para 180 of Rothstein J's reasons.

51 The various s 23 minority language rights are each given to "citizens of Canada."

52 Section 35(4) provides that "(4) Notwithstanding any other provision of this Act, the aboriginal and treaty rights referred to in subsection (1) are guaranteed equally to male and female persons."

a book club, a political platform, or workers' collective bargaining demands and actions.[53]

To be fair, to some extent, Rothstein J's real objection to the approach in *Heath Services* and to the majority's reasons in *Fraser* is to their view that section 2(d) imposes a duty to bargain when it comes to a group of employees, when there is no such duty to bargain when it comes to an individual. From his perspective, both *Health Services* and the *Fraser* majority's approach wrongly results in the group receiving a larger measure of constitutional protection than would individuals if acting on their own.

However, as the *Fraser* majority repeatedly emphasizes, the duty to bargain, which it regards as being included in the protection of collective bargaining under section 2(d), is very much a "derivative" right, that is, a right that, in its view, is necessary to ensure that the protection of collective bargaining is not reduced to a meaningless or vacuous exercise.[54] As discussed below, the majority itself can be criticized for its failure to recognize that the duty to bargain alone is not sufficient to ensure protection for meaningful collective bargaining. However, once it is recognized that the *Fraser* majority extends protection to the duty to bargain only as a derivative right necessary to ensure that the process of collective bargaining protected by section 2(d) is not rendered meaningless, Rothstein J's attack on the majority for defining the content of section 2(d) in a manner which accords greater protection to groups than to individuals would seem misplaced. The duty to bargain is not, on this view, an associational activity that *per se* is protected by section 2(d); rather, the protected associational activity is the workers joining together and seeking to bargain their terms and conditions of employment, with any good faith bargaining duty protected only in a derivative sense as necessary to ensure that the protected associational activity is not rendered illusory or meaningless.

Moreover, in the specific context of collective bargaining, to the extent that collective bargaining is recognized not merely as an extension of individual activity, but as a uniquely or inherently collective activity, criticizing the majority for treating it differently than individual bargaining by deriving a duty to bargain would seem to be

53 This observation is consistent with the Court's recognition in *Lavigne v Ontario Public Service Employees Union*, [1991] 2 SCR 211, that, although individual employees contribute dues to union, the dues once contributed belong to the union and not to the individual employees [*Lavigne*].

54 *Fraser*, above note 1 at paras 46, 54, 66, and 99 of the majority's reasons.

irrelevant.[55] On the broader *Dunmore* conception of freedom of association, protected associational activity need not have an exact individual counterpart. In this sense, Rothstein J's criticism of a derived duty to bargain simply appears to be another way of expressing his disagreement with the *Dunmore* notion that uniquely collective activities may receive section 2(d) protection.

Furthermore, the notion that there is no individual analogue to collective bargaining (in the sense it is understood by the majority, that is, as including a derivative duty to bargain in good faith) is consistent with the approach taken under our Canadian law of labour relations. Both before and outside of the *Charter*, our courts have consistently recognized that collective bargaining cannot be viewed as simply being the collective counterpart to individual bargaining.[56] In any event, even if collective bargaining was considered to be the collective counterpart to individual bargaining, implying or imposing good faith obligations in the context of individual employment is not foreign to Canadian employment law.[57]

---

55 This is, of course, separate from the question of whether, if collective bargaining has no individual counterpart, a duty to bargain should be derived. The majority's view that it must be derived because it is necessary to make bargaining meaningful is one approach. Another approach, at least in the context of agricultural workers, is to recognize that excluding agricultural workers from the generally applicable normative scheme, which includes the duty to bargain in good faith, is intended to have (and has) the practical real world effect of impairing their ability to bargain meaningfully. On this view, it is not that section 2(d) itself includes imposition of a duty to bargain which renders the exclusion of agricultural workers constitutionally infirm, but rather that the legislative exclusion (that is, from the duty to bargain and other critical normative provision of the *LRA*) results in purpose or effect in interference with the freedom to collectively bargain, since it is not practically possible for agricultural workers to engage in meaningful collective bargaining outside of the dominant and comprehensive legislative model.

56 Indeed, in *Dunmore*, the very decision Rothstein J purports to rely on in contesting the view of s 2(d) protection for collective bargaining taken in *Health Services* and by the *Fraser* majority, Bastarache J emphasized the extent to which the attempt to characterize collective bargaining as simply an extension of individual is "contrived," and inconsistent with the legal characterization of collective bargaining by Canadian courts and commentators. Above note 11 at para 16.

57 While the courts may have been reluctant to impose any duty of good faith in the initial negotiation of the employment contract, where there is a subsisting individual employment relationship, the courts have been willing to impose good faith obligations on employers in dealing with employees in some contexts. See, for example, *Greenberg v Meffert*, 1985 CanLII 158 (ON CA); *Wallace v United Grain Growers Ltd*, [1997] 3 SCR 701; *Honda Canada Inc v Keays*, [2008] 2 SCR 362; and *Wronko v Western Inventory Service Ltd*, 2008 ONCA 327.

Thus, at the end of the day, Rothstein J's assertion—that in extending protection to collective bargaining, *Health Services* went beyond the principles established in *Dunmore*—cannot be reconciled with the actual holding and reasons in *Dunmore* concerning the collective dimension of freedom of association. Despite his use of the choir analogy, Rothstein J's reasons are out of tune with the actual chord struck in *Dunmore.*

3) Implications of Justice Rothstein's Equal Protection Approach to Section 2(d) for Protection for Collective Bargaining and Strike Activity

a) Collective Bargaining

As discussed in the preceding section, despite the fact that Rothstein J's view of the extent to which section 2(d) offers protection to collective associational activities is narrower than the approach taken in *Dunmore,* he nonetheless accepts that section 2(d) protects activities performed collectively that are lawful individually. He also accepts that this protection includes circumstances where the group activity may produce qualitatively different results as a result of being carried out collectively.

As we discuss in Section 5, we do not believe that rooting freedom of association primarily in what is essentially a libertarian "equal protection" approach[58] (under which section 2(d) extends constitutional protection only to that collective activity which is not legally prohibited for the individual) gives sufficient scope to the underlying history, philosophy, and purpose of freedom of association. However, in this section, we discuss the extent to which, even under Rothstein J's "equal protection" approach to freedom of association, he accepts that collective bargaining (without a corresponding employer duty to bargain in good faith) falls within the scope of protected associational activity under section 2(d). We also discuss the extent to which his doctrinal approach to section 2(d) also provides support to extension of constitutional protection to the right to strike.[59]

---

58 As Rothstein J puts, "s. 2(d) is intended to protect a sphere of individual autonomy or liberty." See above note 1 at para 202.

59 Justice Rothstein's doctrinal view of freedom of association has also been advanced by Brian Langille. However, based on this approach, Langille argues that since individuals are generally not prohibited from bargaining with their employers or from withdrawing their services in order to secure improved terms of employment, it follows that freedom of association must protect the ability of workers to collect-

Indeed, when it comes to collective bargaining, Rothstein J himself recognizes precisely this to be the case when he asserts that section 2(d) protects "the freedom to engage in a coordinated attempt to negotiate with one's employer,"[60] and that section 2(d) was "intended to secure the individual's freedom to coordinate his or her actions with others and enjoy the benefits that flow naturally from that coordination."[61] As he also emphasizes:

> In my view, s. 2(*d*) protects the liberty of individuals to associate and engage in associational activities. Therefore, s. 2(*d*) protects the freedom of workers to form self-directed employee associations in an attempt to improve wages and working conditions. What s. 2(*d*) does not do, however, is impose duties on others, such as the duty to bargain in good faith on employers.[62]
>
> As I have explained through these reasons, I do not accept that s. 2(*d*) protects a right to collective bargaining. I am, however, of the view that s. 2(*d*) does protect a voluntary association of workers who wish to use their associational freedoms to come together and attempt to improve their wages and working conditions.[63]
>
> Under Canadian law, an individual is generally free to bargain with an employer over terms of employment. Because such individual bargaining is generally lawful, it necessarily follows that the decision of individuals to band together to approach their employer must necessarily be protected. The free decisions of individuals to do in association what they can lawfully do alone lies at the very heart of s. 2(*d*) protection, and it therefore follows that *s. 2(d) must protect the decision of individuals to come together, to form a bargaining position and to present a common and united front to an employer.*[64]

Admittedly, this is a conception of collective bargaining that does not, on Rothstein J's terms, include a corresponding duty on employers to collectively bargain in good faith. But it is nonetheless a conception of section 2(d) that affords protection to not only the right to form and join associations, but also, insofar as workers

---

ively bargain with their employer, and to collectively withdraw their services. For his most recent exposition of this view, see Langille, above note 10.

60 *Fraser*, above note 1 at para 144.

61 *Ibid* at para 292.

62 *Ibid* at para 125.

63 *Ibid* at para 270.

64 *Ibid* at para 271 [emphasis added].

are concerned, the right to bargain in association for the purpose of seeking to protect and improve their conditions of employment. Conceived in the sense that Rothstein J accepts, protection for collective bargaining would at the very least provide some measure of constitutional protection against legislative or governmental actions that prevent workers capacity to "come together and attempt to improve their wages and working conditions," that is, to collectively bargain. At the very least, it should require that workers not be precluded, before or after the fact, from collectively negotiating conditions of employment as a result of legislative prohibition or interference.

Moreover, as we have previously suggested, it is important to recognize the extent to which much of Rothstein J's attack on *Health Services* is not a challenge to the principle that workers have a section 2(d) right to collectively bargain (which, it turns out, he accepts), but rather a challenge to the majority's view that, in addition, section 2(d) can include a derivative positive duty to bargain in good faith, including an obligation on legislatures to enact statutory provisions providing for such a duty (which he does not accept). This distinction is illustrated by his assertion that "collective bargaining" is not protected by section 2(d) because it is "not emergent from an activity that an individual alone could do." However, in advancing this claim, he is explicit in only referring to collective bargaining in the sense of its including "a duty on employers to meet with employees and make a 'reasonable effort to arrive at an acceptable contract,'" that is, as including a duty on an employer to bargain in good faith.[65]

This very same focus on the duty to bargain underlies Rothstein J's critique of the reliance by the Court in *Health Services* on Canadian labour history, on international law, and on *Charter* values for the claim that section 2(d)'s protection for collective bargaining includes a derivative duty to bargain in good faith (a view defended and upheld by the majority in *Fraser*[66]). In all of these areas, his objection is entirely aimed at the assertion that the duty to bargain forms part of section 2(d)'s protection for collective bargaining, but not at the conclusion that collective bargaining should receive no protection at all that section.

Thus, when it comes to Canadian labour history,[67] Rothstein J accepts that Canadian labour history confirms "a long-standing practice of Canadian workers associating for the purpose of bargaining

65 *Ibid* at para 197; see also paras 121–24, 179, 187–90, and 199.

66 *Ibid.* See in particular the reasons of the majority at paras 82–85 and 89–96.

67 *Ibid.* Discussed by Rothstein J in paras 234–46 of his reasons.

collectively with their employers" and that "at least since the Trade Unions Act of 1872 workers enjoyed a legal freedom to associate for the purpose of bargaining collectively with their employers without being prosecuted or sued for simply doing so." Indeed, he goes so far to accept the proposition that collective bargaining (without a corresponding employer duty to bargain) is "the most significant collective activity through which freedom of association is expressed in the labour context." He simply distinguishes between collective bargaining understood as "self-directed activities engaged in by workers without the benefit of statutory enhancements or protection, i.e. workers organizing in order to attempt collective engagement with their employer in the hopes of obtaining better pay and working conditions," and collective bargaining "used as shorthand for a particular kind of statutorily enabled activity," and in particular "a specific set of legislatively imposed obligations, including the requirement of a duty to bargain in good faith."

When it comes to international law,[68] Rothstein J accepts the view that "a freedom of association which includes voluntary collective bargaining . . . [is] more consistent with international norms." The thrust of his critique is that neither Convention No. 87, which Canada has ratified, nor Convention No. 98, which Canada has not ratified, includes a duty to bargain in good faith as part of the guarantee of freedom of association or of collective bargaining. On the

---

68 *Ibid.* Discussed by Rothstein J at paras 247–50 of his reasons. Notably, he fails to consider the ILO's 1998 *Declaration on Fundamental Principles and Rights at Work*, which commits Canada to respect the fundamental right of collective bargaining, including both Convention No 87 and Convention No 98, and which explicitly recognizes in s 2 that "even if they have not ratified the Conventions in question," all members "have an obligation arising from the very fact of membership in the organization, to respect, to promote and to realize, in good faith and in accordance with the Constitution, the principles concerning the fundamental rights which are the subject of those Conventions [including] freedom of association and the effective recognition of the right to collective bargaining . . . ." His reasons also ignore the principle that international human rights norms should inform the interpretation of the scope of fundamental freedoms (regardless of whether Canada has ratified any particular instrument): see, for example, the discussion in *Dunmore* at para 27 ("Although provincial jurisdiction has prevented Canada from ratifying Convention No. 11, together these conventions provide a normative foundation for prohibiting any form of discrimination in the protection of trade union freedoms"), and the fact that, as recognized in *Health Services* (above note 2 at paras 71–74), Canada has ratified two other International Covenants (the ICESCR and the ICCPR), both of which extend protection to collective bargaining, regardless of the scope of Convention No 87. For a critique of Rothstein J's use of international law see Ewing and Hendy in this volume.

basis of this critique, he concludes only that international law does not support the claim in *Health Services* "that Canada's obligations and . . . international norms imply compulsory collective bargaining [that is, a duty to bargain]".

Similarly, nowhere in his discussion of *Charter* values does Rothstein J dispute that collective bargaining without an attached employer duty to bargain is inconsistent with or is not supported by underlying *Charter* values; what he directs his entire argument to is "a right which 'requires both employer and employees to meet and bargain in good faith.'"[69]

What emerges from this review of his critique of the *Health* Services decision, and of the majority's reinforcement of *Health Services* in *Fraser*, is that Rothstein J is not asserting that section 2(d) protection for a process of collective bargaining is inconsistent with Canadian labour history, or international law, or *Charter* values, or that section 2(d) does not provide any protection for collective bargaining. To the contrary, the essence of his position is that collective bargaining protection is supported by these sources, but collective bargaining understood as the freedom of workers to seek to negotiate improvements to their terms and conditions of employment, and not collective bargaining understood as including a reciprocal obligation on employers to bargain in good faith.

This is not to suggest that his analysis appropriately recognizes the extent to which certain rights and obligations under the Wagner Act statutory model can also be the statutory manifestation of underlying section 2(d)'s fundamental freedoms. It is not so easy or appropriate to altogether disentangle the section's protected pre-statutory exercise of the freedom to collectively bargain from its incorporation and regulation under the Wagner Act model (including the duty to bargain), which has been dominant for the last seventy years. Moreover, there is a strong case to be made that it simply ignores labour relations history and reality to treat the "pre-statutory" freedom to collectively bargain as having disappeared into the ether simply because the freedom has been incorporated into, and protected under, a statutory labour relations Wagner model. Rather, the Wagner Act model itself can readily be viewed as a trade-off, under which the constitutionally protected pre-statutory freedoms to bargain and strike (for recognition, for bargaining, and for enforcing collective agreements) were restricted in return for statutory protections. The key elements of this model are majoritarian certifica-

69 *Ibid* at paras 251–55 of Rothstein J's reasons.

tion process based on exclusive bargaining agency, a duty to bargain collective agreements coupled with a right to strike (and lock-out) with tightly circumscribed restrictions (only at the expiry of the collective agreement and then only after a mandatory conciliation process and cooling-off period) for negotiating collective agreements, and a grievance arbitration process for enforcing collective agreements coupled with a duty of fair representation.

Understood in this context, the statutory elements must at least be, to some extent, recognized as the legislative reflection, embodiment, and reinterpretation of the pre-statutory constitutional freedoms; in effect, the fundamental freedom has been transferred and integrated into the Wagner Act model. Indeed, this was the very understanding of the Court in *Health Services*, which recognized the extent to which labour relations statutes in Canada must be viewed as protecting, incorporating, and instantiating the pre-statutory, constitutionally-protected freedom to engage in collective bargaining. As the majority stated:

> [T]he fundamental importance of collective bargaining to labour relations was the very reason for its incorporation into statute . . . . The statutes . . . did not create the right to bargain collectively. Rather, they afforded it protection. There is nothing in the statutory entrenchment of collective bargaining that detracts from its fundamental nature . . .[70]

Moreover, viewed from this perspective, exclusion from or removal of one or more of the critical protections under the Wagner model (including, but not restricted to, the duty to bargain) that instantiates these pre-statutory freedoms (to collectively bargain, and indeed, to strike) may well amount to an unjustified interference with section 2(d) freedoms. It is, at the very least, necessary to take into account the extent to which the seventy years of bargaining under the Wagner Act model has displaced, at the coal face of labour relations, the notional exercise of "pre-statutory collective bargaining," to the point where the fundamental freedoms are now exercised predominantly, if not exclusively, through the statutory vehicle. This is not to claim the Wagner Act model is "constitutional-

---

70 *Health Services*, above note 2 at para 25. See also *Dunmore*, above note 11 at paras 24 and 36, and Langille, "The Freedom of Association Mess" (2009) 54 McGill LJ 177 at 181 and at 211–12 (emphasizing the extent to which "Canadian labour relations statutes are best conceived as our domestic version of a detailed and legally enforceable instantiation of the fundamental freedom of association" and to which the Wagner model is "our way of actually making that freedom available to Canadian workers").

ized" or that there is any permanent or freestanding constitutional entitlement to all of its elements. Rather, it is to suggest that for so long as the Wagner model's protections and restrictions remain in place, the courts must be sensitive to the possibility that removal of or exclusion from one or more key protective elements of the model may have the effect of interfering with the ability of workers to exercise the fundamental freedoms upon which the model is premised, and that it is designed to reflect and protect. We should at least be skeptical of the automatic dismissal of any such claims on the basis that they merely involve an attempt to vindicate statutory rights but not constitutional freedoms.

In addition to advancing an alternative view of section 2(d)'s protection for collective bargaining—one which does not include a corollary duty to bargain —Rothstein J is also at pains in his reasons to criticize the holding in *Health Services* that overriding freely negotiated collective agreement provisions, and prohibiting unions and employers from agreeing in future on certain terms and conditions of employment, can interfere with section 2(d). However, it is difficult to see how these measures would not interfere with freedom of association, even on his more limited conception of section 2(d)'s protection for collective bargaining.

Indeed, Deschamps J recognizes, in her concurring reasons, that even on a conception of section 2(d)'s protection free of any bargaining duty (a conception which she shares with Rothstein J), overriding collective agreements and preventing bargaining over future terms can amount to an infringement of section 2(d). As she points out, the result in *Health* Services did not depend on a *Charter*-based duty to bargain, or on importing "the good faith element that is one of the hallmarks of the Wagner model and that inevitably entails a number of statutory components."[71] Rather:

> [305] All that was required by the questions raised in *Health Services* was a finding that since the employees had a constitutional right to engage in associational activities and act in common to reach common goals, the legislature could not interfere with their right (i) by prohibiting them from addressing certain issues in the collective bargaining process; and (ii) by cancelling negotiated provisions in the agreements and thereby rendering the process meaningless. By enacting legislation that had prohibited the negotiation of certain issues in the course of *Charter*-protected associational activities and rendering useless the efforts expended to achieve a negotiated agreement on certain subjects,

71 *Fraser*, above note 1 at para 304.

> the legislature had interfered with their right. This conclusion did not depend on the employer's being under a duty to bargain in good faith.[72]

At the very least, it would seem that, if constitutional protection for Rothstein J's more limited conception of collective bargaining is to be respected, even it requires at the very least the possibility that a union and employer will be able to agree to include certain negotiated terms and conditions of employment in a collective agreement. Where, as in *Health Services*, legislation prohibits even the possibility of entering into a collective agreement over such terms, there is no point in employees forming a bargaining position and presenting a common front. There is no point in coming together, forming a common bargaining position, and presenting that to the employer if legislation can extinguish any resulting bargain, or prevent any future bargain from being made.[73] Indeed, in his discussion of international law, Rothstein J emphasizes the extent to which international law on freedom of association protects "voluntary" negotiation of collective agreements, and "excludes recourse to measures of compulsion."[74] Overriding collective agreement provisions, or precluding future bargaining, is hardly consistent with an absence of governmental or legislative compulsion in the collective bargaining process.

Justice Rothstein accepts "that s. 2(d) was intended to secure the individual's freedom to coordinate his or her actions with others and enjoy the benefits that flow naturally from that coordination."[75] However, he fails to recognize that what the BC legislature did in

---

72 To be clear, in applying her conception of s 2(d)'s protection for collective bargaining, Deschamps J holds that the *AEPA* does not infringe s 2(d) on the basis of her view that, despite the expanded definition of freedom of association in *Health Services* to include collective bargaining, the *AEPA* did not preclude agricultural employees from acting "in common to reach shared goals relating to workplace issues and terms of employment," and that neither the duty to bargain, nor presumably any other components of the Wagner model, are a "constitutional requirement": *ibid* at paras 306–8. The difficulties with Deshamps J's analysis of the *AEPA* are discussed elsewhere in this paper, including Part A above and Section 4 below.

73 Moreover, under the "equal protection" conception of freedom of association, at the very least, restrictions on *collective* bargaining and *collective* agreements in the absence of restrictions on *individual* bargaining and *individual* agreements must be seen to infringe s 2(d). To the extent that legislation targets concerted associational activity by singling out *collective* bargaining and *collective* agreements for restriction and prohibition, without imposing the same restrictions and prohibitions on *individual* bargaining and *individual* agreements, the legislation has unconstitutionally targeted associational conduct because of its concerted or associational nature.

74 *Fraser*, above note 1 at paras 249–50.

75 *Ibid* at para 144.

Health Services substantially interfered with the ability of workers to "coordinate" their actions and "enjoy the benefits that flow naturally from that coordination"; indeed, it made it impossible and fruitless for them to do so. Perhaps he is so focused on challenging the majority's inclusion of the duty to bargain that he stops short of considering the extent to which, even without a derivative duty to bargain, overriding collective agreements and prohibiting future agreements fails to respect the very process of collective bargaining that he accepts is protected by the freedom of association guarantee.

b) The Right to Strike

Paradoxically, Rothstein J's "equal protection" theory of freedom of association—the view that section 2(d) protects collective activity that is lawfully performed by individuals (regardless of whether there are qualitative differences in the effects of the activity when performed collectively)—also supports the conclusion that section 2(d) can and does extend protection to the right to strike. Given that individuals have the lawful right to quit or withdraw their labour, and if, as he accepts, "the free decisions of individuals to do in association what they can lawfully do alone" are constitutionally protected, this position must mean that individuals also have the right to collectively withdraw their services.[76]

In the *Alberta Reference*, Dickson CJ held that while the right to strike is protected by section 2(d), collective strike activity does not have an individual analogue, because strike (or indeed, bargaining) activity is qualitatively different when carried out collectively.[77] However, as noted in the preceding section, Rothstein J accepts that even where there is a qualitative difference between the effect of individual and collective activity, this distinction cannot disqualify the collective activity from section 2(d) protection. Thus, even if there is a qualitative difference in kind or quality between individual and collective withdrawal of labour, the right to strike would still be a constitutionally protected associational activity (presumably, so long as no law is passed imposing forced labour on individual employees).

Indeed, as he observes, "while greater economic clout or political power may flow from the very act of association in a way that makes the associational activity 'qualitatively' different from the individual activity, the legal rights and freedoms granted to individuals acting in association under s. 2(d) are nonetheless limited to the same rights

76 See text at above note 46.

77 *Alberta Reference*, above note 13 at 367.

and freedoms afforded to individuals acting alone."[78] Moreover, his observation that "the right to make representations in association . . . is meaningful because of the increased persuasive weight carried by collective representations rather than individual representations,"[79] would appear to be equally apposite to the increased persuasive weight of collective as opposed to individual withdrawal of labour.

Thus, while there are additional strong doctrinal and practical reasons for concluding that the right to strike is included in freedom of association, including the extent to which it is recognized as a core component of freedom of association at international law as well as being essential to making collective bargaining meaningful, Rothstein J's own doctrinal approach provides independent and additional support for the proposition that section 2(d) protection extends to the right to strike.

4) Differing Approaches in *Fraser* to Assessing Activities/ Processes Essential for Meaningful Section 2(d) protection

In this section, we turn our focus from an assessment of Rothstein J's reasons to a discussion of the difference between, (1) the majority's reasons, (2) those of the Court of Appeal, and (3) both Abella and Rothstein JJ's reasons, in terms of how to approach the question of which activities or processes are essential to ensure meaningful section 2(d) protection.

As discussed above, while Rothstein J contests the majority's view that section 2(d) includes a derivative duty on employers to bargain in good faith, he agrees with both the Court of Appeal and Abella J that if, contrary to his view, section 2(d) were to include a derivative duty to bargain, that section must also require a dispute resolution mechanism. In this respect, Rothstein J observes:

> [268] . . . for a duty to bargain in good faith not to be an illusory benefit, there must be both a way of dealing with bargaining impasses as well as an effective remedy for persistent breaches of a duty to bargain in good faith. The first requires that there be some default mechanism for resolving the dispute in case an impasse is reached—such as striking or binding arbitration—while the second may require, in extreme circumstances, the imposition by an arbitrator of particular terms of a collective agreement: W. B. Rayner, Canadian Collective Bargaining Law

---

78 *Fraser*, above note 1 at para 172.

79 *Ibid* at para 192.

> (2nd ed. 2007), at pp. 349-55. Each of these goes well beyond a mere process and results in the protection of a particular substantive outcome.[80]

For its part, the *Fraser* majority took a different approach, concluding that a process of good faith bargaining for agricultural workers is, or may be, sufficient to make the process of collective bargaining meaningful.

However, as Rothstein J correctly points out, the majority never explains why it draws the line at the duty to bargain, or views the duty to bargain as the key to making collective bargaining meaningful for agricultural workers in particular or for workers in general. After referring to Winkler CJ's view that without dispute resolution (or for that matter exclusivity), meaningful collective bargaining for agricultural workers would be jeopardized, Rothstein J states:

> Winkler C.J.O.'s concerns present a significant problem that the Chief Justice and LeBel J. do not address in their reasons. They limit constitutionalization to collective bargaining imposing a duty on employers to bargain in good faith. The reasons of the Chief Justice and LeBel J. provide no explanation for why Winkler C.J.O. is wrong. As the majority in *Doucet-Boudreau* said in discussing minority language educational rights: "A purposive approach to remedies in a *Charter* context gives modern vitality to the ancient maxim *ubi jus, ibi remedium*: where there is a right, there must be a remedy" (para. 25). I cannot agree that a right can be workable without the imposition of an appropriate remedy.[81]

Certainly, from a practical and historical perspective, the duty to bargain has never been regarded as the exclusive or most important mechanism for ensuring meaningful collective bargaining. Both prior to the introduction of the Wagner model in Canada, and subsequent to its widespread implementation, the right to strike has been widely regarded as the critical mechanism which makes collective bargaining meaningful.

Over time, under the Wagner model, the right to strike has been legislatively restricted so that it can only take place at certain prescribed times and under certain prescribed conditions. At the same time, as noted earlier, these restrictions have in turn, at least under the industrial pluralist model, been regarded as trade-offs for various other features of the Wagner Act model. However, to imply, as does the *Fraser* majority, that the duty to bargain is somehow the singular or most important vehicle for making collective bargaining

80 *Ibid* at para 268.

81 *Ibid* at para 261.

meaningful is to ignore labour history and practical labour relations reality.[82]

What explains the majority's narrow approach? One possibility is that it stems from a perceived tension within *Health Services* itself. On the one hand, *Health Services* accepts and articulates the principle that section 2(d) protects those processes and activities necessary to make collective bargaining meaningful (including as reflected in international law human rights protection). On the other hand, *Health Services* accepts and articulates the principle that the Wagner model itself should not be constitutionally protected or "constitutionalized." In perceiving a conflict between these two principles, the majority decided to steer clear of the charge of constitutionalizing the Wagner model, restricting protection to the duty to bargain (itself one component of the Wagner model), while dismissing the need for affirmative legislative protection of other elements (such as interest arbitration where the right to strike is restricted), on the basis that it was, at the very least, premature to conclude such elements were necessary to make collective bargaining meaningful.

By contrast, the dissenting reasons of Abella J and of the Court of Appeal did not perceive the same conflict between ensuring meaningful protection of section 2(d)'s bargaining activity or processes for agricultural workers, and avoided permanently constitutionalizing elements of the Wagner model. This is because they more appropriately focused on the real life, contextual, and practical impact of excluding agricultural workers from core features of the Wagner model, which agricultural workers argued deprived them of their section 2(d) right to meaningful collective bargaining. In holding that excluding agricultural workers from the exclusivity and dispute resolution provisions of the normative labour relations scheme applicable to virtually all other Canadian workers, neither the Court of Appeal nor Abella J were suggesting that Wagner Act components—whether exclusivity, the duty to bargain, or a particular statutory method of dispute resolution—were to be constitutionalized for all time. Rather, they recognized that as long as the Wagner Act model was the normative, and indeed, exclusive legislative vehicle for instantiating and giving effect to collective bargaining, exclusion from the rights and protections offered by that collective bargaining regime, as a practical matter, nullified the capacity of agricultural workers to collectively bargain in any meaningful sense.

---

82 See, for example, Judy Fudge & Eric Tucker, "The Freedom to Strike in Canada: A Brief Legal History" (2010) 15:2 CLELJ 333.

This difference in turn appears to be rooted not only in competing assessments on a pragmatic level as to what is required to make collective bargaining meaningful, but also a methodological divide. The Court of Appeal and Abella J adopted a contextual analysis to assess the scope of activities or processes that may be required in order to give meaningful protection to freedom of association. By contrast, the majority can be criticized for employing a more abstract, formal, and detached approach, isolating the duty to bargain as a definitional component of freedom of association without adequately recognizing and assessing the actual impact on meaningful collective bargaining of excluding agricultural workers from the normative legislative regime.[83]

5) Differing Conceptions of the Purpose of the Freedom of Association Guarantee

The differences between the *Fraser* majority and Rothstein J—including which activities are protected as associational freedoms or are necessary to make the exercise of freedom of association meaningful, and the extent to which freedom of association is an individual or collective right—flow from starkly different conceptions of the underlying purposes served by freedom of association.

Justice Rothstein views the underlying purpose of section 2(d)—consistent with his restricting section 2(d) to the equal protection of individuals and associations—as ensuring a content-neutral approach to the legislative or governmental treatment between permitted individual and associational activity, and as between associations. The purpose of section 2(d), in this conception, is to ensure not only that individuals can collectively carry out those activities that are lawfully permitted to individuals, but also that all associations are treated the same by the state, without any assessment made of their role or relative importance to the underlying purpose or history of freedom of association, or to *Charter* values.

Justice Rothstein professes to anchor the need for a "generic" or "content-neutral" approach to freedom of association in the linguistic,

---

83 To some extent, the majority's conclusion can be seen to stem from its assessment that there was insufficient evidence that exclusion from the normative regime adversely impacted the ability of agricultural workers to engage in meaningful collective bargaining. As persuasively documented in other chapters of this book, the majority's assessment of the evidence and of the reality of practical labour relations is difficult to support.

philosophic, and historical origins and context of the freedom, and its relationship to the character and larger objects of the *Charter* itself.

However, other than asserting this purpose, he does not engage in the very philosophical and historical analysis he espouses. Instead, without explanation, he devotes virtually all of his discussion to analogizing freedom of association to those principles the Court has found to be applicable to freedom of religion. On this basis, he simply extends to freedom of association the Court's conclusion that freedom of religion is intended to protect against the state privileging one religion over another, and assumes that the same or similar purpose underlies the freedom of association guarantee.

In support of his view that freedom of association must be content-neutral, Rothstein J cites Langille for the suggestion that it would be "chilling" to assess the functioning or importance of different associations and associational activities.[84] However, apart from simply being intuitively morally unsatisfactory, a "content-neutral" theory of freedom of association that would treat collective worker activity in the same manner as criminal conspiracies such as "Murder Incorporated" and terrorist or criminal organizations such as Al-Qaeda, or as gun clubs, golf clubs, or choirs, also ignores the actual underlying historical purposes and philosophic underpinnings of freedom of association and its relationship to the larger purposes and values of the *Charter* itself—the very historic and philosophical inquiry that Rothstein J acknowledges must animate the inquiry.

Thus, his approach fails to consider the extent to which there can be a meaningful and principled basis for protecting some associational activity, and for distinguishing between different forms and types of associational activity. In other words, while section 2(d) should not protect all associational activity, or all activity essential to any association's purpose, this is not to say that section 2(d) should not protect any associational activities at all. Rather, the determination of whether associational activity falls within the scope of the section 2(d) guarantee requires an inquiry into the activity's relationship to the language, to the historical and philosophical origins, and to the underlying purpose of freedom of association, and into the nature and importance of the association itself to the values and maintenance of a free and democratic society.

Had Rothstein J engaged in the very analysis he advocates, it would be difficult to avoid the actual historical record. This record includes the origins of freedom of association in international law,

---

84 *Fraser*, above note 1 at paras 211–15 of Rothstein J's reasons.

which specifically relate to promoting collective worker activities, in particular, collective bargaining and the right to strike. These associational protections are seen as a necessary bulwark and countervailing force against the significant power of both the state and employers.[85]

In this respect, both courts and commentators have consistently recognized a broader purpose than content-neutrality as underlying freedom of association, including overcoming inequality between individuals and the state and/or employers, and serving as a bulwark against totalitarianism.[86] For this reason, it would seem not only legitimate, but necessary, that when determining the scope and content of section 2(d), to look to the extent to which a particular association (and the particular associational activities engaged in by an

---

85 This history is reflected in the 1919 *Treaty of Versailles*, and in international human rights protections, including the *UN Charter* and various international covenants. Indeed, the relationship of the protection of freedom of association, as the embodiment of collective worker associational activities, to fundamental human rights, and the rationale for such protection, has been explained in the following terms by the former director-general of the ILO, CW Jenks:

> Freedom of association by highly organised and powerful economic interests calls for a counterpart in strong leadership in the public interest by the state. But *strong leadership by the state without the counterpart of such freedom of association can be dangerous for political as well as for economic and social freedom* . . . . Mass production involves large concentrations of economic power which have made the individual craftsman powerless. *In such a situation the alternatives are democratic labour organizations or a slave state. Freedom of association represents the point of contact between industrial relations and human rights and a condition without which no satisfactory solution of the other problems of industrial relations is possible in a free society. Without being in any sense an end in itself, freedom of association for trade union purposes is a major postulate of democratic government in an industrial society.*

From CW Jenks, *Human Rights and International Labour Standards* (New York: Stevens and Sons, 1960) 14 [emphasis added].

86 As Dickson CJ concluded in the *Alberta Reference*, above note 13 at 365–66:

> Freedom of association is most essential in those circumstances where the individual is liable to be prejudiced by the actions of some larger and more powerful entity, like the government or an employer. Association has always been the means through which political, cultural and racial minorities, religious groups and workers have sought to attain their purposes and fulfil their aspirations; it has enabled those who would otherwise be vulnerable and ineffective to meet on more equal terms the power and strength of those with whom their interests interact and, perhaps, conflict . . . .

This view is consistent with the view taken of the history and purpose of freedom of association taken by all members of the Court in *Lavigne*, above note 53; see Wilson J (speaking for three of the seven judges) at 253, La Forest J (speaking for three other judges) at 317, and (then) McLachlin J at 343.

association) further the purposes of freedom of association, and the broader purposes and values of a free and democratic society. Indeed, an inability and unwillingness to draw contextual and purposive distinctions between different associational activities and different associations only serves to undermine and trivialize the importance of section 2(d) protection. As the *Fraser* majority pointed out:

> One of the basic principles of *Charter* interpretation is that rights must be interpreted in a purposive way—having regard for the purposes, or goals, they serve. Thus, in the *Alberta Reference*, McIntyre J. described the core of s. 2(*d*) protection as being association "both to satisfy [a] desire for social intercourse and to *realize common purposes* (emphasis added)." *Dunmore* resolved the issue, not by saying that the s. 2(*d*) right must be content-neutral, but by asserting that it must be interpreted in conjunction with Canada's values and international human rights and labour law commitments. In our view, this is the preferable approach. A content-neutral right is too often a meaningless right.[87]

Moreover, protection of freedom of association is effectively understood by the international community[88] as code for protection of workers' collective action in general, and collective bargaining and the right to strike in particular. Understood in this context, Rothstein J's plea for content neutrality would seem to ignore the actual historical record and purpose which led to the implementation of post-World War I protection for freedom of association (including its origin, evolution, and current meaning at international law).

Ironically, Rothstein J also seems to be unaware of the extent to which the differential treatment of agricultural workers in the *Fraser* case itself runs afoul of his own approach to freedom of association, which requires the state to adopt a posture of content neutrality to all associations. It is hardly a posture of neutrality between different associations of workers for the state to single out associations of agricultural workers for prejudicial treatment and exclusion from

---

87 *Fraser*, above note 1 at para 75.

88 The evolution of the recognition of collective bargaining as a fundament human right and integral component of freedom of association at international law is reviewed in Roy J Adams, "Collective Bargaining: The Rodney Dangerfield of Human Rights" (1999) 50 Lab LJ 204; Adelle Blackett, "Mutual Promise: International Labour Law and *B.C. Health Services*" (2009) 48 Sup Ct L Rev (2d) 365 at 369–77; and Janice Bellace, "ILO Fundamental Rights at Work and Freedom of Association" (1999) 50 Lab LJ 191. See the discussion of the European Court of Human Rights approach (recognizing that both collective bargaining and the right to strike are essential components of constitutional protection of freedom of association) in Ewing and Hendy in this volume.

the protection of the normative labour relations regime available to virtually all other associations of workers. Indeed, extending that positive protection to the overwhelming majority of workers while excluding a small number would seem to be anything but content-neutral. Justice Rothstein's professed concern about content neutrality should, at the very least, have led him to question a legislative scheme that imposes such differential treatment on associations of agricultural workers.

Ultimately, however, in determining whether associational activity is protected under section 2(d), it would seem to be undesirable if not impossible to avoid an assessment of the extent to which that activity furthers the purposes and values of freedom of association, as recognized under international law and elsewhere, and the degree to which it is essential to preserving and sustaining a free and democratic society and promoting fundamental *Charter* values. The history, philosophical origins, and purpose of freedom of association, at the very least, require protection of collective bargaining, and, for that matter, the right to strike. This position is particularly the case, given the extent to which both have been recognized (by the courts and under international human rights law) as essential to the capacity of individuals to join together in attempting to provide a meaningful voice and counterbalance against both employers and the state,[89] to the preservation and promotion of *Charter* values,[90] and more generally, to the functioning and maintenance of a free and democratic civil society.

---

89 In the words of Dickson CJ in the *Alberta Reference*, above note 13 at para 23 (adopted by the Court in *Health Services*, above note 2 at para 84):

> Freedom of association is the cornerstone of modern labour relations. Historically, workers have combined to overcome the inherent inequalities of bargaining power in the employment relationship and to protect themselves from unfair, unsafe, or exploitative working conditions. . As the United States Supreme Court stated in *N.L.R.B. v. Jones & Laughlin Steel Corp.*, 301 U.S. 1 (1937), at p. 33:
>
> > Long ago we stated the reason for labor organizations. We said that they were organized out of the necessities of the situation; that a single employee was helpless in dealing with an employer; that he was dependent ordinarily on his daily wage for the maintenance of himself and family; that if the employer refused to pay him the wages that he thought fair, he was nevertheless unable to leave the employ and resist arbitrary and unfair treatment; . . .

90 As the Court eloquently stated in *Health Services*, above note 2 at paras 82–86, the *Charter* values of "human dignity, equality, liberty, respect for the autonomy of the person and the enhancement of democracy . . . are complemented and indeed, promoted, by the protection of collective bargaining in s. 2(d) of the *Charter*."

CHAPTER NINE
Labour Rights: A Democratic Counterweight to Growing Income Inequality in Canada

Derek Fudge

A. Introduction

The Supreme Court of Canada's 29 April 2011 decision in *Ontario (AG) v Fraser*,[1] upholding the constitutionality of the 2002 *Agricultural Employees Protection Act* (*AEPA*), was both disappointing and astounding. The decision marked the latest chapter in a decades-long legal struggle by the United Food and Commercial Workers (UFCW) Canada to achieve labour rights for the 80,000 domestic and migrant farm workers in Ontario.[2]

The disappointment over the decision is because the Court turned its back on one of the most vulnerable groups of workers in Canada by ruling that farm workers are not entitled to the same collective bargaining rights as almost all other Canadian workers. Ontario is the most intensive agricultural province in Canada, and the agricultural sector's workforce is one of the lowest paid groups of workers in the country and often face deplorable working conditions.[3] With the exception of management employees and certain categories of professional employees, Ontario farm workers are the

---

1 2011 SCC 20 [*Fraser*].

2 For more detail on UFCW Canada's longstanding campaign to improve working conditions and to obtain labour rights for agricultural workers in Canada, see UFCW, *History of Agricultural Workers in Canada*, online: UFCW Canada www.ufcw.ca/index.php?option=com_content&view=article&id=2012&Itemid=250& lang=en. See also Eric Tucker's chapter in this volume.

3 *Fraser v Ontario (AG)*, 2008 ONCA 760 at paras 67–69.

largest occupational grouping in Canada to be denied access to effective collective bargaining rights.

It is difficult to fathom how the Supreme Court could deny this vulnerable group of workers access to a statutory framework for collective bargaining available to virtually all other workers. But upon close examination of the facts of the case and the decision, one can see how *Fraser* got lost in a much larger political battle in which big business and governments used the case as a way to argue the Supreme Court had gone too far in the *BC Health Services* case[4] in protecting collective bargaining rights under section 2(d) of the *Charter.*

It is this larger political battle that is my focus in this chapter, which takes an unabashedly pro-labour stance on the need to protect collective bargaining and other key labour rights, such as the right to strike, as part of the constitutional guarantee of freedom of association. The chapter begins by showing how governments and employer organizations from across Canada ignored the issue in dispute—the right of agricultural workers to bargain collectively—in order to launch an assault on the precedent established in 2007 in *BC Health Services* that collective bargaining was a constitutionally protected right. It then proceeds to show how the *Charter* has failed to provide a robust and secure shield against governments determined to roll back workers' hard won collective rights to bargain collectively and to strike. After briefly recounting the concerted assault on trade union rights that began in the 1980s, I turn to demonstrate the important contribution that unions make toward building a more just and equitable society. Given the significance of trade unions for providing greater income equality in Canada, I argue that it is critical for the labour movement and its allies to launch a vigorous defence of labour rights. I describe some of the initiatives that my union, the National Union of Public and Government Employees (NUPGE), has taken to demonstrate how important unions and labour rights are for a vibrant democracy and sustainable economy.

B. *Fraser* Used as an Attempt to Roll Back *BC Health Services*

In many respects, the Supreme Court's ruling in the *Fraser* case ended up not being about agricultural workers and their right to bargain collectively; rather, it ended up being about *BC Health Services*, which had established that freedom of association protected in the *Charter*

4 *Health Services and Support—Facilities Subsector Bargaining Assn v British Columbia*, 2007 SCC 27 [*BC Health Services*].

includes collective bargaining. Big business, along with the federal government and several provincial governments in Canada, lined up to strategically use *Fraser* as an opportunity to roll back *BC Health Services*, and to some degree they were successful.

The first hint of this retreat was the list of seventeen interveners in the case, twelve of whom argued in favour of the appellant attorney general of Ontario's position. Although *Fraser* dealt specifically with farm workers in Ontario and their right to bargain collectively, only five of the twelve appellant-side interveners had either a direct or a partial interest in agriculture workers. The Ontario Federation of Agriculture and the British Columbia Agriculture Council both represent agricultural employers and had an obvious interest in the outcome of the case. The Alberta government's interest was also clear since its labour law continues to exclude farm workers from the right to bargain collectively. The interests of Quebec and New Brunswick were less clear since their labour laws already extend collective bargaining rights to farm workers except for those on farms with fewer than three or five employees respectively.[5] The direct interests of the federal government and the Government of British Columbia were not easily discernible since the federal government does not have jurisdiction over labour law governing the agricultural sector, and British Columbia already includes farm workers under its collective bargaining laws.

The four interveners representing big business were the Canadian Employers Council, the Coalition of BC Businesses, Conseil du patronat du Québec Inc, and Federally Regulated Employers—Transportation and Communications. Collectively, these four business groups represented a powerful political voice—a voice that was coordinated, was organized, and had a common objective far greater than just denying collective bargaining rights to Ontario farm workers. Five of the six interveners representing business interests were represented by the law firm of Heenan Blaikie LLP, the pre-eminent management-side law firm in Canada.[6]

---

5 *Québec Labour Code*, RSQ, c C-27, s 21; *Industrial Relations Act (New Brunswick)*, RSNB 1973, c I-4, s 1(5)(a).

6 The interveners represented by Heenan Blaikie were: Ontario Federation of Agriculture, the Coalition of BC Businesses and British Columbia Agriculture Council, Federally Regulated Employers—Transportation and Communication, Conseil du patronat du Québec Inc, and the Mounted Police Members Legal Fund. The only business intervener not represented by Heenan Blaikie was the Canadian Employers Council, represented by the law firm Stewart McKelvey.

From the moment *BC Health Services* was released in June 2007, right up until the *Fraser* decision was issued, big business worked to create a national hysteria around *BC Health Services*. Consider this recent quote from the president of the Canadian Association of Counsel to Employers, representing over 350 management-side lawyers across Canada:

> It is impossible to take a step without risking the explosion of a mine laid by the *BC Health Services* case, mines that are causing courts, arbitrators, and mediators to question every aspect of our labour relations system in this country, and mines that are costing employers time, money and productivity. The next step for employers is to defuse some of these mines. [7]

Big businesses' fear over the implications of *BC Health Services* was that the decision might weaken the power of employers within Canada's labour relations system, power, as we will see in the next section, that has been greatly tipped in their favour as a result of a serious erosion of labour rights over the past three decades.

Big business was well prepared and coordinated at the Supreme Court in December 2009, and they hijacked the *Fraser* case. Quarterbacked by Heenan Blaikie, and counsel to the Canadian Employers Council, big business had one objective in the *Fraser* case: to roll back any potential strengthening of the labour rights of Canadian workers resulting from *BC Health Services*. Their concerns found a receptive audience in two of the judges.

Even though no party in the case asked that the precedent in *BC Health Services* be overturned,[8] nearly two-thirds of the 101-page judgment in *Fraser* is devoted to re-litigating *BC Health Services*. Justice Rothstein's lengthy and forceful attack on *BC Health Services*, which he found "was not correctly decided, to the extent that it constitutionalizes collective bargaining,"[9] accounted for half of the decision. In a concurrence backed by Charron J, Rothstein analyzed *BC Health Services*, citing eleven arguments as to why section 2(d) of the *Charter* does not protect the right to collective bargaining.[10]

---

7 Peter McLellan, "Making Sense of the Minefield: Employer Uncertainty and the Constitutional Protectionism of Collective Bargain Rights" (Paper presented to the Freedom of Association Conference, University of Saskatchewan's College of Law, 27 February 2010) [unpublished] at 1 & 2.

8 This point was underscored by the majority, which stated that while it was asked to clarify the ambit of *BC Health Services*, it was not asked to overrule it: *Fraser*, above note 1 at para 59.

9 *Ibid* at para 127.

10 *Ibid* at paras 177–269.

The majority judgment devotes little attention to the *AEPA*, focusing instead on defending *BC Health Services* against Rothstein and Charron JJ's attempt to overrule it. While the majority reaffirmed that the *BC Health Services* decision represents "good law and should not be overturned,"[11] they also appear to have retrenched from the scope of protection *BC Health Services* gave to the right to collective bargaining. *Fraser* seems to have limited the right to collective bargaining to allowing employees to engage in "meaningful association to achieve workplace goals." Only legislation that "makes good faith resolution of workplace issues between employees and their employer *effectively impossible*"[12] will impede the right to meaningful association and therefore will violate section 2(d).

The interveners in *Fraser* representing big business and governments ultimately would have liked the Supreme Court to overturn *BC Health Services*, although they did not specifically request it. As a result of their well-coordinated presentations to the Court, designed to create constitutional hysteria over *BC Health Services*, the Supreme Court handed down a political compromise decision in *Fraser*—one that reaffirms the constitutional right to collective bargaining while limiting the meaningfulness of the right. Unfortunately, the 80,000 vulnerable and marginalized farm workers were the big losers in this political compromise as they continue to be denied any meaningful legal protection or support for collective bargaining.

C. The *Charter of Rights and Freedoms*: A Weak Shield

Unfortunately, the labour movement did not contribute in a major way to the national debate around the drafting of Canada's *Charter* in the early 1980s.[13] In deference to the Quebec Federation of Labour's opposition to the *Charter*, the Canadian Labour Congress did not participate in hearings of the Special Joint Committee of the Senate and the House of Commons, which examined the *Charter*'s terms in detail and recommended amendments.[14] It was hoped that the right to freedom of association contained in section 2(d) of the

---

11 *Ibid* at para 55.

12 *Ibid* at para 98 [emphasis added].

13 Larry Savage, "Organized Labour and the Canadian Charter of Rights and Freedoms" (2007) 36 Sup Ct L Rev 175.

14 Katherine Swinton, "The Charter of Rights and Public Sector Labour Relations" in Gene Swimmer & Mark Thompson, eds, *Public Sector Collective Bargaining in Canada: Beginning of the End of End of the Beginning* (Kingston: Queen's University Industrial Relations Centre Press, 1995) at 59.

Charter would protect the labour movement from a multitude of restrictions on union activities, including limitations on the right to collective bargaining and the right to strike, but it was also feared by unions, including NUPGE, that it would prove to be a double-edged sword, providing support for those who wished to constrict collective labour rights.[15]

In the years since, the *Charter* has proven to be both a weak shield and a weak sword. Until the beginning of the twenty-first century, the *Charter* provided unions with little relief in preventing the erosion of labour rights in Canada as the Supreme Court of Canada held that freedom of association did not limit the power of government to restrict collective bargaining rights or the freedom to strike. During the same period, however, the Court also did not make the *Charter* available as a sword for those who wanted to require governments to limit trade union activity on the basis that individuals were protected against forced associations. However, beginning with *Dunmore* in 2001 up until the period just prior to *Fraser*, which included several subsequent positive decisions flowing from the 2007 *BC Health Services* decision, there has been close to a decade of incremental positive jurisprudence from the courts requiring government to protect vulnerable workers' exercise of freedom of association and limiting governments' power to interfere in a substantial way with collective bargaining.

Without question, *Dunmore, BC Health Services*, and subsequent decisions have been significant cases for the advancement of labour rights in Canada. However, the decision in *Fraser* indicates that we cannot expect the Court to expand *Charter* protection of labour rights in the near future and that, indeed, we may be facing a period in which unions will have to fight to defend the legal victories they have achieved. But an even more important lesson is that the *Charter* is only one factor shaping the development of labour rights and it is not the most important. Rather, as this section demonstrates, the broader political and ideological context exerts far more influence.

---

15 In January 1986, prior to the Supreme Court's "Labour Trilogy" decision, NUPGE published a booklet entitled *The* Canadian Charter of Rights and Freedoms*: A Doubled-Edged Sword for Unions?* This booklet argued that while the *Charter* may enhance some rights of Canadian workers, it might also prove to be a double-edge sword, used by anti-union forces to weaken the freedom of association rights of workers.

1) Three Decades of Expansion, Followed by Three Decades of Retrenchment

There can be no stronger evidence to support the view that courts alone cannot defend labour rights than Canada's legislative record with respect to labour law.

The federal and provincial governments built up a fairly comprehensive legislative framework for collective bargaining in Canada over a thirty-four year period, from 1944 to 1978. The roots of the framework can be traced back to the 1944 federal wartime labour relations regulation, *Privy Council Order 1003*, which established the first nation-wide legal recognition of collective bargaining in Canada based on the US Wagner model. Shortly after, provincial legislatures began to enact their own collective bargaining statutes.

It started with Saskatchewan eight months after *PC Order 1003* was introduced, when its new Co-operative Commonwealth Federation government passed the *Trade Union Act* in November 1944, and continued up until May 1978, when Nova Scotia proclaimed the *Civil Service Collective Bargaining Act*, making it the last provincial government to grant collective bargaining rights to public employees.[16] During that period, a fairly progressive and consistent collective bargaining framework was constructed. Even today, the Saskatchewan *Trade Union Act* remains unique in North America for providing collective bargaining rights to both private sector and public sector employees (although the bargaining rights of public sector employees have become much more restricted by Bill 5, the 2008 *Public Service Essential Services Act*).[17]

Despite some huge gaps across the country in terms of certain groups of workers being denied collective bargaining rights, as well as experiencing restrictions on organizing and the scope of bargaining, the development of collective bargaining laws across the country spurred a wave of unionization that reached a high point in 1984 with 41.8 percent of the Canadian workforce being unionized.

---

16 Derek Fudge, *Collective Bargaining in Canada: Human Right or Canadian Illusion?* (Black Point, NS: Fernwood Publishing, 2006) at 22 [Fudge].

17 SS 2008, c P-42.2. Bill 5 provides for an extremely broad definition of essential services to the extent that practically any public service employee could be designated as an essential employee and therefore not eligible to go on strike. On 6 February 2012, Ball J of the Saskatchewan Queen's Bench declared this legislation to be unconstitutional for violating s 2(d), and he suspended his declaration of invalidity to give the Saskatchewan government twelve months to respond. See *Saskatchewan Federation of Labour v Saskatchewan*, 2012 SKQB 62.

This high point, however, marked the beginning of the erosion of labour rights in Canada.

Since 1982, the federal and provincial governments have passed 199 labour laws and of those 199 labour laws, 194 have restricted, suspended, or denied collective bargaining rights for workers.[18] Restrictions have been placed on the rights of unions to organize and on the scope of workplace issues that can be bargained collectively. Collective agreements have been torn up. Negotiated wages and benefits have been taken away. Employers' positions have been legislatively imposed on workers and the right to strike has been withdrawn. Both public and private sectors have been affected by this phenomenon. The 2011 legislative framework for labour law in Canada is far more restrictive than the framework that existed in 1984, when Canada reached its highest rate of union density and two years after the *Charter* was introduced.

Despite the *BC Health Services* decision in June 2007 and other subsequent legal victories over the past four years, the labour movement has not been able to stop the federal government, nor several provincial governments, from continuing a legislative attack on labour rights. Since that historic decision, fourteen labour laws have been passed in Canada that have restricted the bargaining rights of workers.[19]

2) The Attack on Labour Rights Intensifies in Canada and Internationally

While the attack on labour rights is not a new phenomenon for unions in Canada and around the world, Canada is currently experiencing one of the most intense assaults in decades. Across the globe, 2011 represents what appears to be the beginning of a prolonged, multi-pronged attack on labour rights.

The corporate world has stepped up its anti-union propaganda and has launched an all-out attack on unions, especially those in the public sector.[20] With unions weakened in the private sector, right-

---

18 For an overview of each of the 194 restrictive labour laws, see Fudge, above note 16, as well as NUPGE's Labour Rights are Human Rights website, online: www.labourrights.ca.

19 Summaries of the restrictive labour laws passed in Canada since June 2007 can be found online: www.labourrights.ca/content/summary-legislation-restricting-collective-bargaining-and-trade-union-rights-canada.

20 "The Battle Ahead: Confronting Public Sector Unions" *The Economist* (6 January 2011) online: The Economist www.economist.com/blogs/multimedia/2011/01/confronting_

wing governments around the globe, egged on by corporate big business, are turning their sights on the last bastion of union power—the public sector—where unionization rates remain healthy (71 percent in Canada compared with just 16 percent in the private sector).

Fresh off winning a Conservative majority in the May 2011 federal election, the Harper government was quick to set the tone that it is committed to further weakening labour rights. Under the pretence of protecting Canada's "fragile economic recovery," it declared in June 2011 that it would legislate an end to a sixteen-hour private sector strike between Air Canada and its employees—a rather rapid and incongruous response from a government that purports to be non-interventionist.[21]

Only four days later, it introduced legislation, Bill C-6, *Restoring Mail Delivery for Canadians Act*, forcing locked-out postal workers back to work.[22] The legislation was designed to favour the employer's bargaining position by directing that the arbitrator be "*guided by the need for terms and conditions of employment that are consistent with those in comparable postal industries*"—an industry in which, for the most part, workers do not enjoy the benefit of being unionized like Canada Post workers. It was also vindictive by imposing a wage settlement on postal workers that was less than the employer's last offer. This substantial interference in the collective bargaining process was clearly designed to weaken the bargaining power of the Canadian Union of Postal Workers and its members. This legislation, along with the threat to legislate an end to the Air Canada strike, was intended to send a signal to all Canadian workers that this government will not shy away from opportunities to weaken labour rights.

But the Harper government was not alone in its attack on labour rights; this past year has seen a series of attacks on unions. In February 2011, the Liberal Charest government in Quebec passed Bill 135, *An Act to ensure the continuity of the provision of legal services within the Government and certain public bodies*, to end a two-week strike by the province's 1,500 government lawyers and crown prosecutors and

public-sector_unions; Richard Michael Fischl, "'Running the Government Like a Business': Wisconsin and the Assault on Workplace Democracy" (2010) 121 Yale LJ 39, online: Yale Law Journal yaelawjournal.org/2011/06/21/fischl.html.

21 The government introduced Bill C-5, *Continuing Air Services for Passengers Act*, for First Reading on 16 June 2011. However, the parties negotiated a settlement before the legislation was passed.

22 SC 2011, c 17. Bill C-6 was introduced for First Reading on 20 June 2011 and Royal Assent was received on 26 June 2011.

impose a five-year agreement on them.[23] The Liberal McGuinty government in Ontario, in an attempt to appease the new administration of Toronto City Hall and its right-wing mayor, Rob Ford, passed Bill 150, *TTC Labour Disputes Resolution Act*, in March 2011; that Act took away the right to strike of Toronto's public transit workers.[24]

Although the labour movement cannot solely rely on the courts to defend labour rights, it also appears that it cannot rely on governments to adhere to the decisions of the courts regarding the constitutionality of their legislative actions around labour rights. Based on the fourteen regressive labour laws passed since the 2007 *BC Health Services* decision, it seems many of Canada's governments are prepared to legislate away labour rights at a moment's notice and not consider the constitutionality of their actions until years later, when a challenge finally makes its way to the Supreme Court of Canada. Of all the significant rights and freedoms in our *Charter*, it is only for the freedom of association that governments have demonstrated such a cavalier disrespect.

3) Using the "Deficit Crisis" to Attack Labour Rights is a False Argument[25]

The pretense for the attacks on labour rights, especially those of public sector workers, is that governments are broke and radical measures are required to eliminate budget deficits. Public services and unionized public sector workers are facing a wave of political and media attacks trying to fuel resentment among the private sector's largely non-unionized taxpayers who are being "forced" to pay for "out of control" government spending and the "bloated" wages of public sector workers.[26]

---

23 See NUPGE, "Charest Government Nothing More than Bullies for Passing Unjust Law" (23 February 2011) online: NUPGE www.nupge.ca/content/4072/charest-government-nothing-more-bulllies-passing-unjust-law.

24 See NUPGE, "Proposed TTC Essential Service Law Violates International Labour Standards" (17 March 2011) online: NUPGE www.nupge.ca/content/4137/proposed-ttc-essential-service-law-violates-international-labour-standards.

25 I would like to acknowledge the assistance of my NUPGE staff colleague, Mike Luff, for his contribution to this section. Much of the data, research, and studies quoted in this section have been compiled by him. Mike's valuable work over the past couple years has helped NUPGE build a strong case for the value of public services and the need for greater tax fairness in Canada.

26 See NUPGE, "President's Commentary: Lies About the Deficit" (2 June 2009) online: NUPGE www.nupge.ca/node/2334.

This attack on the public sector is built on a false argument. It is a classic bait-and-switch political tactic intended to steer the public away from the real issue, the serious problem of income inequality, which is being caused by unfair tax policies.

The fact is, Canada is not facing a fiscal crisis. According to the International Monetary Fund (IMF), Canada is in the very best fiscal shape of all the major industrialized countries, known as the G7 countries.[27] Canada's total government net debt is expected to be around 33 percent in 2014. The net debt of all other G7 countries is expected to be over 80 percent. At 33 percent, Canada's debt burden is less than half of what it was (70 percent) when the country hit the so-called "debt wall" in the early 1990s under the Mulroney government. Most government deficits will be eliminated over the next four to six years as the economy recovers. There is no deficit crisis in Canada, and there is no reason for governments to be cutting public services or freezing public sector wages.

Canada also does not have a spending problem. In 1992, total government spending was 53 percent of the GDP. By 2008, it was down to 39 percent. When one compares Canada with the other G7 countries, Canada ranks near the bottom when it comes to total government spending.[28] By the end of 2008, Canada and the US (the supposed greatest free market economy on the planet) actually had the same level of total government spending at 39 percent of the GDP. Only Japan spent less, at 37 percent.

The real fiscal problem in Canada today is that governments are facing a revenue problem by choice. In 1995, total tax revenue collected by governments was 36 percent of the GDP compared with 2008, when the total was 33 percent. Three percent does not sound like a lot, but it represents about $50 billion in lost tax revenue every year for governments.

Contrary to conventional wisdom, Canada is not a high-tax country when it is compared with other developed nations. In the G7, Canada is one of the lowest taxed countries.[29] The US is lowest at 28 percent and Canada is the third lowest at 33 percent; France is

---

27 International Monetary Fund, "World Economic Outlook, April 2009: Crisis and Recovery" (April 2009) online:www.imf.org/external/pubs/ft/weo/2009/01/pdf/text.pdf.

28 Organisation for Economic Co-operation and Development, *OECD in Figures, 2009* (10 September 2009) online: OECD iLibrary www.oecd-ilibrary.org/economics/oecd-in-figures-2009_oif-2009-en.

29 Organisation for Economic Co-operation and Development, "OECD Economic Outlook No. 84" (25 November 2008) online: OECD www.oecd.org/dataoecd/62/55/42181001.pdf.

the highest at 44 percent. In 2005, Canada ranked tenth out of the thirty OECD (Organisation for Economic Co-operation and Development) countries for the lowest total taxes as a percent of the GDP. Canada is substantially below both the OECD average (36 percent) and the European Union average (40 percent).

Throughout most of Canada's history, its tax system was fair and progressive. Unfortunately, today this is no longer true. From the mid-1930s through to the early 1980s, the top marginal income tax rate for the highest incomes in Canada was over 60 percent and at one point reached 90 percent.[30] None of this slowed economic growth or drove rich people and their investments out of the country. In fact, it was a period of unparalleled economic growth and social progress.

Over the past three decades, governments have reduced the top federal-provincial marginal tax rate to 43 percent.[31] The last time the richest Canadians were taxed at a level this low was in the 1920s—just before the Great Depression. Meanwhile, tax rates for middle- and lower-income families over the last thirty years have been steadily rising. Today, the top 1 percent pays a lower share of their total income in taxes than the poorest 10 percent. This is because the richest 1 percent have benefited spectacularly from income tax cuts, while the poorest 10 percent have faced increasing sales, payroll, and property taxes. Our tax system no longer meets the test of fairness across income groups. Tax fairness has been flipped upside down in Canada.

At the same time, governments have been making dramatic cuts to corporate tax rates. Over the last decade, Canada has led the race to the bottom on corporate tax rates, reducing them by 50 percent. By the end of 2012, Canada will have the lowest corporate rates in the entire G7. Despite these massive corporate tax cuts, business investment in equipment is down and productivity is down, but unemployment is up. Predictably, CEO salaries have skyrocketed and corporations are hoarding a record amount of cash. Canadian corporations are now sitting on a huge $700 billion pile of cash, and the lion's share of these extra billions is going into shareholder dividends and compensation hikes for corporate executives. Clearly, the experiment with dramatically lower tax rates for wealthy people and corporations has failed.

---

30 Linda McQuaig & Neil Brooks, *The Trouble with Billionaires* (Toronto: Viking Canada, 2010) at 115 [McQuaig & Brooks].

31 *Ibid* at 116–17 and 216–19.

As a result, governments are facing a serious revenue shortfall and are running much larger deficits. Consider the situation facing the federal government. By 2013, the Harper government's tax cuts since 2006 will have resulted in the loss of a staggering $220 billion. The federal government would not be in a deficit situation today, even after the economic stimulus package, if they had not made these massive tax cuts.

The problem of the lack of tax fairness and lost revenue is the real reason for government deficits. But the unfairness of our tax system is also contributing to a much greater problem facing our society today, that of income inequality.

D. Understanding the Critical Connection between Labour Rights and Income Equality

To appreciate the true significance of the attack on labour rights, one must understand the broad role unions play in society. Unions do far more than negotiate decent wages and benefits for its members; they also play a critical role in ensuring greater economic and social justice for all citizens.

The role of unions in helping to achieve higher levels of economic equality and social rights for all citizens has been well documented over the years by ILO. Most recently, a major 2008 study undertaken by the ILO, looking at a comprehensive set of data covering fifty-one countries, found a clear negative correlation between unionization and income inequality. Its research showed that the countries in which income inequality was on average lower in the period 1989–2005 tended to be those in which a greater proportion of workers were affiliated with trade unions.[32]

The study also noted a positive correlation between income equality and respect for fundamental international labour standards of the ILO that promote unionization and collective bargaining. It found countries that have a greater compliance with two of the ILO's fundamental conventions that define the basic principles of labour rights throughout the world—*Freedom of Association and Protection of the Right to Organize Convention, 1948* (No 87) and *Right to Organize and Collective Bargaining Convention, 1949* (No 98)—tend to have

32 International Labour Organization, *World of Work Report 2008: Income Inequalities in the Age of Financial Globalization* (Geneva: International Institute for Labour Studies, 2008) at 82 [ILO, *World of Work Report 2008*].

lower inequality.[33] Canada has not ratified Convention No 98 but has ratified Convention No 87. Since 1982, seventy-nine complaints have been submitted to the ILO against the federal and provincial governments against labour laws that violate Convention No 87. Of those seventy-nine complaints, the ILO has found that freedom of association principles had been violated in seventy-five of those cases.[34]

The ILO's 2008 study also found that higher rates of union density had a positive impact on the range of social rights afforded to citizens:

> The countries in which union density rates are higher are also the ones in which the welfare state is more developed, taxation levels higher and more progressive, collective bargaining more centralized and labour law both closer to international labour standards and better implemented.[35]

It is important to look at the relationship here in Canada between income equality, labour law, and union density in the past five decades.

1) Labour Rights Expand, Income Inequality Declines

From the 1950s through the early 1980s, we saw an unprecedented period of economic growth and, more importantly, a period during which income growth was shared proportionally across all income groups. Between 1951 and 1981, the bottom 80 percent of Canadian income earners increased their share of total income marginally by 1.2 percent, while the top 20 percent of income earners saw their portion of total income decline by the same percentage.[36]

During the same period, union density in Canada gradually rose from 28.4 percent in 1951 to 37.6 percent in 1981, reaching its highest point of 41.8 percent in 1984.[37] Much of this rise in union density coincided with a major expansion of labour law, which established a comprehensive legislative framework of collective bargaining rights for most Canadian workers. As Michael Lynk noted, there is a broad

---

33 *Ibid* at 84.

34 For a summary of each of the seventy-nine ILO complaints, see NUPGE, "Canada's Record at the International Labour Organization (ILO)" online: www.labourrights.ca/content/canadas-record-international-labour-organization-ilo-updated-april-2011.

35 ILO, *World of Work Report 2008*, above note 32 at 86.

36 Lars Osberg, *A Quarter Century of Economic Inequality: 1991–2006* (Ottawa: Canadian Center for Policy Alternatives, 2008) at 7 [Osberg].

37 Andrew Jackson & Sylvain Schetagne, *Solidarity Forever? An Analysis of Changes in Union Density* (Ottawa: Canadian Labour Congress, 2003) at 14.

consensus among labour law and industrial relations scholars in Canada that labour laws play a significant role in shaping the levels of unionization:

> In Canada, opinion from the Fraser Institute on the political right to trade union researchers on the left have stated that our labour laws are key to the determination of the country's unionization rates, a conclusion that academics have also adopted.[38]

With the expansion of labour laws resulting in greater union density, organized labour was a key political player in leading the advancement of equality and social rights. The labour movement was able to influence important public policy and legislative choices that were designed to invest in the social and economic well-being of all citizens and share Canada's common wealth. The development of a progressive tax system, collective bargaining laws, stronger employment standards, a national public medicare system, a national public pensions system, a broad range of public services, and large-scale investment in public infrastructure all played a key role in creating greater equality for all Canadians.

2) Labour Rights Attacked, Income Inequality Increases

This trend toward greater equality completely changed with the emergence of corporate globalization and the dramatic rise of corporate power in the early 1980s. The gradual trend toward income equality began to reverse itself. The focus was no longer on how federal and provincial governments in Canada fairly distribute the wealth Canadian citizens collectively create. It became driven by greed, which has resulted in a massive concentration of wealth in the hands of a few—so much so that income inequality is now at its highest level since 1928, just before the Great Depression.[39]

The 60 percent of income earners who fall within Canada's three middle income quintiles lost 4.7 percent of all Canadian income from 1981 to 2005, taking home 49.1 percent in 2005 compared with 53.8 percent in 1981, while the bottom 20 percent of income earners lost 0.5 percent during the same period, taking home just 4.1 percent of all Canadian income in 2005.[40] The only group of income earners

---

38 Michael Lynk, "Labour Law and the New Inequality" (2009) 59 UNBLJ 14 at 36-6 (footnotes omitted) [Lynk].

39 McQuaig & Brook, above note 30 at 3–4.

40 Osberg, above note 36 at 7.

to increase their share of Canadian income during this period was the top 20 percent of income earners. Their share increased by 5.3 percent, which resulted in their taking home close to half (46.9 percent) of all income earned in Canada in 2005.[41] These statistics reveal the long-term trend toward greater income inequality, but by themselves do not show how disturbing that trend is.

Let's look at the richest 10 percent of Canadian income earners. In 2007, they took home 41 percent of the nation's total income. The share of all income going to the richest 1 percent (with an average income of $404,500) almost doubled between 1982 and 2007, rising from 7.9 percent to 13.8 percent.[42] If that's not outrageous enough, consider the share of the nation's income the top 0.1 percent earns (those 24,600 Canadians with an average income of $1.49 million). Their share of Canadians' total income was 5.5 percent, more than double their share from the 1980s.[43]

Included in this group of 0.1 percent of top income earners are Canada's 100 best-paid CEOs. During the height of the economic crisis in 2009, these CEOs pocketed an average of $6.6 million, earning 155 times more than the average Canadian income earner ($42,988).[44] They didn't always have it this good; in 1998 the best-paid 100 CEOs pocketed an average of 104 times more than the average Canadian wage earner.[45] It is undisputable that the obscene rise in pay for Canada's top corporate executives is a critical factor causing our widening income gap. In fact, Canada has one of the worst records in the world when it comes to the inequality gap. In 2008, the OECD warned that Canada is on a slippery slope and that our inequality gap is growing faster than that of almost all other developed countries in the world.[46]

So what has happened to labour rights during this period of excessive growth of income inequality? Without question, Canada has seen a major erosion of labour rights over the past three decades. In

---

41 *Ibid* at 7.

42 Armine Yalnizyan, *The Rise of Canada's Richest 1 Percent* (Ottawa: Canadian Center for Policy Alternatives, 2010) at 11.

43 *Ibid* at 12.

44 Hugh Mackenzie, *Recession Proof: Canada's 100 Best Paid CEOs* (January 2011) online: Canadian Center for Policy Alternatives http://www.policyalternatives.ca/publications/reports/recession-proof at 3 & 4.

45 *Ibid* at 4.

46 Armine Yalnizyan, "Growing Income Gap a Warning to Leaders: OECD Report Shows Rift in Canada Increasing at Quick Rate" (22 October 2008) online: Canadian Center for Policy Alternatives www.policyalternatives.ca/publications/commentary/growing-income-gap-warning-leaders.

every jurisdiction in Canada, the labour rights of Canadians have been diminished by the legislative actions of our federal and provincial governments. As previously mentioned, up to and including the Harper government's back-to-work legislation ending the postal workers lockout in June 2011, there have been 194 pieces of legislation since the *Charter* was introduced in 1982 that have restricted, suspended, or denied collective bargaining rights for Canadian workers.[47]

Table 1: Summary of Labour Laws Restricting Collective Bargaining and Trade Union Rights, 1982–2011 (as of January 2012)

Type of Legislation	Jurisdiction											Total
	Fed	BC	AB	SK	MB	ON	QC	NB	PE	NS	NL	
Back to work—dispute sent to arbitration	10	4		3		14	2	2		1		**37**
Back to work—settlement imposed	7	5	4	3		5	16	4		1	3	**48**
Suspension of barg. rights—wage freeze or rollback imposed	6	12		1	2	6	6	2	2	4	3	**44**
Restrictions on certification process		1			1	2					1	**5**
Denial of workers' right to join a union		1	2			3	2					**8**
Restrictions on scope of barg. & other union activities	4	15	4	6	4	6	3	4	1	3	2	**52**
Total	**27**	**38**	**10**	**13**	**7**	**36**	**30**	**12**	**3**	**9**	**9**	**194**

47 Summaries of the 194 restrictive labour laws passed in Canada since 1982 can be found at Canadian Foundation for Labour Rights, "Restrictive Labour Laws in Canada" (October 2011) online: http://www.labourrights.ca/issues/restrictive-labour-laws-canada.

There has been a major change in the frequency and severity of back-to-work legislation in Canada in recent years. Since the early 1980s, the number of instances of back-to-work legislation is higher than it has been in any other period in the history of labour relations in Canada. In the last twenty-nine years, the federal government alone has passed fifteen pieces of back-to-work legislation, while provincial governments across the country have enacted seventy-six pieces of back-to-work legislation. Most of this legislation (fifty-two of the ninety-one pieces of legislation) not only forced workers back to work after they had taken strike action, but also arbitrarily imposed settlements on them.[48]

A common phenomenon in the public sector during this period has been the suspension of collective bargaining rights. Almost all public sector workers have had their collective bargaining rights suspended at some point over the last three decades. Thirty-eight pieces of legislation passed in the federal Parliament and provincial legislatures have suspended the collective bargaining rights of public sector workers. The longest legislative suspension of collective bargaining rights was for a period of seven years. Bill 142, *An Act Respecting the Working Conditions in the Public Sector*, passed by the Charest government in December 2005, had the effect of suspending collective bargaining for the province's 500,000 public sector workers for a seven-year period, retroactively from 2003 to 2010.

Since 1982, there have also been sixty-five instances where federal and provincial labour laws have been amended to further restrict unions' ability to organize. Nine pieces of legislation have actually denied certain categories of workers the right to join a union and five pieces of legislation have restricted the certification process, hurting the labour movement's ability to organize the unorganized. There have been fifty-one instances where the federal and provincial governments passed legislation that restricted the rules and scope of bargaining, denied the right to strike, and limited the mechanisms available for settlement of disputes or allowed for greater government and employer interference in internal union matters.

These thirty years of consistently chipping away at labour rights by Canada's federal and provincial governments has had a detrimental impact on the labour movement in Canada. It has hurt not

48 See Canadian Foundation for Labour Rights (CFLR), *Restrictive Labour Laws in Canada—Summary of Legislation Restricting Collective Bargaining and Trade Union Rights in Canada 1982–2011*, online: CFLR http://www.labourrights.ca/issues/restrictive-labour-laws-canada.

only the labour movement's ability to organize the unorganized but also its capacity to maintain the levels of union density that were achieved in the mid-1980s. During this period of labour rights, retrenchment union density has fallen a full 10 percent to its current level of 30 percent of the Canadian workforce.

Beyond the negative impact on the labour movement's ability for unions to protect the interests of their members, this dramatic drop in union density has had profound implications for Canadian society. As Michael Lynk points out, this should concern all Canadians:

> Labour and employment rights and the laws that buttress them are not the accumulation of privileges by a vigourous lobby of special interests, but the expression of core constitutional and human rights that benefit, directly and indirectly, the majority of citizens living in a modern democratic society.[49]

E. A Vigorous Defence of Labour Rights is Critical

Corporate rights must be curtailed in order to provide a democratic counterweight to the growing power of corporations and the super wealthy. The critical rebalancing of the scales of power between corporations and labour desperately needs to take place. It can only happen with the existence of a strong and vibrant labour movement. Strong labour rights are key to a functioning democracy in which economic justice and social rights can flourish. The labour movement in Canada must continue to make the connection between these issues and mobilize Canadians around them.

How does the labour movement and its allies successfully challenge this dominant corporate greed ideology? How do we as a labour movement change the debate to focus our values, our belief in the common good, and the recognition of the value of sharing our common wealth? Several strategies are outlined below for consideration. These have guided my union (NUPGE) in much of the work we have undertaken to defend labour rights, our members, and the valuable public services they provide.

1) Strategic and Coordinated Approach to the Judicial System

In terms of defending labour rights in the courts, the labour movement needs to take more of a strategic and coordinated approach

---

49 Lynk, above note 38 at 35.

to legal challenges to restrictive labour laws. We cannot allow ourselves to be passive "observers" of future constitutional challenges by an individual union.

The labour movement did not participate in a major way in the national debate around the drafting of Canada's *Charter* in the early 1980s. Nor did it coordinate our approach in bringing forward early *Charter* cases (that is, the Labour Trilogy) in the mid-1980s to advance labour rights. For the most part, this has resulted in twenty years of bad jurisprudence on labour rights in *Charter* cases.

The June 2007 *BC Health Services* decision was a significant legal victory for the Canadian labour movement. Unions celebrated the decision, but they did not collectively consider how to use it to strategically move labour rights ahead in Canada. We must make a greater effort to work in a coordinated way to ensure that the strongest challenges go forward in the courts. The labour movement's approach to the *Fraser* case signified a greater coordinated effort, but paled in comparison to the well-planned and coordinated approach demonstrated by big business.

Unions involved in *Charter* cases and their legal counsel must coordinate future legal challenges in light of these decisions. We need to develop a common understanding of the Supreme Court rulings in both *BC Health Services* and *Fraser* in terms of their scope, limitations, and impact on future legal challenges involving labour rights in Canada. The labour movement needs to provide a forum for the brightest legal minds associated with this movement to meet on a regular basis to discuss the potential impact on labour rights and the perceived strength of all *Charter* challenges in order to strategically co-ordinate the labour movement's approach to constitutional cases.

This goal was part of the intent of NUPGE when it established the Canadian Foundation for Labour Rights (CFLR) in 2010. The Foundation is run by a Board of Directors made up of well-respected human rights activists, progressive labour relations academics, and union-side labour lawyers. NUPGE is promoting CFLR as a vehicle to monitor, provide advice, and offer coordination on legal challenges to labour laws, with a view to strategically moving labour rights ahead in Canada. A concrete example of this is the *Labour After Fraser* seminar, which the CFLR hosted in May 2011. It brought together some thirty prominent labour law academics, union-side labour lawyers, and union leaders to bring timely analysis to the *Fraser* decision and to explore the response from the labour community. A report of the seminar was published in August 2011.[50]

a) Labour Rights are Human Rights

It goes without question that the labour movement needs to defend labour rights beyond the courts. We need to change the public discourse on labour rights by elevating them beyond being just statutory rights. We must reinforce that labour rights are indeed human rights. Entrenching this principle would raise labour rights to the quasi-constitutional level that human rights occupy in Canadian law and open the door for genuine legal protection, rather than occasional judicial endorsements.[51]

The labour movement and its allies must build on the knowledge and evidence concerning the broader role unions play in strengthening democracy and promoting greater economic equality and the social and economic well-being of all citizens. Unions have been, and continue to be, an important force for democracy, not just in the workplace, but also in the community—locally, nationally, and globally. It is no coincidence that in countries where there are free and active trade union movements, there are more democratic, transparent, and representative forms of government.

Not only do democracies benefit from unions, but economies do as well. Beyond the economic benefits provided to workers and their families, unions have historically been an important force in humanizing and democratizing the economies of nations. The erosion of labour rights diminishes our standing as a democracy and threatens the social and economic well-being of citizens. In that regard, another key purpose of CFLR is to create greater public awareness and understanding of labour rights as a key critical component of human rights and to build effective political momentum and public support for progressive labour law reform.

b) Coordinated National Campaigns against New Regressive Labour Laws

The labour movement's approach to any future regressive labour law being contemplated or introduced by a government in Canada

50 *The Labour Movement After Fraser: Report of the Seminar on the Supreme Court Decision AG of Ontario v. Fraser* (Ottawa: Canadian Foundation for Labour Rights and National Union of Public and General Employees, August 2011) online: NUPGE http://www.nupge.ca/files/publications/The_Labour_Movement_After_Fraser.pdf.

51 Remarks made by Michael Lynk at the Canadian Foundation for Labour Rights seminar on the Supreme Court of Canada decision in *AG of Ontario v Fraser* (Toronto: 30 May 2011).

has to be guided by labour's old adage: "*an injury to one is an injury to all.*" We cannot look at a bad law as a single piece of legislation negatively impacting one single sector of our movement in a specific jurisdiction. All too often, this is what we have done in the past. A bad labour law, regardless of what workers and what jurisdiction it affects, negatively impacts the entire labour movement.

It would be hard to argue that the 194 restrictive labour laws passed by federal and provincial governments in Canada since 1982 have not collectively hurt our ability to organize. We also know from experience that a bad labour law introduced in one jurisdiction can lead, and has led, to the introduction of similar laws in other jurisdictions (for example, wage controls and restrictive certification processes).

The introduction of a new restrictive labour law, regardless of jurisdiction, must be met by an effective, quick, and coordinated national campaign by the entire labour movement. It should immediately unleash a national campaign to create public backlash and strong political pressure against the legislation and the government that introduced it. Unions must never lose focus that the fight back against a bad labour law has to be a commitment of the entire Canadian labour movement.

c) Pressuring Governments in Canada to Comply with International Labour Law

All governments in Canada are failing in their responsibility under international labour and human rights law to promote and protect workers' rights. The image of Canada within the international community as a country that respects human rights, especially in the area of labour rights, is an illusion. The reality of Canada's record is quite different: labour rights endorsed so enthusiastically in international forums by Canada have never been fully realized here at home.

The Supreme Court of Canada has made it quite clear that Canada has not only a moral, but also a legal obligation to live up to its international commitments as spelled out in those ILO conventions that Canada has ratified. To quote from the *BC Health Services* decision:

> International Conventions to which Canada is a party recognize the right of members of unions to engage in collective bargaining, as part of the protection for freedom of association. It is reasonable to infer that the Section 2(d) of the *Charter* should be interpreted as recognizing at least the same level of protection.[52]

---

52 *BC Health Services*, above note 4 at para 79.

This view was reaffirmed in *Fraser:*

> Notwithstanding the comprehensive reasons of our colleague, we conclude that *Health Services* is grounded in precedent, consistent with Canadian values, *consistent with Canada's international commitments* and consistent with this Court's purposive and generous interpretation of other *Charter* guarantees.[53]

With courts in Canada increasingly using international labour standards to interpret and rule on the constitutionality of Canadian labour laws, unions should make greater use of the ILO to reinforce judicial challenges to restrictive labour laws.

As the union that has submitted the most formal complaints against regressive Canadian labour laws to the ILO's Freedom of Association Committee, NUPGE gets some satisfaction out of the fact that Canada's international law commitments are being relied on to help interpret the constitutionality of Canadian labour laws. The first complaint NUPGE filed was in 1982 against the government of Alberta's Bill 44, *Labour Statutes Amendment Act*.[54] Since then, NUPGE has filed a total of thirty-two complaints.

There was, justifiably, some skepticism around the value of using the ILO complaints procedure to fight regressive labour laws, as few governments accepted the decisions. NUPGE used it as a political tool to fight bad laws but now appreciate that the body of ILO jurisprudence regarding complaints against Canadian labour laws has guided, and continues to guide, the courts in their deliberations in labour law cases.

d) Ratification of ILO Conventions

As dismal as Canada's record is in failing to abide by the basic freedom of association principles endorsed by the ILO, its record at ratifying ILO conventions is worse. Most of the conventions endorsed so enthusiastically by the Canadian government at the ILO have never been ratified. Of the ILO's 188 conventions, Canada has ratified only thirty in total and only three of the last thirty conventions developed since 1982.

Canada is one of the few countries in the world that has yet to ratify all eight of the ILO conventions recognized as being fundamental

---

53 *Fraser*, above note 1 at para 97 [emphasis added].

54 International Labour Organization, Committee on Freedom of Association (Case No 1234) Report No 241 (*Vol LXVIII, 1985, Series B, No 3)* online: http://webfusion.ilo.org/public/db/standards/normes/libsynd/LSGetParasByCase.cfm?hdroff=1&FILE=1234&PARA=37.

to the rights of human beings at work.[55] The three fundamental ILO conventions that Canada has yet to ratify are: *Convention No 29—Forced Labour* (1930); *Convention No 98—Right to Organize and Collective Bargaining* (1949); and *Convention No 138—Minimum Age* (1973).

On a positive note, the federal government did advise the ILO in June 2011 that it will be ratifying Convention 29 (being one of only eight countries in the world that has yet to do so) and will begin another consultative process with provincial governments regarding the ratification of the other two fundamental ILO conventions.

The official reasons of the federal and most provincial governments for refusing to ratify ILO conventions are sometimes obscure and difficult to understand.[56] There is a real mystery surrounding the federal-provincial-territorial consultation process for ratifying ILO conventions. It is extremely difficult, if not impossible, to find out the precise reasons for the refusal to ratify, including details on which governments have objected to ratification and the exact nature of their concerns.

As demonstrated by the low level of ratification of ILO conventions by Canada, the current system of consultation between the federal and the provincial governments is in serious need of restructuring. Prior to the 1960s, debate and approval by Parliament of international treaties was the norm. This practice is no longer the case.

The labour movement must become more engaged in lobbying the federal and provincial governments to have a more transparent and consultative approach to ratifying ILO conventions. Unions should not accept the hypocrisy of our federal government playing a leadership role at the ILO in developing international labour standards while not being prepared to have them ratified in Canada.

More importantly, we know from the *BC Health Services* and *Fraser* decisions that these international conventions have played, and will continue to play, a major role in the interpretation of Canadian law. As a start, the labour movement should recognize *Convention No 98—Right to Organize and Collective Bargaining* as the number one priority convention for Canada to ratify. Convention No 98, together with *Convention No 87—the Freedom of Association and Protection of the Right to Organize*, is recognized as covering the basic principles of labour rights throughout the world.

---

55 For more information regarding the three fundamental ILO conventions that Canada has not ratified, see NUPGE, *Backgrounder: Canada's Shameful Secret*, online: http://www.nupge.ca/files/publications/Canadas_Shameful_Secret_Backgrounder.pdf.

56 Only the federal government can ratify treaties; however, the federal government has adopted a convention that it will not adopt treaties that provinces are violating.

Convention No 87, which the Supreme Court applied in interpreting the freedom of association guarantee under the *Charter*, was ratified by Canada in 1972. However, Canada is only one of twenty-three countries that have not ratified Convention No 98 and one of only three countries to have ratified Convention No 87, but not Convention No 98 (the other two countries being Mexico and Myanmar). Ratification of this critical convention would provide further guidance to the courts in helping to interpret the right to collective bargaining as providing all Canadian workers with access to a legislative framework that allows them to exercise their right in an equal and meaningful manner.

2) Changing the Discourse on the Value of Public Services and Fair Taxation

In recent years NUPGE has put an increased emphasis on making the connection with its members, their families, and their communities between labour rights and a fair and just economy built on tax fairness and a vibrant public sector. We recognize that along with creating greater awareness around labour rights, we need to foster a greater understanding of how the public sector is a critical positive force not only for the well-being of our citizens, but also for our economy as a whole.

With the current global attack on public services and public service unions, now is not the time to go on the defensive for the important services and programs our members deliver. We need to mobilize an aggressive offensive in promoting the value of the work public service workers do.

We also must aggressively talk about the need for greater tax fairness in Canada. We need to ensure that current political debate on taxation policy focuses on three critical points:

1) It is responsible government spending that allows us to pay for public services;
2) Canadian governments have a revenue problem, not a deficit problem; and,
3) Many well-to-do Canadians are not paying their fair share of taxes.

The labour movement and its progressive allies must not shy away from talking about taxes. We cannot have a responsible conversation about paying for valuable public services and programs unless we are prepared to address issues of tax fairness. Governments in Canada and most of our political leaders are avoiding engaging Canadians in this conversation. For the most part, they have not presented citizens with honest choices but have instead limited public debate around taxation policy based on corporate ideology.

Labour and its progressive allies need to mobilize around our common good and our common wealth. But mobilizing today is not like mobilizing was just a decade ago. It is not just about getting our members out to rallies.

We need to create a movement, not a coalition, if we are going to win this battle of ideas and values. The movement must be unified around the fundamental progressive principle of equality. It cannot be just about single issues such as labour rights, or environmentalism, or education, or health care, or peace. It must seek to change the political discourse by engaging Canadians in a conversation about the moral mission of governments to reduce inequality through a fair tax system and the provision of quality public services.

Since June 2010, NUPGE has been engaged in a national campaign we call *All Together Now!*[57] to defend our members, promote public services, and fight for tax fairness. It includes most of the basic campaign principles we have used over the years, but it is also different in some of the approaches and tools we are using. We are attempting to convert members to activists through engagement and conversations about the value of the work they do, and we're asking them to have similar conversations with their co-workers, their families, and their neighbours.

We have built a cadre of over 100 campaign activists across the country who we have called "Champions for Change." We have trained them and provided them with the resources to take the message about the value of public services and fair taxation out into their workplaces and communities. Over the last year these champions have had conversations with tens of thousands of NUPGE members and other workers in their communities. They have also helped mobilize NUPGE members and others to take direct action in support of public services and tax fairness.

The campaign has achieved a lot in short period of time. By the beginning of 2011, the debate over the value of more corporate tax cuts exploded into the political discourse and became a major issue in the spring federal election campaign. It was also a major issue in several provincial elections held in the fall of 2011. At the same time, the issue of income inequality has gained some traction in the polit-

57 For further information see NUPGE, *All Together Now! A National Compaign for Public Services and Tax Fairness*, online: alltogethernow.nupge.ca.

ical discourse and has appeared in hundreds of media editorials over the last few months.

Another initiative NUPGE recently undertook is the establishment of a second foundation—the Public Services Foundation of Canada (PSFC)—which we intend to build into a national research and advocacy organization dedicated to defending and promoting the value of high-quality public services. We aim to use the foundation to help further foster an understanding of the role of public services in supporting families and communities.

We want it to be a counterweight to right-wing corporate front groups such as the Fraser Institute. We intend to have the foundation conduct rigorous research and analysis of public policy issues, as well as provide access to commentaries and popular education tools. We hope to build it into a strong and credible voice in the mainstream media and social networks, while coordinating advocacy campaigns to convince all levels of government to strengthen and expand quality public services.

F. Conclusion

Increasing corporate power and excessive greed in Canada and around the world has resulted in massive inequality and social exclusion. Continuing along this ill-fated path greatly threatens Canada's ability to build a more egalitarian society based on our common good and common wealth. Our values of compassion, sharing, and caring are in danger of being overtaken by the corporate elite's notions of individual responsibility and survival of the fittest.

Balance must be restored to the scales of economic and social justice. The only democratic counterweight to the power of corporations and the super wealthy is an agenda that supports and promotes strong labour rights and economic justice, which can be achieved only through tax fairness and quality public services. These are key components to a functioning democracy and an equitable and sustainable economy. The labour movement in Canada and its progressive allies must continue to make the connection between these issues and mobilize Canadians around them.

CHAPTER TEN
The International Constitution

Patrick Macklem

So comrades, come rally,
And the last fight let us face.
The Internationale,
Unites the human race.

—Eugène Pottier, "L'Internationale" (1871)

A. Introduction

Twenty-five years ago, the Supreme Court of Canada embarked on what has become a remarkable jurisprudential voyage on the nature and scope of the constitutional guarantee of freedom of association. In 1987, in a trilogy of cases (known collectively as the Labour Trilogy) that cast cold water on the Canadian labour movement's hopes that the guarantee would extend robust constitutional protection for the rights of workers, a majority of the Court held that freedom of association enshrines neither a right to strike nor a right to bargain collectively.[1] At most, it held that the guarantee protects a right of workers to establish, join, and belong to a trade union.

Obliquely acknowledging logical flaws and doctrinal inconsistencies, subsequent cases began to chip away at the Labour Trilogy's

1 *Reference Re Public Service Employee Relations Act (Alta)*, [1987] 1 SCR 313 [*Alberta Reference*]; *RWDSU v Saskatchewan*, [1987] 1 SCR 460; and *PSAC v Canada*, [1987] 1 SCR 424.

holdings.[2] In 2007, the dam finally broke, and the Court explicitly overruled the Trilogy's reasoning and much of its result, holding that freedom of association protects the right of workers to bargain collectively with their employers.[3] Recently, the Court explored some of the implications of this dramatic reversal, holding that freedom of association guarantees a meaningful process that enables employee associations to make representations to employers, which employers must consider and discuss in good faith.[4] On the horizon is litigation over whether freedom of association now enshrines a right to strike.

As remarkable as these constitutional developments are, beneath their collective surface lies a more fundamental transformation—one that relates to Canada's engagement with the international legal order. Unlike the constitutions of some countries,[5] the Constitution of Canada is textually silent on the domestic legal status of international law. Traditionally understood, however, Canada is a dualist jurisdiction, whereby an international treaty obligation does not become domestic law unless it has been implemented in domestic legislation.[6] But this traditional view of the domestic implications of international law has gradually but steadily been replaced by a much more relational understanding of the boundary between the international and national legal spheres.[7]

This contemporary approach reflects an increased willingness on the part of the judiciary in democratic societies to look to comparative, regional, and international legal developments for guidance in constitutional interpretation.[8] The Supreme Court of Canada is a leader among national courts in championing a more relational conception of a domestic constitutional order. Nowhere is this more apparent than in its constitutional jurisprudence on freedom of association.

---

2 See *Dunmore v Ontario (AG)*, [2001] 3 SCR 1016 [*Dunmore*].

3 *Health Services and Support—Facilities Subsector Bargaining Assn v British Columbia*, [2007] 2 SCR 391 [*BC Health Services*].

4 *Ontario (AG) v Fraser*, 2011 SCC 20 [*Fraser*].

5 South Africa's constitution, for example, provides that "in interpreting the provisions of this Chapter [dealing with fundamental rights], a court of law shall promote the values which underlie an open and democratic society based on freedom and equality and shall, where applicable, have regard to public international law applicable to the protection of the rights entrenched in this Chapter, and may have regard to comparable foreign case law."

6 *AG Canada v AG Ontario*, [1937] AC 326 (PC).

7 See Karen Knop, "Here and There: International Law in Domestic Courts" (2000) 32 NYU J Int'l Law & Pol 501.

8 See generally Sujit Choudhry, ed, *The Migration of Constitutional Ideas* (Cambridge: Cambridge University Press, 2006).

This chapter locates current debates on the constitutional dimensions of labour market regulation in light of this transformation in Canada's constitutional relationship with international law. It argues that one of the consequences of this transformation is that the legal capacity of provincial legislatures to tailor labour market regulation to the interests of capital, engage in regulatory competition with other provinces, and experiment with new forms of regulating employment relations, is now curtailed by international standards that receive constitutional expression regardless of whether they have been implemented in domestic legislation. More generally, it explores the nature of Canadian constitutionalism in an age of post-dualism.

Section B provides an account of the demise of dualism's explanatory value in comprehending Canada's constitutional relationship with the international legal order. Section C traces the Court's jurisprudential reversal of its stance toward freedom of association and situates it in light of dualism's demise. Section D addresses some of the implications of these twin developments in the context of contemporary debates over the merits of constitutional oversight of Canadian labour law. The conclusion offers some more general concluding observations on the implications of a constitutional engagement with international law that transcends dualism.

B. Dualism's Demise

At the height of the Great Depression in 1937, the Judicial Committee of the Privy Council audaciously struck down three statutes enacted by the Parliament of Canada extending rights to workers. The legislation sought to implement international treaty obligations that Canada had assumed under the auspices of the International Labour Organization (ILO).[9] Drawing a famous distinction between forming and performing a treaty, the Privy Council held that the federal government possesses the authority to form or ratify a treaty and thereby bind Canada at international law, but the performance of a treaty—its implementation into domestic law—requires legislation. When an international legal obligation is implemented by legislation, its domestic legal force is the product of the implementing statute, not the treaty. A treaty itself creates no domestic legal obligations. The justification commonly offered for this approach is that by entering into treaties with foreign states, the Crown, in its executive

9 *AG Canada v AG Ontario*, [1937] AC 326 (PC) (Lord Atkin).

capacity, should not be entitled to usurp federal or provincial legislative authority.[10]

Because Canada is a federal state, the Privy Council held further that treaty performance depends on the distribution of legislative authority between Parliament and provincial legislatures. Relying on precedent,[11] it concluded that Parliament does not possess the jurisdiction to enact the legislation in question because labour relations, with the exception of those in enterprises under federal authority, fall within the exclusive authority of provincial legislatures.

Neither the Privy Council's dualist stance on Canada's relationship to the international legal order nor its implications for the federal distribution of legislative authority have been explicitly revisited by the Canadian judiciary. As a result, the political capacity to regulate relations between capital and labour has been diffused throughout the federation, with democratic contestation over the appropriate relationship between market and state occurring in multiple jurisdictions. This diffusion of regulatory power has hampered the capacity of the Canadian state to provide for uniform and national levels of worker protection consistent with its international obligations.[12] Instead, it has empowered provincial majorities to engage in regulatory competition with each other and other jurisdictions to attract capital investment by reducing costs associated with worker protection.

In recent years, however, the Supreme Court of Canada has effectively rendered obsolete Canada's dualist engagement with international law. By extension, it has cast serious doubt on the substantive value of the principle that implementation of international legal norms is subject to the distribution of legislative authority be-

---

10 See *Capital Cities Communications v CRTC*, [1978] 2 SCR 141 at 173, Laskin CJ ("[C]ertainly the convention [the 1937 Inter-American Radio Communications Convention] per se cannot prevail against the express stipulations of the Act"); *Daniels v White and the Queen*, [1968] SCR 517, Hall J dissenting, but not on this point, and with the concurrence of Ritchie and Spence JJ ("[I]f a statute is unambiguous . . . its provisions must be followed even if they are contrary to the established rules of international law [specifically, the 1916 Canada-U.S. Migratory Birds Convention]"); *Re Arrow River and Tributaries Slide & Boom Co Limited*, [1932] SCR 495 at 510, Lamont J. See generally Irit Weiser, "Undressing the Window: Treating International Human Rights Law Meaningfully in the Canadian Commonwealth System" (2004) 37 UBC L Rev 113.

11 *Reference re Regulation and Control of Radio Communication in Canada*, [1932] AC 304 (PC); and *Toronto Electric Commissioners v Snider*, [1925] AC 396 (PC).

12 See Adelle Blackett, "Mutual Promise: International Labour Law and B.C. Health Services," (2009) 48 SCLR (2d) 365 at 368–9 [Blackett].

tween Parliament and provincial legislatures. Five related developments account for this fundamental shift in Canada's constitutional relationship to the international legal order.

First, the Court relies on international law to determine the constitutional distribution of legislative authority between Parliament and the provincial legislatures. In *R v Crown Zellerbach*,[13] the Court was asked to determine the constitutionality of a provision in a federal statute apparently enacted to implement international legal obligations Canada had assumed by ratifying an international treaty governing marine pollution. The provision in question encroached on provincial legislative authority over provincial waters. The federal government nonetheless argued that marine pollution constituted a matter of national concern that fell under its peace, order, and good government power.

The Court agreed, holding that marine pollution was a subject that possesses the requisite singleness or indivisibility to be assigned to Parliament as a matter of national concern. One of the reasons the Court offered in support of this conclusion was that the international treaty in question, the Convention on the Prevention of Marine Pollution by Dumping of Wastes and other Matter, treats marine pollution as "a distinct and separate form of water pollution having its own characteristics and scientific considerations."[14]

The terms of an international treaty, in other words, are relevant to determining whether Parliament or provincial legislatures possess the authority to legislate in relation to a particular subject matter. While *Crown Zellerbach* formally does not disturb the *Labour Conventions* holding that implementation of treaty obligations is subject to the distribution of legislative authority, it does a substantive end run around the rule. The implementation of international treaty obligations itself does not fall within federal jurisdiction, but the presence of an international treaty suggests that its content constitutes a matter of national concern assigned to Parliament under its peace, order, and good government power.

Second, the Court relies on international law to determine the extraterritorial reach of the *Canadian Charter of Rights and Freedoms*. For example, at issue in *R v Hape* was whether RCMP officers were subject to the *Charter* when participating in a search and seizure in the Turks and Caicos Islands during an investigation of suspected money-laundering activities of a Canadian businessman. Justice

13 *R v Crown Zellerbach Canada Ltd*, [1988] 1 SCR 401 [*Crown Zellerbach*].

14 *Ibid* at para 38.

LeBel, for a majority of the Court, held that, generally speaking, the *Charter* does not apply to Canadian officials participating in another state's investigation so as to require it to conform to Canadian law. Justice LeBel relied on the relationship between principles and obligations of customary international law, on the one hand, and the common law, on the other, in support of this conclusion.[15]

The international legal customs on which LeBel J relied involved principles relating to the limits of a state's jurisdiction, the sovereignty and domestic affairs of other states, and the comity of nations. It is not at all controversial to hold that these principles form part of the common law. As noted by LeBel J, unlike international treaty obligations, customary international law does not require implementing legislation to acquire domestic legal force. Canadian courts have long followed the English tradition[16] that customary international law forms part of the common law.[17]

To hold that customary international law is relevant to the scope of the *Charter*, however, circumvents the dualist requirement that legislatures are to determine whether international legal principles receive domestic legal force. Although courts presume legislation to conform to international law,[18] dualism authorizes legislatures to contradict international legal norms that crystallize domestically in the common law. By relying on customary international law to determine the territorial reach of the *Charter*, *Hape* instead suggests that international law assists in determining the limits and possibilities of legislative authority.

Hape thus affirms a conception of the relationship between the international and domestic legal orders markedly different than the dualist vision. Justice Bastarache in *Hape* was quick to realize the implications of this approach. Concurring with Lebel J in the result, Bastarache J argued that relying on international law to "strike a balance between effective participation by Canadian officers in fighting transnational crime and the protection of fundamental human rights"

15 *R. v Hape*, [2007] 2 SCR 292 [*Hape*].

16 See, for example, *Trendtex Trading Corp v Central Bank of Nigeria*, [1977] 1 QB 529 (CA).

17 *The Ship "North" v The King*, (1906) 37 SCR 385 at 394; *Reference as to Whether Members of the Military or Naval Forces of the United States of America are Exempt from Criminal Proceedings in Canadian Criminal Courts*, [1943] SCR 483 at 502; *Reference as to Powers to Levy Rates on Foreign Legations and High Commissioners' Residences*, [1943] SCR 208; *Saint John (Municipality of) v Fraser-Brace Overseas Corp*, [1958] SCR 263; *Mack v Canada (AG)* (2002), 60 OR (3d) 737 (CA); *Bouzari v Islamic Republic of Iran* (2004), 71 OR (3d) 675 (CA).

18 See, for example, *Daniels v White*, [1968] SCR 517 at 541, Pigeon J.

wrongly replaces constitutional norms with international norms. He countered that "constitutions operate to define the sphere of legitimate governmental action."[19] In his view, courts should rely on constitutional—not international—norms to determine the territorial reach of the *Charter*.

Not only does international law underpin a general rule governing the *Charter*'s exterritorial reach; it also underpins an exception to this general rule. The groundwork for this exception was laid in *Hape*, when LeBel J held that that the deference required by the principle of comity "ends where clear violations of international law and fundamental human rights begin."[20] It was brought to the surface in *Canada v Khadr*,[21] where the Court held that the American military commissions did not possess the status of "a regularly constituted court, affording all the judicial guarantees which are recognized as indispensable by civilized peoples," as required by Common Article 3 of the *Geneva Conventions*, to which Canada is party.[22]

This was sufficient for the Court in *Khadr* to conclude that the general rule established in *Hape* that the *Charter* does not apply to Canadian participation in the activities of a foreign state is subject to an exception that prevents Canadian authorities from engaging in activities abroad that violate Canada's international obligations. In such circumstances, the *Charter* binds Canada to the extent that Canadian officials abroad violate international law. Like *Hape*, *Khadr* illustrates the replacement of the traditional dualist view of the domestic implications of international law with a much more porous conception of the boundary between the national and international. In addition to customary international law, Canada's treaty obligations participate in determining the scope of constitutional—and, by extension, legislative—authority.

Third, the Court relies on international human rights treaties to which Canada is party to interpret the content of the *Charter*. The *International Covenant on Civil and Political Rights* (*ICCPR*) and, to

---

19 *Hape*, above note 15 at para 125.

20 *Ibid* at para 52 (LeBel J); see also paras 51 and 101.

21 *Canada (Justice) v Khadr*, [2008] 2 SCR 125 [*Khadr*].

22 Ibid at para 23, citing Common Article 3 of *Geneva Convention for the Amelioration of the Condition of the Wounded and Sick in Armed Forces in the Field*, 75 UNTS 31, Can TS 1965 No 20 at 25; *Geneva Convention for the Amelioration of the Condition of Wounded, Sick and Shipwrecked Members of Armed Forces at Sea*, 75 UNTS 85, Can TS 1965 No 20 at 55; *Geneva Convention Relative to the Protection of Civilian Persons in Time of War*, 75 UNTS 287, Can TS 1965 No 20 at 163; and *Geneva Convention Relative to the Treatment of Prisoners of War*, 75 UNTS 135, Can TS 1965 No 20 at 84.

a lesser extent, the *International Covenant on Economic, Social and Cultural Rights* (*ICESCR*) figure prominently in *Charter* interpretation. Since the inception of the *Charter* in 1982, the Court has invoked provisions of the *ICCPR* in at least thirty-three cases,[23] whereas it has invoked the *ICESCR* in at least thirteen cases.[24] In several cases, the Court has also made reference to legal instruments and jurisprudence under the auspices of the ILO.[25]

Of particular relevance is the Court's treatment of these three international legal sources in *BC Health Services*.[26] The Court in *BC Health Services* noted that Canada, strictly speaking, is a dualist jurisdiction, but proceeded to treat Canada's international legal obligations to protect freedom of association as enshrined in the *ICESCR*,

---

23 *R v Big M Drug Mart Ltd*, [1985] 1 SCR 295; *Mills v The Queen*, [1986] 1 SCR 863; *R v Oakes*, [1986] 1 SCR 103; *R v Smith (Edward Dewey)*, [1987] 1 SCR 1045; *Alberta Reference*, above note 1; *R v Milne*, [1987] 2 SCR 512; *Edmonton Journal v Alberta (AG)*, [1989] 2 SCR 1326; *Reference Re Canada (Human Rights Commission) v Taylor*, [1990] 3 SCR 892; *R v Zundel*, [1992] 2 SCR 731; *R v Keegstra*, [1990] 3 SCR 697; *R v Brydges*, [1990] 1 SCR 190; *McKinney v University of Guelph*, [1990] 3 SCR 229; *Kindler v Canada (Minister of Justice)*, [1991] 2 SCR 779; *R v Tran*, [1994] 2 SCR 951; *R v Prosper*, [1994] 3 SCR 236; *B(R) v Children's Aid Society of Metropolitan Toronto*, [1995] 1 SCR 315; *Chan v Canada (Minister of Employment and Immigration)*, [1995] 3 SCR 593; *R v O'Connor*, [1995] 4 SCR 411; 2747-3174 *Québec Inc v Quebec (Régie des permis d'alcool)*, [1996] 3 SCR 919; *R v Lucas*, [1998] 1 SCR 439; *Reference re Secession of Quebec*, [1998] 2 SCR 217; *Quebec (Commission des droits de la personne et des droits de la jeunesse) v Montréal (City); Quebec (Commission des droits de la personne et des droits de la jeunesse) v Boisbriand (City)*, [2000] 1 SCR 665; *R v Sharpe*, [2001] 1 SCR 45; *United States v Burns*, [2001] 1 SCR 283; *R v Advance Cutting & Coring Ltd.*, [2001] 3 SCR 209; *Suresh v Canada (Minister of Citizenship and Immigration)*, [2002] 1 S.C.R. 3 [*Suresh*]; *Lavoie v Canada*, [2002] 1 SCR 769; *Chamberlain v Surrey School District No 36*, [2002] 4 SCR 710; *Sauvé v Canada (Chief Electoral Officer)*, [2002] 3 SCR 519; *Canadian Foundation for Children, Youth and the Law v Canada (Attorney General)*, [2004] 1 SCR 76; *Harper v Canada (Attorney General)*, [2004] 1 SCR 827; *BC Health Services*, above note 3; *Fraser*, above note 4.

24 *Alberta Reference*, *ibid*; *Slaight Communications Inc v Davidson*, [1989] 1 SCR 1038 [*Slaight Communications*]; *Irwin Toy Ltd v AG Quebec*, [1989] 1 SCR 927; *Reference re Secession of Quebec*, [1998] 2 SCR 217; *Canadian Egg Marketing Agency v Richardson*, [1998] 3 SCR 157; *Delisle v Canada (Deputy AG)*, [1999] 2 SCR 989; *Quebec (Commission des droits de la personne et des droits de la jeunesse) v Montréal (City); Quebec (Commission des droits de la personne et des droits de la jeunesse) v Boisbriand (City)*, [2000] 1 SCR 665; *R v Sharpe*, [2001] 1 SCR 45; *R v Advance Cutting & Coring Ltd*, [2001] 3 SCR 209; *Gosselin v Québec (AG)*, [2002] 4 SCR 429; *Quebec (Commission des droits de la personne et des droits de la jeunesse) v Maksteel Québec Inc*, [2003] 3 SCR 228 [*Maksteel Québec*]; *BC Health Services*, above note 3; *Fraser*, above note 4.

25 See, for example, *Alberta Reference*, *ibid*; *RWDSU v Saskatchewan*, above note 1; *Dunmore*, above note 2; *Maksteel Québec*, *ibid*; *BC Health Services*, above note 3.

26 *BC Health Services*, *ibid*.

the *ICCPR*, and ILO Convention No 87 concerning freedom of association and protection of the right to organize[27] as relevant to the interpretation of the *Charter*'s guarantee of freedom of association. The scope of protection accorded to the right to bargain collectively in these international legal instruments was one of several reasons why the Court held that the constitutional guarantee includes a right to bargain collectively and requires legislative action to secure its protection.

Notwithstanding its nod to dualism, *BC Health Services* decisively departs from the dualist requirement that international treaty obligations require legislative implementation to acquire domestic legal force. While treaty obligations do not assume legislative status absent legislative action, they now participate in the imposition of constitutional obligations on legislatures. *BC Health Services* also renders practically moot that fact that, as a result of *Labour Conventions*, provincial legislatures, generally speaking, possess the legislative authority to implement international labour law. If legislatures fail to implement international labour law, they risk running afoul of the *Charter*.

Fourth, the Court does not solely look to treaties that Canada has ratified for guidance when interpreting the *Charter*.[28] In *Suresh v Canada (Minister of Citizenship and Immigration)*, for example, the Court relied on the *European Convention on Human Rights*,[29] the *African Charter on Human Rights*, and the *American Convention on Human Rights*—in addition to treaties to which Canada is party—to reach the conclusion "that international law rejects deportation to torture, even where national security interests are at stake," and that this norm "best informs the content of the principles of fundamental justice under s 7 of the *Charter*."[30]

---

27 68 *UNTS* 17 (entered into force 4 July 1950).

28 See Stephen Toope, "Canada and International Law" (1998) 27 Proc Can Council Int'l L 33 at 36 ("[A]t the Supreme Court of Canada there appears to be no great distinction between treaties actually ratified by Canada and those to which Canada is not and could not be a party.").

29 The jurisprudence of the European Court of Human Rights on the *European Convention on Human Rights* plays an especially prominent role in *Charter* interpretation. See, for example, *R v Oakes*, above note 23; *R v Jones*, [1986] 2 SCR 284; *R v Nova Scotia Pharmaceutical Society*, [1992] 2 SCR 606; *R v Advance Cutting & Coring Ltd*, above note 23; *Sauvé v. Canada (Chief Electoral Officer)*, above note 23; *Charkaoui v Canada (Citizenship and Immigration)*, [2007] 1 SCR 350; and *Alberta v Hutterian Brethren of Wilson Colony*, [2009] SCR 567.

30 Suresh, above note 23.

It is one thing to rely on treaties to which Canada is bound when interpreting the scope of domestic constitutional authority. Such a departure from dualism can be papered over by presuming that the drafters of the Constitution enacted the *Charter* with an eye to Canada's international legal obligations. However, relying on treaties that Canada has not ratified—and, in some cases, could not ratify—to interpret the scope of constitutional authority casts Canada's constitutional relationship to the international legal order in entirely different terms. Gone is any pretence of voluntarism. International legal principles possess domestic constitutional significance not because political authorities have actually or fictively consented to be bound by them; they possess domestic constitutional significance simply because of their international legal stature.

Fifth, the Court invokes non-binding international instruments, commonly known as "soft law," to interpret the scope and content of constitutional provisions. It has done so even where Canada is not—and, in all likelihood, never will be—a signatory of the instrument in question. In *Suresh,* for example, the Court cited the *Universal Islamic Declaration of Human Rights* in support of its conclusion that deportation to torture offends constitutional principles of fundamental justice.[31]

The Court has also relied on soft law initiatives still in draft form for interpretive guidance. In *Mitchell v MNR,*[32] for example, Binnie J, in a concurring judgment, referred to the draft *Inter-American Declaration on the Rights of Indigenous Peoples*[33] and the then-draft *UN Declaration on the Rights of Indigenous Peoples*[34] in the course of an analysis of the transnational dimensions of Aboriginal rights recognized and affirmed by section 35(1) of the *Constitution Act, 1982*. These cases further underscore the demise of dualism. A dualist legal order only concerns itself with binding international legal norms; a non-binding international legal norm would have no domestic legal consequences whatsoever. Now even nonbinding international legal norms possess constitutional significance.

Nowhere is the Court's reliance on international legal norms to determine the limits of constitutional authority more striking than when international law serves as a basis for a reversal of constitutional precedent. In 1991, the Court rendered reasons in *Kindler v*

---

31 Suresh, ibid.

32 Mitchell v MNR, [2001] 1 SCR 911.

33 Inter-American Commission on Human Rights (18 September 1995).

34 Sub-Commission on Prevention of Discrimination and Protection of Minorities, United Nations—Res 1994/45 (26 August 1994).

Canada, a case involving the constitutionality of the minister of justice's decision to surrender a fugitive to the United States without seeking assurances from American officials that the death penalty would not be imposed or, if imposed, not carried out.

A majority of the Court, garnered by separate judgments by McLachlin and LaForest JJ, held that the minister's decision to surrender the fugitive violated his rights to life and liberty but was in accordance with the principles of fundamental justice. According to LaForest J, the ministerial decision could not be said to "shock the conscience of the Canadian people nor be in violation of the standards of the international community."[35] According to McLachlin J, the situation faced by the fugitive upon extradition could not be said to be "simply unacceptable."[36] Both saw the reasons for extradition as compelling and the American procedural guarantees afforded to the individual as adequate, and both emphasized the need to confer extensive deference on ministerial extradition decisions when assessing their constitutionality.

Ten years later, in *United States v Burns*, the Court effectively reversed its holding in *Kindler*, holding that assurances from a foreign jurisdiction that the death penalty would not be imposed or, if imposed, not carried out, are constitutionally required in all but exceptional cases. Casting *Kindler* as establishing a balancing test for determining the constitutionality of extradition without assurances, the Court in *Burns* held that "a balance which tilted in favour of extradition in *Kindler* . . . now tilts against the constitutionality of such an outcome."[37]

One of the reasons for this tilt, according to the Court, is that "[t]he international trend against the death penalty has become clearer" since its decision in *Kindler*. The Court acknowledged that international law has yet to yield a legal "norm against the death penalty, or against extradition to face the death penalty," but the lack of a binding legal international legal obligation did not stop the Court from relying on international legal sources in support of overturning *Kindler*.[38] It referred to numerous hard and soft international

---

35 *Kindler v Canada (Minister of Justice)*, [1991] 2 SCR 779 [*Kindler*]. See also *Reference re Ng Extradition (Can)*, [1991] 2 SCR 858.

36 Kindler, *ibid*.

37 *United States v Burns*, [2001] 1 SCR 282 at para 144 [*Burns*].

38 Compare to *Hape*, above note 15 at para 55, where LeBel J held that both international obligations and principles of international law are relevant to *Charter* interpretation: "This Court has also looked to international law to assist it in interpreting the *Charter*. Whenever possible, it has sought to ensure consistency

legal instruments and initiatives that suggest "significant movement towards acceptance" of such a norm.[39] These included both instruments and initiatives to which Canada both is and is not a party or participant, namely, the *European Convention on Extradition*, the United Nations *Model Treaty on Extradition*, and calls by the UN Commission on Human Rights, the UN Secretary-General, the UN Special Rapporteur on Extrajudicial Executions, the Parliamentary Assembly of the Council of Europe, and the European Parliament.[40]

International legal instruments thus possess domestic constitutional significance to the distribution of legislative authority between Parliament and provincial legislatures and the scope and content of the *Charter*. They do so not simply because they might impose binding international legal obligations on Canada. The Court relies on international instruments to which Canada is not bound, instruments to which Canada could not be bound, and instruments that create no binding legal obligations whatsoever, to both develop and overrule domestic legal doctrines governing the nature and scope of the Canadian constitutional order.

To the extent that dualism requires international legal norms to be implemented by legislation to receive binding legal force, dualism is alive in Canada in name only. Such international legal norms are not domestically binding, but ratified and non-ratified, hard and soft, and finalized and draft international legal norms form a backdrop to judicial determinations of constitutional power, which are, of course, domestically binding. As the next section explains, the key to understanding the Court's constitutional jurisprudence on freedom of association is that its trajectory runs parallel to the emergence of this new conception of Canada's constitutional relationship to the international legal order.

---

between its interpretation of the *Charter*, on the one hand, and Canada's international obligations and the relevant principles of international law, on the other."

39 *Burns*, above note 37 at para 89. For more discussion of the role that international law plays in extradition cases, see Ed Morgan, "In the Penal Colony: Internationalism and the Canadian Constitution" (1999) 49 UTLJ 447.

40 See, respectively, *European Convention on Extradition*, Eur TS No 24, signed 13 December 1957; *Model Treaty on Extradition* (passed by the General Assembly in December 1990); UN Commission on Human Rights, Resolutions, 1999/61 (adopted 28 April 1999 and 2000/65 (adopted 27 April 2000); *Extrajudicial, Summary or Arbitrary Executions: Report by the Special Rapporteur*, UN Doc E/CN 4/1997/60 at para 79; *Extrajudicial, Summary or Arbitrary Executions: Note by the Secretary-general*, UN Doc A//51/457 at para 145; Council of Europe, Parliamentary Assembly, Resolution 1044 (1994); European Parliament, Resolutions B4-0468, 0487, 0497, 0513 and 0542/97 (1997).

C. The Post-Dualist Trajectory of Freedom of Association

The Court's jurisprudence on freedom of association commenced in the early years of the *Charter.* At issue in the lead case of the Labour Trilogy—the *Alberta Reference*—was the constitutionality of several provincial statutes prohibiting strikes by public service employees, firefighters, hospital employees, and police officers, and substituting an arbitration scheme for resolving bargaining disputes.[41] The plurality decision by LeDain J held that freedom of association protects the ability to establish, belong to, maintain an association, and participate in its lawful activities, but not a right of workers to bargain collectively or strike.

In a concurring judgment, McIntyre J held that freedom of association includes the ability to carry out collectively those activities that are lawful for the individual, but not activities which cannot be performed by an individual. Even if such activities are essential to the purposes of the organization, they cannot come within the scope of freedom of association since a group can only possess the same rights as its individual members. Because there is no individual analogue to striking, according to McIntyre J, these actions are not protected as of constitutional right.

In his dissent, Dickson CJ, presciently planting the seeds of dualism's demise, stated that:

> The various sources of international human rights law—declarations, covenants, conventions, judicial and quasi-judicial decisions of international tribunals, customary norms—must, in my opinion, be relevant and persuasive sources for interpretation of the Charter's provisions.[42]

Chief Justice Dickson also stated that "the *Charter* should generally be presumed to provide protection at least as great as that afforded by similar provisions in international human rights documents which Canada has ratified."[43] International instruments, including the *IC-*

---

41 *Alberta Reference*, above note 1.

42 *Alberta Reference, ibid* at para 57. See also *Godbout v Longueuil (City)*, [1997] 3 SCR 844 at para 69, La Forest J (art 12 of the *ICCPR* supports interpreting s 7 of the *Charter* as protecting a right to an abode); *R v Jones*, [1986] 2 SCR 284, Wilson J (art 8(1) of the *European Convention* supports interpreting s 7 of the *Charter* as protecting a right of parents to educate children in accordance with their religious and philosophical convictions).

43 But see *B(R) v Childrens Aid Society of Metropolitan Toronto*, [1995] 1 SCR 315 at 349–50, where restrictive decisions by the Human Rights Committee under the *ICCPR* were relied on to exclude certain economic interests from the scope of s 7 of the *Charter.*

CPR, the *ICESCR*, and ILO Convention No 87, according to Dickson CJ, extended international legal protection to the right to bargain collectively and the right to strike as incidents of freedom of association, which in turn figured prominently in his reasons why they ought to receive constitutional protection.

The Court reiterated its majority holdings three years later in *PIPS*,[44] a case dealing with whether public sector employees had to belong to a union other than the one to which they belonged in order to bargain collectively with their employer. Justice Sopinka's plurality judgment held explicitly that collective bargaining is not an activity protected by freedom of association. He distilled the *Alberta Reference* down to four propositions:

> [F]irst, that s. 2(d) protects the freedom to establish, belong to and maintain an association; second, that s. 2(d) does not protect an activity solely on the ground that the activity is a foundational or essential purpose of an association; third, that s. 2(d) protects the exercise in association of the constitutional rights and freedoms of individuals; and fourth, that s. 2(d) protects the exercise in association of the lawful rights of individuals.[45]

Justice Sopinka was of the view that restrictions on the activity of collective bargaining do not amount to an interference with the freedom to form or join a trade union. Moreover, while collective bargaining may be an essential purpose of a trade union, s 2(d) does not protect essential purposes of associations for the reasons provided in the Labour Trilogy.[46] Finally, Sopinka J held that there is no individual analogy to the right to bargain collectively; individuals at common law are not entitled to force employers to bargain with them over terms and conditions of employment. An employer is free at common law to contract or refuse to contract with whomever she so desires.[47] According to Sopinka J, if there is no individual duty to

---

44 *Professional Institute of the Public Service of Canada v Northwest Territories (Commissioner)*, [1990] 2 SCR 367 [*PIPS*].

45 *Ibid* at para 73.

46 In the *Alberta Reference*, LeDain J described the view that s 2(d) ought to protect activity essential to the existence of an association as "sweeping" (above note 1 at 239). Justice McIntyre stated that to accept the proposition "would be to accord an independent constitutional status to the aims, purposes, and activities of the association, and thereby confer greater constitutional rights upon members of the association than upon non-members" (*ibid* at 225).

47 See, for example, *Christie v York*, [1940] SCR 139.

bargain with an employee, freedom of association cannot be said to require an employer to bargain collectively with its employees.

As many were quick to point out, the majority judgments in the Labour Trilogy and *PIPS* misunderstand important features of the private and public dimensions of labour law.[48] Although it is the case that there are qualitative differences between individual and collective employee action, contrary to McIntyre J's assertion that there is no individual analogue to a right to strike, individual employees do possess the freedom to refuse to work for an employer upon the expiry of a contract of employment. And contrary to Sopinka J's assertion that there is no individual analogue to collective bargaining, employees do possess the freedom to bargain individually with their employers. Subsequent decisions exposed these internal flaws even as they attempted to fix them.

Delisle v Canada, for example, concerned a provision in a federal statute that excluded RCMP members from its definition of "employee" for the purposes of collective bargaining. Delisle, an RCMP member, argued that this provision made it impossible for him to organize and therefore violated the constitutional guarantee of freedom of association.[49] Writing for the majority, Bastarache J provided a narrow interpretation of what little remained of freedom of association in the context of work after the Labour Trilogy and its progeny, namely, the simple right to form an association. He noted that the statute in question did not prohibit RCMP officers from forming a union. It prohibited RCMP officers from forming a union that could access the statutory rights that the Act extended to qualified public sector unions, such as the right to bargain collectively and, in some circumstances, the right to strike. Justice Bastarache then held that, except in exceptional circumstances, freedom of association does not impose on Parliament a positive obligation to provide a statutory collective bargaining regime in which its employees can exercise their freedom of association; it imposes only a negative obligation not to prevent employees from forming an association. Since the legislation did not breach such an obligation, it did not violate the guarantee.

---

48 See, for example, David Beatty & Steven Kennett, "Striking Back: Fighting Words, Social Protest and Political Participation in Free and Democratic Societies" (1988) 67 Can Bar Rev 573; and Patrick Macklem, "Developments in Employment Law: The 1991 Term" (1993) 3 Sup Ct L Rev 227. See also Brian Langille & Patrick Macklem, "The Political Economy of Fairness: The Labour Law Jurisprudence of Frank Iacobucci" (2007) UTLJ 343.

49 *Delisle v Canada (Deputy AG)*, [1999] 2 SCR 989.

With the Court's ruling in *Dunmore*,[50] it was only a matter of time that the reasons offered by the majority in the Labour Trilogy would be exposed as doctrinal disasters. At issue in *Dunmore* was the constitutionality of a statutory provision excluding agricultural workers from the protection of a provincial collective bargaining regime. The effect of the exclusion was to render it virtually impossible for agricultural workers to form a union to represent their interests to employers.

Justice Bastarache, again for a majority of the Court, held that the collective bargaining regime in question "provides the only statutory vehicle by which employees in Ontario can associate to defend their interests and, moreover, recognizes that such association is, in many cases, otherwise impossible."[51] Although the Court was careful to state that freedom of association does not require the state to provide extensive statutory protection of freedom of association, it held that the exclusion from a statutory regime otherwise available to most workers in the province had a chilling effect on the agricultural workers' freedom of association. The Court ordered the legislature to provide a statutory framework that secures the right of agricultural workers to form a union and protects freedoms essential to its exercise, such as freedom of assembly; freedom from interference, coercion, and discrimination by an employer; and freedom to make lawful representations and participate in the lawful activities of a union.

In so holding, Bastarache J accepted the dissenting account of freedom of association offered by Dickson CJ in the *Alberta Reference*, who rejected McIntyre J's assertion in that case that only those activities that can be performed by individuals fall within the scope of the guarantee. Chief Justice Dickson had argued that freedom of association should also protect activities that possess no individual analogue, because of their uniquely social quality. In Dickson CJ's view, freedom of association recognises "the profoundly social nature of human endeavours," protects "the individual from State-enforced isolation in the pursuit of his or her ends," and is a vital means of "protecting the essential needs and interests of working people."[52]

In *Dunmore*, Bastarache J similarly argued that an association of individuals is qualitatively distinct from the individuals who comprise it: individuals associate not simply because there is strength

50 Above note 2.

51 *Ibid* at para 36.

52 *Alberta Reference*, above note 1 at para 86.

in numbers, but because a collectivity can embody objectives that individuals cannot. Such objectives include aggregating individual interests into collective representations to an employer and federating with other associations. On this account, the purpose of freedom of association is to protect not simply the collective exercise of lawful individual actions but also actions that are uniquely social—precisely because of their uniquely collective nature.

Justice Bastarache was careful to pay lip service to the majority holding in the *Alberta Reference*, noting that the right to bargain collectively was not at issue in the case, and the legislature is not obligated to provide agricultural workers with the full panoply of statutory protections typically associated with a collective bargaining regime. The logic of his reasons, however, extends well beyond the right to form a union. Given the Court's previous holdings that there is no individual analogue to collective bargaining and striking, *Dunmore* implied that, in some circumstances at least, the *Charter* guarantee of freedom of association protects collective actions associated with collective bargaining and striking.

Dunmore is particularly noteworthy for its post-dualist engagement with international labour law. In support of his holdings, Bastarache J referred not only to ILO Convention No 87,[53] which Canada has ratified, but also ILO Convention No 11 concerning the rights of association of agricultural workers[54] and ILO Convention No 141 concerning organizations of rural workers, neither of which Canada has ratified. The fact that the latter two instruments did not impose binding international legal obligations on Canada possessed no significance to Bastarache J's reasoning. They lent persuasive force to his conclusion that freedom of association, in some circumstances, requires legislatures to legislate for its protection.

Justice Bastarache also relied on the jurisprudence of the ILO's Committee on Freedom of Association (CFA), a body not responsible for delineating binding obligations arising from ILO Conventions. The CFA does not enforce or monitor state compliance with ILO Conventions—the ILO Constitution provides for other formal legal processes for allegations of noncompliance with a Convention by a state party to its terms; for the making of authoritative findings of fact in this regard; for authoritative judicial interpretations of treaty obligations; for the articulation of recommendations; and ultimately for remedies for breach. The CFA hears cases brought against mem-

---

53 67 UNTS 17.

54 38 UNTS 153.

ber states of the ILO alleging failures to adhere to various principles that relate to freedom of association, and renders its views on the admissibility and merits of such complaints.

In rendering its views, the CFA often makes reference to the terms of various Conventions, including Conventions that the state in question has failed to ratify, but it does not do so in ways that suggest that a state owes obligations under a Convention that it has not ratified. Instead, it makes reference to Conventions to illuminate the nature and scope of the principles of freedom of association that it is charged with promoting. The CFA has consistently treated the right to bargain collectively as an incident of freedom of association.[55]

By invoking treaties that Canada has not ratified in addition to Convention No 87, and the views of an international body devoted to the production of soft international legal norms, *Dunmore* affirms a conception of the relationship between the national and international legal orders markedly different than the dualist vision. Notably, it did so at the very moment when the Court began to dismantle the doctrinal framework that it constructed in the Labour Trilogy to give meaning to the constitutional guarantee of freedom of association.

The Court completed the circle in *BC Health Services*. It did so by explicitly overruling the Labour Trilogy, in no small measure because of the Labour Trilogy's incompatibility with international legal norms. At issue in *BC Health Services* was legislation that unilaterally introduced changes to existing rules governing employee transfers, job security, and layoffs and invalidating inconsistent provisions of existing collective agreements. Expressly overturning the Labour Trilogy, the Court held that freedom of association protects the right to bargain collectively and imposes a duty on employers to negotiate the terms and conditions of collective agreements in good faith. Specifically, McLachlin CJ and LeBel J stated:

> [89] The constitutional right to collective bargaining concerns the protection of the ability of workers to engage in associational activities, and their capacity to act in common to reach shared goals related to workplace issues and terms of employment. In brief, the protected activity might be described as employees banding together to achieve particular work-related objectives. Section 2(d) does not guarantee the particular objectives sought through this associational activity. However, it guarantees the process through which those goals are pursued. It means

55 See Patrick Macklem, "The Right to Bargain Collectively at International Law: Workers' Right, Human Right, International Right?" in Philip Alston, ed, *Labour Rights as Human Rights* (Oxford University Press, 2005).

> that employees have the right to unite, to present demands to health sector employers collectively and to engage in discussions in an attempt to achieve workplace-related goals . . . .
>
> [90] . . . [T]he state must not substantially interfere with the ability of a union to exert meaningful influence over working conditions through a process of collective bargaining, conducted in accordance with the duty to bargain in good faith. Thus the employees' right to collective bargaining imposes corresponding duties on the employer. It requires both employer and employees to meet and to bargain in good faith, in pursuit of a common goal of peaceful and productive accommodation.

As noted in Section B, the Court in *BC Health Services* relied on the *ICCPR*, the *ICESCR*, and ILO Convention No 87, all ratified by Canada, in support of these conclusions. Vindicating Dickson CJ's dissent in the *Alberta Reference*, it held that "the *Charter* should be presumed to provide at least as great a level of protection as is found in the international human rights documents that Canada has ratified."[56]

But, as in *Dunmore*, it also relied on principles developed by the ILO's Committee on Freedom of Association that inform the international guarantee of freedom of association.[57] In addition, it relied on the 1998 ILO *Declaration on Fundamental Principles and Rights at Work*,[58] stating that it reveals a "global consensus" and "the current state of international thought on human rights."[59] The 1998 Declaration, a soft international legal instrument, defines freedom of association as including the right to bargain collectively. Like *Dunmore*, *BC Health Services* demonstrates the central properties of a post-dualist conception of the constitutional salience of the international legal order, one where "the current state of international thought on human rights"—whether expressed in hard or soft legal norms—is relevant to determining the contours of Canada's constitutional order.

D. Re-engaging the International

Understanding the trajectory of constitutional jurisprudence on freedom of association in terms of a post-dualist engagement with

56 Above note 3 at para 70.

57 See Bernard Gernigon, Alberto Odero, & Horacio Guido, "ILO Principles Concerning Collective Bargaining" (2000) 139 Int'l Lab Rev 33 at 51–52.

58 6 IHRR 285 (1999).

59 Above note 3 at para 78.

international law makes sense of sharp disagreements over the stability of the majority's reasons in *BC Health Services*. *BC Health Services* enlisted international legal norms in support of its holding not only that a right to bargain collectively is an incident of freedom of association but also that freedom of association requires a process that ensures that employers bargain with employee representatives in good faith. The latter holding was arguably tangential to the facts in the case as the legislation in question violated freedom of association primarily by voiding terms of existing collective agreements. As a result, the Court spent little time addressing the merits and implications of a constitutional duty to bargain in good faith.

However, these were the main issues raised in *AG Ontario v Fraser*,[60] a case that dealt with the constitutionality of legislation designed to comply with the Court's ruling in *Dunmore*. Enacted before the Court's ruling in *BC Health Services*, the *Agricultural Employees Protection Act, 2002* (*AEPA*)[61] granted farm workers statutory rights to form and join an association, participate in its activities, make collective representations to their employers on the terms and conditions of employment, and be protected against interference and discrimination in the exercise of their rights. It also required employers to give employees an opportunity to engage in collective representation, and to listen to such representations, but it did not explicitly impose on employers a duty to negotiate in good faith.

Confronted by a vigorous dissent by Rothstein J arguing that *BC Health Services* should be overturned, McLachlin CJ and LeBel J, for a majority of the Court, held that *Health Services* "affirms a derivative right to collective bargaining, understood in the sense of a process that allows employees to make representations and to have them considered in good faith by employers, who in turn must engage in a process of meaningful discussion."[62] The *AEPA* did not violate freedom of association because, according to McLachlin CJ and LeBel J, its provisions requiring an employer to listen to the collective representations of its employees imply that employers are to consider them in good faith.

Significantly, the majority Justices and Rothstein J in *Fraser* square off over the role that international law should play in constitutional interpretation. Justice Rothstein sounds two alarms over the *BC Health Services*' reliance on international law. First, he notes

60 *Fraser*, above note 4.

61 SO 2002, c16.

62 Above note 4 at para 54.

that the majority's invocation in that case of ILO Convention No 87 ignored the fact that Convention No 87 deals only with freedom of association and does not specifically refer to a right to bargain collectively. Convention No 98 enshrines the right to bargain collectively but, as Rothstein J notes, Canada has not ratified Convention No 98 and therefore has no binding obligations under that Convention. Second, even if Convention No 98 were applicable to Canada, it does not support constitutional recognition of a duty to bargain in good faith.

Justice Rothstein's first critique blithely ignores the fact that *BC Health Services* equally relied on the *ICCPR* and the *ICESCR*, to which Canada is party, in support of its conclusion that the right to bargain collectively is an incident of freedom of association in international law. More importantly, assuming that he was correct to characterize *BC Health Services* as wrongly conflating Convention No 87 and Convention No 98,[63] his concern makes sense only if Canada's constitutional relationship with the international legal order remains dualist in nature. Were it dualist, then implicit reliance on an international treaty provision that does not bind Canada internationally to interpret a constitutional provision would amount to a significant legal error. However, by the time *BC Health Services* was decided, Canada was dualist in name only.

Even if the Court in *BC Health Services* had explicitly relied on Convention No 98, it would have posed no legal problem in our post-dualist times. The Court regularly relies on hard and soft international legal norms by which Canada is not and could not be bound, as well as norms that have yet to acquire the status of international hard or soft law, to interpret the nature of the Canadian constitutional order. If the *Universal Islamic Declaration of Human Rights* is relevant to *Charter* interpretation,[64] then an international convention to which Canada is not party but which had been developed under the auspices of an international organization to which Canada has long been a member, surely is as well.

Dualism's demise also pulls the rug out from under Rothstein J's second critique that international law does not impose a requirement on states to legislate a duty to bargain in good faith. Although indeterminacy runs especially rampant in international law, on this point he is right,[65] and the majority in *BC Health Services* erred to the

---

63 The Court made no reference to Convention No 98 in *BC Health Services*.

64 *Suresh*, above note 23.

65 See Brian Langille, "Can We Rely on the ILO?" (2007) 13 Can Lab & Emp LJ 273.

extent that it interpreted international legal norms in this manner. But the majority also noted that legislative recognition of a duty to bargain in good faith is "consistent" with international legal norms, and, on this point, the majority is also right. As the ILO has repeatedly reassured Canada, a constitutional duty to bargain is not inconsistent with the protection that its instruments and principles extend to freedom of association.[66]

Justice Rothstein claims that consistency with international law is an insufficient basis on which to align constitutional with international norms. In his view, international law must require domestic legal recognition of a norm before it possesses constitutional significance. But while dualism requires a requirement, post-dualism is consistent with consistency. It doesn't matter whether an international legal norm imposes a binding obligation on a post-dualist state. What matters is simply consistency with "the current state of international thought on human rights."[67]

Especially striking in *Fraser* is the fact that international legal norms figure prominently in the majority's defense of the Court's decision in *BC Health Services* to overturn the Labour Trilogy. Chief Justice McLachlin and LeBel J note that the ILO's CFA had reviewed the legislation at issue in *BC Health Services* and had concluded that it violated the principle of freedom of association because voiding the terms of existing collective agreements "may have a detrimental effect on workers' interests in unionization . . . if the results of bargaining are constantly cancelled by law."[68] Oddly enough, the views of the CFA were not referred to by the majority in *BC Health Services* although they predated the Court's decision in that case by four years. But they served as *ex post* validation of *BC Health Services*' reversal of key holdings of the Labour Trilogy.[69] Nonbinding international legal norms, in other words, served as a basis for affirming a reversal of constitutional precedent.

Even more striking is the fact that Rothstein J relies on international law to press for reversing the reversal. A proper understanding of international law, according to Rothstein J, supports overturning *BC Health Services* and restoring the Labour Trilogy's

---

66 See, for example, *ILO Committee of Experts on the Application of Conventions and Recommendations, Freedom of Association and Collective Bargaining* (1994) at para 243. See generally, Blackett, above note 12.

67 *BC Health Services*, above note 3 para 78.

68 *CFA Report No 330 (2003)*, vol LXXXVI, Series B, No 1 at para 304.

69 Equally odd is the fact that the majority in *Fraser* did not refer to the CFA's criticism of the *AEPA* itself: see *CFA Report No 358 (2009)*, vol XCIII, 2010, Series B, No 3.

holding that freedom of association does not protect a right to bargain collectively. Exactly what aspect of the Labour Trilogy Rothstein J seeks to rehabilitate is unclear. While he is of the view that freedom of association should not include a duty to bargain in good faith, he is also of the view that it protects "the decision of employees to come together, to form a bargaining position and to present a common and united front to an employer."[70] But McIntyre J in the Labour Trilogy held that such a decision was not protected by freedom of association as collective bargaining did not possess an individual analogue. This ambiguity notwithstanding, Rothstein J's dissent effectively adds international legal requirements to the list of considerations relevant to deciding whether to overturn constitutional precedent.

Elsewhere the Court has identified the considerations relevant to deciding whether to overturn constitutional precedent. They include whether the prior decision departed from the purpose of a constitutional guarantee; whether it is unworkable as its application is unnecessarily complex and technical; whether it is contrary to "sound principle"; and whether it results in unfairness.[71] Justice Rothstein's reasons suggest the current state of international law assists in determining whether a precedent is contrary to "sound principle." On his account, international law not only supports reversing constitutional precedent, it also supports restoring overturned precedent to the status of constitutional validity.

E. Conclusion

In 1934, Hans Kelsen identified two different ways of explaining why a constitutional order might regard international law as possessing domestic legal significance. The first locates the origins of the significance of international law in a domestic act of recognition. On this account, international law possesses constitutional relevance to the extent a domestic constitution deems it relevant. The second locates the significance of international law in the validity of the international legal order itself. On this account, international law confers on states the authority to arrange the constitutional distribution and exercise of sovereign power.[72]

---

70 Above note 4 at para 271.

71 *R v Henry*, [2005] 3 SCR 609 at paras 45–46, Binnie J.

72 Hans Kelsen, *Pure Theory of Law*, 2d ed, translated by Max Knight (Clark, NJ: Lawbook Exchange, 2005) at 333–44.

A post-dualist conception of Canada's constitutional relationship with the international legal order raises many questions about its normative basis and constitutional consequences. From a theoretical perspective, the most fundamental relates to the reason why international legal developments—whether they take the form of ratified or non-ratified treaties, hard or soft law, or finalized or draft instruments—possess domestic constitutional significance. Is it simply because the Constitution of Canada, as interpreted by the judiciary, deems them relevant? If this is the case, merely pointing to their international legal stature does not provide a persuasive account of their relevance. Or is it because the international legal order normatively grounds domestic constitutional arrangements? If this is the case, then what is needed is a normative account of the primacy of international law over domestic legal orders.

International human rights law may intuitively share common features with constitutional orders that seek to restrain the arbitrary exercise of state power and promote more just societies. Such a convergence might explain the relatively placid acceptance of post-dualism in the age of the *Charter*. But champions of post-dualism should not overlook the fact that international human rights law also includes doctrines that place limits on the exercise of human rights and privileges certain human rights at the expense of others.[73] It also conceives of the legitimacy of human rights primarily in terms of universal features of what it means to be human, a stance that does not always fit comfortably with constitutional arrangements designed to promote social justice within particular political communities. Moreover, many processes responsible for the production of international legal norms lack democratic accountability, and privilege the interests of certain segments of civil society—and certain states—over others.

Closer to home, the Court's jurisprudence on freedom of association—in tune with international human rights law and international labour law—now formally restricts the capacity of Parliament and provincial legislatures to tailor labour market regulation to the interests of capital. However, just as there was more to international politics than international solidarity when Eugène Pottier penned

73 The Court has relied on international human rights instruments to interpret limitations on *Charter* rights in several cases. See, for example, *Slaight Communications*, above note 24; *R v Keegstra*, above note 23; *R v Zundel*, above note 23; *Suresh*, above note 23; *Canada (Human Rights Commission) v Taylor*, above note 23; *Edmonton Journal v Alberta (AG)*, above note 23, La Forest J, dissenting; and *R v Sharpe*, above note 24, L'Heureux-Dubé, Gonthier, and Bastarache JJ.

the original lyrics of "L'Internationale" in 1871, today there is more to international law than international human rights. For example, much has been written on international law's participation with processes of economic globalization. Does international economic law now possess domestic constitutional significance?[74] Are international legal norms governing terrorism relevant to determining the nature and scope of Canadian constitutional authority?[75] In other words, what kind of cat has post-dualism let out of the constitutional bag?

It would be surprising if future cases do not invite the Court to cast a more critical gaze on the invocation of international legal norms when interpreting the nature and scope of constitutional authority. But this chapter is not meant to advocate a return to dualism.[76] In contrast to the constitutional insularity prevalent south of the border, an engaged constitutional stance toward the international legal order promotes open-minded constitutionalism.[77] Nor, however, is it meant to celebrate the new role that international law currently plays in determining the nature and scope of the Canadian constitutional order. Open-mindedness notwithstanding, post-dualism needs more normative justification than what has been offered to date in the jurisprudence. What remains to be explained is exactly when and why international law matters to constitutional interpretation in a post-dualist age.

---

74 For a critical assessment of linkages between international investment law and constitutional norms, see David Schneiderman, *Constitutionalizing Economic Globalization: Investment Rules and Democracy's Promise* (Cambridge: Cambridge University Press, 2008).

75 For a critical assessment, see Kent Roach, *The 9/11 Effect: Comparative Counter-Terrorism* (New York: Cambridge University Press, 2011) especially c 2.

76 But see Gib van Ert, *Using International Law in Canadian Courts*, 2d ed (Toronto: Irwin Law, 2008) especially at 349–51, for a principled defence of dualism that emphasizes a rebuttable presumption of constitutional conformity with international law.

77 For an eloquent defence of post-dualism along these lines, see Knop, above note 7.

CHAPTER ELEVEN

Giving Life to the ILO—Two Cheers for the SCC

*KD Ewing and John Hendy, QC**

I

Fraser is an important case, with a significance that extends well beyond Canada's long border. For those of us who work outside the jurisdiction, the use of international human rights treaties by the Supreme Court of Canada (SCC) in both *Health Services* and *Fraser* is particularly interesting, not least because it reflects developments taking place in courts elsewhere in the world.[1] One of the most significant examples was the recent decisions of the European Court of Human Rights (ECtHR), which has for some time relied upon international human rights instruments (including International Labour Organization (ILO) conventions) to give substance to the right to freedom of association to be found in the European Convention on Human Rights, Article 11. The parallels between the ECtHR and the SCC are particularly significant in view of the fact that like the SCC, the ECtHR had a major conversion, repudiating in 2008 a body of learning that tended towards a narrow rather than an expansive

* The authors wish to thank Dr Alan Bogg, Hertford College, Oxford, for his generous support in the preparation of this paper.

1 See *Bakery, Confectionery, Manufacturing and Allied Workers' Union v Wrigley Ltd*, [2007] eKLR (Kenya); *Mkwezalamba v Malawi Posts Corporation* [IRC 154/2001], *Makande v Malawi Telecommunications Ltd* [IRC 81/2001] (Malawi); *South African Police Service v Police and Prisons Civil Rights Union*, [2011] ZACC 21 (RSA); and *RMT v Serco Ltd; ASLEF v London and Birmingham Railway Ltd*, [2011] EWCA Civ 226; [2011] ICR 848 (UK).

reading of freedom of association guarantees than now is the case.[2] There are, however, important differences in the way in which these two courts now approach ILO standards, with the SCC content to incorporate the principles, and the ECtHR insisting that the principles must be adopted as applied by the ILO supervisory bodies.

As contributors observing the Canadian scene from afar, it is with some humility that we enter what has become a lively and sometimes testy debate about the *Fraser* decision and its implications. We do feel, however, that there are important points to be made about the role of ILO principles, conventions, and jurisprudence in the decision of the SCC, and that some of the arguments that have been made in Canada about the use made of this material by the SCC are at best highly contentious. In our view, it was perfectly proper for the SCC to rely on the ILO, the principles of which relating to collective bargaining *do* impose obligations on Canada. Where the SCC erred in our view, however, was in failing to make clear *why* it was perfectly proper to rely on these, particularly in view of the fact that Canada has not ratified a particular ILO Convention (Convention No 98). More importantly, however, having embraced ILO principles as a source of *Charter* interpretation, the SCC also erred, in our view, by embarking on a frolic of its own, and by failing to apply these principles in accordance with the appropriate ILO jurisprudence.[3]

In this chapter, we consider the relevant ILO Conventions relating to collective bargaining and trace the approach of the Canadian courts to international labour conventions, beginning not with the famous labour conventions case of 1937,[4] but with the rather less well known decision of the Alberta Court of Queen's Bench in 1981.[5] We consider how the approach of the Canadian courts to the importance of ILO Conventions gradually evolved through the 1980s "Labour

---

2 *Demir and Baycara v Turkey*, [2008] ECHR 1345 [*Demir and Baycara*].

3 See especially *Health Services and Support—Facilities Subsector Bargaining Assn v British Columbia*, 2007 SCC 27, [2007] 2 SCR 391 at para 92 [*Health Services*].

4 *Canada (AG) v Ontario (AG)*, [1937] AC 32.

5 *Re Alberta Union of Provincial Employees and Alberta* (1980), 120 DLR (3d) 590 (Alta QB) [*AUPE*]. For an excellent discussion of the international and domestic implications of this case, see Michael Bendel, "The International Protection of Trade Union Rights: A Canadian Case Study" (1981) 31 Ottawa L Rev 169.

Trilogy,"[6] to the new trilogy of *Dunmore*,[7] *Health Services*,[8] and *Fraser*,[9] and consider the claim that it was inappropriate for the SCC to rely on Convention No 87 as an interpretive source for the proposition that the *Charter* right to freedom of association includes a right to bargain collectively. In addressing these matters, we also explain why, in our view, the government of Canada is bound by membership of the ILO to promote collective bargaining, and why, as a result, the SCC was fully entitled to rely on ILO principles relating to collective bargaining in construing the *Charter*. We also explain why the SCC's decision fails to implement these principles, and how this failure could have been avoided if the decision had been more deeply rooted in ILO standards.

II

The main international instruments dealing with collective bargaining are ILO Convention Nos 98, 151, and 154. Convention No 98 is probably the most important international treaty dealing with collective bargaining, providing that:

> Measures appropriate to national conditions shall be taken, where necessary, to encourage and promote the full development and utilisation of machinery for voluntary negotiation between employers or employers' organisations and workers' organisations, with a view to the regulation of terms and conditions of employment by means of collective agreements.[10]

The scope and content of these various measures have been determined by the supervisory bodies established by the ILO to supervise the application of international labour conventions, notably the Committee of Experts on the Application of Conventions and Recommendations (CEACR) established for this purpose in 1926, and the Freedom of Association Committee of the Governing Body (CFA), established in 1951.[11]

6 *Reference re Public Service Employee Relations Act (Alta)*, [1987] 1 SCR 313 [*Alberta Reference*]; *PSAC v Canada*, [1987] 1 SCR 424; *RWDSU v Saskatchewan*, [1987] 1 SCR 460 [*RWDSU*].

7 *Dunmore v Ontario (AG)*, 2001 SCC 94, [2001] 3 SCR 1016 [*Dunmore*].

8 *Health Services*, above note 3.

9 *Ontario (AG) v Fraser*, 2011 SCC 20 [*Fraser*].

10 *Right to Organise and Collective Bargaining Convention 1949*, art 4 [Convention No 98].

11 For a good account, see Bendel, above note 5. The former is a body of eminent jurists whose number in the past has included Earl Warren and Archibald Cox from the United States, while the latter is a tripartite body reflecting the traditional

ILO Convention No 98 does "not deal with the position of public servants engaged in the administration of the State," though it is not to "be construed as prejudicing their rights or status in any way."[12] The ILO supervisory bodies have narrowly interpreted this exclusion in order to enhance the scope of application of Convention No 98.[13] However, Convention No 98 is complemented by Convention No 151, which "applies to all persons employed by public authorities, to the extent that more favourable provisions in other international labour conventions are not applicable to them."[14] By Article 7, Convention No 151 provides that

> Measures appropriate to national conditions shall be taken, where necessary, to encourage and promote the full development and utilisation of machinery for negotiation of terms and conditions of employment between the public authorities concerned and public employees' organisations, or of such other methods as will allow representatives of public employees to participate in the determination of these matters.

It will be noted that Article 7 of Convention No 151 includes a qualification to the general duty to promote collective bargaining that is not to be found in Convention No 98, authorizing the contracting parties to adopt "other methods as will allow representatives of public employees to participate in the determination of these matters," which are normally to be dealt with by collective bargaining. It is true that Convention No 151 is not directly relevant to *Fraser* (agricultural workers in Ontario not being public servants). However, this aspect of the Convention is not without significance, for it demonstrates that in the public sector traditional forms of collective bargaining are not the only way by which a state can meet its obligations to workers. Convention No 98, in contrast, imposes a

---

forms of governance within the ILO, consisting of nine members and nine deputies from each of the government, employers', and workers' groups of the ILO. It is important to recall that from the founding of the CFA, the CFA has always had jurisdiction to entertain complaints in respect of states that had not ratified the relevant Convention in respect of which the complaint is brought (Convention No 98, above note 10 at art 6). Among many sources, see the *Introduction to the ILO Digest of Decisions and Principles of the Freedom of Association Committee of the Governing Body of the ILO*, revised 5th ed (1 November 2006) online: ILO www.ilo.org/global/standards/information-resources-and-publications/publications/WCMS_090632/lang--en/index.htm at 2 [*Digest*]. As we shall see, this proposition has been expressed by the CFA specifically in relation to Canada.

12 Convention No 98, above note 10 at art 6.

13 See the discussion in *Demir* and *Baycara* above note 2 at para 43.

14 *Collective Bargaining Convention 1981*, art 1.

duty to promote the machinery of collective bargaining, to which no alternatives are specified.

Further support for the principle of collective bargaining is provided by Convention No 154, the preamble to which declares that "it is desirable to make greater efforts to achieve the objectives of these standards and, particularly, the general principles set out in Article 4 of the *Right to Organise and Collective Bargaining Convention, 1949*." Unlike Convention Nos 98 and 151, Convention No 154 attempts to define collective bargaining by providing that:

> [T]he term ***collective bargaining*** extends to all negotiations which take place between an employer, a group of employers or one or more employers' organisations, on the one hand, and one or more workers' organisations, on the other, for —
>
> (a) determining working conditions and terms of employment; and/or
>
> (b) regulating relations between employers and workers; and/or
>
> (c) regulating relations between employers or their organisations and a workers' organisation or workers' organisations.[15]

By Article 7, Convention No 154 reinforces the obligations in Convention Nos 98 and 151 by stating again that "measures adapted to national conditions shall be taken to promote collective bargaining." It also states specifically, however, that

- collective bargaining should be made possible for all employers and all groups of workers in the branches of activity covered by the Convention;
- collective bargaining should be progressively extended to all matters covered by subparagraphs (a), (b) and (c) of Article 2 of the Convention;
- the establishment of rules of procedure agreed between employers' and workers' organisations should be encouraged;
- collective bargaining should not be hampered by the absence of rules governing the procedure to be used or by the inadequacy or inappropriateness of such rules;
- bodies and procedures for the settlement of labour disputes should be so conceived as to contribute to the promotion of collective bargaining.

---

15 *Ibid*, art 2 [emphasis in original].

III

Although a founding member of the ILO, Canada has not ratified any of the collective bargaining conventions.[16] Nevertheless, *Health Services* was by no means the first occasion on which an attempt was made to give legal effect (directly or indirectly) to the ILO freedom of association Conventions in the Canadian courts. Although it has not ratified any of the collective bargaining conventions, Canada has ratified Convention No 87 on freedom of association and the right to organize. This provides basic guarantees that workers should be free to join trade unions "without previous authorisation" (Article 2), and that trade unions should be free from state control "to draw up their constitutions and rules, to elect their representatives in full freedom, to organise their administration and activities and to formulate their programmes" (Article 3). This last provision has been the basis for the development of the right to take collective action by the ILO supervisory bodies (to which we return below), though it is not typically thought to be the basis of the right to engage in collective bargaining.[17]

Convention No 87 was one of three international instruments which formed the basis of an audacious attempt to challenge the *Public Service Employee Relations Act, 1977*, passed by the Alberta legislature to ban all public service strikes. The other two instruments were the ILO Constitution 1919 (said to have been enforceable in Canada by virtue of the *Treaties of Peace Act*, SC 1919, c 30), and the

16 Convention No 98 is one of the most heavily ratified of all ILO Conventions. By September 2011, it had been ratified by 160 of the 183 ILO Member States. The countries which had not ratified it include: Afghanistan, Bahrain, Brunei Darussalam, Canada, China, India, Islamic Republic of Iran, Republic of Korea, Lao People's Democratic Republic, Marshall Islands, Mexico, Myanmar, Oman, Qatar, Saudi Arabia, Solomon Islands, Somalia, Thailand, United Arab Emirates, United States, and Vietnam: http://www.ilo.org/ilolex/cgi-lex/ratifce.pl?C098. Interestingly, as recently as June 2011 Canada ratified three further Conventions (Nos 29, 144, and 187).

17 But see *Alberta Reference*, above note 6 at 355 (Dickson CJC), *Health Services*, above note 3 at para 74, and *Fraser*, above note 9 at para 94. Convention No 98 was in draft when Convention No 87 was opened for ratification and was itself opened for ratification within a year (1948 and 1949 respectively). Nonetheless, since the right to strike protected by Article 3 of Convention No 87 has been considered for over half a century as "one of the essential means through which workers and their organizations may promote and defend their economic and social interests" (*Digest*, above note 11 at para 522), it must follow that the right to engage in collective bargaining would have been equally so regarded had Convention No 98 not appropriated that territory.

International Covenant on Economic, Social and Cultural Rights 1966 (*ICESCR*), Article 8. The latter provides that:

> 1 The States Parties to the present Covenant undertake to ensure:
>
> (a) The right of everyone to form trade unions and join the trade union of his choice, subject only to the rules of the organization concerned, for the promotion and protection of his economic and social interests. No restrictions may be placed on the exercise of this right other than those prescribed by law and which are necessary in a democratic society in the interests of national security or public order or for the protection of the rights and freedoms of others;
>
> (b) The right of trade unions to establish national federations or confederations and the right of the latter to form or join international trade-union organizations;
>
> (c) The right of trade unions to function freely subject to no limitations other than those prescribed by law and which are necessary in a democratic society in the interests of national security or public order or for the protection of the rights and freedoms of others;
>
> (d) The right to strike, provided that it is exercised in conformity with the laws of the particular country.
>
> 2 This article shall not prevent the imposition of lawful restrictions on the exercise of these rights by members of the armed forces or of the police or of the administration of the State.
>
> 3 Nothing in this article shall authorize States Parties to the International Labour Organisation Convention of 1948 concerning Freedom of Association and Protection of the Right to Organize to take legislative measures which would prejudice, or apply the law in such a manner as would prejudice, the guarantees provided for in that Convention.

This pioneering action was led by Tim Christian, a brilliant young Edmonton labour lawyer, a generation ahead of his time in his attempts to use international standards in the domestic courts to enhance trade union rights. The action predated the *Charter*, and was based on the argument that the right to strike was part of customary international law, and that the Alberta legislature did not have the power to legislate contrary to Canada's international obligations. The argument was rejected on a number of grounds, with Sinclair CJ being firmly of the view that "it is not part of the customary international law that there is a right to strike in the public service except in the case of essential services."[18] Thus,

> none of the ILO documents [referred to] expressly mentions the right to strike at all, but only the right of association and of collective bargaining. On the other hand the UN Covenant mentions both the right of association and the right to strike, but place a restriction on such rights on persons involved in the administration of the State.[19]

Although it was argued that the right to strike was inherent in Convention No 87 and acknowledged by the ILO Freedom of Association Committee, Sinclair CJ said that "the effect of all this material from a legal point of view is that the Government of Alberta is in no way bound by the ILO Recommendations which do not and have never formed part of the law of Alberta."[20]

The foregoing decision was soon followed by another challenge led by Tim Christian to the *Public Sector Employee Relations Act*, this time arguing that the restrictions on the right to strike in the latter were inconsistent with the *Charter*, introduced since the decision by Sinclair CJ.[21] Here too the action was kicked out of the Alberta courts as it revealed no breach of the *Charter* guarantee of freedom of association.[22] The action was also lost in the SCC, despite heavy reliance on a number of international treaties cited to shape the construction of the *Charter*, including the *ICESCR*, the *International Covenant on Civil and Political Rights* (*ICCPR*), and ILO Convention No 87.[23] No mention was made of this material in the majority decisions of the court, in which the justices in question were unwilling to "constitutionalize a particular feature of labour relations by entrenching a right to strike [, which] would have other adverse effects."[24] However, a rather different view was taken in the remarkable minority judgment of Dickson CJC, according to whom "the various sources of international human rights law—declarations, covenants, conventions, judicial and quasi-judicial decisions of international tribunals, customary norms—

18 *AUPE*, above note 5 at 620.

19 *Ibid.*

20 *Ibid* at 621. Here Sinclair CJ was referring to a recommendation of the CFA.

21 *Alberta Reference*, above note 6.

22 *Reference re: Public Service Employee Relations Act (Alta)* (1984), 16 DLR (4th) 359.

23 On which see the dissenting judgment of Dickson CJC, *Alberta Reference*, above note 6 at paras 57–72.

24 *Alberta Reference*, *ibid* at para 183, McIntyre J.

must . . . be relevant and persuasive sources for interpretation of the Charter's provisions."[25] To this end:

> As a party to these human rights documents, Canada is cognizant of the importance of freedom of association to trade unionism, and has undertaken as a binding international obligation to protect to some extent the associational freedoms of workers within Canada. Both of the U.N. human rights Covenants contain explicit protection of the formation and activities of trade unions subject to reasonable limits. Moreover, there is a clear consensus amongst the ILO adjudicative bodies that Convention No. 87 goes beyond merely protecting the formation of labour unions and provides protection of their essential activities—that is of collective bargaining and the freedom to strike.[26]

But although the chief justice (along with Wilson J) was prepared to give due weight to international standards, to read the *Charter* widely in order to include the right to strike, and to say that the limits in this case could not be justified under section 1, they were unable to persuade the rest of the SCC.

As is often the case, however, it is the well-reasoned minority decision that foreshadows history, and although neither *Health Services* nor *Fraser* go as far as Dickson CJC, they are closer to him than to the majority in the *Alberta Reference*, and the game is by no means over. However, it should be pointed out that Dickson CJC was not always a consistent keeper of the faith, in the sense that the *Charter* guarantee of freedom of association must be construed consistently with ILO standards, as these standards are understood by the ILO supervisory bodies. In the *Dairy Workers* case,[27] the chief justice repeated his wide interpretation of section 2(d), but appeared to yield very easily on section 1 to a strike by dairy workers, which had been declared unlawful by the provincial legislature.[28] This drew the following rebuke from Wilson J who shared the minority opinion in the *Alberta Reference*:

> In the *Reference re Public Service Employee Relations Act (Alta)* (judgment released concurrently herewith), Dickson CJ concluded that the fact that employees were providing "essential services" justified the substitution of an adequate scheme of compulsory arbitration for the freedom to strike. He adopted the definition of an "essential service" reflected in

25 *Ibid* at para 57.

26 *Ibid* at para 72.

27 *RWDSU*, above note 6.

28 *Ibid* at paras 29–44.

> decisions of the Freedom of Association Committee of the International Labour Office. These decisions have consistently defined an essential service as a service "whose interruption would endanger the life, personal safety or health of the whole or part of the population" (*Freedom of Association: Digest of Decisions and Principles of the Freedom of Association Committee of the Governing Body of the ILO*, 3rd ed Geneva, International Labour Office, 1985). The Chief Justice appears now to be engrafting a substantial extension on to that definition. He is sanctioning in this case the abrogation of the freedom to strike when the economic interests of a particular group are threatened. The implications of this for the collective bargaining process are extremely far-reaching since some measure of damage to the economic interests of the parties and the public is an inevitable concomitant [of] every work stoppage. Indeed, the effectiveness of this negotiating tool depends upon it.

IV

In *Health Services*, the SCC completed a move from (1) the position in *AUPE* of refusing to apply international labour conventions in domestic law, overtaking (2) the position in the Labour Trilogy in which these conventions were adopted by a minority, to reach (3) the position in which they have become (where relevant) part of Canadian law. Although this process reached its apotheosis in *Health Services*,[29] its seeds were sown in the *Alberta Reference* and its young shoots nurtured by Bastarache J in *Dunmore v Ontario*,[30] where the SCC held that the exclusion of agricultural workers from the *Labour Relations Act, 1995* was a violation of the *Charter* right to freedom of association. In the course of doing so, Bastarache J said that "the collective dimension of s. 2(*d*)" being developed in that case was "consistent with developments in international human rights law, as indicated by the jurisprudence of the Committee of Experts on the Application of Conventions and Recommendations and the ILO Committee on Freedom of Association."[31]

In holding that the exclusion of agricultural workers was inconsistent with *Charter* rights, Bastarache J referred specifically to Convention No 87, Article 2, which provides that "[w]orkers and employers, without distinction whatsoever, shall have the right to

---

29 *Health Services*, above note 3 at paras 69–79.

30 *Dunmore*, above note 7 at paras 16 and 27.

31 *Ibid* at para 16.

establish and . . . to join organisations of their own choosing." These "broadly worded provisions" were said to confirm precisely that "discriminatory treatment implicates not only an excluded group's dignity interest, but also its basic freedom of association," a view said to be "further confirmed by the fact that Article 2 operates not only on the basis of sex, race, nationality and other traditional grounds of discrimination, but on the basis of any distinction, including occupational status."[32] Reference was also made to Convention No 11, dealing specifically with the rights of association of agricultural workers, applying to "all those engaged in agriculture,"[33] making "no distinction as to the type of agricultural work performed."[34] While accepting that Convention No 11 had not been ratified by Canada, it was said to provide *"a normative foundation for prohibiting any form of discrimination in the protection of trade union freedoms."*[35]

Although it did not address the Convention No 11 point, the SCC in *Health Services* developed the principles adopted by Bastarache J in relation to international labour conventions. Matters got off to a good start in *Health Services* when, according to the SCC, "Canada's adherence to international documents recognising a right to collective bargaining supports recognition of the right in s 2(d) of the Charter," the latter being "presumed to provide at least as great a level of protection as is found in other international human rights documents that Canada has ratified."[36] But although international documents do support recognizing a right to collective bargaining, it is not clear that the SCC chose the best examples to establish this development, as in the process of doing so, it left itself open to the criticism we consider below. It was the reliance on ILO Convention No 87 that was especially unfortunate,[37] giving the SCC's critics a heavy stick with which to beat it. Unfortunate, but understandable in view of the fact that Convention No 87 had been relied upon by

---

32 *Ibid*, citing Lee Swepston, "'Human Rights Law and Freedom of Association: Development though ILO Supervision'" (1988) 137 International Labour Review 169 at 179–80.

33 *Rights of Association and Combination of Agricultural Workers Convention*, 1921, art 1. This provides that "Each Member of the International Labour Organisation which ratifies this Convention undertakes to secure to all those engaged in agriculture the same rights of association and combination as to industrial workers, and to repeal any statutory or other provisions restricting such rights in the case of those engaged in agriculture."

34 *Dunmore*, above note 7 at para 27.

35 *Ibid* [emphasis added].

36 *Health Services*, above note 3 at para 70.

37 *Ibid* at para 76.

Bastarache J as an authority to guide an interpretation of the *Charter* in the direction of recognizing the right to bargain collectively.[38]

As we indicate above, it is probably not the case, however, that Convention No 87 "has been understood to protect collective bargaining as part of freedom of association"[39]—Convention No 87 traditionally being regarded, perhaps misleadingly, as addressing the relationship between the trade union and the state, rather than the relationship between the trade union and an employer.[40] However, the SCC did not rely only on Convention No 87, but also referred to a well-known article in the International Labour Review,[41] which "summarized a number of principles concerning collective bargaining."[42] The SCC does not suggest that these principles are drawn from Convention No 87, but cites a passage in the article that makes it clear that the right to collective bargaining exists independently of any Convention obligations:

> The right to collective bargaining is a fundamental right endorsed by the members of the ILO in joining the Organization, which they have an obligation to respect, to promote and to realize, in good faith (ILO Declaration on Fundamental Principles and Rights at Work and its Follow-up).[43]

The SCC then rehearsed a number of other principles outlined in the article, principles relating to collective bargaining which are drawn from the jurisprudence of the ILO supervisory bodies, which the SCC had already accepted were a "cornerstone" of international labour law.[44]

Careful reading of the decision thus reveals that although the SCC stated that ILO Convention No 87 has been understood to pro-

---

38 *Dunmore*, above note 7 at paras 16 and 27; *Health Services*, *ibid* at para 76.

39 *Health Services*, *ibid* at para 75.

40 While the lines between the two are blurred (for example, employer sanctions against strikers violates Convention No 87), it is nevertheless the case that it is Convention No 98 and not Convention No 87 that is normally associated with the promotion of collective bargaining.

41 Bernard Gernigon, Alberto Odero, & Horacio Guido, "ILO Principles Concerning Collective Bargaining" (2000) 139 International Labour Review 33. For a parallel study of the right to strike (based on Convention No 87), see Bernard Gernigon, Alberto Odero, & Horacio Guido, "ILO Principles Concerning the Right to Strike" (1998) 137 International Labour Review 441.

42 *Health Services*, above note 3 at para 77.

43 *Ibid.*

44 Citing Michael Forde, "The European Convention on Human Rights and Labor Law" (1983) 31 Am J Comp L 301 at 302 [Forde]. The principles in question derive of course from Convention Nos 87 and 98.

tect collective bargaining, the case made by the SCC for extending collective bargaining to the *Charter* was based at least in part on Canada's obligations arising by virtue of membership of the ILO. These obligations were powerfully reaffirmed in the Declaration of Philadelphia in 1944, when Canada was party to the unanimous ILO conference decision, which "recognizes the solemn obligation of the International Labour Organization to further among the nations of the world programmes which will achieve," among other things, "the effective recognition of the right of collective bargaining."[45] Although the SCC did not refer to the latter Declaration, it did refer to the ILO's *Declaration on Fundamental Principles and Rights at Work of 1998* for its "usefulness in interpreting s 2(d) of the Charter."[46] However, in our view, in light of the Declaration of Philadelphia, it is probably not the case that "a global consensus on the meaning of freedom of association did not crystallize" until the promulgation of the 1998 Declaration,[47] which was little more than a reaffirmation of certain core principles recognized by the ILO for decades. Nevertheless, in attaching importance to the latter, the Supreme Court said that:

> For one thing, the Declaration was made on the basis of interpretations of international instruments, such as Convention No 87, many of which were adopted by the ILO prior to the advent of the Charter and were within the contemplation of the framers of the Charter. For another, the Charter, as a living document, grows with society and speaks to the current situations and needs of Canadians. Thus Canada's current international law commitments and the current state of international thought on human rights provide a persuasive source for interpreting the scope of the Charter.[48]

V

And so to *Fraser*, and the interesting contribution of a Canadian expert in international labour law, who in two articles had strongly criticised the SCC for its reliance on ILO sources, arguing that Canada had no obligations under the ILO in relation to collective

45 Declaration of Philadelphia 1944 (appended as an Annex to the ILO Constitution), Part III(e) [*Declaration of Philadelphia*]. It was also affirmed that "the principles set forth in this Declaration are fully applicable to all peoples everywhere."

46 *Health Services*, above note 3 at para 78.

47 *Ibid.*

48 *Ibid.*

bargaining, and that even if it did, the Wagner Act was not an appropriate way of complying with that duty.[49]

These views appear to have been adopted in *Fraser* by Rothstein J, whose judgment is an excoriating attack on *Health Services*. On the aspect of the *Health Services* decision dealing with international labour standards, Rothstein J said that the SCC had reached a wrong conclusion, having committed "two errors."[50] First, it had conflated two ILO Conventions, namely Convention Nos 87 (which Canada has ratified) and 98 (which it has not). Noting that the SCC had discussed at length an article from the International Labour Review, Rothstein J points out that the authors were "actually discussing the scope of [Convention No 98], which deals more specifically with collective bargaining."[51] Citing one of the academic articles criticizing the use of ILO material by the SCC, Rothstein J concluded that "Canada has no obligations under that Convention," with the result that it was "therefore inappropriate to interpret the scope of Canada's obligations on the basis of that Convention."[52] Justice Rothstein did not, however, discuss other sources of obligation referred to in *Health Services*, namely the obligations of membership of the ILO, as referred to in the aforementioned article, or the signing of the 1998 Declaration. No explanation for this omission was given.

In any event, claimed Rothstein J, "even if Convention No. 98 were applicable to Canada, the majority in *Health Services* would still have erred in relying on that Convention to constitutionalize a version of collective bargaining that includes a duty to bargain in good faith."[53] This is because Convention No 98 "conceives of collective bargaining as being a process of 'voluntary negotiation' that is fundamentally distinct from the model of collective bargaining incorporated in the Wagner model."[54] Drawing again on academic literature, Rothstein J noted in particular that Convention No 98 does not contemplate the imposition of a duty on parties to bargain in good faith.[55] And in inflicting the ultimate indignity upon the major-

---

49 Brian Langille, "Can We Rely on the ILO?" (2007) 13 CLELJ 363 [Langille, "Can We Rely"]; Brian Langille, "The Freedom of Association Mess: How We Got Into It and How We Can Get Out of It" (2009) 54 McGill LJ 177 [Langille, "The Freedom"].

50 *Fraser*, above note 9 at para 247.

51 *Ibid* at para 248.

52 *Ibid.*

53 *Ibid* at para 249.

54 *Ibid.*

55 *Ibid*, citing Langille, "Can We Rely," above note 49.

ity in *Health Services*, Rothstein J quoted back to them from the very article on which they had purported to rely:

> The Committee on Freedom of Association, following this line of reasoning, has stated that *nothing in Article 4 of Convention No. 98 places a duty on a government to enforce collective bargaining with a given organization by compulsory means*, and that such an intervention by a government would clearly alter the nature of bargaining (ILO, 1996a, para 846).[56]

Relying on other passages to the effect that it "*cannot therefore be deduced from the ILO's Conventions on collective bargaining that there is a formal obligation to negotiate* or to achieve a result (an agreement)," Rothstein J repeated his view that the majority in *Health Services* "was in error when it concluded that international law pointed to compulsory collective bargaining."[57]

The majority in *Fraser* responded to Rothstein J's claims that they had been in error in *Health Services*, though their response could have been more powerful. As to the first point (reliance on an unratified Convention), the majority accepted that it had relied on Convention No 87, but in doing so drew attention to a report of the ILO Freedom of Association Committee, which "concerned the very conflict that formed the factual background of the decision in *Health Services*."[58] According to the SCC:

> After applying Convention 87 and noting that Canada had not ratified *Convention (No. 98) concerning the application of the principles of the right to organise and to bargain collectively* . . . , the CFA concluded that the action of the government of British Columbia violated the employees' right to freedom of association. It stated that the unilateral cancellation of collective agreements "may have a detrimental effect on workers' interests in unionization, since members and potential members could consider it useless to join an organization the main objective of which is to represent its members in collective bargaining, if the results of bargaining are constantly cancelled by law" (Report No. 330 (2003), vol LXXXVI, Series B, No 1, at para 304).[59]

This, however, sheds no light on the question of whether the right to collective bargaining is protected by Convention No 87,[60] and over-

56 *Ibid* [emphasis in original].

57 *Ibid* at para 250 [emphasis in original].

58 *Ibid* at para 94.

59 *Ibid.*

60 Though it is true that the BC government defended itself on the basis of arguments wrapped in the rhetoric of Convention No 87. See especially paras 271, 277, and 286.

looks more compelling sources for Canada's ILO obligation to promote collective bargaining.

As to Rothstein J's second point (no duty to bargain in good faith in any event implied in Convention No 98), this was perhaps of secondary importance: the question ought not to have been whether there was a duty to promote a duty to bargain in good faith, but whether the right to make representations in *AEPA* was consistent with the duty to promote collective bargaining. Here the majority replied, perhaps more convincingly than in response to Rothstein J's first point, by saying that:

> While voluntariness is a component of the international model of collective bargaining—as noted by the majority in *Health Services* (para 77, citing B Gernigon, A Odero and H Guido, "ILO principles concerning collective bargaining" (2000) 139 *Int'l Lab Rev* 33, at pp 51-52)—the ILO Committee of Experts has not found compulsory collective bargaining to be contrary to international norms. The 1994 Report of the Committee of Experts discussed the domestic schemes that compelled employers to bargain with unions, listing Canada, and approvingly stated that such schemes illustrated "the principle that employers and trade unions should negotiate in good faith and endeavour to reach an agreement" (Committee of Experts on the Application of Conventions and Recommendations, *Freedom of Association and Collective Bargaining* (1994), at para 243). This is precisely the general principle that *Health Services* endorses.[61]

In our view, however, discussions of this latter kind were unnecessary. As already suggested, the task of the SCC in *Health Services* and *Fraser* ought to have been simply whether the contested legislation in each case was consistent with ILO principles relating to collective bargaining. This is a question that could have been answered without a detailed examination of the full scope and depth of the ILO duty, the question for the SCC in *Health Services* being simply whether the withdrawal of bargaining rights was a violation of ILO principles, and in *Fraser* whether a right to make representations was consistent with the right to bargain collectively. In both cases, the ILO Freedom of Association Committee had already answered that the legislation was not consistent.[62]

---

61 *Fraser*, above note 9 at para 95.

62 *CFA Report No 330 (2003)*, vol LXXXVI, 2003, Series B, No 1; *CFA Report No 358 (2009)*, vol XCIII, 2010, Series B, No 3.

VI

We confess to being perplexed by the view that Canada has no obligations in relation to the ILO, and that the SCC in *Health Services* was wrong to conclude otherwise. We confess to being even more perplexed that this view should have been taken so seriously by the SCC in *Fraser.* It has been boldly claimed that there is a "fundamental legal truth,"[63] namely that "the relevant ILO law is not what the Court thinks it is—and, in any event, Canada is not a party to it."[64] Far from it; this is a conclusion that does not appear to be sustainable on consideration of the jurisprudence of the ILO, or of the legal obligations of any member state of the ILO.

Beginning at the beginning, it has been asserted that "the key point, which so many overlook" is that under the ILO's Constitution, ratification of ILO treaties (called "conventions") is an entirely voluntary matter.[65] This is plainly correct. It is then argued that the ILO Constitution expressly states that a member state's "sole obligation" is to place a convention, "newly minted in Geneva" before the appropriate domestic authority for possible voluntary ratification.[66] We believe this to be incorrect; there are secondary obligations that flow from this obligation that need not be explored here.[67] It is then argued further that if a country fails or decides not to ratify, then according to the constitution, "no further obligation shall rest upon the Member."[68] We believe this to be incomplete. After the words "no further obligation shall rest upon the Member," Article 19(5)(e) continues as follows:

> [E]xcept that it shall report to the Director-General of the International Labour Office, at appropriate intervals as requested by the Governing Body, the position of its law and practice in regard to the matters dealt with in the Convention, showing the extent to which effect has been given, or is proposed to be given, to any of the provisions of the Conven-

63 Langille, "The Freedom," above note 49 at 194.

64 *Ibid* at 197.

65 *Ibid* at 194.

66 *Ibid.*

67 See for example ILO Constitution, art 22:

> Each of the Members agrees to make an annual report to the International Labour Office on the measures which it has taken to give effect to the provisions of Conventions to which it is a party. These reports shall be made in such form and shall contain such particulars as the Governing Body may request.

This provision is in fact acknowledged by Professor Langille. See Langille, "Can We Rely," above note 49 at 374.

68 Langille, "The Freedom of Association," above note 49 at 194.

> tion by legislation, administrative action, collective agreement or otherwise and stating the difficulties which prevent or delay the ratification of such Convention.

These, however, are not the obligations we are concerned with, even though they do arise under the Constitution.

Apart from obligations in relation to Conventions, there may be other obligations on states. Indeed, in his 2007 article,[69] the academic critic of *Health Services* himself accepted that "simply by virtue of membership in the ILO, though not bound by the provisions of any non-ratified Convention, member states are nevertheless bound to 'promote' the 'principles' underlying the core ILO value of freedom of association."[70] We believe this to be correct, though we also believe that it understates the duty as expressed in paragraph 2 of the *Declaration on Fundamental Principles and Rights at Work of 1998* that:

> [A]ll Members, even if they have not ratified the Conventions in question, have an obligation arising from the very fact of membership in the *Organization to respect, to promote and to realize*.[71]

Thus, Canada is bound by obligations relating to freedom of association by virtue of membership of the ILO. This is an obligation reinforced not only by the 1998 Declaration but also by the Declaration of Philadelphia in which Canada recognized (along with the other ILO member states) a "solemn obligation" to "further" programmes that will "achieve the effective recognition of the right to collective bargaining."[72] This does not necessarily contradict the view that only ratification can give rise to obligations under conventions (in the sense that ratification is a source of obligation under conventions). But it does make clear that membership alone is another source of obligation, this time to "principles concerning the fundamental rights."[73]

So far, so good. Unfortunately, however, the position appears to be obfuscated by the contention that:

> In hearing complaints against ratifiers and non-ratifiers, the CFA may refer to conventions relevant to that principle [the principle of freedom of association], but it is it not limited to them. And the one thing the

---

69 Langille, "Can We Rely," above note 49.

70 Langille, "Can We Rely," *ibid* at 372.

71 Adopted by the International Labour Conference at its Eighty-sixth Session, Geneva, 18 June 1998 (Annex revised 15 June 2010) [emphasis added].

72 *Declaration of Philadelphia*, above note 45 at Part III(e).

73 ILO, *Declaration on Fundamental Principles and Rights at Work* above note 71 at para 2.

> CFA cannot do is impose obligations under those conventions upon non-ratifying members. It can only draw attention to the "principles," in a constitutional effort to "promote" them.[74]

As already explained, however, in our view, Canada clearly has obligations relating to collective bargaining deriving from the fact of membership of the ILO alone. It is true that a complaint that Canada has failed to comply with these obligations may be made to the CFA. But in considering such complaints, we do not believe that the CFA is imposing on member states obligations arising under un-ratified conventions, even if in performing its duties, it has regard to the same underlying principles of freedom of association that may also have informed those who drafted the freedom of association conventions. As a matter of legality, by submitting to the jurisdiction of the CFA, Canada is NOT submitting to un-ratified conventions.

To suggest otherwise appears to us to interweave two different processes, each of which gives rise to a different obligation. In our view, it is important not to conflate the legal obligation of the state "*to respect, to promote and to realize*"[75] freedom of association principles (which are indisputable), with arguments about the powers of a supervisory committee (which in any event appear to us to support the proposition that collective bargaining obligations exist regardless of ratification of Convention No 98). We nevertheless accept that the SCC put too much weight on Convention No 87 (in both *Dunmore* and *Health Services*). But neither muddled reasoning nor over-reliance on Convention No 87 alter the fact that the SCC in *Health Services* was absolutely right in its conclusion by reference to the International Labour Review that "the right to collective bargaining is a fundamental right endorsed by the members of the ILO in joining the Organization, which they have an obligation to respect, to promote and to realize, in good faith."[76] It is a matter of regret that the SCC did not further develop this point from *Health Services* rather than returning once again to the ill-judged deployment of ILO Convention No 87. The majority in *Fraser* were, nevertheless, quite right to hold that a constitutional duty to promote collective bargaining was consistent with "Canada's international and human rights commitments."[77] Although the means by which the majority

---

74 Langille, "Can We Rely," above note 49 at 373.

75 Above note 43 [emphasis added].

76 Gernigon, Odero, & Guido, "ILO Principles Concerning Collective Bargaining," above note 41 at p 51.

77 *Fraser*, above note 9 at para 92.

justified this statement may give rise to regret, this does not render the statement inaccurate as a matter of law. Where in our view the SCC erred in *Fraser* was in the application of these ILO principles to the legislation in dispute, that is to say the *AEPA*.

VII

We thus disagree with the view that Canada has no ILO obligations in relation to the right to bargain collectively. Where we part company with the SCC, however, is in relation to its decision that the *AEPA* is consistent with Canada's duty to promote that principle. We have no desire to engage with the argument whether the Wagner model is or is not consistent with the ILO freedom of association principles. We would be happy to accept the position advanced by Rothstein J that these principles permit, but do not require, a system of what was referred to as "compulsory collective bargaining" (which we understand to mean the Wagner model, and in particular the duty to bargain in good faith).[78] Consequently, we would also accept the view of Rothstein J that other forms of worker representation are also consistent with the freedom of association principles.[79] What we are clear about, however, is that the procedure for making representations introduced by the *AEPA* is not consistent with the ILO duty to promote collective bargaining, even allowing for the constitutional air blown into the statute by the majority of the SCC in *Fraser*,[80] air that requires these representations to be considered in good faith.[81] As already suggested, the SCC should have been asked to rule on the question whether the *AEPA* was consistent with ILO principles, not on the question of whether *AEPA* should have embraced the Wagner model.

It is true that the majority in *Fraser* purported to reaffirm the finding in *Health Services* that the right to freedom of association includes a right to collective bargaining.[82] The problem, however, lies with the definition of collective bargaining for this purpose as "a process of collective action to achieve workplace goals," albeit one "requiring engagement by both parties."[83] Whatever the SCC may say about the agricultural workers of Ontario being entitled "to mean-

78 *Ibid* at para 250.
79 *Ibid*.
80 *Ibid*. See especially paras 98–113.
81 *Ibid* at para 107.
82 *Ibid*. See especially paras 40, 41, and 97.
83 *Ibid* at para 117.

ingful processes by which they can pursue workplace goals," it is not the same meaningful process that would be open to other workers protected by the labour relations statute.[84] If the SCC had addressed the question we believe that it should have addressed, it seems to be implausible that it could have answered in the affirmative. It would then have been for the Ontario legislature to come back with an upgraded version of the *AEPA*—one that met Canada's international obligations. That may have been a Wagner-style statute (or a simple removal of the exclusion of agricultural workers from the *Labour Relations Act*), or it could have been a different representative model altogether, perhaps along the lines pressed eloquently and persuasively by Professor Roy Adams for many years.[85] Either way, there would first have to be a finding that *AEPA* was in breach of Canada's international obligations. In our view, there is little room for doubt on this point, given that ILO standards emphasise three essential features of collective bargaining, which do not appear to be acknowledged in the *AEPA* if it is construed literally, or in the *AEPA* even as inflated by *Fraser*.

For ILO purposes, collective bargaining is (1) a defined process (*negotiation*), for (2) a specific purpose (*regulation of terms and conditions of employment*), with (3) a view to a prescribed outcome (a *collective agreement*).[86] A gloss on these three features is to be found in ILO Convention No 154, which so far as (1) (the process) is concerned, proposes that negotiations should take place within established "rules of procedure agreed between employers' and workers' organizations," even if "collective bargaining should not be hampered by the absence of rules governing the procedure to be used or by the inadequacy or inappropriateness of such rules."[87] And so far as (2) (the purpose) is concerned, Convention No 154 provides that measures are to be taken progressively to extend collective bargaining to all of the following matters: determining working conditions and terms of employment; regulating relations between employers and workers; and/or regulating relations between employers or their organizations and a workers' organization or workers' organizations.[88] By any standard, the rudimentary procedure in the *AEPA* falls short of each of these essential features. First, because the right to make

---

84 *Labour Relations Act*, SO 1995, c 1, s 3(b1).

85 For a recent contribution, see Roy J Adams, "Collective Bargaining as a Minimum Employment Standard" (2011) 22 Economic and Labour Relations Review 1.

86 See *Digest*, above note 11 at paras 880 and 882.

87 ILO Convention No 154, art 5(c) and (d).

88 *Ibid*, art 2.

representations is not a right to enter into negotiations; and second, because the right to make representations respecting terms and conditions of employment is without indication as to the purposes for which these representations may be made;[89] and third, because no provision is made for the outcome of this process by way of a collective agreement, the terms of which should be binding.[90]

Our confidence that the *AEPA* procedure is not consistent with ILO principles is reinforced by a most authoritative source. That source is a report of the CFA published between the date of the hearing in *Fraser* and the date of the decision.[91] The report was published following a complaint by the UCFW that the *AEPA* breached ILO principles. In dealing with the complaint, the CFA had to first deal with the question of jurisdiction we discussed above, and with the argument by the Ontario government that collective bargaining is dealt with in Convention No 98, which Canada had not ratified, and could therefore not be bound by (Rothstein J's first point). This drew the following response for the CFA:

> While taking due note of the Provincial Government's reminder that Canada has not ratified Convention No 98, the Committee recalls that the purpose of the procedure on freedom of association is to promote respect for trade union rights in law and practice, therefore complaints lodged with the Committee can be submitted whether or not the country concerned has ratified the freedom of association Conventions.[92]

The *APEA* complaint is thus important for further affirming to those who are unconvinced that Canada is bound by its membership of the ILO to promote the full range of freedom of association principles, including the right to bargain collectively. But it is also important for the finding that the *APEA* violated these principles (Rothstein J's second point, as well as the position of the majority). Thus:

> Fully recognizing the importance it places on the voluntary nature of collective bargaining, the Committee recalls that the voluntary *negotiation of collective agreements*, and therefore the autonomy of the bar-

89 And quite apart from that, the statutory procedure fails to provide any obligation on the employer to consider representations for the establishment of a process within which such representations may be made.

90 *Digest*, above note 11 at para 939.

91 Complaint against the Government of Canada presented by the United Food and Commercial Workers Union Canada (UFCW Canada) supported by the *Canadian Labour Congress and UNI Global Union Report No 358*, Case(s) No(s) 2704: ILO, Vol XCIII, 2010, Series B, No 3.

92 *Ibid* at para 355.

> gaining partners, is a fundamental aspect of the principles of freedom of association. (see Digest, op. cit., para 925). The Committee also recalls that measures should be taken to encourage and promote the full development and utilization of machinery for *voluntary negotiation* between employers or employers organizations and workers organizations, with a view to *the regulation of terms and conditions of employment by means of collective agreements*.[93]

Consequently, the Committee concluded that "the absence of any machinery for the promotion of collective bargaining of agricultural workers constitutes an impediment to one of the principal objectives of the guarantee of freedom of association—the forming of independent organizations explicitly capable of concluding collective agreements," and requested the government "to take the necessary measures to ensure that the Provincial Government puts in place appropriate machinery and procedures for the promotion of collective bargaining in the agricultural sector."[94] Crucially, "appropriate machinery can be adapted to national circumstances provided the principles reflected above are fully respected."[95]

To say the least, it is a matter of great regret that this decision was not considered by the SCC, and a matter of even greater regret that the SCC did not consider whether the *AEPA* (even as inflated) was consistent with Canada's international obligations, in light of these findings of the supervisory body.[96] The CFA was aware that the matter was under consideration by the SCC at the time of its report, and asked to be kept informed of the decision as soon as it was handed down, and to be made aware of "any implications this decision may have on the question of bargaining rights in the agricultural sector of Ontario."[97] The reconsideration of the matter by the CFA in the light of the SCC decision will be an extremely important opportunity

93 *Ibid* at para 357 [emphasis added].

94 *Ibid* at para 361(a).

95 *Ibid.*

96 From NUPGE, "Fraser Decision 'Troubling' According to Lead Counsel for UFCW" (31 May 2011) online: NUPGE www.nupge.ca/content/4309/fraser-decision-troubling-according-lead-counsel-ufcw:

> [Paul] Cavalluzzo noted that while the majority's ruling noted the relevance of international law and the International Labour Organization (ILO) decisions in informing the interpretation of s 2(d) of the *Charter of Rights and Freedoms*, they failed to refer to two ILO rulings concerning the AEPA in the record of evidence. "Both of these ILO decisions found the legislation violates Canada's obligations under international human rights law by failing to provide agricultural workers with collective bargaining rights."

97 Complaint, above note 93 at para 361(b).

for the committee to restate the principles of collective bargaining, and to assess the extent to which the rhetoric of the majority decision meets the requirements of these principles. As matters currently stand, however, it seems implausible that the CFA could be satisfied with the SCC decision, simply because both the CFA and the relevant ILO Conventions appear to emphasize a definition of collective bargaining which is at some stages removed from the right to make representations as set out in the *APEA*.

VIII

The SCC is by no means alone in wrestling with the reconciliation of ILO principles and human rights standards. Different courts have responded in different ways, and some operate under different rules. In the case of South Africa, for example, the Constitutional Court is mandated to consider international law when interpreting the Bill of Rights.[98] We would suggest, however, that the ECtHR stands as an example to courts everywhere in its treatment of this matter. The leading case is now *Demir and Baycara*,[99] a decision of the Grand Chamber of seventeen judges on 12 November 2008. It is a great surprise that this decision was not referred to by the SCC, especially in view of the *Charter* provision that any limits must be "demonstrably justified in a free and democratic society." It is also particularly surprising that *Demir and Baycara* was not discussed given our understanding that it was cited to the SCC, that it was directly on point, and that it would have provided a comparative perspective on a difficult area of international law.

The facts of *Demir and Baykara* are fairly straightforward. The applicants were a member and president respectively of a trade union called Tum Bel Sun, which in 1993 negotiated a two-year collective agreement with the Gaziantep Municipal Council. The agreement concerned all aspects of the employment relationship, including wages, allowances, and welfare services. When within a few months the local authority failed to comply with the agreement, legal proceedings were brought against it by the officers of the union, the

---

98 Constitution of the Republic of South Africa, s 39(1)(b). On the right to strike, see *South African Police Service v Police and Prisons Civil Rights Union*, [2011] ZACC 21, judgment delivered by Justice Nkabinde.

99 [2008] ECHR 1345, discussed in Keith D Ewing & John Hendy, QC, "The Dramatic Implications of *Demir* and *Baycara*" (2010) 39 Indus LJ 2, reproduced in part in (2010) 15 CLELJ 165.

action succeeding in the District Court. On an appeal by the local authority, this decision was reversed by the Court of Cassation, which referred the matter back to the District Court. But the District Court stuck to its guns, and the matter was brought back before the Court of Cassation, which also upheld its original decision. The basis of the latter court's decision was that although trade unions in Turkey were free to exist, they had no legal capacity to enter into collective agreements. As a result, the agreement contested in the case was held invalid *ex tunc*, and following an audit of the local authority's accounts, those who benefited from it were ordered to repay the benefits secured.

Domestic legal proceedings concluded on 10 April 1996. The union officers thereupon brought proceedings against Turkey in the ECtHR, alleging that the invalidation of the collective agreement violated their right to freedom of association, as protected by the *European Convention on Human Rights*, Article 11. This provides that:

> Everyone has the right to freedom of peaceful assembly and to freedom of association with others, including the right to form and to join trade unions for the protection of his interests.

The difficulty in bringing a claim under this provision in relation to collective bargaining rights is that—as in Canada—there was a legacy of conservative jurisprudence in which the Court had previously held that the right to freedom of association did not include the right to bargain collectively. Indeed, the Council of Europe had its own trilogy of cases, in which, in the 1970s, the ECtHR had held that the right to freedom of association did not include the right to be consulted, the right to bargain, or the right to strike, while accepting that these were all legitimate trade union methods.[100]

This jurisprudence was, however, not immutable, and by 2002 it was beginning to crumble.[101] In the instant case, in 2006, the second chamber of the ECtHR held unanimously that there had been a breach of Article 11. On an ill-advised application by the Turkish government, the matter was referred to the Grand Chamber,[102] which in 2008 duly returned a 17:0 decision upholding the second chamber. In a noteworthy and extensive judgment, the ECtHR relied heavily on

---

100 *National Union of Belgian Police v Belgium* (1975), 1 EHRR 578; *Swedish Engine Drivers' Union v Sweden* (1976), 1 EHRR 617; and *Schmidt and Dahlstrom v Sweden* (1976), 1 EHRR 632. See Forde, above note 44, for a seminal discussion of these and other cases.

101 Notably in *Wilson v United Kingdom* (2002), 35 EHRR 523.

102 For details of this procedure, see ECHR, art 43.

a number of other international treaties, including ILO Conventions Nos 98 and 151, both of which Turkey had ratified. It also relied on the Council of Europe's Social Charter, Article 6(2), which Turkey had not accepted, and the *EU Charter of Fundamental Rights*, which Turkey was not in a position to ratify, not being a member of the EU. In considering these sources, the ECtHR made clear that it was deferring to the relevant supervisory bodies (the ILO Committee of Experts and the Council of Europe's Social Rights Committee) for their interpretation of the relevant provisions.[103] The ECtHR also looked to law and practice of other European states and found that

> in the vast majority of them, the right of civil servants to bargain collectively with the authorities has been recognised, subject to various exceptions so as to exclude certain areas regarded as sensitive or certain categories of civil servants who hold exclusive powers of the State. In particular, the right of public servants employed by local authorities and not holding State powers to engage in collective bargaining in order to determine their wages and working conditions has been recognised in the majority of Contracting States.[104]

Having regard to the foregoing, the ECtHR overruled the old caselaw, emphasizing the need to keep abreast of the "perceptible evolution" of the law, both internationally and in the member states of the Council of Europe.[105] The ECtHR made clear that this was not a step to be taken lightly: "[I]n the interests of legal certainty, foreseeability and equality before the law [. . .] the Court should not depart, without good reason, from precedent established in previous cases."[106] Here, there was good reason:

> [H]aving regard to the developments in labour law, both international and national, and to the practice of Contracting States in such matters, the right to bargain collectively with the employer has, in principle, become one of the essential elements of the 'right to form and to join trade unions for the protection of [one's] interests' set forth in Article 11 of the Convention, it being understood that States remain free to organise their system so as, if appropriate, to grant special status to representative trade unions.[107]

This led the ECtHR to conclude that:

---

103 *Demir* and *Baycara*, above note 2 at paras 43, 50, and 166.
104 *Ibid* at para 151.
105 *Ibid*.
106 *Ibid* at para 153.
107 *Ibid* at para 154.

> The absence of the legislation necessary to give effect to the provisions of the international labour conventions already ratified by Turkey, and the Court of Cassation judgment of 6 December 1995 based on that absence, with the resulting *de facto* annulment *ex tunc* of the collective agreement in question, constituted interference with the applicants' trade-union freedom as protected by Article 11 of the Convention.[108]

IX

The significance of the *Demir and Baykara* case for present purposes relates not only to the fact that the ECtHR—like the SCC—held that the right to bargain collectively is encapsulated by the principle of freedom of association. There is a major difference between the two courts in terms of the meaning of the right to bargain collectively and the influence of ILO standards for this purpose. In the first place, the ECtHR held that the right to collective bargaining must be set at the standards set by the ILO. Thus, in the crucial paragraph of the judgment (para 157), Turkey was found in breach because there was an "absence of the *legislation necessary to give effect to the provisions of the international labour conventions* already ratified by Turkey" (emphasis added). This is important, because what the Court appears to be saying is that the standard of the ECHR is the standard set by the ILO. This is very different from the position in Canada where the SCC appeared to adopt its own autonomous meaning of the term collective bargaining, which is inconsistent with the meaning attributed to it by the ILO.[109]

But not only that—also important is the response of the ECtHR to the restrictions and qualifications that may be imposed on Convention rights. In the case of Article 11, it is provided by Article 11(2) that:

> No restrictions shall be placed on the exercise of these rights other than such as are prescribed by law and are necessary in a democratic society in the interests of national security or public safety, for the prevention of disorder or crime, for the protection of health or morals or for the protection of the rights and freedoms of others. This article shall not prevent the imposition of lawful restrictions on the exercise of these

---

108 *Ibid* at para 157.

109 Indeed, as we have seen, the legislation upheld by the SCC had already been condemned by the CFA.

> rights by members of the armed forces, of the police or of the administration of the State.

The last sentence mirrors the provisions of ILO Convention No 98, Article 6, which provides that the "Convention does not deal with the position of public servants engaged in the administration of the State, nor shall it be construed as prejudicing their rights or status in any way."

The Turkish government in *Demir and Baycara* seized upon the second sentence of the European Convention on Human Rights (ECHR), Article 11(2), which it argued applied here to excuse the exclusion of local government employees from the right to bargain collectively. Not so, said the ECtHR:

> There is no evidence in the case file to show that the applicants' union represented "public servants engaged in the administration of the State", that is to say, according to the interpretation of the ILO's Committee of Experts, officials whose activities are specific to the administration of the State and who qualify for the exception provided for in Article 6 of ILO Convention No. 98.[110]

The ECtHR has thus accepted that ILO Convention No 98 is determinative of the scope and content of a permitted exemption from the right to bargain collectively in Article 11(2), as well as determinative or partly determinative of the scope and content of the Article 11(1) right itself. In that determinative application of ILO standards, the ECtHR defers to the judgments of the ILO supervisory bodies, in defiance it seems of the view that "the 'comments' of the distinguished Committee of Experts are not, and constitutionally cannot be, 'authoritative.'"[111]

Before leaving these matters, there are two points that perhaps ought to be addressed. One point alluded by the ECtHR in both paragraphs 157 (establishing the right) and 166 (resisting attempts to qualify the right) is that Turkey (unlike Canada) had ratified Convention No 98. Indeed all forty-seven member states of the Council of Europe have ratified Convention No 98. This, however, should not give comfort to critics of the decision of the SCC, for it is not evident that Turkey's ratification of Convention No 98 had any relevance to the disposal of the ECtHR case. Turkey was not being challenged for breach of Convention No 98, but for breach of the ECHR, Article 11. Convention No 98 was relevant only to the extent that, along with

---

110 *Demir* and *Baycara*, above note 2 at para 166.

111 Langille, "Can We Rely," above note 49 at 375.

other instruments, it helped to determine the scope and extent of Article 11. The ECtHR having used ILO Convention No 98 as a source of interpretation, the fact that Turkey had ratified it was irrelevant for the purposes of its obligations under the Convention, just as it was irrelevant that Turkey had not accepted or ratified the other international instruments on which the Court relied as sources of interpretation. It is most improbable that the ECtHR would adopt a two-tier approach to the interpretation of the European Convention (one for countries that had ratified Convention No 98, and another for those that had not).

The other point worth emphasizing is the extent to which the ECtHR relied upon the jurisprudence of the ILO supervisory bodies (both the Committee of Experts and the CFA) as sources of authority for the interpretation of ILO Conventions, and on the Social Rights Committee of the Council of Europe (which performs a similar task in relation to the European Social Charter). So far as the ILO bodies are concerned, in an extensive discussion of a number of relevant international treaties, the ECtHR quoted freely from the *Digest of Decisions* by the CFA, and from the *General Survey* by the Committee of Experts.[112] This is surely to be expected, and any suggestion that this body of jurisprudence should be ignored seems curious. These supervisory bodies have created what is in effect the "cornerstone" or (as we would prefer) a "common law" on freedom of association, which adds flesh to the bare bones of the treaties to which they relate. Like any legal instrument, the general terms of these treaties are incomplete and may be misleading without an understanding of the jurisprudence of those adjudicative fora formally established to supervise their operation, and best placed to decide what they mean.[113]

112 This was foreshadowed in earlier cases, and has been adopted subsequently: *Cheall v UK* (1985), 8 EHRR 74; *Sigurjonsson v Sweden* (1993), 16 EHRR 462 at para 35; *Wilson, Palmer*, [2002] IRLR 568 at paras 30, 35, 36, & 37; *ASLEF v UK*, [2007] IRLR 361 at paras 22 and 25; and most recently *Vörður Ólafsson v Iceland*, Application No. 20161/06 (27 July 2010), and *Palomo Sanchez v Spain*, Application Nos. 28955/06, 28957/06, 28959/06, and 28964/06 (12 September 2011) at paras 24 (extensively), 67, 72, & 73.

113 Note also that when the Dutch Hoge Raad applied the *European Social Charter* in domestic law, it did so having regard to the jurisprudence of the Committee of Independent Experts (now the European Committee on Social Rights): *NV Dutch Railways v Transport Unions FNV, FSV, CNV*, (1986) 6 International Labour Law Reports 57.

X

We have come a long way since Tim Christian, QC, sought to persuade Sinclair CJ of the merits of international labour standards, and to persuade the SCC of the need to give *Charter* protection to the right to strike. The SCC has now embraced these standards and is now using them to interpret *Charter* rights. That is a considerable advance—two cheers for the SCC. What is now needed is for the SCC to take the final step, which is to follow the example of the ECtHR and apply not only international labour principles, but also international labour principles as elaborated by the supervisory bodies of the ILO, in its cautious but impressively extensive body of jurisprudence. Litigation being a dynamic and evolving process, it seems inevitable that the SCC will be called upon to do just that at some time in the future, no doubt in the most unpredictable of circumstances.

In the meantime, although *Fraser* has been seen by the Canadian unions as a setback, it is a defeat rather than a conquest. It is in the nature of litigation that gains will be made and losses incurred. The fact is that legal reasoning is now at least moving in a progressive direction, that the tribunal set up under *AEPA* knows that the *Charter* is breathing down its neck, and that there will inevitably be a third *Charter* challenge on behalf of the agricultural workers of Ontario. But more than that: how can the decisions in *Health Services* and *Fraser* be confined to collective bargaining? Suppose the Ontario farm workers were to make representations, that these representations reach "impasse," and there is no way to resolve the dispute but by strike action? There is no protection for the right to strike in the *AEPA*, which means that it would be governed by common law rules—that is to say, it may be a breach of contract on the part of those taking the action, and tortious on the part of those organizing it, raising the spectre not only of injunctions, but also unlimited damages at the suit of the employer.[114]

Which brings us back to *Demir and Baykara*, the progeny of which have extended the right to bargain collectively to include the right to take collective action (in other words, the right to strike).[115]

114 It has been found by the ILO supervisory bodies in complaints from both Australia and the UK that the common law position relating to industrial action breaches Convention No 87.

115 See *Federation of Offshore Workers Trade Unions v Norway*, Application No 381/97, (2002) ECHR 2002-VI, 301; *UNISON v UK*, [2002] IRLR 497; *Wilson, Palmer and ors v UK*, [2002] IRLR 568; *Enerji Yapi-Yol Sen v Turkey*, Application No 68959/01, judgment dated 21 April 2009; *Danilenkov and ors v Russia*, Application No 67336/01, 30 July 2009, definitive version 10 December 2009; *Urcan v Turkey*, Application

The logic that demands that freedom of association includes the right to bargain is the same logic that demands that it also includes the right to strike, at least so far as this is a process driven by the need to comply with international standards. The right to strike is protected not only by the ILO constitutional principle of freedom of association already considered, but also by Convention No 87, in relation to which a sophisticated jurisprudence has been developed, by both the Committee of Experts and the CFA. This ought to go some way towards addressing Canadian academic concerns that a relevant obligation must derive from a convention that has been ratified by Canada. However, we fear that ratification of Convention No 87 may not be enough on its own for all critics, given that the right is not expressly protected, but rather is a product of its interpretation by the supervisory bodies, said not to be "authoritative."[116]

It will no doubt surprise those who have relied heavily on the supervisory bodies of the ILO (including the seventeen judges of the Grand Chamber of the ECtHR) to discover that the "interpretations" by these bodies are not "authoritative," and that the right to strike exists under Convention No 87 only because it has been acknowledged by an ILO Commission of Inquiry.[117] We believe this thesis to be unsustainable.[118] We also express grave concern that international labour rights—already under siege from employers and governments—will be seriously undermined by diminishing the processes

No 23018/04 etc, 17 July 2008, definitive judgment 17 October 2008; *Saime Özcan v Turkey*, Application No 22943/04, 15 September 2009; *Kaya and Seyhan v Turkey*, Application No 30946/04, 15 September 2009; *Karaçay v Turkey*, Application No 6615/03, 27 March 2007, definitive version 27 June 2007; and *Dilek et al v Turkey* judgment of 17 July 2007 sub nom *Satlimiş v Turkey*, final version 30 January 2008, rectified on 28 April 2008 and name corrected to *Dilek v Turkey*, Application Nos 74611/02, 26876/02, and 27628/02. For a full treatment, see KD Ewing & J Hendy, QC, *Days of Action: The Legality of Protest Strikes against Government Cuts* (Institute of Employment Rights, 2011).

116 Langille, "Can We Rely," above note 49 at 375.

117 See *Alberta Reference*, above note 6 at para 68, Dickson CJC: "A Commission of Inquiry, appointed to investigate a complaint against Greece, held that strike activity is implicitly protected by Convention No. 87: *ILO Official Bulletin: Special Supplement*, vol. LIV, No. 2, 1971." The significance of a Commission of Inquiry is that according to Professor Langille, *ibid*, it is one of the few formal means under the ILO Constitution for the issuing of authoritative outcomes to complaints, citing ILO Constitution, art 26.

118 We note that in the *Alberta Reference*, *ibid*, the chief justice was as respectful of the Committee of Experts and the CFA as he was of the Commission of Inquiry (paras 68–69), and that he found "the decisions of the Freedom of Association Committee of the I.L.O. to be helpful and persuasive" (at para 106).

through which they are developed. However, in the meantime, we are optimistic that the SCC is set on a course that will inevitably lead to a constitutional recognition in Canada of a right to strike. We are optimistic too that this right will be developed in line with the minimum standards of the ILO, by which Canada is bound.[119]

---

119 For a promising start, see *Saskatchewan Federation of Labour v Saskatchewan* [2012] SKQB 62. Thanks to Professor David Doorey's excellent blog.

10) For a promising start, see *Saskatchewan Federation of Labour v Saskatchewan* [2012] SKQB 62. Thanks to Professor David Doorey's excellent blog.

CONTRIBUTORS

Steven Barrett practices in the areas of labour, administrative, and constitutional law. He joined Sack Goldblatt Mitchell in 1985, has been a partner since 1988, and has served as managing partner since 2006. In addition to litigating before a variety of labour and administrative tribunals, representing trade unions and employee associations in collective bargaining negotiations and interest arbitration in the broader public sector, and arguing many judicial review applications and appeals before Ontario courts, Steven has an active practice litigating under the *Charter*, including appearing as counsel before the Supreme Court of Canada in various freedom of association cases (*Delisle, Dunmore, Health Services,* and *Fraser*).

Paul JJ Cavalluzzo, O. Ont., LSM, was called to the Bar in 1973. He received his LLB from Osgoode Hall Law School and his LLM from Harvard. Paul is the senior partner in Cavalluzzo Hayes Shilton McIntyre & Cornish, a public law firm in Toronto. Paul has argued many leading constitutional, administrative, and labour law cases before the Supreme Court of Canada, the courts of Ontario, and administrative tribunals. He acted as counsel to the United Food and Commercial Workers Union in *Fraser* and *Health Services* before the Supreme Court of Canada. Apart from a busy public law practice, Paul acted as commission counsel to the Walkerton Inquiry and the Arar Inquiry. More recently, Paul has been appointed by the Federal Minister of Justice to act as a special advocate in security certificate cases.

In this regard, Paul represents the interests of persons alleged to be threats to the national security of Canada in top-secret hearings before the Federal Court of Canada in Ottawa. Paul lectures frequently at law schools and professional seminars, and has numerous published articles in the areas of constitutional, administrative, labour, and national security law. At the present time, Paul has a number of *Charter* cases pending before the courts.

Fay Faraday is a social justice lawyer in Toronto, representing community groups and coalitions, unions, and individuals. With a practice focusing on constitutional and appellate litigation, labour, human rights, and administrative/public law, she has extensive experience with *Charter* litigation at all levels of court, including numerous cases before the Supreme Court of Canada and the Ontario Court of Appeal. Fay has a particular interest in the rights of migrant workers and other workers in precarious employment. She was counsel to UFCW Canada in four constitutional challenges advocating for the rights of domestic and migrant agricultural workers, including *Fraser v Ontario (AG)*, 2011 SCC 20 and UFCW's intervention in *BC Health Services*, 2007 SCC 27. In her legal practice, Fay has also addressed a wide range of social justice issues relating to women's equality, race discrimination, gender and work, rights of persons with disabilities, employment equity, poverty, income security, international human rights norms, and homelessness and the right to adequate housing. Fay is an adjunct professor at Osgoode Hall Law School and has published extensively on constitutional law and human rights.

Derek Fudge is the national director of policy development for the National Union of Public and General Employees (NUPGE), one of Canada's largest unions. He has coordinated NUPGE's ongoing *Labour Rights are Human Rights* campaign for the past six years. The foundation of this campaign was a book authored by Derek entitled *Collective Bargaining in Canada: Human Right or Canadian Illusion* (Black Point, NS: Fernwood Publishing, 2006). He serves as the secretariat of NUPGE's Canadian Foundation for Labour Rights. He is also he editor of NUPGE's *Labour Rights are Human Rights* e-bulletin, a monthly electronic newsletter containing news, research, and trends on labour rights from across the country and around the world.

Judy Fudge is the Lansdowne Professor in Law at the University of Victoria, which she joined in 2007 after twenty years of teaching employment and labour law at Osgoode Hall Law School. She is a member the Inter-University Research Centre on Globalization and Work (CRIMT, or le Centre de recherche interuniversitaire sur la mondialisation et le travail) and a member of the board of the Canadian Foundation for Labour Rights.

Keith Ewing has been professor of Public Law at King's College, London since 1989. He is also president of the Institute of Employment Rights and vice-president of the International Centre for Trade Union Rights.

Wayne Hanley is the national president of UFCW Canada. UFCW Canada is the country's largest private-sector union with more than 250,000 members. Members work primarily in the food sector, including in a number of agricultural workers' bargaining units. For more than two decades, UFCW Canada has led a campaign for the labour, human, and legal rights of domestic and migrant agriculture workers across Canada, and is the union behind the *Fraser* case.

John Hendy, QC is a barrister specializing in industrial relations law and Standing Counsel to eight British trade unions. He is a visiting professor in the School of Law, King's College, London, and in the Faculty of Laws, University College, London. He is also chair of the Institute of Employment Rights and president of the International Centre for Trade Union Rights.

Patrick Macklem is the William C. Graham Professor of Law at University of Toronto and a fellow of the Royal Society of Canada. He holds law degrees from Harvard and Toronto, and an undergraduate degree in political science and philosophy from McGill. He is a recurring visiting professor at Central European University. He is the author and editor of numerous books and essays on international law, constitutional law, labour law, human rights, and indigenous rights.

Vincenzo Pietropaolo is an award-winning photographer. He is celebrated for his artistry, empathetic approach, and social commitment. His work has been exhibited and published widely, and is included in public collections such as the Art Gallery of Ontario. In 2010 he received the Cesar E. Chavez Black Eagle Award for his photographs of migrant farm workers.

Ethan Poskanzer is a partner at Sack Goldblatt Mitchell with a research-based practice. He has been involved in the preparation of legal cases before administrative tribunals and all levels of courts, primarily in cases relating to labour, administrative, and constitutional law. Ethan obtained both his BA and LLB from the University of Toronto and was called to the Ontario Bar in 1979.

Kerry Preibisch is an associate professor at the University of Guelph. A sociologist specializing in international migration, her research focuses on temporary migration programs, migrant rights, and development; labour and globalized agro-food systems; gender, migration, and rural livelihoods in Latin America; and im/migration and social change in rural Canada. She has published in *International Migration Review, Signs,* and *International Migration,* among others.

Eric Tucker has been a professor at Osgoode Hall Law School, York University, since 1981. He has published widely the in area of labour and employment law and occupational health and safety regulation, including *Administering Danger in the Workplace* (Toronto: University of Toronto Press, 1990) and *Labour Before the Law* (Toronto: University of Toronto Press, 2004, with Judy Fudge).

Printed and bound by CPI Group (UK) Ltd, Croydon, CR0 4YY
15/09/2026
14962401-0003